1391

The Principal and Individually Guided Education

The Principal and Individually Guided Education

James M. Lipham
Marvin J. Fruth

University of Wisconsin—Madison

Addison-Wesley Publishing Company
Reading, Massachusetts • Menlo Park, California
London • Amsterdam • Don Mills, Ontario • Sydney

CARNEGIE LIBRARY
LIVINGSTONE COLLEGE
SALISBURY, N. C. 28144

This book and the correlated films and filmstrips are in the
Leadership Series in Individually Guided Education,
Herbert J. Klausmeier, Editor.
Development of this series was funded by
The Sears-Roebuck Foundation.

Copyright © 1976 by The Board of Regents of the University of Wisconsin System.
Philippines copyright 1976 by The Board of Regents of the University of Wisconsin
System.

All rights reserved. No part of this publication may be reproduced, stored in a re-
trieval system, or transmitted, in any form or by any means, electronic, mechanical,
photocopying, recording, or otherwise, without the prior written permission of the publisher. Printed in the United States of America. Published simultaneously in Canada.
Library of Congress Catalog Card No. 75-14797.

ISBN 0-201-19811-8
ABCDEFGHIJ-HA-798765

372.1394
L764

Editor's Foreword

These are exciting and challenging times in American education. Personnel in local school districts, intermediate education agencies, state education agencies, and teacher education institutions are cooperating as never before to improve the quality of education for children, high school youth, and college students. Bringing Individually Guided Education, a new approach in education, to an ever increasing number of students provides the focus for many of these cooperative efforts. This Leadership Series in Individually Guided Education consists of ten sets of printed materials and correlated sound/color films and filmstrips and is designed to aid teacher educators and other educational leaders in their improvement efforts. The materials have been developed for use both in credit courses conducted on college campuses and local schools and in noncredit staff development programs carried out in the local schools.

The set of materials for the principal and Individually Guided Education consists of this textbook; a 20-minute sound/color film, *The Principal in an IGE School,* and three problem films of about 10 minutes each: *Helping Janice Teach Effectively, Who Should Spend the Money?* and *Parents Want to Participate.* Other films and filmstrips that can be used effectively with this package include a 25-minute film, *Making Unit Meetings Effective* and two filmstrips: *The Multiunit School Organization*—20 minutes—and *Instructional Programming for the Individual Student*—20 minutes. An accompanying instructor's manual provides aids to instructors for meeting the needs of their students in their particular situations.

The authors of this book, James M. Lipham and Marvin J. Fruth, have

98766

been involved in preparing principals and other school administrators for many years. They have formulated many of the concepts and competencies required of successful IGE principals and have offered intensive workshops and graduate courses for principals and other school administrators. To assist in writing this book, many able contributing authors have been recruited, each of whom has expertise in a particular area of the administration of IGE schools.

I have enjoyed the cooperative and productive working relationships with these scholars, the film producers, the publisher, and others in developing this comprehensive set of multimedia materials. To assure that the users of this and other sets of materials in the Leadership Series get attractive, high quality, usable materials and also are not presented with conflicting interpretations of IGE in either the books or the visuals, I personally reviewed each book from its first chapter outline, through its several field-tested drafts, and the final manuscript. I did the same for each visual from the initial content outline, through the several drafts of the script, rough cuts, and fine cuts. Many other persons also participated in the production, review, and quality control process.

In this regard I am pleased to recognize the many school personnel, state education agency personnel, professors, and students who participated in field tests and review sessions; the consultants with expertise in the various subject matter fields or in the filmic quality and instructional effectiveness of the visuals; Anthony E. Conte, James M. Lipham, Wesley C. Meierhenry, and William Wiersma for serving on the Project Publications Board; Judith Amacker, William R. Bush, James R. Dumpson, Martin W. Essex, Nancy Evers, Lovelia P. Flournoy, John R. Palmer, Edward C. Pomeroy, Richard A. Rossmiller, B. Othanel Smith, Lorraine Sullivan, and James Swinney for serving on the Project Advisory Committee; Leslie C. Bernal, G. R. Bowers, Eleanor Buehrig, Xavier Del Buono, Lee M. Ellwood, G. W. Ford, Marvin J. Fruth, George Glasrud, James Hixson, Ronald Horn, Terry Jackson, L. Wayne Krula, Max Poole, Kenneth B. Smith, James Stoltenberg, Michael F. Tobin, Philip Vik, James E. Walter, S. Edward Weinswig, and William Wiersma for serving on the Project Steering Committee; and the staff of the IGE Teacher Education Project. Particular recognition is given to the members of minority groups who reviewed the visuals in order to avoid having any unintentional racism or sexism appear in them.

The development of these materials became possible through a grant by The Sears-Roebuck Foundation in 1973 to the IGE Teacher Education Project at The University of Wisconsin—Madison. The authors, editor, and others associated with the Project receive no royalties from the sale of these materials. However, the royalties that accrue will be returned to The University of Wisconsin—Madison to support continuing research, development, and implementation activities related to Individually Guided Education.

> Herbert J. Klausmeier
> Series Editor and Director
> IGE Teacher Education Project
> The University of Wisconsin—Madison

Preface

The purpose of this book is to provide present and prospective principals with the understandings, skills, and attitudes required to implement effectively the program of Individually Guided Education (IGE) in the elementary school. The system of IGE is a major educational change which has great potential for substantially improving the education of our children and youth. The leadership of the principal is crucial to the successful implementation of this major educational change.

This textbook consists of two parts. The first part consists of nine substantive chapters which treat the principal's leadership role in each of the basic components of IGE. Each chapter is introduced by a brief overview of underlying administrative and instructional theories from which operational procedures and practical guidelines are drawn for the principal in implementing IGE. In several of the chapters, recent research findings from IGE schools are cited to substantiate the suggested concepts and competencies.

The second part of the book, Chapter 10, consists of eight case studies which serve as the basis for analysis, discussion, and action on the part of the IGE school principals. Although abbreviated, each case is reality based. The questions for analysis at the end of each case are suggestive only of the issues to be considered in relation to the substantive chapters in the first part of the book.

To be of further help to university professors of educational administration and school district inservice personnel, an Instructor's Manual to Accompany the Principal and Individually Guided Education is also available. Moreover, an overview film, *The Principal in an IGE School,* and three problem films, *Helping Janice Teach Effectively, Who Should Spend the Money?* and *Parents Want to Participate,* have been prepared. These and other print and audiovisual materials in the Leadership Series in Individually Guided Education should be used to develop and refine the leadership skills required of the effective IGE school principal.

This work represents the efforts of many individuals whose contributions we are pleased to acknowledge. First, Herbert J. Klausmeier, Director of The University of Wisconsin/Sears-Roebuck Project in Teacher Education and the former Director of the Wisconsin Research and Development Center for Cognitive Learning at the University of Wisconsin—Madison, not only pioneered in the conceptual development of IGE, but also provided the resource, managerial, and technical input required for a project of this magnitude. As Editor, his indefatigable review and helpful suggestions at each step in conceiving, preparing, testing, and revising the work have been an inspiration to all of us. It has been a distinct privilege to work with an editor who not only can detect a problem, but also can suggest how to remedy it.

Next, this book would not have been possible except for the knowledge and efforts of its contributing authors: B. Dean Bowles, Nancy A. Evers, Albert M. Holmquist, Herbert J. Klausmeier, William H. Klenke, Walter E. Krupa, Joseph J. Marinelli, William R. Miles, Douglas A. Paul, Richard A. Rossmiller, Dennis W. Spuck, James E. Walter, and Kenneth W. Wright. Hopefully, their expertise is accurately reflected and acknowledged in the several chapters and cases.

For assistance in preparing the manuscript, we wish first to express appreciation to our friend and colleague, the former Dean of the Graduate School of Education at the University of Chicago, Francis S. Chase, who suggested several substantive changes in the organization and content of the manuscript. To our graduate assistants in the Department of Educational Administration at the University of Wisconsin—Madison, Barbara H. Bocian, Charles G. Goodridge, Diana R. Mendenhall, and Conrad W. Sigurdson, we are indebted for their conscientious attention to the many details required in preparing the manuscript for publication.

To members of our graduate course in the IGE School Principalship conducted at the University of Wisconsin—Madison during the fall of 1974, we are indebted not only for their critical critiques of the pilot manuscript, but also for their refreshing and realistic suggestions for its improvement. The members of this class were: Wayne R. Bobholz, Barbara H. Bocian, Barun K. Dutta, Charles G. Goodridge, Thomas E. Grannis, Patricia J. Hoffman, Khanda H. Humuri, Lynn G. Karges, Virgil C. Leopold, Michael J. Maier, Diana R. Mendenhall, Constance M. Nerlinger, Marlene E. Powell, Joan M. Rebeck, Conrad W. Sigurdson, and Warren F. Turner.

For permission to utilize previously published materials, appreciation is expressed to the following: the Wisconsin Research and Development Center for Cognitive Learning at the University of Wisconsin—Madison, the Evaluation Center of University of California at Los Angeles, the Midwest Administration Center at the University of Chicago, Harper & Row Publishers, and McCutchan Publishing Company.

Finally, we wish to express appreciation to our secretary, Carol Jean Roche, who was able to type and retype manuscripts faster than all of us could revise them.

Madison, Wisconsin   J. M. L.
January 1976   M. J. F.

Contents

1

Development and Description of IGE

James M. Lipham
Herbert J. Klausmeier

Objectives

After reading this chapter, the reader will be able:

- To recall the main events in the historical development of IGE.
- To understand the seven major components of an IGE school.
- To know how the seven major components are interrelated.
- To recognize the importance of the principal's role in an IGE school.

Any significant change in the educational program of the school requires thorough understanding of that change on the part of the principal. Since Individually Guided Education (IGE) represents a change of great magnitude, the principal initially must understand the full meaning of the concept as a basis for subsequently developing the skills and attitudes required for effective and efficient performance in the role as principal of an IGE school.

The purpose of this chapter is to acquaint prospective and practicing principals with the development, definition, and description of IGE as an educational system. IGE is conceptualized as a comprehensive alternative form of schooling designed to produce higher educational achievements through providing well for differences among students in rate of learning, learning style, and other characteristics.*

To place IGE in an appropriate historical perspective, certain prevailing conditions in American education which gave rise to the need for a new form of schooling are first described. By contrast, there are delineated some desirable conditions for teaching and learning which led to the origin and development of IGE. Next, a brief overview of the system of IGE is presented wherein each of the seven basic components is operationally defined and briefly described. It is then shown how certain promising educational purposes, programs, and practices are encompassed within each component of IGE. The chapter concludes with an introductory overview of this book which deals with the understandings, skills, and attitudes required for effective performance as principal of an IGE school.

HISTORY OF IGE

To understand the development of IGE, consideration must be given to certain conditions prevailing in American schools which suggested an urgent need for a viable alternative form of education. Description of these conditions is followed in this section by a discussion of desirable conditions for teaching and learning. Then, the origin and historical development of IGE are traced.

Prevailing Conditions in American Education

By any criterion, the American educational system is truly remarkable. The progress made in education is evidenced by many statistics. For example, 75 percent of the pupils entering the fifth grade in the fall of 1964 graduated from high school in 1972 and about 23 percent of them are expected to graduate from college with a bachelor's degree. The comparable percentages

---

*   Herbert J. Klausmeier 1975. IGE: an alternative form of schooling. In H. Talmage (ed.), *Systems of individualized education*, Berkeley, Calif.: Mc-Cutchan, pp. 48–83. Sections of this chapter are based on this reference.

ten years earlier, in 1962, were about 67 and 17 percent, respectively (U.S. Department of Health, Education, and Welfare 1975, p. 33). Moreover, the quality of the product of American schools compares favorably with that of any other nation. For example, the recent findings of the International Association for the Evaluation of Educational Achievement revealed that in reading comprehension the top 10 percent of American high school seniors performed better than similar groups in 15 other nations, including Australia, England, France, West Germany, Sweden, and Japan (Thorndike 1973). Further, many children of low socioeconomic status in the United States get more schooling than do their counterparts in 19 other nations. In reporting the findings, Hechinger (1973) stated:

> The increasingly vocal critics of our schools, in keeping with the current mood of American self-criticism, have assumed an isolationist or at least a provincial tone. It is, of course, true that American schools have discriminated against the poor and against minority groups. American education policy has not always made the climb up the ladder of success as easy or as equal as envisioned by the American dream. But a look at the schools of Germany, England, and France, where stratification is still far more rigid, puts the American achievement in a much brighter light, clearly at the head of the international parade.

The achievements of the schools, however, cannot allay concern about major inadequacies in American education. The critics of the schools can point to statistics such as the following which indicate that education in the United States has not been a successful experience for some young people: one out of four students has a significant reading deficiency, one-half of our unemployed youth are functionally illiterate, and approximately 2.5 percent of our nation's youth drop out of school by the eighth grade (U.S. Department of Health, Education, and Welfare 1969).

These distressing findings appear to be related to practices and conditions which are typical in the schools:

- Students are required to adjust to uniform educational programs, and provisions for differences in rate of learning, style of learning, and other characteristics are inadequate.
- Students are placed in age-graded classes and are expected to attain the same instructional objectives by studying the same graded basic textbooks and supplementary materials.
- Students are frequently evaluated using norm-referenced tests of intellectual ability and educational achievement, and such tests are often used for categorizing and grading students, and not for improving their instruction.
- Teachers are treated as if they are equally competent in all subject fields and in all media and methods of instruction; and appropriate

provisions are seldom made for differences among teachers in interests, knowledge, experience, and expertise.

- Teachers spend nearly all their time throughout the school day with children, leaving little time for planning and evaluating instructional activities.

- The principal tends to be a building manager rather than an educational leader; the teacher is an independent ruler of a classroom rather than a cooperative team member; and administrative arrangements discourage cooperative planning and decision making.

- The staff spends most of its energy in keeping the school going. Little effort is devoted to research and development activities that are essential to continuous improvement of educational practice.

- The staff of each school functions in relative isolation from other schools; communication networks for sharing creative ideas, materials, and instructional approaches function only sporadically, causing many to "reinvent the wheel."

- The typical school building is not well adapted to effective instruction; access to library, audiovisual, and other instructional materials and aids is circumscribed; and space configurations impede varied types of grouping and learning activities.

- Parent contact with the schools is largely negative, being concerned primarily with problems of school finance or student discipline, and the primary means for communication between the school and the home is by report cards or parent-teacher conferences supplemented occasionally by a school newsletter.

Early it was recognized that the preceding obsolete conditions should be remedied without destroying public education or eliminating any effective practices. One solution was seen as being a new form of tax-supported education within local school districts to serve as an alternative to the self-contained, age-graded system of elementary education which has not changed much since 1850. The development of a suitable, carefully designed and tested alternative to the traditional school would facilitate the adoption of practices conducive to more effective teaching and learning in the schools. IGE was conceived and developed as a response to the need for such an alternative.

Desirable Conditions for Teaching and Learning

First and foremost, the educational process should focus attention on the individual learner as a person with unique characteristics, capabilities, concerns, need-dispositions, and motivations. Focusing attention on the individual learner can be accomplished through the following four operations.

1. Assessing the level of achievement, learning style, and motivation of each student by the use of criterion-referenced tests, observation schedules, or work samples prior to beginning instruction.

2. Setting specific instructional objectives for each student to attain over a short period of time.

3. Planning and conducting instructional activities suitable for each student through varying the amount of direction by the teacher; the amount of time spent in interaction among students; the use of resources, materials, equipment, and direct experience; and the amount of time spent by each student in different types and sizes of learning groups.

4. Assessing each student for attainment of the student's initial objectives in order to set the next instructional objectives to be attained.

Principals and teachers will immediately recognize that this system of individually guided instruction removes the heavy dependence on standardized texts and tests for structuring the form and content of instruction. Instead, a wide variety of quality curricular materials, audiovisual equipment, and assessment devices is required to vary sizes of groups, use of time, and teacher and student activities. For example, some concepts may be introduced to a large group through a sound motion picture, extended in a smaller group through slide films and discussion, and developed independently through use of printed or audiovisual sets of curricular materials or programmed instructional packages. Although a wealth of materials may be available, in many instances it is necessary for the principal to provide teachers the time and encouragement to develop and refine curricular materials and assessment instruments and procedures.

To implement IGE, the principal must demonstrate one of the essential qualities of leadership—that of initiating change in the organizational structure of the school. The organizational design of the school should foster open communication, systematic planning, cooperative decision making, intra- and intergroup coordination, and instructional accountability at all levels. Moreover, the administrative and instructional units should be small enough to allow each person to be known and treated as an individual, yet large enough to permit role differentiation and complementarity of contributions. The organizational structure must affix role responsibilities and clarify working relationships among administrators, specialists, teachers, teacher interns, aides, students, and other participants in the educational process. Moreover, the organizational structure of the school should provide for adequate and appropriate involvement of each participant in the decision-making process.

To identify and satisfy the educational needs of individual students, the principal and staff must employ systematic problem-solving processes. Each step in planning, developing, conducting, and evaluating instruction should be treated as a problem to be solved. The inputs, processes, and outcomes of each subunit within the school not only must be articulated with those of other subunits and with other schools in a district, but also with other agencies, such as state education departments, teacher education institutions, and research and development centers which foster and sustain educational change. Continuous research and development, utilizing problem-solving processes, is vital to the success of the school.

The activities of the principal and the staff in planning instructional activities, developing curricular materials and assessment procedures, and conducting research and development activities obviously constitute the core of a continuous program of staff development. The principal must assume the primary leadership responsibility not only for staff development, but also for staff identification, selection, orientation, assignment, and evaluation. These activities are of critical significance since communication, interaction, and interdependence are increased in schools that individualize instruction.

To provide a desirable environment for learning, the principal also plays a key role in obtaining the necessary financial and physical resources. Buildings must be planned, or in many instances remodeled, to permit maximum flexibility and to provide an environment conducive to the many types of learning activities. Large instructional spaces which permit varied types of instructional groupings are required, as is a central instructional materials center which includes library and audiovisual materials and equipment readily accessible to staff and students. Even in older buildings, inexpensive alterations, imaginative use of corridors, and ingenious adaptation of space to educational needs may improve the total climate for learning.

Increasingly, parents and other citizens want assurance that the schools are productive, that students are achieving well in the 3 Rs and other curricular areas, and that they are developing culturally, socially, and emotionally as responsible individuals and productive citizens. Major attention must be given to home-school-community relations by increasing the interaction and involvement of parents and citizens in planning educational programs, providing educational activities, and evaluating educational outcomes. Parents should be able to convey information, values, and attitudes; teachers, parents, and students should be involved in reporting practices; and a systematic program of home-school-community relationships should be developed.

Origin and Development of IGE

The system known as IGE was started by personnel of the Wisconsin Research and Development Center for Cognitive Learning and cooperating school systems as an efficient alternative to age-graded, self-contained schooling at both elementary and middle school levels. Every element and phase in the development, refinement, and implementation of the system is designed to create the conditions and stimulate the activities essential to effective educational planning, teaching, and learning.

IGE started in embryonic form when a project called Maximizing Opportunities for Development and Experimentation in Learning in the Schools was begun at the Wisconsin Research and Development Center under the direction of Herbert J. Klausmeier as principal investigator (Klausmeier, et al. 1966). As a first practical result of this project, four school districts, with the assistance of Center personnel, started the first 13 nongraded, Instruction and Research Units as replacements for age-graded classes in schools of Madison, Janesville, Milwaukee, and Racine, Wisconsin, in the second semester of the 1965–66 school year (Klausmeier et al. 1967). In 1966–67, the number of functioning I & R Units was increased to 19.

In 1967–68, for the first time, seven elementary schools were completely organized into I & R Units, and the term Multiunit Elementary School was coined to designate these schools (Klausmeier et al. 1968). Also, the other two elements of the organizational-administrative arrangements, Instructional Improvement Committees (ICC) at the school level, and Systemwide Program Committees (SPC), at the school district level, were formed.

The Wisconsin Department of Public Instruction selected the Multiunit School for statewide demonstration and implementation during the 1968–69 school year. Thereafter, as implementors were educated regarding IGE and as materials and programs were developed to assist local schools in changing to IGE, many agencies became involved, and the number of IGE multiunit schools increased rapidly: 50 in 1969–70, 50 in 1971–72, approximately 700 in 1973–74, and over 2500 in 1974–75. Projections for the future indicate that accelerated expansion will continue throughout the 1970s. Some events associated with this rapid and continual growth merit attention.

In 1968, the staff of the Wisconsin Research and Development Center, with assistance of personnel of the Wisconsin Department of Public Instruction and the local schools, developed a book and 15 videotapes for use in implementing IGE by state education departments, teacher education institutions, and other interested educational agencies. These materials were used until 1971. In 1969, the Wisconsin Research and Development Center and the Institute for Development of Educational Activities (/I/D/E/A/) signed an agreement whereby /I/D/E/A/ was authorized to use the preceding materials in producing a more sophisticated set of inservice materials. /I/D/E/A/ incorporated into the new materials insights from their own study of educational change. In 1970–71 and thereafter, /I/D/E/A/ used these IGE "Change Program" materials to prepare "facilitators" to establish multiunit schools (Education USA Special Report 1972).

The Wisconsin Research and Development Center also used the same materials until 1972 when the requirements of /I/D/E/A/ for using the "Change Program" materials were found to be incompatible with the federally funded implementation activities of the Wisconsin Center. The Wisconsin Research and Development Center then had to develop new inservice materials in order to continue its implementation of IGE as provided for in an agreement with the Office of Education.

Early in 1971, the Multiunit Elementary School was selected by the United States Office of Education for nationwide implementation, and this brought the Wisconsin Research and Development Center into its first large-scale implementation effort as noted earlier. The Research and Development Center was funded by three federal agencies to carry out a comprehensive implementation strategy during 1971–72 and 1972–73. The National Institute of Education funded a small effort during 1973–74. In preparation for the national effort, a four-phase implementation strategy was formulated consisting of the following stages: awareness, first-year implementation, second-year maintenance and refinement, and institutionalization of IGE.

The awareness phase was carried out by the Wisconsin Research and Development Center only once in 1971. First-year implementation was systematized primarily by coordinators in nine state educational agencies— Colorado, Connecticut, Illinois, Indiana, Minnesota, New Jersey, Ohio, South Carolina, and Wisconsin—and by other agencies in California, Nebraska, New York, and Virginia. Sufficient funding was not available to respond to the interest in the other states. Approximately 275 IGE schools were started each year in these states. Maintenance and refinement activities, in the form of one-week institutes for experienced IGE personnel, were conducted by seven teacher education institutions in Connecticut, Ohio, and Wisconsin. Approximately 700 unit leaders, 300 building principals, and 100 teachers of reading of functioning IGE schools attended these institutes (Sipes 1972). Institutionalization (defined as teacher education institutions developing on-campus programs and preparing building principals, unit leaders, and leaders for their IGE roles) also was started in 1971–72 with federal funding. This support was provided, however, for only that year.

In 1972, the Sears-Roebuck Foundation invited a proposal that led to funding of the project of which this book is a part—the UW/SRF IGE Teacher Education Project (Klausmeier 1972). The major thrust of this project was the development of printed and audiovisual instructional materials for use in undergraduate programs to prepare teachers for IGE schools and in graduate programs to prepare staff teachers, unit leaders, school principals, and other administrators for leadership in IGE schools. The materials are also for use in inservice performs to aid schools in changing over to IGE and in their refinement of IGE practices. A second purpose of the project was to assist personnel of various states to form state IGE networks coordinated by the state educational agency. The mutual expectations are that the educational agencies and teacher education institutions of each state will have the capability to start and maintain IGE schools, to prepare prospective IGE teachers through on-campus programs, and to prepare unit leaders and building principals for service in IGE schools through on-campus graduate programs and continuing inservice programs.

Another significant event was the establishment, by the IGE coordinators of 12 states, of a national IGE organization. In November of 1973, the Association for Individually Guided Education (AIGE) was organized at Madison, Wisconsin, and held its first annual meeting which was attended by over 400 persons representing state education departments, teacher education institutions, and public and private schools in 30 states. At the second annual meeting of the Association, held in Chicago in 1974, over 1200 persons were in attendance. At these meetings, new theoretical conceptualizations, reports of research, and practical ideas for the implementation and refinement of IGE were shared and exchanged.

As the chronicle of preceding developments indicates, continuing cooperative efforts by many persons and agencies have been required to develop the various components of IGE, start the early IGE schools, and carry out the implementation process in numerous school districts in many states. Unlike a curricular package that can be distributed commercially and used by teachers without fundamental changes in school organization or instruction, IGE requires many changes within schools that are possible only if there is early inservice education, followed by continuing staff development within each IGE school. Each of the major components of IGE has far-reaching implications for school board members, superintendents, principals, specialists, teachers, students, parents, and others vitally concerned with improving the educational process.

THE COMPONENTS OF IGE

The system of IGE includes seven basic components, each of which is relatively complex. Succeeding chapters will treat more fully each of the following basic components introduced here: the multiunit organizational-administrative arrangements, instructional programming for the individual student, evaluation for educational decision making, curricular materials compatible with IGE, home-school-community relations, facilitative environments for IGE, and the continuing research and development required to improve IGE. These basic components are shown in the model in Figure 1.1.

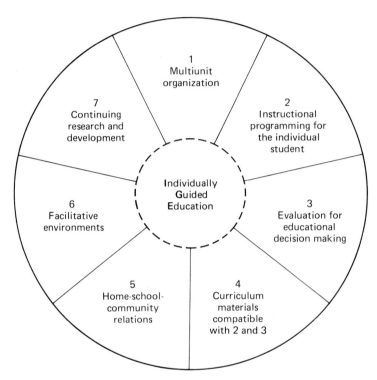

Fig. 1.1 Components of Individually Guided Education. Based on H. J. Klausmeier, M. R. Quilling, J. S. Sorenson, R. S. Way, and G. R. Glasrud 1971. *Individually guided education and the multiunit school: guidelines for implementation,* Chapter 2. Madison, Wisc.: Wisconsin Research and Development Center for Cognitive Learning.

The Multiunit Organizational Structure

The multiunit organizational structure was designed to produce an environment in a school building which would facilitate instructional programming for the individual student and the introduction and utilization of the other components of IGE (Klausmeier, *et al.* 1968, p. 18). The multiunit school is a new organizational structure that has emerged from a synthesis of organizational theory and practice in education. The multiunit structure is designed to: articulate vertical and horizontal relationships, affix organizational roles and responsibilities, facilitate immediate and long-range planning, increase involvement in educational decision making, and improve communication among school personnel. The anticipated results are fuller commitments to shared goals, higher educational achievement, and increased satisfaction for each person involved in the educational process.

Admittedly, organizational change alone cannot meet simultaneously such ambitious theoretical and practical goals. Significant changes of the kinds described are possible, however, if other essential supportive components are combined with substantial restructuring to create an environment which motivates and reinforces contributions to learning.

The instruction and research unit (I & R unit).   At the instructional level in the multiunit school is the I & R Unit. The nongraded I & R Unit replaces both the age-graded, self-contained classroom and the departmentalized form of organization for instruction. Each typical unit includes the following personnel: a unit leader, three to five other staff teachers, a first-year or resident intern teacher, an instructional or clerical aide, and 100 to 150 students.

The main functions of the I & R Unit are: to plan, carry out, and evaluate instructional programs for each student in the unit; to engage in continuous inservice staff development programs; to provide preservice teacher education activities; and to plan and conduct cooperatively, perhaps with other agencies, a systematic program of research and development. Since all units must continuously conduct practical research to devise and evaluate an instructional program appropriate for each student, research is included in the title to reflect clearly this emphasis.

The instructional improvement committee (IIC).   The IIC is at the second scalar level of the organization, the school building level. This committee comprises the principal and the unit leaders and is organized and chaired by the principal.

The four main functions for which the IIC takes primary initiative are: (a) stating the general educational objectives and outlining the educational program for the entire school building, (b) interpreting and implementing systemwide and statewide policies that affect the educational program of the building, (c) coordinating the activities of the I & R Units to achieve continuity in all curricular areas, and (d) arranging for the use of the time, facilities, and resources that are not managed independently by the units. The IIC thus deals primarily with planning, decision making, and coordinating the activities related to instruction.

The systemwide program committee (SPC).   The SPC is at the third or district level of the organization. In earlier literature this structure was called the Systemwide Policy Committee since policy changes are often necessary to move from a self-contained classroom form of organization to that required in IGE. Since the board of education is the policymaking body, however, the designation Systemwide Program Committee is more appropriate. The committee is chaired by the school superintendent or an appropriate designee and includes representative central office consultants, principals, unit leaders, teachers, and parents or citizens.

The four decision-making and facilitative responsibilities for which the SPC takes primary initiative are: (a) identifying the functions to be performed in each IGE school of the district, (b) recruiting personnel for each IGE school and providing for their inservice education, (c) providing the essential physical resources and instructional materials, and (d) planning an effective program of home-school-community relations. An alternative central office structure other than the SPC may be responsible for these functions; considerable flexibility is required since local school districts differ greatly in size and other characteristics.

Differentiated roles.   Unlike some differentiated staffing programs that create a complex hierarchy and call for a proliferation of new roles and titles for school personnel, the multiunit organizational pattern establishes only one new position, that of the unit leader. However, basic changes are made in the roles of the principal and teacher and in other roles that are integrated into the unit, such as teacher aide, instructional secretary, and intern teacher. The multiunit organization does not preclude the identification and establishment of other specialized roles, such as those concerned with instructional media, pupil personnel services, or home-school-community relations. It does assume, however, that the unit leader and the unit staff who work directly with the students and their parents are the key individuals in the instructional process. The multiunit pattern also calls for a direct concentration of the personnel and material resources of the school district in the daily program of instruction. In the discussion that follows, the key roles of unit leader, staff teacher, and principal are described briefly.

The unit leader is a member of the IIC, the leader of a unit, and a teacher in the unit. As a member of the IIC, the unit leader contributes to planning the entire program of the school primarily by defining the program of the unit in relation to that of other units. As the leader of the unit, the unit leader plans and coordinates the instructional activities in the unit; allocates and manages materials and resources; fosters and maintains effective working relationships within the unit and between the unit staff and others; and instructs unit members, including beginning teachers and instructional aides. As a teacher, the unit leader spends from 50 to 80 percent of the time interacting directly with students—the proportion of time depending on the size of the unit, the amount of research and development, and the extent of preservice teacher education activities being conducted in the unit. The unit leader is a career teacher who takes the initiative in developing, utilizing, and testing new materials and instructional approaches.

The role of the staff teacher is altered considerably by the multiunit organization. The staff teacher participates in unit planning sessions, is involved with a large number of children in the unit, and performs more professional and less routine work. The collaborative planning, instruction, and evaluation called for in IGE demand specialization of tasks according to the capabilities and interests of each staff member. For example, the teacher who is strong in a given curricular area takes greater initiative for planning unit activities, teaching other staff members, and actually teaching children in that area. Teachers also may be strong or weak in certain instructional groupings. One teacher may be excellent in tutorial activities; another, in small group activities; and still another, in large group activities. The tasks of identifying instructional materials, developing assessment tools and procedures, planning home-school-community activities, or conducting other specialized functions are assigned according to each teacher's characteristics. Although each teacher takes the initiative in areas of strengths or interests, one does not become completely specialized.

In the IGE school the role of the principal is changed substantially in that the principal assumes greater and more direct leadership responsibility for the improvement of instruction. The principal organizes and leads the IIC which serves as the vehicle for open communication and systematic planning. The principal assists the committee in making decisions which can be implemented effectively. The principal selects, assigns, and orients the staff members to their differentiated roles and encourages each person to participate in a meaningful program of professional growth and development. As the leader of the staff, the principal's interpersonal relationships and behavior influence the organizational climate and morale of the entire school. As the administrator of the school, the principal is responsible for obtaining and managing the financial and physical resources required for the program. Finally, the principal initiates and fosters extraorganizational relationships and resources to provide effective programs of home-school-community relations, preservice and inservice training, and continuing research and development to improve instructional programming for the individual student.

The Instructional Programming Model

At the heart of IGE is the Instructional Programming Model for the individual student (Klausmeier, *et al.* 1971, p. 19). This model specifically takes into account each student's beginning level of performance, rate of progress, style of learning, motivational level, and other characteristics in the context of the educational program of the school. Instructional programming for the individual student must be appropriately planned and implemented in the cognitive, psychomotor, and affective domains. The model is used with explicitly stated instructional objectives and criteria of mastery which indicate that every student should attain mastery of the objectives to the stated criterion level in a given phase of learning before proceeding to the next objective or item in a curricular sequence. It is also used with expressive objectives in the affective and psychomotor domain when the same level of mastery is not sought by all students. Therefore, instructional programming for the individual student should not be interpreted to mean that all students engage in the same number or kinds of activities, or reach an identical level of achievement, interest, or motivation. The Instructional Programming Model also implies that objective-based instruction may proceed differently in various curricular areas, rather than prescribing that objective-based instruction should proceed in an identical manner in all curricular areas.

Regardless of the nature and specificity of the objectives and the criteria for mastery, seven sequential steps are followed in implementing instructional programming for the individual student.

Step 1 is the setting of general educational objectives to be attained by the student population of a school within a period of a year or longer in terms of level of achievement or other criteria related to each curricular area. The initiative for setting schoolwide objectives is taken by the IIC with appropriate input from unit staff members, central office personnel, parents, and others concerned with the educational priorities of the school. In formulating the schoolwide objectives, the staff gives attention not only to priorities, but also to the programs to be utilized and the criteria to be accepted as evidence that the objectives have been attained.

Step 2 is the identification of the range of objectives that may be attainable for subgroups of the student population. The initiative for this step is taken by the unit leader and staff of each I & R Unit. Certain general objectives, for example, are more suitable for students in upper intermediate units than for those in primary units.

Step 3 is the actual assessment of each student's level of understanding, skill, or attitudinal development, either by administering tests, observing performance, or utilizing other measures. Criterion-referenced tests are particularly useful for assessing mastery of instructional objectives related to clearly delineated skills, such as those in reading, spelling, and mathematics. When the appropriate subset of objective-related tests is administered, the capabilities and deficiencies of each student are pinpointed, and the instructional objectives for the individual student can be identified.

Step 4 is the setting of instructional objectives for each student in the unit to attain over a short period of time. Particular understandings and attitudes which the student has not yet acquired become that student's instructional objectives.

Step 5 is the planning and implementing of an instructional program whereby the student attains the objectives. The plan is implemented by varying (a) the amount of attention and direction by the teacher, (b) the use of printed materials, audiovisual materials, and direct experiences, (c) the use of space and equipment, and (d) the amount of time spent by each student in independent study, in one-to-one interactions with the teacher or media, in adult- or student-led small group activities, and in adult-led large group activities.

Generally, each teacher instructs one or more groups of students who are working toward mastering the same objective or set of objectives. In each small group, materials, methods, and use of time are matched to individual pupils with consideration given to their present level of skill development, rate of learning, preferred learning style, and other characteristics. Personal variables, such as sociability, motivation, and emotional maturity, are also given attention. To the extent that staff is available, goal-setting conferences and individual tutoring are provided for each student.

Step 6 is the assessment of students to determine their attainment of objectives. According to *Step 7,* if a student has failed to attain an objective, the student's readiness to attain it must be evaluated, as should other aspects of the instructional programming sequence. A student who has attained an instructional objective or set of objectives moves ahead to the next objective or set of objectives.

Implementation of instructional programming for the individual student requires a schoolwide effort. In the IGE school, instructional programming is done by the unit leaders and teachers with assistance from the staffs of other units and the central office. However, specialized assistance must also be provided to develop suitable instructional materials in the various curricular areas, prepare criterion-referenced tests and other assessment techniques, and obtain and summarize evaluative data required for making effective educational decisions.

Evaluation for Educational Decision Making

The third major component of IGE is a model of evaluation for making effective educational decisions at all levels of the organization. Evaluation processes pervade the IGE school, relating to such essential functions as staff personnel, curriculum development, resource management, and home-school-community relations, but they converge critically on instructional programming for the individual student.

Decision making as a rational process includes the following six steps or stages:

1. Identifying the problem: defining and establishing priorities for the decision to be made
2. Setting the decision criteria: determining what information and values are relevant to the decision
3. Obtaining information: utilizing appropriate mechanisms to collect, summarize, and deliver the required data at the appropriate time

4. Formulating alternatives: relating the data to the decision criteria

5. Making the decision: choosing an alternative

6. Implementing the decision: assessing progress and outcomes (Lipham 1974)

Klausmeier and Goodwin (1975) developed the following decision-making model concerning student process:

Formulate instructional objectives and set related criteria of attainment $\longrightarrow$ measure $\longrightarrow$ relate measurement to criteria $\longrightarrow$ judge $\longrightarrow$ act on judgment.

The sequence may be applied both to cognitive learning and to other forms, such as the affective domain. It also applies either to short parallel instructional sequences, such as topics or units in science and social studies, or to completely sequenced programs extending through an entire level of schooling. In IGE, the evaluation of the student's learning characteristics and performance is aimed at providing information at three stages: (1) at the beginning of a unit of instruction, (2) key stages in the instructional sequence, and (3) at the end of a unit of instruction.

Compatible Curricular Materials

The success of IGE depends heavily on the availability of curricular materials compatible with both the Instructional Programming Model and the availability of appropriate evaluative procedures. As Klausmeier indicated, curricular materials, whether developed for IGE or any other instructional system, should incorporate four main attributes (Klausmeier 1975). First, the content incorporated in the material should be accurate and reliable. For example, scholars in a particular discipline should agree that the content is free of cultural bias, factual errors, and possible misinterpretations of the information.

Second, the content should be learnable by the particular students for whom it is prepared. Here, the concern is that the content items (facts, concepts, and skills) are properly paced sequentially—the steps in the sequence are not so large or abrupt that the student cannot accomplish them, or so small and repetitive that student curiosity and creativity give way to disinterest and distaste.

Third, the materials and related activities should be teachable. To be compatible with the Instructional Programming Model and the evaluation needed, each set of materials in any curricular area should include: (a) clearly stated objectives, either behavioral or expressive; (b) assessment tools and procedures directly related to each objective that will aid teachers in the initial, formative, and summative evaluation of student learning; (c) print and nonprint instructional materials that will enable students to attain each objective; and (d) suggestions to teachers concerning possible instructional activities that effectively combine the use of materials with student and teacher activities. This last attribute of curricular materials assumes that each teacher, in order to attain any particular objective that may be common for students, must be able to vary the instructional activities for particular students in order to provide for individual differences.

Fourth, the materials should be suitable in terms of cost, attractiveness, and the amount of inservice teacher education required. Neither IGE nor any other form of schooling will improve education when the materials of instruction are either unattractive to children and teachers, or so costly that school districts cannot afford them. Similarly, while it is expected that new materials will require some inservice training, it is futile to incorporate new content and methodology which will require massive inservice education before it can be handled by teachers.

Many professors, scientists, and other personnel at the Wisconsin Research and Development Center have developed curricular materials that are intended to meet these criteria and therefore are suitable for use in IGE schools. Included are exemplary programs in reading (Otto, et al. 1973), prereading (Venezky, et al. 1974), mathematics (Romberg, et al. 1974), and student motivation (Klausmeier, et al. 1973). These, as other programs, require careful evaluation prior to adoption for use in any school or school district.

The availability of instructional materials suitable for use in IGE schools continues to increase. In addition to the Wisconsin Research and Development Center, other centers, regional educational laboratories, colleges and universities, and nonprofit and profit-making organizations are producing a wide variety of quality curricular materials. Procedures recommended to schools for identifying and using instructional materials follow this general sequence: First, broad terminal educational objectives related to the major curricular areas are formulated at state and school district levels. Then, available printed and audiovisual instructional materials are identified by a representative committee of teachers and administrators. From this large list, the IIC and I & R Units of a school select the materials which are appropriate for each student to attain specified instructional objectives. Each building staff continuously recommends to the district committee the specific materials needed for the students in a particular school and community.

Home-school-community Relations

Since no system of public education is any better than the public's understanding of the program of the school, the successful implementation of IGE depends in large measure on an active program of home-school-community relations. Three general aims of a home-school-community relations program are:

1. To make the staff more aware of available resources and more responsive to the educational expectations of the community, parents, and students.
2. To make the community, parents, and students more aware of and responsive to the requisites of the instructional program implemented through IGE.
3. To identify and utilize ways and means of actively involving both staff and community in the awareness, commitment, changeover, refinement, and renewal stages of IGE (Fruth, Bowles, and Moser. In press).

Within the system of IGE, the program of home-school-community relations operates at three interdependent levels: the school district level, the local school level, and the I & R Unit level. At the level of the school district, the larger community controls the schools through its willingness to expend its power and resources on programs which reflect its values and interests. If the values held in the broader community are communicated and if the school is responsive to these educational expectations, then the community will use its power and resources to support the instructional program. If the schools do not meet the expectations held by citizens—whether because of dissimilarities in values, lack of expertise, or faulty communication—the community will likely withdraw its support and will use its power to reallocate resources or to replace the staff with personnel who will accomplish the expected tasks in an acceptable manner. The staff, on the other hand, has power in its expertise. The staff expects that the community will furnish the resources to implement the instructional program. Although the staff has power to withdraw services if it does not receive adequate resources, staff members are, in the final analysis, agents of the community and ultimately must either accommodate to its demands or set about to change them. Open and clear channels of communication must be initiated and maintained in order to optimize the success of the instructional program.

The second level focuses on the local school community. At this level, particular attention is accorded parents. Parents often hold expectations for the school which are more specific, and perhaps less objective, than those of the wider community. Parents also have a direct effect on the input of each child into the instructional program. Because of their intense interest in the school's available means and projected ends, the parents collectively constitute the most influential school-related group; they have the greatest impact on actual awareness and potential political actions within the larger community.

At the third level the focus is directly on instruction. Parents must have a clear understanding of the school's aims regarding the cognitive, affective, and psychomotor development of their children. Because roles and functions may differ in the IGE school, parents also must understand the organization, program, and procedures used. To develop such understandings, the unit staff must provide an effective program of home-school-community relations. At the level of instruction, the family impacts directly on the individual student's abilities, skills, and attitudes.

Facilitative Environments

Early it was recognized that a system of supportive and facilitative environments is required to maintain and strengthen each IGE school so that, in fact, each school becomes increasingly self-renewing. The system of facilitative environments is conceptualized as consisting of the requisite inputs, personnel, material, and resources, in two categories: intraorganizational system variables and extraorganizational system variables. Concerning intraorganizational variables, the multiunit organizational structure was conceptualized to produce the facilitative environment at both school and school district levels. Intraorganizational facilitative environments focus particularly on obtaining, providing, and managing the physical and material resources which constitute the learning environment. For example, the change to IGE often requires that existing school facilities be remodeled or that projected facilities be planned to provide maximum flexibility in learning spaces. Moreover, to maximize the instructional accountability inherent in the system of IGE, attention must be given to systematic planning, programming, budgeting, and evaluating the equipment and materials that facilitate the teaching-learning process.

The system of extraorganizational facilitative environments includes the linkages and relationships which must be established and sustained between the school district and the larger environment, including other school districts, the state education agency, teacher education institutions, and other groups, such as teachers' association and parents' organizations—all of which share in policy development and program implementation processes. As in the multiunit organizational structure, a trilevel hierarchical arrangement should be utilized to structure extraorganizational relationships (Klausmeier, et al. 1974). At the lowest level in this structure are the Systemwide Program Committees of school districts, which, it will be remembered, include the administrative officer of the school district or designee, other members of the central office staff, representative building principals of IGE schools in the district, and representative unit leaders, teachers, and parents from the IGE schools.

At the next level of organization a Regional IGE Coordinating Council should be formed consisting of representatives of intermediate agencies in some states, a representative of at least one teacher-education institution of the region, and a representative of the state education agency. The Regional Council includes a regional IGE coordinator and representatives of the agencies which together are able to start and maintain IGE schools in that region of a state. The representatives from Systemwide Program Committees provide the linkage between the Regional Council and the individual IGE schools of each district. The representative from the state educational agency on the Regional Council provides the linkage with the statewide educational system.

At the third organizational level is the State IGE Coordinating Council. Chaired by the chief state school officer or designee, the State Council should include at least one state IGE coordinator, other key personnel of the state agency, and representatives of each Regional Council including a teacher educator, a representative of an intermediate agency, and a representative of a Systemwide Program Committee. Two important criteria for membership are: having the specialized knowledge to contribute to the success of IGE, and having the authority to represent the particular agency. For example, when providing a preservice IGE teacher-education program, the persons responsible for teacher certification, the teacher education program in a college, and the placement of student teachers in local IGE schools are essential participants.

This pattern of facilitative environments was used as the frame of reference by personnel in 23 states where IGE state networks had been formed by 1975. A recent comparative study by Paul (1974) of the facilitative environments in three states (Connecticut, Ohio, and Wisconsin) revealed that the greater the dynamic linkages, the clearer coordinating structures, and the greater the resource capabilities between and among the agencies, then the more complete is the diffusion and integration of IGE into the target user system, the public schools. Paul also documented that variations in the structure of the state IGE Coordinating Council are necessary among the states because of differences in kinds of governmental units, constitutional and legislative provisions regarding education, area, population, and other characteristics.

Continuing Research and Development

The seventh and final component of IGE is that of a program of continuing research and development to produce validated instructional materials and procedures. Research to generate knowledge and theory dealing with the various components of IGE is essential since it is a dynamic system that must change and continually improve. Various kinds of research and development related to IGE must be conducted by many individuals and agencies.

Local schools continuously conduct evaluative research when implementing instructional programs for the individual student and evaluating the effectiveness of the programs. Larger school districts and state education agencies also evaluate their IGE programs. Development-based research is being conducted by many agencies to develop each component of IGE, including curricular materials and measurement tools. The development and refinement of the specific components of IGE and of other comprehensive educational systems and products require the specialized capabilities found in colleges and universities, research and development centers, regional educational laboratories, state education agencies, and other profit and non-profit organizations.

Long-term development and refinement of curricular materials and procedures related to reading, mathematics, motivation, and other domains require the cooperative efforts of many personnel and agencies. Subject matter specialists, methodologists, and behavioral scientists provide the essential input of substantive and procedural knowledge. School personnel and those from state education departments assist in determining how well the new materials and methods work. Through an interactive cycle of developing the materials, testing them in school settings, and revising as necessary, the Wisconsin Research and Development Center, for example, has been able to develop materials for particular target groups of students, teachers, and other educational personnel. In revising the material, information is secured to determine (1) how well students learn from materials or procedures in near-final form, (2) how much time is required on the part of the teacher to use it, and (3) how well the students and teachers like it.

Knowledge-generating research has many variants, including short-term horizontal descriptive research and controlled experimentation. Usually, experimental research is not directly related to the instructional program of the school, although it could be, and the results sometimes have neither immediate nor long-term implications for improving IGE or any other form of schooling. Despite this, such research may be of great significance in extending knowledge about a component of the instructional system and in refining administrative and instructional theory and practice in education.

OVERVIEW OF THE PRINCIPAL'S ROLE IN IGE

The chapters that follow are directed toward a synthesis of the knowledge and understandings, leadership and administrative skills, and values and attitudes required of the IGE school principal.

The first section of this book describes the concepts and competencies required in each functional area of the principal's role. Chapter 2 treats the principal's role in moving from a traditional to the multiunit form of organizational structure of the school. Chapter 3 is concerned with the heart of the IGE program, the principal's responsibilities in implementing instructional programming for the individual student. Closely related to instructional programming is the domain of initial, formative, and summative evaluation required for educational decision making which is described in Chapter 4. Staff recruitment, assignment, orientation, motivation, development, and evaluation constitute the personnel function which is highlighted in Chapter 5. Chapter 6 describes the role of the principal in planning, obtaining, programming, budgeting, and managing the financial resources, educational equipment, curricular materials, and school plant facilities required for IGE. The centrality of the principal's role in designing and implementing an effective program of home-school-community relations is treated in Chapter 7. The extraorganizational environment and continuing research and development to install and improve IGE are discussed in Chapter 8. An overview of the IGE school principalship both now and in the future constitutes Chapter 9. Chapter 10 consists of case studies which pose practical problem situations sometimes encountered in administering an IGE school. The cases deal with issues such as the following: adopting an implementation strategy, selecting unit leaders, implementing instructional programming for the individual student, evaluating teachers, allocating resources, remodeling school facilities, improving home-school-community relations, and strengthening facilitative environments. Analysis, discussion, and solution of the issues posed should help the principal to develop the understandings, skills, and attitudes required to implement IGE effectively.

Four instructional films have been produced to accompany this textbook:

1. *The Principal in Individually Guided Education* is designed for use, first with graduate students in elementary school administration, second with practicing principals, unit leaders, and teachers in inservice programs, and third with special groups interested in the principal's role in an IGE school. This overview film describes the principal's role in an IGE school in terms of providing leadership in instruction, implementing the multiunit organization, conducting a staff development program, obtaining financial resources, and coordinating home-school-community relations. This film highlights the mechanisms and procedures for involving others in decision making, and stresses that being a principal of an IGE school is a demanding but rewarding role.

2. *Helping Janice Teach Effectively,* a problem film, poses a situation which emphasizes that evaluation of teaching effectiveness is a critical function. The following issues in staff evaluation are considered: formulating criteria and procedures to be used, involving the IIC in staff evaluation, and involving teachers in evaluating instruction.

3. *Who Should Spend the Money?* a problem film, poses a situation concerning the need for flexibility in budgetary procedures and for involving the SPC in obtaining and allocating resources for IGE schools. This film emphasizes the principal's leadership role in articulating needs, representing the school, and negotiating change in school district policies, programs, and resources.

4. *Parents Want to Understand,* a problem film, poses a situation which helps the principal to recognize the importance of effective home-school-community relations, to communicate effectively with parents and others, and to involve parents and other community groups in the changeover to IGE.

An instructor's guide also has been prepared to assist professors in colleges and universities conducting preservice preparatory programs and to help school systems conducting inservice training programs for practicing and prospective principals of IGE schools. The *Instructor's Guide for the Principal and Individually Guided Education* enumerates the cognitive and affective competencies to be developed, shows the relationship of the cases and films to the competencies, includes several useful instruments and procedures, suggests additional learning activities, and lists additional references for further study.

SUMMARY

This introductory chapter was designed to develop the following knowledge and understandings on the part of present and prospective principals concerning the definition of IGE, the stages in the historical development of IGE, the meaning of the seven basic components of IGE, and the interrelationships of the seven basic components of IGE. Hopefully, information also has been presented which will lead the principal to accept the need for a viable alternative form of schooling and to feel that IGE holds considerable potential for improving education.

REFERENCES

Education USA Special Report, 1972. Individually guided education and the multiunit school. Arlington, Va.: National School Public Relations Association.

Fruth, M. J., B. D. Bowles, and R. H. Moser. In press. *Home-school-community relations* in H. J. Klausmeier, R. A. Rossmiller, and M. Saily (eds.) *Individually guided elementary education: concepts and practices.*

Hechinger, G. U.S. schools *are* number one. In M. O. Donley, Jr. (ed.), *NEA Reporter* **12** (October), 2.

Klausmeier, H. J., and W. Goodwin 1975. *Learning and human abilities: educational psychology.* 4th ed. New York: Harper & Row.

————— 1975. IGE: an alternative form of schooling. In H. Talmage (ed.), *Systems of individualized education.* Berkeley, Calif.: McCutchan.

—————, J. E. Walter, and L. J. Lins 1974. *Manual for starting and maintaining state IGE networks.* Madison, Wisc.: University of Wisconsin/Sears-Roebuck Foundation IGE Teacher Education Project.

—————, J. T. Jeter, M. R. Quilling, and D. A. Frayer 1973. *Individually guided motivation.* Madison, Wisc.: Wisconsin Research and Development Center for Cognitive Learning.

————— 1972. *An invitation to the Sears-Roebuck foundation to improve elementary schooling through implementation, refinement, and institutionalization of IGE/MUS–E.* Madison, Wisc.: School of Education, University of Wisconsin.

—————, M. R. Quilling, J. S. Sorenson, R. S. Way, and G. R. Glasrud 1971. *Individually guided education and the multiunit elementary school: guidelines for implementation.* Madison, Wisc.: Wisconsin Research and Development Center for Cognitive Learning.

—————, R. G. Morrow, and J. E. Walter 1968. *Individually guided education in the multiunit elementary school: guidelines for implementation.* Madison, Wisc.: Wisconsin Research and Development Center for Cognitive Learning.

—————, D. M. Cook, W. L. Goodwin, G. E. Tagatz, and L. Pingel 1967. *Individualizing instruction in language arts through development and research in R & I units of local schools, 1965–66.* Technical Report No. 19. Madison, Wisc.: Wisconsin Research and Development Center for Cognitive Learning.

—————, W. L. Goodwin, J. Prasch, and M. R. Goodson, with an introduction by W. G. Findley 1966. Project MODELS: maximizing opportunities for development and experimentation in learning in the schools. Occasional paper, No. 3. Madison, Wisc.: Wisconsin Research and Development Center for Cognitive Learning.

Lipham, J. M. 1974. Making effective decisions. In J. A. Culbertson, C. Henson, and R. Morrison (eds.), *Performance objectives for school principals.* Berkeley, Calif.: McCutchan.

Otto, W., *et al.* 1973. *Wisconsin design for reading skill development: rationale and guidelines.* Minneapolis: National Computer Systems.

Paul, D. A. 1974. *The diffusion of an innovation through interorganizational linkages.* Technical report No. 308. Madison, Wisc.: Wisconsin Research and Development Center for Cognitive Learning.

Romberg, T., *et al.* 1974. *Developing mathematical processes.* Chicago: Rand McNally.

Sipes, W. H. 1972. *Preliminary report on results of one-week institutes for experienced multiunit personnel.* Madison, Wisc.: Wisconsin Research and Development Center for Cognitive Learning.

Thorndike, R. L. 1973. *International studies in evaluation III: reading comprehension education in fifteen countries.* Stockholm, Sweden: Almqvist and Wiksells.

U.S. Department of Health, Education, and Welfare 1969. *Digest of educational statistics.* Washington, D.C.

―――― 1973. *American education.* Washington, D.C.

Venezky, R., *et al.* 1974. *Prereading skills program.* Chicago: Encyclopedia Britannica Educational Corporation.

2

Implementing the Multiunit Organization

James E. Walter
James M. Lipham

Objectives

After reading this chapter, the reader will be able:

- To understand the theoretical foundation of the multiunit organizational structure.
- To comprehend the functions of the I & R Unit, the IIC, and the SPC.
- To describe the roles of the principal, unit leaders, teachers, and other personnel in an IGE school.
- To identify the phases and activities in implementing IGE.
- To understand the role of the principal in implementing IGE.

The multiunit organization, a functional modification of the traditional school structure, is designed to facilitate learning and teaching through the establishment of semiautonomous instructional units. The new organization not only creates the pivotal role of unit leader but also gives new depth and range to the roles of principal and teacher. Moreover, the provisions for intra- and interunit planning foster participation in decision making and the assumption of responsibility for implementing decisions. The multiunit structure is designed to increase interpersonal and group interaction within the school and to pave the way for more fruitful relationships between the school and its larger environment. To realize these gains in school operation requires a sound theory of organization which is incorporated in a carefully delineated practical structure made dynamic through continuous fine tuning of the several components.

In this chapter, the theoretical foundations of the multiunit school are first traced in terms of established principles of organization. Next, a prototypic model of the multiunit organization is shown. A description then follows of the major structural and operational components and of the major changes required in roles and responsibilities in the transition to the multiunit form of organization. The chapter concludes with a discussion of the understandings and attitudes required of the principal in order to implement this major organizational change.

THEORETICAL FOUNDATIONS

The move from traditional to individualized education requires several significant shifts compatible with emerging educational practice: in student placement, from age grading to multiaging; in instructional methods, from didactic teaching to discovery learning; in instructional grouping, from class sized to varied patterns; in learning activities, from limited choice to extensive choice; in instructional materials, from required texts to multimedia; in student evaluation, from testing to multiple criteria; and in school architecture from a traditional classroom configuration to flexible open space. Many of these substantive changes are explored in greater detail in subsequent chapters. But what are the basic principles of organization that undergird the multiunit form of organization which was designed to facilitate IGE practices?

It is generally agreed among organizational analysts that at least two types of organizations may be posited. On the one hand, there is the "bureaucratic," "mechanistic," or "closed" organization which emphasizes authority of position, hierarchical structure, status differences, formalized rules, centralized decision making, high role specificity, and routinization. On the other hand is the "dynamic," "organic," or "open" organization which emphasizes professional autonomy and authority, low stratification, informal relationships, involvement in decision making, low role specificity, innovativeness, and job satisfaction (McGregor 1960, pp. 119–125, and Hage 1965, pp. 289–320). No organization, including the school, is either of these "pure" types, yet the multiunit school was designed to be more "open," "organic," or "dynamic" than the traditional school in terms of its authority structure, role relationships, and decision-making processes.

Authority Structure of the School

The school, as does any social institution, consists of a hierarchy of superordinate-subordinate roles and relationships which, as Weber has indicated, is the most commonly utilized means for channeling authority and responsibility in an organized manner (Weber 1959, p. 173). Functionally, this hierarchy of relationships is the locus for allocating and integrating personnel and material to achieve the goals of the system (Getzels, *et al.* 1968, p. 52). The traditional structure of the school, typically represented by a pyramid, stresses formal power relationships—tending to view the school board and superintendent as "top management," the school principal as "middle management," and the teachers and students at the "bottom" level of the organization. In fact, in the traditional school the control function of administrators typically is emphasized while the leadership function is often ignored (Lipham 1964, pp. 119–141).

Parsons (1958, pp. 41–47) has pointed out that there are critical points at which one finds qualitative breaks in the simple continuity of "line" authority in the school organization. Those at the higher levels cannot tell those at lower levels "what to do," because the functions at each level, particularly in organizations made up of professionals, are different. In schools, for example, it is not the administrators but the teachers who possess professional instructional expertise. Consequently, teachers have "power over" those at managerial levels—to plan, implement, and evaluate program activities. Because of this circumstance, the multiunit structure was designed to establish the appropriate coordinating mechanisms so that professionals at the instructional, school, and school district levels could govern their activities, thereby maximizing collegial authority.

Quantitatively, as well as qualitatively, the conventional structure of the school makes little allowance for overloads in the line authority when large numbers of persons often must be supervised directly. In many schools the span of control of the principal is excessive, requiring the direct supervision of many teachers and other school personnel—not to mention the multitude of mandatory personal contacts with students, parents and other citizens. In conventional schools the time constraint alone tends to formalize and stratify working relationships. The result is that the school's authority structure is characterized by directive and mechanistic interactions.

The multiunit form of school organization makes suitable provisions to counteract quantitative as well as qualitative breakdowns in the authority structure of the school. To manage the quantity of interaction, a new leadership role between the principal and the teachers is created to assist in the coordination of instruction, thereby altering the number and nature of activities for which the principal is to provide leadership. The multiunit organizational structure is designed to reinforce the basic organizational principle that the authority structure of the school should emphasize professional rather than positional role relationships.

Role Relationships within the School

As Getzels (1958, p. 153) observed, a role representing the dynamic aspects of a position, office, or status within an institution has certain normative rights and duties called role expectations which define within limits what one should or should not do as the incumbent of a particular role within an institution. Regarding complementarity, roles are interdependent in that each role derives its meaning from other related and interlocking roles within the organization. Indeed, the rights of one role often become the obligations of a second role, and the expectations for the first role may form the sanctions for the second—as in the case of principal-teacher and teacher-student roles (Getzels, *et al.* 1968, p. 63). In the multiunit form of school organization attention is paid to this quality of complementarity, in that the major expectations for each role within the school are defined in terms of relations among the interlocking roles. Thus, the roles are fused into coherent, interdependent units of the organization.

Concerning the issue of role definition, all organizational roles are more or less flexible and the associated behaviors may be thought of as lying along a continuum from "required" to "prohibited" (Getzels, *et al.* 1968, p. 62). Certain behaviors crucial to the role are held as mandatory, whereas other behaviors are forbidden. Within the multiunit school organization, with its emphasis on instructional programming for the individual student, the role expectations of principals, teachers, and students are described so as to foster discretionary judgment. For example, teachers are encouraged to utilize and experiment with a wide variety of instructional approaches, grouping patterns, and materials. As Hull observed, the IGE school grants considerably more freedom of role behavior than does the age-graded, self-contained form of school organization (Hull 1973, pp. 169–173). Such role flexibility helps both staff and students to identify with and internalize the goals of the school, thereby becoming active participants in the decision-making process.

Decision Making in the School

In a complex organization such as the school most decisions are shared; that is, more than one role incumbent is typically involved in the decision-making process. Such involvement, moreover, may range from that of providing information only, to developing alternatives, to recommending an alternative, to actually making the decision (Lipham 1974, p. 103). Several studies have revealed that typically in the school, involvement in decision making by students, teachers, parents, and others has been quite circumscribed—limited primarily to a low level of providing information only, and even then concerning routinized decisions (cf. Lipham and Hoeh, Jr. 1974, pp. 165–171). Still other studies have revealed dysfunctions in decision making in the school to result not so much from lack of involvement as from lack of clarity concerning decision content—"who" should make "which" decisions (Lipham and Hoeh, Jr. 1974, pp. 161–165).

The multiunit form of organization was specifically designed to maximize meaningful mutual participation in the decision-making process. Appropriate organizational mechanisms are established which foster shared decision making, and it is to a description of this structure that we now turn.

THE MULTIUNIT SCHOOL ORGANIZATION *

The multiunit school organization is a structure that has emerged since 1965 from a synthesis of theory and practice. The focus of IGE, of which the multiunit school is the organizational component, is on providing appropriate alternative instructional programs for the individual student. In 1965, this focus led to issues about organizing school staffs appropriately, enhancing role clarity and flexibility, increasing involvement in decision making, and improving communication. Clearly, an alternative to the age-graded, self-contained classroom type of organization, prevalent in American education for nearly 100 years, was needed. In a series of iterations, university personnel, school administrators, and teachers cooperatively designed the multiunit school to produce an environment in which instructional programming and other components of IGE could be introduced and refined to provide for responsible participation and accountability at appropriate levels.

Figure 2.1 depicts the prototypic organizational structure of the multiunit school. The organizational hierarchy consists of interrelated groups at three distinct levels of operation: at the instructional level there is the I & R Unit, at the building or school level there is the IIC, and at the school district level there is the Systemwide Program Committee or similar administrative arrangement. This structure possesses several practical implications concerning decision making, division of labor, and leadership.

---

* The material in this section is based on H. J. Klausmeier, *et al.* 1971. *Individually guided education in the multiunit elementary school: guidelines for implementation.* Madison, Wisc.: Wisconsin Research and Development Center for Cognitive Learning.

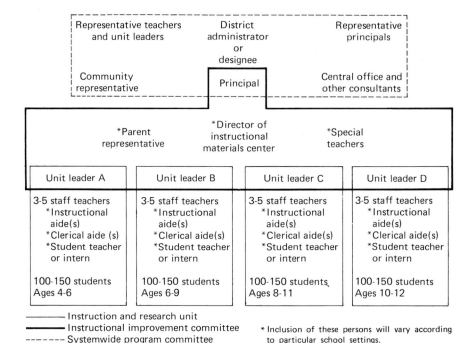

Fig. 2.1 Multiunit organization of an IGE school of 400–600 students. Adapted from H. J. Klausmeier, R. G. Morrow, and J. E. Walter 1968. *Individually guided education in the multiunit school.* Madison, Wisc.: Wisconsin Research and Development Center for Cognitive Learning.

The multiunit organization facilitates shared decision making about instruction and other matters. At the instructional level, a group of teachers, rather than individual teachers, are responsible for the instruction of a large group of children. Decisions about the use of such instructional resources as time, materials, and facilities can be made cooperatively. At the building level, the principal and representatives from the unit (unit leaders) constitute the IIC which also makes decisions cooperatively. This committee makes decisions about schoolwide policies, objectives, and programs. At the school district level, another group, the SPC, identifies resources and establishes policies which will facilitate making and implementing wise and workable decisions by the IICs. At all levels, decisions which must be made at that level are shared decisions. For example, the specific instructional plans for the children are developed and executed by the staff of the unit. The objectives or goals for the school serving a particular community are developed by the IIC. Decisions having districtwide impact or implications are made by the SPC.

The multiunit structure not only permits horizontally shared decision making, characterized by the groups above; it also fosters vertically shared decision making. A major role expectation for both the principal and the unit leader is that each is a member of another level in the hierarchy. Principals not only head the IIC, but they also are members of the Systemwide Program Committee. Likewise, unit leaders not only head the I & R Units but they also are members of the IIC. Moreover, the composition of the IIC includes central office consultants, and that of the SPC includes representative teachers and unit leaders. Representative parents and citizens may serve on any or all committees. A consequence of these vertical arrangements is that while each level takes the initiative for certain decisions, each has information from the other levels.

Regarding division of labor in the I & R Unit, teachers are expected to cooperate in planning and executing instructional programs for students. This cooperative environment makes a flexible division of labor possible in two major respects. With regard to instructional matters, no teacher is expected to be proficient or expert in teaching all the curricular and instructional areas. The skills and understandings in which one teacher may feel less confident can be complemented by those of another teacher in the unit. Some teachers may assume the responsibility for the long-range planning in a unit of study on one occasion, whereas other teachers may assume this task at another time. With respect to routine matters, in all instructional settings there are myriad tasks, such as record keeping, collecting money, and the like. In the multiunit school, teachers are relieved of routine tasks by a secretary or aide. Research has revealed that the IGE school is characterized by a functional, flexible, and dynamic division of labor (Pellegrin 1969).

With regard to leadership, the multiunit organizational structure not only affixes positional leadership responsibilities, but also fosters emergent leadership behavior. Concerning positional leadership, the principal, for example, serves as Chairperson of the IIC. Through the sharing of decision making with the unit leaders, the principal gains the understandings and expertise required to propose knowledgeable solutions to problems, becoming an emergent leader in meetings of both the SPC and the I & R Units. Positional and emergent leadership on the part of unit leaders, teachers, parents and citizens are similarly enhanced at all levels in the organization.

THE ORGANIZATIONAL FUNCTIONS
AT THE THREE LEVELS

As shown in Figure 2.1, the multiunit organization is operative at three levels: the I & R Unit, the IIC, and the SPC, each of which has a designated structure and certain unique functions.

The I & R Unit

In IGE schools, the nongraded I & R Unit replaces age-graded, self-contained classrooms. Each unit has a unit leader, three to five staff teachers, one first-year or resident teacher, one instructional secretary, one teacher intern, and 100 to 150 students.

The age range of students within a unit varies from two to four years with the children assigned to units primarily on the basis of years of school attendance. Within each unit, grade lines should be abandoned as children will be able to work in one-to-one, small group, class-size group, and unit-size activities. It is also possible, and sometimes necessary, for students to be involved in instructional activities in other units.

Four basic functions are performed by the staff of the I & R Unit. As a team, each unit must plan for instruction, teach the children, evaluate their learning, and relate home, school, and community. Other activities associated with these functions are: (1) engaging in on-the-job, inservice training activities; (2) conducting research to devise and evaluate instructional programs appropriate for each child; (3) planning or conducting research and development activities cooperatively with other agencies; and (4) providing clinical and internship experiences for students enrolled in teacher education programs.

The unit staff should meet as a group for at least two hours weekly to plan and evaluate the instructional and other functions, as well as to solve operational problems that may arise. At least all certificated members of the unit are expected to attend these meetings; instructional aides or secretaries may attend to keep abreast of unit activities, since they often can provide valuable information to the professional staff in making decisions. As necessary, parents, consultants, or others may also attend unit meetings. The agenda should be supplied by the unit leader.

Time for unit meetings may be found three ways: (1) by scheduling special teachers (art, music, or physical education) into a unit en bloc, the unit staff can be freed two or three times weekly; (2) by arriving early at school and using teacher aides to supervise homeroom or large group activities, the unit can meet from 30 to 45 minutes daily; or (3) by lengthening four school days during the week, students can arrive at school late or be dismissed early on the fifth day, thus freeing the unit to meet for about two hours. While each of these solutions has advantages and disadvantages and other solutions are possible, it is essential that sufficient time be found for unit staffs to meet.

Unit staffs are more likely to be successful when they: (1) arrange sufficient time for planning and evaluating the instructional program; (2) cooperate fully in expertise exchange; and (3) divide labor according to talents. Unit staffs which meet only to coordinate individual plans will not be successful in carrying out their functions.

The instructional improvement committee (IIC). The IIC is the second organizational level in the multiunit school. As shown in Figure 2.1, the IIC is made up of the building principal and the unit leaders. Since this committee is responsible for schoolwide concerns, it can be organized only when the total building staff is organized into units.

The functions of the IIC are to plan, implement, and evaluate matters associated with curriculum and instruction, staffing, home-school-community relations, and the financial and physical resources. These functions lead to two basic sets of activities, planning and coordinating. With regard to planning, the IIC is responsible for stating the school's educational objectives and outlining its educational program, formulating the school's inservice program, designing the home-school-community relations program, and assessing the financial and physical resources of the building. As it coordinates the implementation and evaluation of these plans, the IIC ensures that the plans and activities of the school's units achieve continuity in all curricular areas, that the use of facilities and materials that are common to two or more units are arranged, and that the programs and activities carried out in cooperation with teacher education institutions and other agencies are coordinated.

The primary responsibility of the IIC is to assume the initiative in identifying and developing the educational objectives of the school and outlining on the basis of these the school's educational program. The committee should also develop the means by which the educational objectives and program are to be evaluated. These efforts lead naturally to guidelines for identifying, developing, and utilizing instructional materials and evaluation tools and procedures. The Instructional Programming Model, discussed in the next chapter, provides the guiding framework in these matters.

Planning, implementing, and evaluating must, of course, be done in the context of state and school district policies and regulations. The IIC ensures that such policies and/or regulations are interpreted and implemented appropriately.

Designing and conducting the school's inservice program is crucial to the success of IGE. Initially, the IIC must plan and carry out inservice activities for the entire staff both before and during the changeover to IGE. The committee is also responsible for providing inservice for personnel who join the staff after the changeover has occurred. Once the school has begun implementing IGE, the committee is responsible for a continuing inservice program that not only will reinforce basic IGE concepts and practices but also will refine the requisite skills and understandings for the continued renewal of IGE. All of these activities should be carefully evaluated by the committee.

Coordinating is also a primary responsibility of the IIC. Only as the committee carries out this function can it encourage consistency of IGE practices, achieve continuity in the curriculum across units, and ensure that implementation accords with appropriate policies. The committee must also ensure the flexible and equitable utilization of facilities, materials, and equipment which is used by the several units. A Wisconsin IGE principal expressed the benefits of coordination by the committee in this way: "I no longer have to stick my neck out alone. The unit leaders and I go out on the limb together!"

Additional coordinative concerns arise out of the school's relationships with other agencies and with the community. If an IGE school is cooperating with a teacher education institution in student teaching or intern programs, for example, the committee is the proper group to ensure that the expectations of the preservice teacher, the school, and the teacher education institution are mutually compatible. Since many IGE schools cooperate with other agencies in research and development activities, the committee must see to it that balance in the school's program is maintained while accommodating the needs of such agencies. Participation in teacher education and research and development experiences can be very rewarding if properly coordinated.

The IIC also assumes a key role in planning and coordinating an effective program of home-school-community relations. Responsibilities of the committee in this domain are described fully in Chapter 6.

Both the planning and coordinating responsibilities of the IIC involve teachers and other personnel in the I & R Units through the unit leader. The unit leaders perform a significant representation function in that they convey the concerns, insights, and other information upward from the unit staffs to the committee (Nerlinger 1975). Plans and guidelines developed by the committee are transmitted to the unit staffs by the unit leaders. Thus the unit leader not only is responsible for managing the activities of the unit, but also for representing the unit members. The principal, as the school's instructional leader and administrator, must see to it that each unit staff executes its responsibilities in the school's total program. The IIC, therefore, has program development and coordination responsibilities but does not assume management responsibilities.

The IIC typically meets a minimum of once a week for at least two hours. Since the schedules of the unit leaders and principal are somewhat flexible, they experience less difficulty than the units in finding time to meet. Instructional planning is the most difficult job for the IIC and the major portion of its agenda should be related to this area. The principal, as chairperson, should formulate the agenda in consultation with the unit leaders and avoid the routine matters frequently associated with faculty meetings. Even so, occasional meetings of the total staff may still be required.

The systemwide program committee (SPC).   Substantial changes are required to move from the self-contained classroom organization to IGE. The SPC facilitates this transition. As shown in Figure 2.1, this committee, chaired by the superintendent or designee, includes consultants and other central office staff, and representative principals, unit leaders, teachers, and community representatives. Since local school districts differ greatly in size and other characteristics, it has been found appropriate in some school systems (for example, those in large, urban districts) to utilize some arrangement other than the SPC. Even so, it is necessary to have some structural arrangement which will assume responsibility for the functions of the SPC.

The primary functions of the SPC are to plan, implement, and evaluate in connection with the matters of curriculum and instruction, staffing, home-school-community relations, and financial and physical resources. The main responsibility of the SPC in terms of these functions is to establish the operational guidelines for the schools in the district which adopt IGE and to recommend changes in school district policies in order to facilitate the implementation of IGE. The guidelines should deal with such matters as endorsing the programmatic thrusts in IGE schools, recruiting IGE personnel and providing for their inservice training, obtaining instructional materials and other resources, and fostering improved community relations in the school district.

The four programmatic thrusts of IGE schools discussed earlier include instructional programming for the individual student, staff development or inservice, preservice teacher education, and research and development. Although all IGE schools must be involved in the first two functions, involvement in the latter two is optional. Initially, an IGE school can easily become overextended if it becomes involved in all four functions. The SPC must provide guidelines for helping each school decide which of the latter two functions will be emphasized.

Once the decision relative to the thrusts of the IGE school is made, it is important that the necessary material and human resources be made available to the school. Systemwide guidelines must be devised for acquiring and providing the necessary resources.

A capable building principal, qualified unit leaders, dedicated teachers, and other personnel who are compatible in their roles are essential to a successful IGE operation. The identification and recruitment of the initial staff in an IGE school is especially critical; the recruitment of new staff for vacancies in existing IGE schools is likewise important. Continuous staff development is necessary to refine and improve the IGE program. Depite careful recruitment and staff development efforts, some personnel may find the role demands in the IGE school to be incompatible with their personal needs and dispositions and may wish to transfer to other schools. It is, therefore, important for the SPC to develop and recommend school district policies concerning staff recruitment, development, and transfer.

The implementation of IGE with its changes in staff and student roles, functions, and processes requires that appropriate means must be established for the involvement of parents, other citizens, and other community subpublics. These efforts are particularly significant, both at the point in time that schools are deciding whether or not to adopt IGE and after implementation has started. The SPC should establish the guidelines for communicating with and involving extraorganizational participation in the school program.

While the SPC meets less frequently than either the IIC or the I & R Units, its operation is important to the success of the IGE school. Three important criteria for membership on the SPC are that its members (1) have decision-making power, (2) have specialized knowledge to contribute to the success of IGE, and (3) represent all levels of the organization. For example, when the school is making a systematic effort to implement an individually guided program in reading, the reading consultant not only should serve on the SPC but also should meet regularly with the IIC and the I & R Units.

Role Responsibilities in the Multiunit School

The multiunit organization possesses important implications for the role responsibilities of all staff members. Unless the expectations are clear to everyone and are carried out as expected, the designated functions at each organizational level will not be adequately fulfilled.

There are three major characteristics of roles in the multiunit school. First, roles are differentiated. Such differentiation is not highly specific, but it does incorporate one new role, the unit leader; it also outlines the major duties of each role in the school. Second, the roles of the principal, staff teachers, and paraprofessionals are changed; they are qualitatively and quantitatively different from those in the traditional school. In part, the change is one of emphasis. For example, the principal is directly involved in providing instructional leadership in small group settings more than with the staff as a whole or with individual teachers. The change is also in kind. The principal, for example, becomes chairperson of the IIC which changes the number and nature of the principal's interactions. The third major characteristic is that in the multiunit school roles become more interdependent. Teachers are dependent on each other to accomplish objectives, and they are dependent on the unit leader for leadership and representation. The unit leaders depend on the principal for overall leadership and coordination. In this interdependent setting the likelihood of conflict arising out of role interaction is increased, but it can be ameliorated by ensuring that all staff members clearly understand the major expectations of the respective roles, including that of school superintendent, school principal, unit leader, staff teacher, and instructional aide.

The superintendent of schools.   The superintendent of a district implementing IGE has two major responsibilities: to support educational change and to evaluate the progress of implementation. To fulfill these responsibilities the superintendent must be fully informed and appropriately involved.

To support the implementation of IGE, the superintendent initially must fully understand its philosophy, practices, and requirements for implementation. Requirements for implementation include securing qualified staff, obtaining appropriate instructional materials and facilities, and providing adequate resources for inservice training. The superintendent may also need to secure changes in certain school district policies or procedures. The changeover will certainly require that important constituencies be informed, and it may require negotiations with the board of education, community groups, and professional organizations. Finally, the superintendent will need to ensure that a timely sequence of implementation activities is planned and executed.

The superintendent is responsible for establishing the SPC or a similar suitable arrangement at the district level, since central office support must be provided for IGE schools. If the superintendent cannot chair this committee, then another member of the central office staff should be appointed. In large districts where IGE is being implemented in several schools, the superintendent may need to appoint a local IGE coordinator. Another important supportive effort of the superintendent and the SPC is to protect the efforts of the IGE staff from unwarranted attacks which any innovative program incurs simply because it is receiving special attention. As all school superintendents will recognize, the IGE program must also be compatible with federal, state, and system goals, purposes, and procedures. In summary, the change effort must at the same time be protected and channeled within overall guidelines.

In an era of accountability the superintendent must also ensure that appropriate evaluation occurs so that corrective actions can be taken promptly. An adequate evaluation plan will help the superintendent to identify both successful and inadequate execution of the concepts and practices of IGE. While such evaluation may be conducted by the local school staff, the superintendent, through the SPC, must be active in developing the overall evaluation plan and in analyzing the evaluative results for dissemination.

The school principal.   This and succeeding chapters in this book are, of course, concerned with the major dimensions of the principal's role in IGE.

Suffice it here, however, to observe that in the IGE school the principal's role is changed in both of its major dimensions, leadership and administration (Lipham 1964, pp. 119–141). Regarding leadership, many IGE principals report that with their reduced span of control and their sharing of decision making with the IIC they are able to devote sustained and meaningful attention to the instructional program. In IGE, their major instructional leadership responsibilities include initiating and refining the system of instructional programming; implementing staff development programs; supervising preservice teacher education programs, and coordinating research and development activities.

Much variability in instructional leadership styles is to be expected among principals. It is not assumed that the principal is an expert in all functions of the school. Concerning instructional programming, for example, the principal must rely heavily on staff members and consultants for the knowledge base for these decisions. On such issues as the content of instruction, materials and media, student activities, teacher activities, evaluation of student performance, and the placement of students, for example, the unit leaders may possess more information and expertise than the principal. Although subject matter specialists and experts from the central office or other agencies may be available to assist the principal, the IIC and teachers provide leadership in these important responsibilities.

Concerning administration, the principal is expected to be strong in providing the conditions essential for the staff to carry out their instructional responsibilities. In meeting this responsibility, the principal must supervise and evaluate educational personnel, obtain and administer resources, and relate effectively to students, parents, and other subpublics.

With regard to staffing the school, the principal is responsible for recruiting, supervising, and evaluating all the certificated and noncertificated staff. In choosing personnel for the IGE school, the principal must first recognize that the units should be staffed by persons who wish to be in such a setting. Typically, time must be allotted for teachers with no previous experience in cooperative planning to develop into effective unit members. During this time of adjustment, the principal must give effective support. Moreover, in the event a teacher does not wish to work in an IGE school, suitable means should be arranged for transfer. Finally, the central office staff, building principal, IIC, and unit staff must agree on how and when to replace a unit leader, a teacher, or an aide who for any reason seriously impedes the functioning of a unit.

Another responsibility of the principal is that of initiating, developing, and implementing a staff development program which includes both on-the-job and special purpose components. This responsibility, conducted in cooperation with the IIC, should include both certificated and noncertificated personnel. Staff development programs should ensure that the staff will learn the skills required to implement IGE effectively.

Involvement of the IGE school in preservice teacher education requires that the principal work closely with persons from outside the building in two important ways. First, the principal is responsible for developing the training program for interns or student teachers in cooperation with the IIC, central office staff, and representatives from teacher education institutions. Second, in coordinating and supervising the program, the principal must ensure that there are not too many adults in any one unit and that pre-service teachers are not utilized for routine chores.

Concerning other educational personnel from outside the building, the principal must deal with specialized consultants and representatives from outside agencies conducting research and development. Central office consultants, special teachers, and others can strengthen the staff's efforts in instructional programming for students. The principal may ensure the effectiveness of such assistance by having them meet with the IIC and the I & R Units.

Concerning research and development activities by outside agencies, the principal is responsible for coordinating research and to ensure that relevant results are communicated within the school, to other schools of the school system, and to other relevant groups. In such research, the principal must also assist unit leaders in arranging experimental treatments which ensure adherence to the quality research designs.

Brief mention should be made concerning the professional preparation and personal characteristics required of the principal who would lead and administer an IGE school. In addition to the usual requirement of success-ful teaching, experience as a unit leader or as a member of a teaching team is, of course, helpful. Graduate preparation should include work in organiza-tional theory, human learning and development, staff personnel, instruc-tional supervision, and research. Commitment to the principalship as a career should also be demonstrated by efforts to expand one's knowledge by further study through attendance at professional meetings, workshops, or institutes designed to develop skills in communicating, planning, organiz-ing, and evaluating educational activities. Requisite attitudes include a willingness to share authority and responsibility, to involve others in decision making, to foster change and innovation, and to assist others in the achievement of both organizational and individual goals.

The unit leader.* The position of unit leader, the only new role created in the multiunit organization, interlocks with its complementary roles of principal and teacher in numerous meaningful ways. First, the unit leader has responsibilities at two levels of the multiunit organization—as a mem-ber of the I & R Unit and as a member of the IIC—since the unit leader

*   For a comprehensive treatment of the role of the unit leader, see J. S. Sorenson, et al. 1976. *The unit leader and individually guided education.* Read-ing, Mass.: Addison-Wesley.

is the link between the two levels. As a result, vertical communications can be opened wherein decisions made at both levels reflect information and concerns of the other. Second, creation of the position of unit leader makes the principal's span of control more manageable. In IGE, the principal's leadership can be focused on fewer people, rather than on many, through frequent contacts with large groups or individual staff members. Unit leaders are expected to perform an important representation function by communicating the progress, plans, and problems of the units in regular meetings of the IIC. Third, the unit leader is primarily a teacher with some responsibilities differentiated from those of the staff teachers. The unit leader should not be considered a quasi-principal. Leadership responsibilities of the unit leader are exercised primarily in planning and coordinating instructional programs.

The responsibilities inherent in the role of the unit leader relate to three broad areas: membership in the IIC, leadership of the I & R Unit, and teaching. As a member of the IIC, the unit leader helps to plan and coordinate the instructional programming and staff development functions of the building. The unit leader also helps to plan and coordinate the programs associated with the preservice teacher education and research and development functions. The unit leader is also responsible for the efficient utilization of unit staff members, materials, and other resources.

With regard to the school's instructional programming function, the unit leader, as a member of the IIC, works with the principal, subject matter specialists, and other consultants in formulating the schoolwide educational objectives. The unit leader helps develop the broad outlines of the school's instructional program and contributes to the establishment and maintenance of an effective program of home-school-community relations relative to these matters.

Instructional improvement activities often result in the need for staff development activities. Here too, the unit leader, as a member of the IIC, cooperates in the development of a buildingwide staff development program for both certificated and noncertificated personnel.

Should the IGE staff participate in the preservice teacher education function, the unit leader, as a member of the IIC, will also have certain major responsibilities. The efficient utilization of interns or student teachers requires careful planning so that the school benefits from the presence of the preservice teacher and the intern or student teacher has appropriate opportunities to develop the understandings, skills, and attitudes required of the effective teacher. The unit leader is responsible for both unit and schoolwide teacher education activities.

Some IGE schools may be involved in research and development activities either in cooperation with some other outside agency or as a result of local school district initiative. In this function, the unit leader, as a member of the IIC, is responsible for planning and conducting research activities in the unit and the school.

As head of the I & R Unit, the unit leader has another set of responsibilities. The unit leader is responsible to the principal for planning and carrying out the unit's programs. This responsibility holds in all the functions in which the unit is involved. The unit leader ensures that all relevant persons including the principal, central office staff, outside consultants, and specialists are adequately involved at appropriate junctures. As in the case of the principal, the unit leader should seek to maximize staff involvement in decision making, since it is expected that each teacher in the unit will share fully in making decisions.

The unit leader must see to it that the staff development program is carried out in the unit. The unit leader provides inservice for the unit staff by demonstrating the proper use of an innovation or by arranging for outside consultants to provide the requisite inservice. So that noncertificated members of the unit can contribute and participate actively, the unit leader must develop and conduct, with the assistance of the others, a program of staff development for each person in the unit.

Even though the unit leader is involved in the IIC and is a leader of the unit, the unit leader is still primarily a teacher. It is recommended that the unit leader have direct contact with children up to 80 percent of the typical school day. Of course, it will be difficult for the unit leader to fulfill successfully the responsibilities as a leader of the unit and as a member of the IIC unless some released time from teaching duties is allotted. If the school is involved in either preservice teacher education or research and development activities, then the unit leader's amount of released time from teaching should be enlarged another 10 to 20 percent.

To investigate the nature of this new position in education, Sheridan (1974) recently conducted empirical analysis of the unit leader's role. From an analysis of the literature and practices in IGE schools, Sheridan developed and validated a survey instrument, the Unit Leader Role Analysis, which was administered to principals, unit leaders, and teachers in 48 IGE schools. From a factor analysis of the results, it was discovered that all respondents viewed the significant dimensions of the unit leader's role to include providing instructional coordination, maintaining extraorganizational relationships, and managing unit activities. Although the unit leader's role is a new position, there was agreement among principals, unit leaders, and teachers on many of the expectations they held for the unit leader's role. Such agreement, moreover, was found to be significantly and positively related to many variables, including staff participation in orientation activities prior to implementing IGE.

The preceding analysis of the unit leader's role suggests several issues which the principal must consider. Because unit leaders have expanded professional responsibilities, they should receive higher salaries than staff teachers. For this additional remuneration, the unit leader should expect to work more hours per week and more weeks per year. It is also apparent that unit leaders must continually improve their professional capabilities by pursuing further education and gaining relevant experiences.

The responsibilities of a unit leader suggest several personal characteristics and professional experiences which should be considered in selecting unit leaders. The unit leader should have had some experience as a teacher, three years as a minimum, and preferably in a team-teaching situation. While the beginning unit leader may not be required to have a master's degree, it is expected that the unit leader be progressing toward such a degree by taking advanced graduate courses in human learning and development, curriculum and instruction, and research and development. It is mandatory that unit leaders have positive attitudes toward change. Since the implementation of IGE requires adaptive behavior, the unit leader should be flexible and inventive. Because the role emphasizes coordination, the unit leader must be skilled in recognizing and utilizing the capabilities of all personnel in the unit. Because the unit leader is a linking role, one must be able to communicate with and maintain effective interaction with various personnel at several levels both within and outside the school and district. Because the role is a leadership position, the unit leader must be willing and able to assume leadership responsibilities. Finally, because the unit leader is also a teacher, one must exemplify the best in appropriate and effective teaching behavior.

The staff teacher.   Three characteristics distinguish the role of the staff teacher in IGE: planning and working cooperatively with other members of the unit, working with many children rather than with a fixed number of children, and performing at a highly professional level. One way in which a higher level of professional activity in IGE is manifested concerns how time is utilized. In IGE, the teacher spends time developing and evaluating several components of the instructional system, such as objectives for each child, assessing each child's characteristics, using new materials and equipment, and trying out new instructional procedures. Planning and participatory decision making also provide the teacher with experiences not found in the age-graded, self-contained classroom situation. The teacher also participates actively in preservice teacher education and in research and development activities. Through time, the teacher in an IGE school can become proficient in all of these areas.

In IGE, the teacher is expected to develop and clarify instructional objectives, design and implement a program based on the assessment of each child, and then continually evaluate both the child's progress and the instructional program. The teacher should understand the basic concepts and skills in at least one broad subject area and within that area arrange a valid sequence of content. Concerning the complementarity of teachers in the unit, a teacher in Connecticut commented as follows:

> We must recognize that teachers, as well as students, are individuals . . . and should be treated as such. A unit needs a balance of personalities as well as skills. If you really believe in individualizing, there's a place for all kinds of teachers on your team.

With regard to the first-year teacher in the multiunit school, it may be helpful for the principal to consider this person as a resident teacher. In the IGE school, the expectation is not that a first-year teacher can perform successfully all of the tasks of experienced teachers. Instead, the first-year teacher is expected to perform without assistance certain instructional tasks, and to perform with assistance those in which further experience is needed. This generalized statement of role expectations assumes assessment of the strengths and weaknesses of each first-year teacher. Such assistance in assessment comes in several forms. Initially, there is a direct partnership between the first-year teacher and the unit leader or other staff member in planning, carrying out, and evaluating the performance of a task. Subsequently, assistance may be necessary only in planning or evaluation. Finally, planning, implementation, and evaluation can all be conducted by the resident. Accommodations may need to be made for the number of pupils, groups, and parents with which the first-year teacher works. For example, initially one may have responsibilities for fewer students and for reporting to fewer parents.

Most elementary schools have special teachers in such areas as art, music, physical education, and remedial reading. These teachers are typically utilized in three ways: as visiting teachers with responsibilities in several buildings, as specialists assigned to one building, or as central office consultants. Due to varying policies and guidelines in districts, it is not possible to provide explicit direction about the proper role of these individuals in unit operations or in the IIC. Nonetheless, each school must decide who is responsible for determining the scope and sequence of instruction in the special areas, who assesses the students, and who carries out the instruction. To the fullest extent possible, the principal should bring special area personnel into the planning of the IIC and the planning and teaching in the units. Special area teachers should also participate fully in providing staff development to improve teacher competencies. In this way, staff teachers can better support special area teachers when they are not able to be in any one unit.

The preservice teacher.   The role of the preservice teacher is important in two respects. First, the preservice teacher provides an important link between the school and the district to the resources of the teacher education institution. Second, the preservice teacher provides additional personnel resources for the unit.

In a recent study of IGE in three states, Paul (1974) discovered that the relationship between local IGE schools and nearby teacher education institutions was perceived by professors, principals, unit leaders, and teachers as the most powerful force for initiating, sustaining, and refining educational change and improvement. He further found that the use of teacher interns not only strengthened the linkage between local schools and universities but also contributed significantly to the infusion of manpower and expertise to the schools. Conversely, the teaching interns contribute significantly to the knowledge and research capability of the teacher education institutions. He concluded that the use of teacher interns in the IGE school possesses great potential for strengthening both theory and practice in the field of education.

As teacher education institutions expand their programs for preservice teachers to include additional clinical experiences, it is becoming increasingly common for student teachers to spend full time in schools for either a semester or an academic year as teacher interns. Accordingly, the following discussion is focused primarily on the teacher intern, although the basic principles are relevant to the role of any student teacher in the IGE school.

The teacher intern is usually assigned to one unit in semester-type programs; or to two units, changing from one to the other at the end of the first semester, in academic-year programs. The latter procedure works particularly well when at least two interns are assigned to the same school. Since a large I & R Unit can readily incorporate two interns per semester, a five-unit school of about 700 students can accommodate as many as twenty interns per academic year. Preinternship observation and participation experiences may also be effectively conducted in the multiunit school. So that clinical experiences for prospective teachers do not overshadow the primary functions of the unit, however, principals of some schools will need to be careful concerning possible overload in preservice training activities.

In the IGE school, the intern engages in professional activities—not in routine, clerical duties. The latter are performed by the instructional secretary or aide. Workshops conducted prior to the opening of school are useful in providing interns with an overview of school operations and unit functions. Adequate provisions should be made for interns to become acquainted with the roles of all personnel in the building, as well as with the functions and procedures of the units to which they will be assigned. The objective is for the intern to engage in observation and minor participation at first, but then to move rapidly to full responsibility at a level similar to that of a first-year teacher.

A well-prepared intern who has previously observed and participated in school workshops or similar orientation activities may assume full responsibility for one-to-one, small group, and class size activities within two weeks after the opening of the semester. Initially, the intern does not assume decision-making responsibilities for the instructional program of the unit, as do the unit leader and experienced teachers, but the intern does participate in unit meetings to plan and subsequently to execute decisions.

Instructional and clerical aides.   Two kinds of noncertificated members of units are instructional aides and secretaries. The wise use of their abilities and expertise is the responsibility of the unit leader, in cooperation with the unit staff, the Instructional Improvement Committee, and the principal. The clerical aide performs a number of responsibilities, such as keeping attendance records, collecting and keeping records of money collected from students, duplicating materials, making lists of pupil supplies, typing, and filing.

The precise responsibilities of these noncertificated personnel vary greatly and are directly related to their previous training and experience. For example, a person with a college degree in education or a subject field will perform activities different from those of the high school graduate—the former may serve as an instructional aide, the latter, as a clerical aide. Even though no common set of specific activities can be prescribed, there are many areas in which aides are useful. They perform many housekeeping chores connected with lighting, ventilation, cleanliness, and instructional materials and supplies. Also, they may provide assistance to children in caring for clothing, moving from one part of the building to another, or receiving attention from a specialist such as a nurse or social worker. Often, they supervise lunchroom and playground activities. Since aides and secretaries often live within the school's attendance area, they also provide invaluable insights in planning and conducting a viable program of home-school-community relations for the units and the total school. Teachers report that instructional aides are especially helpful with the one-to-one, small group, and independent activities inherent in the implementation of IGE.

IMPLEMENTING IGE

The implementation of IGE must be viewed from both long-term and short-term perspectives. In other words, IGE cannot be implemented quickly; yet there are critical short-term considerations to which the principal must attend. In this section attention is directed to the phases of implementation, an overview description of an IGE school in operational terms, inservice and staff development activities, a support system for IGE schools, and certain specific concerns of the principal.

The Phases of Implementation

The implementation of IGE may be viewed in terms of a five-phase model, originally conceived in 1971, which over the years has been refined and validated in practice by the Wisconsin Research and Development Center in cooperation with personnel in state education agencies, teacher education institutions, and local school districts (Wisconsin Research and Development Center for Cognitive Learning 1971). In the 1974–75 school year, hundreds of persons from these agencies in twenty-three states were cooperating in the implementation of IGE.*

The five-phase model, as defined by Evers and others (1974) for local schools, is as follows:

1. *Awareness Phase.* In this phase, school district decision makers are given (1) overview information about IGE in order to stimulate them to adopt IGE and (2) information regarding required school district commitments and how to gain the commitments necessary to make the decision to adopt IGE.

2. *Commitment Phase.* In this phase, school district decision makers compile the necessary information and secure the necessary commitments, approvals, and cooperation of the potential IGE schools' staffs, parents, community groups, and the school board. At the end of this phase, the decision to adopt or not to adopt is made. To assist school personnel in influencing the decision to adopt, school district decision makers are provided with information describing IGE, cost factors, evaluation results, commitments of the implementation agency, and commitments of the school district. The decision to adopt IGE is usually formalized by the school district's entering into a written agreement with an implementation agency.

3. *Changeover Phase.* In this phase, which follows the decision to adopt IGE, the school staff is prepared to make the changeover to IGE. First, the principal and unit leaders are identified, receive instruction regarding IGE concepts and practices, and develop plans for the first year. Second, the principal and unit leaders with the assistance of an implementing agency instruct the staff of their school in IGE concepts and practices after which the school staff develops specific plans for the first year. Third, the school staff participates in ongoing first-year staff development.

4. *Refinement Phase.* After schools have begun implementing IGE, they find that new understandings and skills are required to refine their implementation efforts. The need for such refinement emerges out of the fact that the principal, unit leaders, and teachers are expected to per-

---

* These states were California, Colorado, Connecticut, Florida, Illinois, Indiana, Kentucky, Massachusetts, Michigan, Minnesota, Missouri, New Hampshire, New Jersey, New York, Ohio, Pennsylvania, Rhode Island, South Carolina, South Dakota, Texas, Utah, Virginia, and Wisconsin.

form their responsibilities in a new organizational setting and that the Instructional Programming Model requires unit leaders and teachers to plan and carry out instruction in a manner quite different from that in non-IGE schools.

5. *Renewal.* Built into the system of IGE are the means for the individuals and agencies cooperating in the implementation of IGE to: (1) identify and resolve unanticipated problems; (2) develop improved ways of implementing the concepts of IGE; and (3) prepare successive generations of personnel to fill IGE roles in the various agencies. These conditions can be realized when state IGE networks become fully functional with agencies assuming their appropriate roles (Evers, *et al.* 1974, pp. 17–19).

What Is an IGE School?

There are two ways of defining an IGE school. In one definition the major characteristic is that the IGE school is a self-renewing organization constantly refining and improving both its organizational and programmatic characteristics. At one point in time it may have certain characteristics, but at a later time these characteristics may have changed. In this view, the definition of an IGE school depends upon the local situation and the length of time that a school has been implementing IGE. Such a definition, however, is not of very much practical assistance. Another definition of an IGE school is specifically descriptive, defining in operational terms the most salient characteristics. This definition is given in the following paragraphs. The principal of an IGE school should be cognizant of this definition to assess the progress of the school in implementing IGE.

Stated in general terms, an IGE school is a school in which the staff of the building:

1. Has reorganized into the multiunit organizational pattern, including the SPC,
2. Is implementing the Instructional Programming Model in one curricular area in its first year and in additional areas in successive years,
3. Has identified and/or developed and is utilizing assessment and evaluation tools and procedures with regard to both student progress and overall program concerns,
4. Has established a program of home-school-community relations,
5. As an optional activity is a member of a regional IGE coordinating council of a state IGE network, and
6. As an optional activity is participating with a teacher education institution in a preservice teacher education program or with another agency in research and development activities, or has a locally designed research and development effort.

Each of the major, general characteristics listed above has further aspects that one must consider. With regard to the multiunit school organization, one important criterion is that the school is completely organized into Instruction and Research units. In other words, a staff which has units for only primary or intermediate aged students is not a multiunit school. Units should have not fewer than three nor more than six certificated teachers (Pellegrin 1969), one of whom is the unit leader. Each unit should have at least two hours per week during school hours for the unit members to plan as a group. The unit leader should be released from direct contact with children at least 20 percent of the time. Finally, each unit incorporates children of at least a three-year age range, i.e., the units are multiaged. Another important criterion for the organizational pattern is that an IIC is established and comprises at least the unit leaders, the principal, and a parent or community representative. This committee should meet weekly for a minimum of one to two hours and be able to have occasional meetings, for up to one-half day, particularly when consultants are available. The IIC should be chaired by the principal, and the agenda should show a primary focus on matters related to implementation of the Instructional Programming Model. The third organizational criterion is that an SPC be established with members as indicated in Figure 2.1. This committee will meet less frequently than the IIC but often enough to consider matters which affect the operation of IGE schools in the district.

As the school staff implements the Instructional Programming Model, it should consider several important aspects. First, in the subject matter field or fields to which the model is being applied, the IIC should formulate a buildingwide educational objective which will guide the activities of the staff and which can be used to evaluate the progress of the instructional program. Second, a range of appropriate instructional objectives should be identified for each I & R Unit. There also should be evidence that the range of instructional objectives is being modified as appropriate. Third, the school staff should be using a variety of assessment techniques including paper-and-pencil tests, work samples, observation, and performance tests to assess achievement levels, motivation for learning, preferred types of learning materials and situations, and other characteristics of the students. Finally, when learning and teaching activities are designed and executed they should reflect a variety of techniques, materials, modes of instruction, and grouping patterns.

Evaluation of an IGE school's program serves two purposes. It helps identify areas or aspects of the program which need improvement and also provides information relative to the progress of the staff towards reaching its educational objectives. One of the characteristics of IGE is that its implementation involves an iterative process whereby the staff of a school is continuously refining its implementation. At initial stages, the implementation of IGE will require changes on the part of the staff as they adjust to

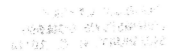

new roles and procedures. Consequently, the staff can expect that they will not function as smoothly as they might desire. Appropriate evaluation of the implementation of all the components of IGE, however, will provide the staff with information which will help them become effective and efficient. Evidence of such evaluation includes not only data such as pupil performance on tests but also the observations and perceptions of the staff. Both input from tests and the professional judgment of the staff are used in refining the implementation of IGE.

Home-school-community relations programs will vary substantially from district to district and state to state. Minimally, however, an IGE school should be able to interpret and report the progress of the school to its constituent community. A variety of techniques can be employed for such communication—a newsletter, home visitations, representatives from the community on the IIC and SPC, and mass media. An IGE school is also expected to utilize appropriate procedures for interpreting and reporting student progress to parents. Such procedures commonly include parent visits to the school alternating with written reports to the parents. Finally, an IGE school should include in its home-school-community relations program the use of community volunteers who participate in the instructional program.

It is helpful for the staff of an IGE school to participate in a regional network of other IGE schools which includes cooperating teacher education institutions and representatives from the state education agency. Such an agreement provides both a peer support system and ready access to external sources of support. Many IGE schools have found that sharing problems and solutions with each other through a formal means for communicating with other IGE schools has helped them avoid mistakes and duplication of effort. IGE staffs also frequently encounter situations wherein they will need to seek help from such sources as teacher education institutions and state education agencies. Personnel from these agencies have information and skills which many local school districts do not possess. When an IGE school is associated with a regional IGE coordinating council or similar arrangement, access to support from other IGE schools and other agencies provides continuous assistance.

Should an IGE school be in close proximity to a teacher education institution, its staff may have the opportunity to participate in the institution's preservice program or in a research and development program. An IGE staff involved in either of these efforts should establish clear statements of roles and relationships between the school and the agency with which it is cooperating so that the mutual expectations are clearly understood and mutually beneficial.

The indicators just described are the major ones for defining an IGE school in operational terms. By this definition, it may take from five to seven years for a school staff to become a completely functioning IGE

CARNEGIE LIBRARY
LIVINGSTONE COLLEGE
SALISBURY, N. C. 28144

school. However, as the list of implementation phases suggests, a school staff should never assume that it has "arrived." Persons involved in implementing IGE have observed a tendency for some school staffs to seek early closure and to feel they have done all that can be done in implementing IGE. Even though a school may have implemented all the components of IGE in all of its programs, there is an important sense in which a staff should always seek better ways of improving its implementation.

As a guide for helping the staff of an IGE school to make progress in implementation, the Wisconsin Research and Development Center has developed a set of performance objectives. Some of these objectives are related to ongoing processes; others are related to outcomes that can be observed at certain points in time. (These performance objectives are provided in Appendix A of this book.)

Inservice and Staff-development Activities

The inservice and staff-development activities in which a school staff will be involved parallel the phases of implementation described earlier. Figure 2.2 is a chart describing a prototypic sequence of implementation activities. Each of the activities in the phases is now generally described. They subsequently are discussed fully in Chapter 5.

The school superintendent, selected central office staff such as director of elementary education, and building principals are all involved in the *awareness* phase. In addition to what they may have read about IGE in professional journals or heard about it from colleagues or at professional conferences, they may receive specially targeted communications from either the state education agency or a regional implementation agency, such as an intermediate education agency or a teacher education institution. Such communications may include brochures or invitations to a one-day awareness conference held in the vicinity. Very often school districts also send representative teachers and school board members or parents to such conferences. The major objective of this conference is to give school personnel enough information about IGE so that they can make a decision about whether or not they wish to attempt to secure school district approval to proceed. Generally, awareness conferences are held in October and November of each year.

During the *commitment* phase, those persons attending the one-day awareness conference engage in activities to secure the support and approval of other persons in the school district. Building principals present information and hold discussions with their staffs to secure a favorable consensus. The superintendent or other central office personnel present information to parents and school board members and obtain official action. This phase normally occurs between November and February.

Once a favorable decision is reached and the school(s) to begin implementation of IGE are identified, the principal(s) and prospective unit lead-

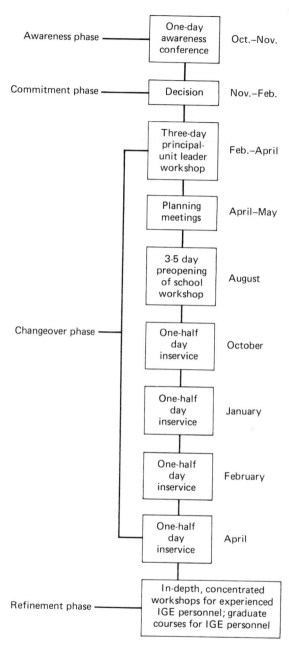

Fig. 2.2 Prototypic sequence of inservice activities for local school districts. Based on H. J. Klausmeier, *et al.* 1974. *Manual for starting and maintaining state IGE networks.* Madison, Wisc.: University of Wisconsin/Sears-Roebuck Foundation IGE Teacher Education Project, p. 47.

ers attend a three-day (or longer) principal and prospective unit leader workshop.

In this workshop, which begins the *changeover* phase and is normally held in February or March, the participants acquire the necessary understandings and skills relative to the concepts and practices of IGE. When the participants leave the workshop they should have prepared a plan for providing inservice to the remainder of the school staff. On returning to their schools, the principal and unit leaders hold planning meetings and begin to involve the rest of the building staff. These meetings typically occur during April and May. In August preceding the opening of school, the principals and unit leaders conduct a total staff workshop for three to five days similar to the workshop they attended. Some schools hold this workshop during the summer months and add an additional week for in-depth planning. During the first year as an IGE school, each staff should spend a minimum of four one-half days of inservice activities for the purpose of reviewing basic concepts and practices in order to evaluate their implementation progress.

At the end of the first year of the changeover to IGE, school staffs and central office personnel evaluate the first year of implementation and assess which basic IGE concepts and practices need to be reinforced and what additional skills and understandings are required to refine their implementation plans. The school has now entered the *refinement* phase. The IIC and the SPC jointly discuss these needs and plan appropriate staff development activities to ensure that the needs are met. Depending on the size and sophistication of the district, the persons who conduct the inservice training may or may not be in the district. Early in the refinement phase, schools may tend to be either totally independent of other agencies or totally dependent upon other agencies. As they participate fully in activities of a state IGE network, they will grow to a realistic comprehension of when to seek outside help and when they can resolve their own problems. As they begin to realize such considerations they are beginning to enter into the *renewal* phase.

Implicit in this discussion is the fact that some person, properly trained as an IGE implementor from the state education agency, intermediate education agency, and/or teacher education institution has been working closely with the school district. Such a person participates in conducting the awareness activities, providing expert assistance during the commitment phase activities, conducting the changeover phase activities, and assisting in the evaluation of the first year of operation. This person or agency is a prime resource during the refinement and renewal phases.

An IGE Support System

IGE is a relatively complex set of concepts and basic principles which require substantial change in the behaviors of persons involved in its implementation. The matter of new behaviors on the part of individuals implementing IGE is approached through redefining organizational and individual roles and providing the requisite understandings, skills, and attitudes to fulfill the redefined roles. IGE does not comprise totally new concepts; rather, it consists of many familiar and innovative ideas. Therefore, while changes in roles may be threatening to some, the familiarity of many of the ideas in IGE makes it acceptable to most educators.

IGE is also an open system that can be easily adapted to local circumstances, and it is divisible, i.e., some of the components can be adopted initially and other components later. The implementation of IGE can be handled flexibly and paced comfortably.

The characteristics of IGE suggest approaches to designing inservice activities and materials. For one approach, prototypes for the various components of IGE were developed. These prototypes were described explicitly so that adopters could anticipate some of the consequences of modifications and make appropriate allowances for such consequences as they adapt the prototypes to local circumstances. Second, inservice activities and materials were designed to provide enough information and experiences to help individuals make the changeover to IGE successfully. Third, the skills and understandings required for successful implementation are learned through activities and materials which focus primarily on those aspects of IGE that are uniquely IGE or essential to its successful operation. The basic concepts and principles are first explained and then illustrated with examples of excellent IGE practices. By such approaches only a minimal investment of time and money is required for the inservice activities.

Implementation of IGE has proceeded by disseminating information broadly and then providing inservice to those schools and agencies which choose to implement it. Agencies were provided opportunities to learn the minimally required skills and understandings for the successful changeover to IGE and, at the same time, an IGE support system was developed so that agencies could continue to be successful.

The IGE support system comprises four basic components: state IGE networks (Klausmeier, Walter, and Lins 1974); the Association for Individually Guided Education; leadership development activities sponsored by the Wisconsin Research and Development Center, the University of Wisconsin/Sears-Roebuck Foundation Project, and other cooperating agencies; and Multistate IGE Institutes. These compose the facilitative environments component of the IGE system which is described more fully in Chapter 8. This system of facilitative environments is predicated on the experience of those agencies which implemented IGE. This experience has shown that workshops alone are not sufficient. There needs to be a continuing cooperative relationship between the sources of assistance and the users, particularly the principal concerned with implementing IGE in the school.

Specific Implementation Concerns of the Principal

It is not the purpose of this chapter to direct attention to all of the concerns that a principal may expect to encounter in the process of implementing IGE. Matters associated with instructional programming, evaluation, staff development, use of resources and facilities, home-school-community relations, and so on are treated extensively in subsequent chapters of this book. There are, however, specific concerns associated with implementing the multiunit school organization.

When embarking on the implementation of IGE, the principal should be aware that the building staff will be engaged in a long-term process. As indicated earlier, the implementation of IGE requires from five to seven years to implement fully all seven components of IGE and to utilize the Instructional Programming Model in all of the different curricular and instructional areas of the school's program. Some research on this matter has shown that there is a tendency for schools to reach premature closure in implementing IGE (Packard 1973). The principal, therefore, must help the staff to realize that they will always be refining or improving their implementation of IGE.

In changing to a new organizational structure, a major leadership concern of the principal is that of maintaining a healthy amount of tension among the staff. It has been observed that an IGE staff can easily become quite committed to the concepts and practices of IGE. The resultant common failing is that they often attempt too much too soon. For example, a school probably should not try to implement the IPM in more than one curricular area at a time. However, many schools have become so enthusiastic about this approach to instruction that they attempt to implement the IPM in additional curricular areas before they are ready to do so. In such circumstances, a staff can become exhausted, causing unnecessary problems to emerge. Principals must pace the implementation of IGE in such a way that demands are not excessive. On the other hand, too leisurely an approach to the implementation of IGE can be debilitating.

With thousands of schools implementing IGE, it is only natural to find that some staffs are not realizing the success they had originally anticipated. Typically, the difficulties which arise out of poor execution of the concepts and practices of IGE can be attributed to problems in staffing, lack of resources, and insufficient planning for the early stages of implementation, particularly during the first year. An adequate evaluation program will help in identifying problem areas and in obtaining the information needed to establish IGE as a permanent alternative form of schooling in the schools. A set of IGE Performance Objectives has been developed as one of the important means for assessing the implementation progress of the school. As one principal commented, the principal should use these objectives to help "keep the school on track."

Shared decision making is a basic distinguishing characteristic of the

IGE multiunit school. The principal must strike an appropriate balance between the involvement of the staff on the one hand, and the principal's responsibility for making decisions and taking action on the other. The principal must identify the appropriate level of staff involvement, while at the same time responding to staff expectations for the assumption of responsibility. When staff members are not involved sufficiently, they will tend to implement decisions with somewhat less than full commitment. Conversely, the staff may feel at a loss when the principal does not exercise sufficient authority and assume responsibility. Regarding this delicate balance, a principal of a school that had been implementing IGE for four years stated: "Occasionally you and the IIC together must say, 'We think this is a better way, so let's get on with it! Then, if it doesn't work, we try something else.'"

The concept of shared decision making possesses numerous implications for the proper use of time. Participatory decision making requires considerable time for the IIC and the I & R Units to define a problem, provide information, and arrive at a decision relative to a solution. It is absolutely essential, therefore, that time be spent only on the most important problems and not on details. Many decisions can be left to the professional judgment of the individual staff members, provided that they fully understand the organizational structure, fully internalize their respective role expectations, and fully accept the responsibility for their decisions and actions.

Another ingredient which is important to the success of the IGE school is that of securing important information and expertise from extraorganizational agencies and individuals. One source of such information is that of consultants both from the district and other agencies. The principal, for example, should make arrangements so that the IIC can meet occasionally for periods of up to a half day to take advantage of such resources. Such consultants can provide specialized knowledge regarding content, methodology, materials, evaluation and similar matters. When district consultants are used they can effectively link the school's program to the systemwide program. When external consultants are used, the staff can become active participants in workshops, conferences, training experiences, visitations, and research. The principal must plan time for the appropriate utilization of district, state, and regional resource personnel.

To summarize, the principal must exercise leadership in "keeping the school on track," the sharing of decision making, and utilizing time and consultants to implement the multiunit school organization appropriately. Subsequent chapters of this book are devoted to these and other skills required of the principal of the IGE multiunit school.

SUMMARY

The multiunit organizational structure was created to maximize professional autonomy, clarify role relationships, facilitate shared decision making, and enhance emergent leadership at all levels of the school organization. In the first part of this chapter, the mechanisms for achieving intra- and intergroup communication and coordination were described: the I & R Units, at the learning and teaching level; the IIC, at the school building level; and the SPC, at the school district level. A prototypic organizational structure was depicted, including a description of the membership, functions, responsibilities and relationships at each level in the multiunit school. The major expectations for the new role created, that of unit leader, were described along with the major changes in emphasis required in the existing roles of school superintendent, school principal, staff teacher, preservice teacher, and instructional aide or secretary. It was shown how the new structure increases interpersonal and intergroup participation in planning, implementing, and evaluating instructional programs for the individual student.

To assist the principal in changing to IGE, the implementation process was described in terms of the following five phases: awareness, commitment, changeover, refinement, and renewal. Requisite staff development activities in each of the phases were discussed, and it was shown how the principal can utilize the IGE support system to facilitate the implementation process. The concluding section admonished the principal to pace change appropriately, share decision-making responsibility, and utilize time and resources appropriately in implementing IGE.

REFERENCES

Evers, N. A., M. J. Fruth, J. J. Heffernan, M. L. Karges, and W. E. Krupa 1975. *IGE implementor's manual*. Madison, Wisc.: Wisconsin Research and Development Center for Cognitive Learning.

Getzels, J. W. 1958. Administration as a social process. In A. W. Halpin (ed.), *Administrative theory in education*. Chicago: Midwest Administration Center, University of Chicago.

————, J. M. Lipham, and R. F. Campbell 1968. *Educational administration as a social process*. New York: Harper & Row.

Hage, J. 1965. An axiomatic theory of organizations. *Administrative Science Quarterly* **10** (December).

Hull, R. E. 1973. Selecting an approach to individualized education. *Phi Delta Kappan* **55** (November).

Klausmeier, H. J., J. E. Walter, and L. J. Lins 1974. *Manual for starting and maintaining state IGE networks*. Madison, Wisc.: University of Wisconsin/Sears-Roebuck Foundation IGE Teacher Education Project.

————, M. R. Quilling, J. S. Sorenson, R. S. Way, and G. R. Glasrud 1971. *Individually guided education and the multiunit elementary school: guidelines for implementation*. Madison, Wisc.: Wisconsin Research and Development Center for Cognitive Learning.

————, R. G. Morrow, and J. E. Walter 1968. *Individually guided education in the multiunit school*. Madison, Wisc.: Wisconsin Research and Development Center for Cognitive Learning.

Lipham, J. M. 1974. Improving the decision-making skills of the principal. In J. A. Culbertson, C. Henson, and R. Morrison (eds.), *Performance objectives for school principals*. Berkeley, Calif.: McCutchan.

————, and J. A. Hoeh, Jr. 1974. *The principalship: foundations and functions*. New York: Harper & Row.

————, 1964. Leadership and administration. In D. E. Griffiths (ed.), *Behavioral science and educational administration*. Sixty-third Yearbook, National Society for the Study of Education. Chicago: University of Chicago.

McGregor, D. 1960. *The human side of enterprise*. New York: McGraw-Hill.

Nerlinger, C. M. 1975. Participative decision making in IGE schools. Doctoral dissertation, University of Wisconsin—Madison.

Packard, J. S. 1973. Changing to a multiunit school. In W. W. Charters, Jr. et al. (eds.), *Contrasts in the process of planned changes of the school's instructional organization*. Eugene, Ore.: Center for the Advance Study of Educational Administration.

Parsons, T. 1958. Some ingredients of a general theory of formal organization. In A. W. Halpin (ed.), *Administrative theory in education*. Chicago: Midwest Administration Center, University of Chicago.

Paul, D. A. 1974. *The diffusion of an innovation through interorganizational linkages*. Technical report No. 308. Madison, Wisc.: Wisconsin Research and Development Center for Cognitive Learning.

Pellegrin, R. J. 1969. Some organizational characteristics of multiunit schools. Working paper No. 22. Madison, Wisc.: Wisconsin Research and Development Center for Cognitive Learning.

Sheridan, T. J. 1974. *Perceived role and effectiveness of the unit leader in conducting unit functions*. Technical report No. 318. Madison, Wisc.: Wisconsin Research and Development Center for Cognitive Learning.

Weber, M. 1959. Bureaucracy. In J. A. Litterer (ed.), *Organizations*. New York: Wiley.

Wisconsin Research and Development Center for Cognitive Learning, 1971. *Project plan and budget request for the nationwide installation of multiunit schools*. Madison, Wisconsin.

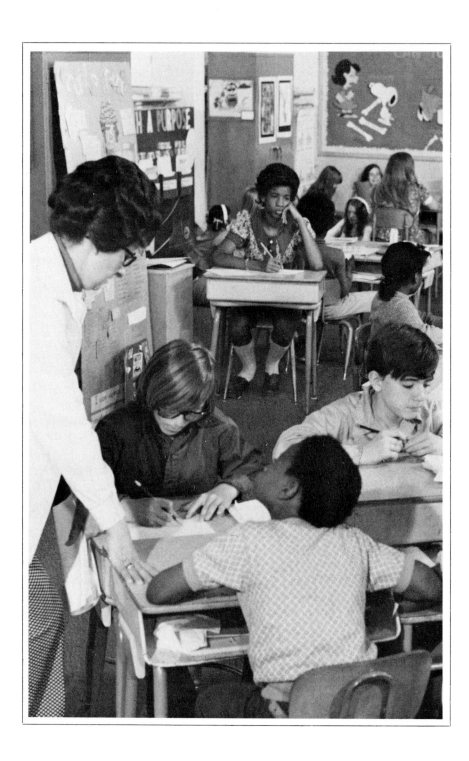

3

Implementing Instructional Change

Nancy A. Evers
William H. Klenke

Objectives

After reading this chapter, the reader will be able:

- To understand how instruction in IGE is adapted to meet children's individual needs.
- To comprehend how educational change is accomplished through utilization of the Instructional Programming Model.
- To identify the steps in the Instructional Programming Model.
- To understand the eight patterns of instructional programming for the individual student.
- To recognize the principal's responsibilities in the school's implementation of the Instructional Programming Model.
- To identify the instructional leadership responsibilities of the principal in the IGE school.

Within the comprehensive educational system of IGE the role of the principal, first and foremost, is to provide instructional leadership. Although much has been written about the necessity for the principal to be an instructional leader, very little has been done previously to define instructional leadership clearly or to describe operationally the instructional leadership role of the principal.

This chapter first presents a definition of instructional leadership. Second, the seven major steps in the IGE Instructional Programming Model are described. Third, the major part of the chapter focuses on the principal's instructional leadership role which is described in terms of specific behaviors to be demonstrated in planning and implementing instructional change. The concluding section reports research which shows the relationship of the leadership behavior of the principal to the effectiveness of the I & R Units in IGE schools.

INSTRUCTIONAL LEADERSHIP DEFINED

Administrative positions similar to the elementary school principalship were found in some large city school systems as early as the first half of the nineteenth century. In 1850, the duties of "head teachers," "principal teachers," or "headmasters" were limited to discipline, routine administrative acts, and grading pupils in the various rooms. In addition to performing limited administrative duties as local representatives of the school superintendent, they also were expected to teach. As schools increased in number and size and as educational and organizational problems became more complex, school districts began to release "principal teachers" from part of their classroom duties to devote more time to administration.

During the last half of the nineteenth century, the administrative responsibilities of principals, particularly in large cities, gradually changed from performing routine clerical duties to managing the entire school. By 1900, the powers and responsibilities of the position had increased considerably, and the principal became recognized as the formal intermediary between the district office and the teachers. As the principalship developed into a full-time administrative position, increased attention was given to the instructional program—particularly to the enforcement of district supervisory policies as a means for coordinating learning activities within the school.

Some individuals recognized early the opportunities for leadership in the elementary principalship. A major impetus toward this new conception of the role came with the formation of a professional association, the Department of Elementary School Principals of the National Education Association, in 1921. From the beginning, the publications of this association stressed the leadership responsibilities of the principal. Principals were urged to work closely with their staffs to improve the quality of curriculum and instruction and to devote less time to the routine management aspects of the role. That the principal must provide instructional leadership has been the predominant theme in the literature for many years.

The principal must provide effective leadership if IGE or any major educational change within the school is to be successful. As Lipham (1964, pp. 119–141) indicated, a distinction may be drawn between the administration of the instructional program, which implies maintenance activities, and leadership of the instructional program, which connotes change and improvement of the existing program. Instructional leadership is here defined as those behaviors of an individual which initiate new goals, structures, and relationships in the instructional program. Within this definition, "individual" refers not only to the principal, but also to unit leaders, teachers, students, parents, central office personnel, consultants, or others. This chapter, however, highlights the instructional leadership activities required of the IGE school principal.

The principal's primary concern must be for the improvement of the instructional program of the school. All other concerns, such as school organizational patterns, curriculum development, improvement of staff personnel, evaluation, home-school-community relations, allocation of resources, and establishing linkages with other agencies must focus on improving the instruction of each student. The IGE principal must work with the unit leaders and other staff to ensure that instructional programming for the individual student is initiated in selected curricular areas. Later the principal must perform those functions necessary for the implementation of instructional programs in the various curricular areas. It is within this dynamic concept of instructional leadership that the role of the IGE principal gains its greatest significance.

INSTRUCTIONAL PROGRAMMING IN IGE

As Chapter 1 indicated, IGE is a comprehensive alternative system of education and instruction designed to produce higher educational achievements through providing for differences among students in their rates of learning, learning styles, levels of motivation, and other characteristics. IGE is more comprehensive than "individualization" which typically is viewed as students progressing at their own rate of speed along some predetermined learning continuum and interacting on a one-to-one basis with a teacher, a learning machine, or a prepackaged instructional program.

IGE demands the use of multiple strategies in planning and implementing the instructional programs of students. It calls for the use of a variety of group sizes, multifaceted instructional activities, and diverse teaching methods, each being appropriate for each student. The heart of IGE is the guidance of individual and group learning by an instructional team which plans, initiates, and evaluates activities conducive to learning. Rather than prescribing an identical grouping pattern for all students, or a set of predetermined instructional activities which individualize only the rate at which the student learns, IGE emphasizes the harmonious blending of group size, instructional activity, teaching style, and instructional methodology with the student's instructional needs, level of motivation, learning style, and any other characteristics appropriate to that learning activity.

Planning, implementing, and evaluating the appropriate instructional activities within an IGE framework is very demanding. It requires an approach much different from traditional methods typically utilized in the school. Reliance on district curriculum guides, teacher's manuals, and prepackaged learning sequences, although helpful, will not be adequate, either singly or in combinations, to serve as the means by which instructional programming in IGE can be accomplished. What is necessary is a procedure which systematically brings all available material and human resources to bear directly on the instructional programming process. Rather than permitting conditions in which instructional programming results from uncoordinated activities, an environment is created in which instructional programming is systematically effected. The Instructional Programming Model was developed to facilitate the instructional programming for individual students in IGE.

The Instructional Programming Model (IPM)

The Instructional Programming Model provides a framework for the staff of the school to participate in planning, implementing, and evaluating an instructional program for each student in a given unit of instruction. This model may be applied to any curricular area. Objectives in the cognitive, psychomotor, and affective domains can be achieved within it.

As may be seen in Figure 3.1, in *Step 1,* the educational objectives to be attained by the student population of a school are to be adapted or developed in terms of level of achievement, values, and action patterns. These terminal objectives extend for one year or longer and represent the end results of the instructional activities provided in the school.

The initiative for the development of these objectives rests with the principal and the IIC with appropriate input from unit staff members, central office personnel, parents, and others concerned with the educational priorities of the school.

No one procedure has been established for formulating the school's educational objectives but two primary procedures are prevalent. According to the first procedure, the specific instructional objectives for each I & R Unit are identified. The children are categorized by the number of years of schooling completed, and their achievements related to each objective during the preceding school year are summarized in terms of the percentage of

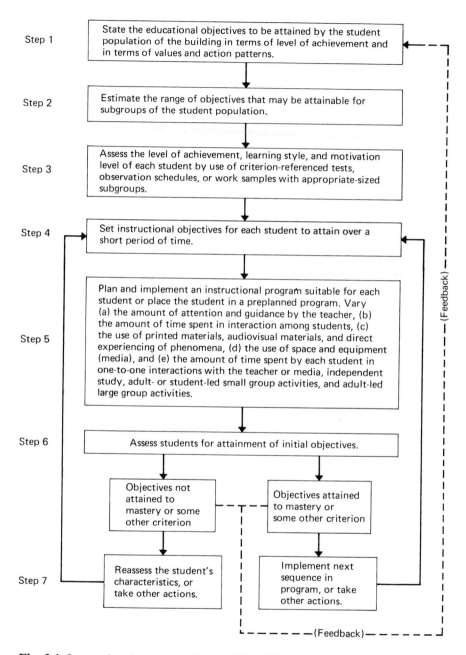

Step 1 — State the educational objectives to be attained by the student population of the building in terms of level of achievement and in terms of values and action patterns.

Step 2 — Estimate the range of objectives that may be attainable for subgroups of the student population.

Step 3 — Assess the level of achievement, learning style, and motivation level of each student by use of criterion-referenced tests, observation schedules, or work samples with appropriate-sized subgroups.

Step 4 — Set instructional objectives for each student to attain over a short period of time.

Step 5 — Plan and implement an instructional program suitable for each student or place the student in a preplanned program. Vary (a) the amount of attention and guidance by the teacher, (b) the amount of time spent in interaction among students, (c) the use of printed materials, audiovisual materials, and direct experiencing of phenomena, (d) the use of space and equipment (media), and (e) the amount of time spent by each student in one-to-one interactions with the teacher or media, independent study, adult- or student-led small group activities, and adult-led large group activities.

Step 6 — Assess students for attainment of initial objectives.

Objectives not attained to mastery or some other criterion

Objectives attained to mastery or some other criterion

Step 7 — Reassess the student's characteristics, or take other actions.

Implement next sequence in program, or take other actions.

(Feedback)

(Feedback)

Fig. 3.1 Instructional programming model in IGE. Adapted from H. J. Klausmeier, M. R. Quilling, J. S. Sorenson, R. S. Way, and G. R. Glasrud 1971. *Individually guided education in the multiunit school: guidelines for implementation.* Madison, Wisc.: Wisconsin Research and Development Center for Cognitive Learning, p. 19.

children of each year of school attendance who attained each objective. Next, the percentage of all the children for each respective year of school attendance who should attain each particular objective the next year is set. These projections of the percentage of students who should attain the objectives become the schoolwide objectives for the ensuing year. Individual children are not named nor are the projections related to individual children. Rather, the projections are based on the assumption that children attending the school during the ensuing year will have characteristics and capabilities similar to those whose achievement of the prior year were summarized. Of course, many children will continue into the next year, but the variables associated with student turnover must also be considered. The main variant to this procedure is to select certain key objectives for each year of school attendance completed, rather than to deal with all the objectives. Usually this means omitting the intermediate process objectives that lead to the attainment of a terminal objective for an instructional sequence.

Another procedure in formulating the school's objectives is to state the objectives at a higher level of generality than the specific instructional objectives. For example, one general objective related to science might be that all the children will, before leaving the elementary school, demonstrate ability to engage in the basic science processes at appropriate levels. The basic processes are then listed. Based on this general objective, each I & R unit then identifies or formulates specific instructional objectives that they estimate are attainable by the particular children of that unit. The unit staff determines the instructional objectives that are attainable by the particular child.

In utilizing either approach to the formulation of a statement of objectives for a school initially, the IIC typically reviews published statements of objectives, modifies them, and draws up its own statement based on the modifications. It is not necessary, therefore, for the IIC to develop a totally new objective-based curriculum. There are two main sources of objectives and assessment items from which the IIC can make selections that are consistent with the student population to be served. The first source is from commercially available, objective-based programs, such as the *Wisconsin design for reading skill development* (Otto 1973) or *Developing mathematical processes* (Romberg 1974). The second source is from collections of objectives and assessment items. The following sources, for example, provide objectives and assessment items in mathematics at a nominal cost:

IOX—Instructional Objective Exchange
P.O. Box 24095
Los Angeles, California   90024

Institute for Educational Research
1400 West Maple Avenue
Downers Grove, Illinois   60515

The final set of objectives agreed upon serves to focus the instructional activities of each unit in the school in desired directions, coordinate the efforts of each I & R Unit, and provide for continuity of instructional programs between and among units. Similar to the IIC, the staff of each I & R Unit reviews, selects, modifies, or develops objectives for their particular students. With each year of experience, the stated objectives are reviewed and revised.

Step 2 of the IPM calls for the identification of the range of objectives that may be attainable by subgroups of the student population. This step includes the development and assignment of specific instructional objectives for the students within each I & R Unit. These objectives, when completed, lead toward the attainment of the schoolwide educational objectives set in Step 1. While the educational objectives in Step 1 are comprehensive in scope and are for longer periods of time, the instructional objectives developed in Step 2 are specific and are for shorter periods of time.

As noted by the two-way arrows in Figure 3.1, this step can precede the establishment of schoolwide objectives, and it often does come first during the changeover year when the school first moves to objective-based instruction.

To provide for continuous pupil progress on a schoolwide basis, instructional continuity is of great importance. To prevent gaps from occurring in the instructional program, the IIC must review the scope and sequence in which the specific objectives are placed and assign appropriate portions of that scope and sequence to each I & R Unit, thereby ensuring accountability for each instructional objective. To accommodate the wide range of individual student learning needs, some specific instructional objectives may become the responsibility of more than one unit. If a unit provides instructional activities based on an objective which is the primary responsibility of another unit, it is important that the other units be informed of such activities—as well as the instructional outcomes.

Step 3 calls for the assessment of student needs in relationship to the desired outcomes of the specific instructional objectives. Such assessment is designed to discover several areas of instructional needs for each child within the I & R Units. In addition to the assessment of specific instructional objectives, this step should also focus on the assessment of specific characteristics of the student so that appropriate learning environments may be provided for each child. While this step is actually implemented by the several I & R Units, it is essential that the total assessment program be coordinated by the principal and the IIC in order to provide program continuity, eliminate duplication of effort, and, most importantly, provide equivalent measures of the objectives throughout the assessment process.

The specific assessment procedures utilize several different techniques, among which are paper-and-pencil tests, work samples, observations, and performance tests. While certain of the assessment techniques will be more appropriate for either a particular objective and/or student, they should all utilize a criterion-referenced base and format.

Completion of the assessment activities reveals the extent to which the several objectives have been mastered by each student, as well as the instructional needs of each student. Assessment at this step should include the full range of behaviors in cognitive, affective, and psychomotor domains. This assessment goes beyond determining only the cognitive needs of students; it leads to questions such as, "What type of instructional setting provides the appropriate environment conducive to learning?" "Can students work in groups of varying sizes to which they may be assigned?" "Does each student possess the necessary learning skills for participating in independent activities?" and "How does each child approach learning?" These are but a few of the many questions that must be considered when assessing the needs of each child in order to provide the appropriate instructional objective and the most conducive learning environment for each student.

In *Step 4* specific instructional objectives are established for each student. This decision is made by the entire staff of the I & R Unit utilizing the information obtained from Step 3, as well as information supplied by previous units and other support staff. This step may appear to be somewhat routine and automatic—simply assign an instructional activity which will lead to achievement of the objective that was identified in Step 3. However, since many objectives are usually assessed during Step 3, extreme care must be exercised by the unit staff in setting objectives for each child to ensure that the resultant instructional program is appropriate.

IGE encourages student involvement in the selection of instructional objectives. While there will be a difference in the degree of involvement among the students, it is important for the children to develop and use decision skills and attitudes. These practices should begin at an early age and continue throughout the child's educational experience so that greater involvement can occur with the increased decision skills. It is equally important to emphasize the need for proper guidance by the I & R Unit staff when assisting students in selecting the most appropriate objectives.

Step 5 is that of planning and implementing the specific learning activities whereby each student attains his or her objectives. This is usually completed in three phases. First, a unit of instruction is developed by the total I & R Units. The term "unit of instruction" is defined to include any grouping of related instructional activities in any curricular area for which there is a beginning point and a terminal point. The activities in each unit of instruction may vary according to subject matter. For example, activities in units of instruction in music are usually different from those in reading or in science. The time required for each unit of instruction may also vary. For example, a unit of instruction may be as short as a week or as long as a school year. Finally, a unit of instruction may vary according to the frequency of student participation. For example, a unit of instruction may occur for thirty minutes each school day while another may occur for only thirty minutes three days of the week. The time spent by each student participating may also vary.

In the second phase, the personnel of the I & R Unit meet to establish the appropriate instructional groupings for all of the students in the unit based upon the identified individual instructional objectives and other learner characteristics. In this phase the leadership responsibilities of the unit leader are particularly important.

The third phase begins when each individual teacher plans the specific activities in detail. It is in this phase of Step 5 that the instructional activities are tailored to meet the specific needs of each student. Each teacher is typically responsible for a number of students. Since multiple sets of activities will have to be provided for the varying needs and characteristics of students, subgroups will undoubtedly be necessary. Some children may be working in pairs or in groups as large as 20, others may be working with an aide, and still others with a student tutor or a teacher. The types of learning activities will also vary. Some students may be involved in programmed lessons or with lessons based upon a filmstrip or tape, and still others may be completing a structured lesson presented by a teacher. The examples above of activities are not meant to be exhaustive, rather they are only illustrative of Step 5—showing that while all students may be working toward attaining the same objective, to mastery or some other criterion, a wide variety of grouping patterns, teaching methods, and instructional activities are employed during this phase.

The assessment in *Step 6* occurs after instruction. This assessment is made to determine the student's level of attainment of the objectives toward which the student was striving. As in Step 3, this assessment procedure may employ a variety of criterion-referenced assessment techniques. Two basic differences between Step 6 and Step 3 are the variety of objectives being assessed and when the assessment occurs. In Step 6 the assessment is only completed for the objectives in which the student received instruction. The assessment in Step 6 occurs after the instructional sequence is completed for the particular student or when the teachers think the student has attained the objectives.

Following assessment, *Step 7* of the Instructional Programming Model indicates two possible outcomes for students. If students are successful in attaining the objectives to mastery or to some other desired criterion, they proceed to a new set of objectives, and follow the same process through the model. If students do not attain the objectives to the criterion, they may be reassessed. The unit staff reexamines its decisions about the instructional activities in which these children participated to discover what necessa adjustments will be needed to enable them to attain the desired outcomes. The unit staff may decide to have students participate in a new set of instructional activities designed to assist them achieve the same instructional objectives or students may move to different instructional objectives. If the latter decision is made, it may be necessary for students to participate at some later time in instructional activities related to the objectives that they had not attained.

These seven steps reveal how instructional programming may proceed generally. However, not all instruction in IGE schools should be carried out in an identical manner. There are eight basic patterns of instructional programming which the principal must thoroughly understand.

Patterns of Instructional Programming*

Three critical matters dealing with instructional programming are: (1) whether the same objectives are to be attained by all students, (2) whether the criteria that are specified for attainment of the objectives are the same for all students, and (3) whether the units of instruction are to be taken in a fixed sequence. These three matters are handled differently both among various curricula and among units of instruction within the same curricular field. For example, in a unit in social studies dealing with map reading skills, attaining identical objectives may be required of all students; in another unit of instruction dealing with climates of the world, not all students may be required to attain identical objectives. In the same way, the criteria that are established for attaining objectives may be identical for all students in a unit of instruction dealing with basic reading skills, e.g., 80 percent correct on a test; in another unit dealing with creative expression, the criteria may be stated variably in terms of each student's characteristics, e.g., each student will participate from one to ten times monthly in an activity. In a certain curricular field, such as mathematics, the units of instruction covering one or more years of schooling may be invariantly sequenced either because mastering each unit is prerequisite to starting the next one or because it is convenient to teach the units in an invariant sequence. In another curricular field, any unit of instruction may be started at any point in time during a given school year and completing one unit is not prerequisite to starting other ones.

There are eight possible combinations of common or variable objectives for students, full mastery or variable criteria of attainment of objectives,

* The material in this section is taken from H. J. Klausmeier, Instructional programming for the individual student, in H. J. Klausmeier, R. A. Rossmiller, and M. Saily (eds.). In press. *Individually guided elementary education: concepts and practices.*

and invariant or variable sequence of instructional units as illustrated in Figure 3.2.

The sequence for attaining objectives within a unit of instruction also may be invariant or variable. Adding this important dimension to the combinations in Figure 3.2 doubles the number of combinations to 16. The word, *variable,* as used in Figure 3.2, implies a range. For example, in connection with objectives it implies all the possibilities, ranging from most but not all the objectives being the same for many individuals to no objectives being the same for any two individuals. In connection with sequence, it implies, for example, that if there are six units of instruction undertaken during a year, they may be taken in any of the possible combinations or that only one or two of the units may be taken out of sequence. Variable level of attainment means that not all students will attain a particular ob-

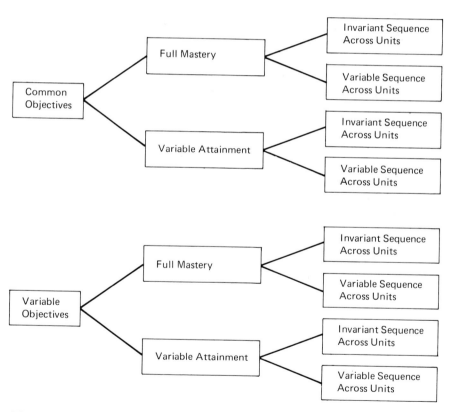

Fig. 3.2 Eight possible patterns of instructional programming. From H. J. Klausmeier, Instructional programming for the individual student, in H. J. Klausmeier, R. A. Rossmiller, and M. Saily (eds.). In press. *Individually guided elementary education: concepts and practices.*

jective or set of objectives to a fixed specified level. For example, in certain cognitive skill areas, most but not all children may be required to attain mastery. Objectives in the psychomotor and affective domains usually are also variable; for example, "each student will hit from one to eight out of ten free throws," or "each student will manifest a positive attitude (but certainly not identically strong) toward children, regardless of their socio-economic status."

Brief descriptions of how instruction may proceed under the eight patterns of objectives, criteria of attainment, and sequencing follow.

Pattern a. Common objectives, full mastery, and invariant sequence across units. Instructional programming for the individual student may be organized for parts of certain curricular areas so that all students proceed through the same sequence of units and attain the same objectives to the same criteria of full mastery. Within a unit, the objectives may or may not be sequenced invariantly. When this pattern is implemented, each student attains the objectives at an individual rate, but not all students attain the same number of objectives during a year, or some other time interval. Instruction in many basic skill areas, such as skill development in reading and mathematics, typically follow this pattern.

It should be clear that when objectives are stated at either a general level or a more specific level, the amount of time students spend on attaining a particular objective also either decreases or increases. This, in turn, greatly affects the amount of assessing, grouping, and record keeping required to manage instructional programming for the individual student.

Pattern b. Common objectives, full mastery, variable sequence across units. Instruction may be organized for parts of some curricular areas so that all students pursue the same units of instruction to attain the same objectives to the same criterion of full mastery; however, mastery of one unit is *not* a prerequisite for starting another one. Therefore, a student may start any one of the several units at any point in time during a semester or year, and groups of students may be pursuing different units during any given week or month. Students who complete a particular unit attain the same objectives of the unit to full mastery but not all complete the same number of units during a given year, nor do all students necessarily attain all the objectives of a unit before starting another unit. Objectives may or may not follow an invariant sequence within each unit.

As practicing principals will easily recognize, some parts of the substantive areas of language arts, science, and social studies may follow this pattern. When students are grouped for instruction, provisions are needed for early attainers and late attainers. This generally requires that several units, preferably of variable difficulty level but of about the same duration, be available simultaneously for students to pursue. It should be noted, however, that when the objectives in *Pattern b* are stated at the same level of generality as in *Pattern a,* management of instruction in terms of frequency of assessment, securing materials as needed, grouping and regrouping, and record keeping are similar.

Pattern c. Common objectives, variable attainment, invariant sequence across units.   According to this pattern, all students pursuing a particular unit attain the same objectives, but not to the same criterion. The criteria of attainment are set so as to be different but appropriate for particular students. For convenience in managing instruction or because of prerequisite knowledge and skills, the units of instruction are sequenced invariantly during the school year. Some knowledge about a topic may be essential for proceeding to the next one, but the amount may vary among students. The objectives may or may not be sequenced within a particular unit.

Some units of instruction in mathematics and science may follow this pattern. All students are to attain certain objectives within each unit to the level appropriate to them and, because of the hierarchical nature of the subject matter, the units follow an invariant sequence. Variable attainment of objectives is specified, because not all students are required to attain the objectives to the identical criteria of mastery.

When *Pattern c* is used, students are placed initially in a proper unit and are grouped for instruction. Frequent regrouping is not essential inasmuch as there are not identical criteria of attainment; however, the amount of assessing, record keeping, and materials handling for any instructional group is large because of the fact that the objectives are attained at different levels and the actual levels attained must be recorded.

Pattern d. Common objectives, variable attainment, and variable sequence across units.   Instruction proceeds here much as in *Pattern c,* except that the units of instruction are not undertaken in a fixed sequence. This instructional pattern is illustrated by programs in self-directed, interpretive, and creative reading and in programs designed to increase the motivation of individual students. In these programs, the same objectives may be held for all students. However, the criterion for attaining the objectives is that each student is to attain the objectives at a level judged by the teacher to be "satisfactory" for the particular student. In this connection, any student rated satisfactory by the teacher on all the objectives of a particular procedure does not participate in it. Moreover, the objectives are not sequenced and most or all the objectives may be pursued simultaneously. Much instruction in the affective domain also proceeds according to this pattern. For example, teachers usually want all students to develop a favorable attitude toward reading or an increasing amount of self-directedness. But they do not expect all students to reach the same level nor is any common set of activities used to attain the objectives.

Pattern e. Variable objectives, full mastery, invariant sequence across units.
Instruction may be arranged so that not all students attain the same objectives; however, each objective set for any student is mastered to the same criterion. The units of instruction are undertaken in an invariant sequence. Instrumental music may follow this pattern. Here, the students who learn to perform on different instruments have different objectives. Those learning to play the same instrument, however, might take successive units in an invariant sequence and also might be required to reach the same level of full mastery before proceeding from one unit to the next.

Pattern f. Variable objectives, full mastery, variable sequence.   Instruction in this pattern follows the same as that of *Pattern e*, except that the units are not sequenced. In connection with the previous example from instrumental music, for example, the difference according to this pattern is that the sequence by which the students attain their objectives is not fixed or invariant.

Pattern g. Variable objectives, variable attainment, invariant sequence across units.   In connection with variable objectives, some schools may include certain objectives only for some students. Moreover, not all students are required to attain the different kinds of objectives to the same criteria. However, when any student does pursue the objectives, the units which deal with various topics follow an invariant sequence. The principal should recognize that some strands in mathematics follow this pattern.

Pattern h. Variable objectives, variable attainment, variable sequence across units.   Principals will immediately recognize that many elective activities, such as outdoor education, and several cocurricular activities, such as clubs, student organizations, and other inschool enrichment activities follow this pattern. Also, some instruction in the affective domain follows this pattern.

From the preceding we see that the instructional programs for individual students attending any particular school may include some of the same objectives for all students, and that all students are to master those particular objectives at some time during their elementary school years. Schools generally have identified a large number of common objectives in the basic skills and a smaller number in science, social studies, music, art, and physical education. Schools also have identified other objectives, particularly in the affective domain and expressive areas, that all students are to attain to a greater or lesser degree. There are also other objectives that only certain children may attain to mastery or to some other criterion. These are usually the students who master the basic skill objectives more rapidly.

Mode of Instruction

In any of the preceding combinations, instruction may possibly be arranged so that students proceed through units of instruction by means of independent study, on a one-to-one basis, as members of small or large groups, or in a combination of these modes. One-to-one instruction of a child by a teacher is possible only for a limited number of children since there is usually about one teacher for twenty to thirty children. A one-to-one arrangement of a student interacting with instructional materials is feasible for certain knowledge and skills. All kinds of one-to-one instruction permit students who can learn with considerable independence of the teacher to proceed at their own individual rates in attaining sequenced objectives. In connection with all the patterns previously discussed, students should be aided in attaining any objectives independently which can be so attained.

Learning stations and small group instruction monitored and directed by teachers are used widely in IGE. Learning stations are often arranged so that certain objectives can be attained by students working at the specified stations. At the learning stations, children may work individually, in pairs, or in small groups. To attain their objectives the teachers move from one child or group to another, assisting, monitoring, and evaluating. Learning stations are excellent for children who can attain their objectives without much teacher-directed instruction. To attain the objectives of some units of instruction, teacher-directed instruction of small groups has proven effective. Sometimes, the teacher may instruct the entire group at the learning station.

When group instruction is used with either *Pattern a* or *b* involving full mastery of identical objectives for all students or with *Patterns d* and *f* that may require full mastery of the same objectives for certain groups of students, but not others, the proper management of instruction is of crucial importance to the success of IGE. More specifically, early attainers of the common objective(s) for any unit of instruction must be identified, and alternative arrangements must be worked out for them. As an example, three possible alternatives for the earlier attainers may be to move with other early attainers to the next unit, to stay with the present group but work toward a different objective, or to tutor a classmate. Also, nonattainers at the end of a fixed time interval for a particular unit of instruction also require preplanned alternatives, for example, the nonattainer might continue with the group into the next unit and try to attain both sets of objectives, move from the group and join other nonattainers and attempt again to attain the same set of objective(s), or move to another group and work toward different and sometimes lower-level objectives.

Student Participation in Determining Instructional Objectives

In the preceding *Patterns a* and *c,* characterized by common objectives for all students and an invariant sequence across units, if there is also an invariant sequence within units, students do not participate in determining their own instructional objectives. In these same patterns, when the objectives are not sequenced within the unit, the student may decide on the order of attaining the objectives, but not on whether to attain them. Giving the students this choice about order of attainment must be weighed against the additional amount of time required for instructional management and other factors, including the student's ability to understand and choose objectives, the availability of appropriate materials, the availability of staff, and other factors.

In *Patterns b* and *d,* both of which show common objectives for all students and a variable sequence of units, the students may make the decision on the order of taking the units of instruction (and thereby also the order of attaining the objectives); however, the student does not decide on whether or not to take the units. Choice of the order of pursuing objectives within a unit is possible only if the objectives are not sequenced within the units. Not permitting students to choose whether or not to attain the objectives in *Patterns a, b, c,* and *d* follows logically from the initial curricular decision that all students should attain the same common objectives. In view of this, each school staff should carefully consider whether to require all students, or groups of students, to attain common objectives. Perhaps the decision is more nearly how many and which objectives to require of all students and how many and which to encourage students to elect.

The preceding *Patterns e, f, g,* and *h* incorporate variable objectives, meaning that not all students attain the same objectives. However, *Patterns e* and *g* call for an invariant sequence across units. If the student chooses a set of objectives to attain initially, there is little or no choice thereafter until the invariant sequence of units is complete. On the other hand, *Patterns f* and *h* show variable sequence across units, so initial choice is possible and also later choice of the order of the units. In all four patterns, if the objectives are not sequenced within a unit the student may choose the order of attaining objectives within the unit. Thus, it is mandatory to involve students as well as staff in planning and implementing the instructional program.

PLANNING AND IMPLEMENTING INSTRUCTIONAL CHANGE

In broad terms, there are three major stages of instructional leadership and change: planning, implementing, and evaluating. The role of the IGE principal in the planning and implementing stages of instructional change is discussed here. The principal's role in evaluating instructional change is discussed in Chapter 4.

Planning for Instructional Change

The implementation of IGE involves many changes, each of which should be carefully planned. It is recommended that the multiunit school organizational change precede the instructional programming change. The multiunit school organizational pattern facilitates the operationalization of instructional programming for the individual student.

In IGE, an initial major concern of the school staff is, "In which curricular area should we first apply instructional programming for the individual student?" At this juncture, the school staff begins earnestly to plan for major change in the instructional program. The process of planning for instructional change consists of three phases (1) analyzing and appraising present instructional programs, (2) identifying and setting priorities for curricular areas in need of instructional change, and (3) strategizing an action pattern for implementation.

Prior to initiating a major change, the school's present instructional program should first be carefully analyzed and appraised. The major goals, objectives, procedures, and activities in the present program should be critically examined and judgments made concerning the worth of each aspect of the instructional program. In making such value judgments, the staff must agree on the relative emphasis to be given to the various tasks of education, the demands society places on the school, and the needs of learners in the particular community. Since ultimately the goal of the school's program is to provide a program tailored to the needs of each student, the analysis of the unique needs of the learners is obviously important. It may also be necessary to assess the expectations held by the community for the school as an institution in order to provide a relevant, contemporary curriculum. (Some techniques for performing this needs assessment are described in detail in Chapter 4.)

Based on the analysis of needs, targeted curricular areas are identified and priorities established. It is the responsibility of the principal and the IIC to perform this function. In the process of identifying and setting priorities for the curricular areas in need of improvement, the following are important considerations:

1. Student needs
2. Consistency of the change with the value structures of the following:
   - students
   - parents and community
   - staff
3. Staff personnel
   - curricular expertise of staff members
   - staff experience in instructional programming

4. Resources
   - adequacy
   - flexibility of allocation and expenditures
5. Instructional facilities
   - adequacy of space
   - flexibility of space for various instructional grouping patterns

After identifying and setting priorities for the curricular areas in need of improvement, the principal and the IIC must develop an action pattern for implementation of the instructional change program. The ultimate responsibility for instructional programming for the individual student rests with the principal and it is through the principal's instructional leadership that this may be accomplished.

The leadership behavior of the principal is of course influenced by some conditions external to the school and by other conditions existent within the school. External conditions, for example, may include specific "instructional and curricular" clauses contained in a negotiated master contract, as well as established policies, procedures, and practices regulating the nature of curricular offerings within the district. Within each school, such factors as the curricular expertise, readiness, and commitment of the staff to IGE are among the first variables that must be considered.

The transition from planning to implementing is that of transforming thought into action. After program needs have been identified and priorities have been established, it is necessary to implement successfully that action plan.

Implementing Instructional Change

A new or beginning IGE principal may ask, "What specifically should I do to implement instructional programming for the individual student?" The response to this question is that the principal is responsible for activities in four functional subcategories of the implementation process: initiation, coordination, facilitation, and evaluation. Initiation is the process of introducing change into the social system of the school. For example, when talking with the unit leaders about possible schoolwide objectives or when suggesting objectives to other staff members, the principal is engaging in the initiation process.

Coordination is the process of bringing the activities of people and resources to bear upon the initiated change. For example, when principals ask the school district reading consultants to attend meetings of the IIC to provide help with formulating schoolwide objectives, they are engaging in the coordination process—bringing the activities of the committee and the reading consultant toward common action—the formulation of schoolwide objectives.

Facilitation is the process of rendering less difficult the actions required to introduce the change. For example, when the principals arrange for "released time" for committee members to meet and formulate schoolwide objectives, they are engaging in the facilitation process by providing an intraorganizational environment conducive to completion of the task.

Evaluation is the process of ascertaining the effect of the change on individuals in the social system. For example, when principals suggest using the criteria of consistency between schoolwide objectives and existing district policies, they are engaging in the evaluation stage of the implementation process.

In each of the four processes and at each of the seven steps in implementing the IPM the principal engages in many different leadership activities. To be of specific help to the principal, an exemplary, but by no means exhaustive, enumeration of these activities is shown in Table 3.1. In the flowchart of activities presented, it is assumed that the principal and the IIC are directly involved in completing each of the tasks in each step. It should be pointed out, however, that several alternative strategies may be possible, depending on such factors as size of the school, previous experience and training in IGE by the staff, or availability of consultant and other resources. For example, some IGE schools have found it advantageous to utilize task forces or ad hoc committees for certain of the processes—particularly in Steps 1 through 3 of implementing the IPM. It should be cautioned, however, that if such groups are used, (1) their functional responsibilities should be clearly delineated; (2) communicative and coordinative mechanisms will need to be established; and (3) they still are to report to the principal and the IIC who hold the leadership responsibility for the instructional program of the school.

LEADERSHIP BEHAVIOR OF IGE PRINCIPALS

In providing instructional leadership the central issue remains: "What specific types of leadership behavior of the principal are related to the effectiveness of the instructional program in IGE schools?"

To examine this issue, Gramenz (1974) recently completed a nationwide empirical study of the relationship of the leadership behavior of the principal to the effectiveness of the instructional program in IGE multiunit elementary schools. Utilizing social systems theory as a frame of reference, Gramenz hypothesized that (1) the "real" or actual leadership behavior the principal, (2) the "ideal" or desired leadership behavior of the principal, and (3) the difference between the real and the ideal leadership behavior of the principal would be meaningfully and systematically related to the effectiveness of the I & R Units within the IGE school.

To obtain descriptions of the real and ideal leadership behavior of the principal, House's Leader Behavior Description (1971), which is con-

Table 3.1 Activities of the IGE Principal in Implementing Instructional Programming for the Individual Student

	Step 1 Setting Schoolwide Objectives	Step 2 Establishing the Range of Objectives
INITIATION	1. Communicates the need for instructional change 2. Places discussion of the IPM on the IIC agenda 3. Suggests educational objectives to be considered by the IIC 4. Encourages others to suggest their educational objectives to the IIC	1. Communicates the importance of forming a scope and sequence of specific objectives for the entire school to provide for continuous pupil progress 2. Communicates objectives or means of assisting in the development of objectives to be considered by the IIC 3. Encourages others to suggest their specific objectives to the IIC
COORDINATION	1. Encourages all IIC members to contribute their ideas 2. Encourages the staff to respond to the objectives during their development 3. Coordinates the development of the objectives to ensure consistency with local district or state regulations 4. Coordinates requests of the IIC for resource material and personnel to assist in the development of objectives	1. Encourages all IIC members to contribute their ideas 2. Encourages the staff to respond to the objectives during their development 3. Coordinates the development of the objectives to ensure consistency with local district or state regulations 4. Coordinates requests for resource materials and personnel to assist in the development of objectives 5. Coordinates the development of the specific instructional objectives to ensure continuous pupil progress within and among I & R Units
FACILITATION	1. Arranges for the necessary IIC meeting time 2. Arranges released time for IIC members to accomplish individually assigned tasks 3. Provides the needed personnel and resource materials within situational limitations	1. Arranges for the necessary IIC meeting time 2. Arranges released time for IIC members to accomplish individually assigned tasks 3. Provides the needed personnel and resource materials within situational limitations

Step 1 (*continued*)	**Step 2** (*continued*)
EVALUATION 1. Suggests criteria on which the objectives can be evaluated 2. Encourages teachers, unit leaders, and curriculum consultants to suggest criteria on which the objectives can be evaluated 3. Ensures that objectives are consistent with any local, state, or national curricular constraints	1. Suggests criteria upon which the objectives can be evaluated 2. Encourages teachers, unit leaders, and curriculum consultants to suggest criteria on which the objectives can be evaluated 3. Ensures that objectives are consistent with any local, state, or national curricular constraints 4. Ensures that the specific instructional objectives are compatible with the long-range, schoolwide educational objectives

Step 3 Assessing Each Student	**Step 4** Setting Each Student's Objectives
INITIATION 1. Suggests specific ideas in the development of the assessment program 2. Encourages others to suggest their ideas in the development of the assessment program 3. Provides rationale for criterion-referenced assessment	Introduces the staff to new ideas, techniques, and methods to assist in the setting of objectives and the formation of instructional groups
COORDINATION 1. Coordinates the assessment program and schedules of the units to provide continuity and the elimination of duplication 2. Coordinates the development of appropriate record-keeping procedures to guarantee continuity as a child progresses through the school 3. Coordinates the school assessment schedules with the district testing program	

Table 3.1 Activities of the IGE Principal in Implementing Instructional Programming for the Individual Student (*continued*)

	Step 3 (*continued*)	Step 4 (*continued*)

FACILITATION	1. Provides access to technical assistance in identifying instruments and procedures that will be used in assessing each child's
	   a. level of motivation
	   b. interests and attitudes
	   c. learning characteristics
	   d. special problems (personal and learning)
	2. Participates in the assessment program by:
	   a. conducting assessment sessions
	   b. collecting, recording, and analyzing data
		1. Serves as a resource
		2. Provides time and resources to assist units in making program improvements

EVALUATION	Ensures that the assessment program and procedures are being conducted properly	Monitors the units to ensure that appropriate goals are established for each student

	Step 5 Implementing a Program for Each Student	Step 6 Assessing Attainment of Initial Objectives
INITIATION	1. Initiates instructional improvement by introducing staff to new teaching strategies, materials, and resources 2. Establishes program and activities to encourage the sharing of ideas, methods, and materials and the working together as a unit	1. Provides mechanisms by which each unit leader can inform the other unit leaders as to unit progress 2. Provides within the ICC the opportunity for each unit leader to report postassessment techniques and general results

	Step 5 (*continued*)	**Step 6** (*continued*)
COORDINATION	Coordinates the development system to make all school materials and resources available to each unit	
FACILITATION	1. Serves as a technical resource to the units by capitalizing on own areas of curricular expertise 2. Teaches, if possible 3. Secures personnel and material resources, as requested by the units 4. Ensures consistency in the organization of instruction in relationship to the objectives of the curriculum 5. Provides location for and access to materials in order to eliminate duplication of effort by units	Provides assistance, personnel, and material for postassessment activities
EVALUATION	Monitors the general program development of the units	Monitors postassessment results in relationship with the overall program objectives

Step 7
Reassessing Students or Implementing Next Sequence

INITIATION	1. Introduces the staff to new teaching strategies, materials, and resources 2. Encourages the staff to reassess their instructional strategies employed with students who did not achieve their objectives 3. Encourages the units to develop mechanisms for continuous pupil progress

Table 3.1 Activities of the IGE Principal in Implementing Instructional Programming for the Individual Student (*continued*)

Step 7 (*continued*)

COORDINATION	Coordinates the management system for continuous pupil progress among units
FACILITATION	Provides the staff assistance in further refining their instructional strategies
EVALUATION	Monitors the activities of each unit to ensure continuous pupil progress

ceptually derived from the Ohio State University Leader Behavior Description Questionnaire (Halpin 1956), was administered to principals, unit leaders, and staff teachers in a randomly selected sample of fifty IGE elementary schools which were in their third year of implementation. This leadership questionnaire provides descriptions of the principal's behavior in the three important categories defined as follows:

1. Instrumental leadership—behaviors which define roles and relationships, stress rules and regulations, schedule work to be done, stress standards of performance, and explain why tasks should be done.
2. Supportive leadership—behaviors which build interpersonal relationships, make it pleasant to be a member of the group, help others in overcoming problems, and facilitate change.
3. Participative leadership—behaviors which include working directly with others, listening to what subordinates say, asking for suggestions, and involvement of others in making decisions.

To obtain a measure of the effectiveness of the instructional program, Gramenz administered to unit leaders and staff teachers the Instruction and Research Unit Operations Questionnaire, developed jointly with Evers (1974), which measures the extent to which fifty-one performance objectives which are the responsibilities of the I & R Unit are being achieved. A factor analysis of this instrument revealed that instructional effectiveness in IGE schools includes the following categories: (1) instructional program; (2) organizational operations, procedural and substantive; (3) school-community relations; and (4) staff development.

The findings of Gramenz were straightforward and confirmed the basic hypotheses. A positive and significant relationship was found between the unit leaders' and unit teachers' perceptions of the instrumental, supportive, and participative leadership behavior of their principal and the effectiveness of the instructional program in IGE schools. Moreover, in situations wherein there was high agreement on the ideal leadership behavior of the principals, the instructional program also was perceived as highly effective. These findings are compatible with other leadership studies which have shown that both the nature of the behavior of the leaders (for example, whether they exhibit instrumental, supportive, and participative behavior) and the degree of correspondence between what is held as ideal behavior and what is actually practiced are significantly related to productive organizational outcomes.

Hypothesizing that a similar dynamic would be operative at the unit level as well as schoolwide, Evers (1974) conducted a study of the relationship of the leadership behavior of the unit leader to the effectiveness of the Instruction and Research units in IGE schools. In this nationwide study, also utilizing a random sample of fifty IGE schools, House's (1971) Leader Behavior Description—modified to assess the behavior of the unit leader—and the Instruction and Research Unit Effectiveness Questionnaire were administered. Again, the basic hypothesis was confirmed. Evers concluded:

> The unit leader's instrumental leadership behavior, the unit leader's supportive leadership behavior, and the unit leader's participative leadership behavior significantly influenced each of the measures of Instruction and Research Unit effectiveness.

Research to date leads to the conclusion that the principal contemplating implementation of IGE would do well not only to have "knowledge about" the leadership activities required to implement the Instructional Programming Model, but also to have "understanding of" his or her unique and personalistic leadership style in relation to the great situational demands that are required in moving from a traditional to an IGE school. Not all principals are equally proficient, for example, in the instrumental, supportive, and participative categories of behavior. As indicated in Table 3.1, moreover, a wide variety of leadership behaviors are appropriate at the seven steps in implementing the IPM.

As Getzels and Guba (1957, pp. 423–441) observed, at various junctures and under differing circumstances it is necessary to vary one's leadership style—at some times stressing organizational or instrumental factors and at others emphasizing individual or supportive factors. In this regard, for example, we may consider only the domain of participative leadership. The principal's participative leadership is high in the school in which the

IIC is directly involved in all steps of the instructional programming process. By contrast, the task force or ad hoc committee approach requires less of a participative leadership style in the instructional programming process. The principal who desires little involvement in instructional programming would be well advised not to consider IGE.

SUMMARY

In this chapter the instructional leadership role of the principal was defined as those behaviors which initiate new goals, structures, and relationships in the educational program of the school. The IPM was posited as an appropriate conceptual framework for bringing to bear the human and material resources of the school to provide a program of individually guided instruction for each student. Each of the seven steps in the IPM was defined and described, as well as the dynamic relationships among the steps. The utility of the model was shown and examples were cited concerning eight patterns of instructional programming frequently used in IGE schools. These patterns represent the viable combinations possible when three basic variables, commonality of objectives, level of attainment, and variability of sequence, are considered.

A brief discussion of instructional planning introduced consideration of the major thrust of this chapter, the instructional leadership activities required of the principal in implementing IGE. Such implementation was conceived as consisting of four interrelated processes, initiation, coordination, facilitation, and evaluation, and some exemplary activities of the principal were cited concerning each process in each of the seven steps of the Instructional Programming Model.

Research conducted to date regarding the leadership of IGE principals was cited, revealing that a systematic, positive, and significant relationship exists between the instrumental, supportive, and participative leadership behavior of the principal and the effectiveness of the instructional program in the IGE school. From these studies it was suggested that the principal not only be knowledgeable about but also skilled in exercising differential leadership behavior if the instructional program of the school is to be improved.

REFERENCES

Evers, N. A. 1974. *An analysis of the relationship between the effectiveness of the multiunit elementary school's instruction and research unit and interpersonal behaviors.* Technical report No. 298. Madison, Wisc.: Wisconsin Research and Development Center for Cognitive Learning.

Getzels, J. W. 1963. Conflict and role behavior in the educational setting. In W. W. Charters, Jr., and N. L. Gage (eds.), *Readings in the social psychology of education.* Boston: Allyn and Bacon.

————, and E. G. Guba 1957. Social behavior and the administrative process. *School Review* **65.**

Gramenz, G. W. 1974. *Relationships of principal leader behavior and organizational structure of the IGE/MUS–E to I & R unit effectiveness.* Technical report No. 320. Madison, Wisc.: Wisconsin Research and Development Center for Cognitive Learning.

Halpin, A. W. 1956. *The leadership behavior of school superintendents.* Columbus, Ohio: Bureau of Business Research, The Ohio State University.

House, R. J. 1971. A path goal theory of leadership effectiveness. *Administrative Science Quarterly* **16** (September).

Klausmeier, H. J. In press. Instructional programming for the individual student, in H. J. Klausmeier, R. A. Rossmiller, and M. Saily (eds.), *Individually guided elementary education: concepts and practices.*

————, M. R. Quilling, J. S. Sorenson, R. S. Way, and G. R. Glasrud 1971. *Individually guided education in the multiunit school: guidelines for implementation.* Madison, Wisc.: Wisconsin Research and Development Center for Cognitive Learning.

Lipham, J. M. 1964. Leadership and administration. In D. E. Griffiths (ed.), *Behavioral science and educational administration.* Sixty-third Yearbook, National Society for the Study of Education. Chicago: University of Chicago.

Otto, W. *et al.* 1973. *Wisconsin design for reading skill development: rationale and guidelines.* Minneapolis: National Computer Systems.

Romberg, T. *et al.* 1974. *Developing mathematical processes.* Chicago: Rand McNally.

4

Evaluation for Effective Decision Making

Dennis W. Spuck

Objectives

After reading this chapter, the reader will be able:

- To recognize the significance of information in the decision-making process.
- To comprehend the nature of needs assessment, program planning, formative evaluation, and summative evaluation.
- To identify techniques useful in needs assessment, program planning, formative evaluation, and summative evaluation.
- To understand the relationship between the evaluation model and the Instructional Programming Model.
- To understand the role of the principal in evaluation for effective educational decision making.

Evaluation for educational decision making is a basic component of IGE. The IPM, discussed in Chapter 3, calls for considerable measurement and evaluation of individual student performance. Moreover, the multiunit school organization places great emphasis on involvement by all staff members in the decision-making process. For such participation to be effective, attention must be given to evaluative processes in the school. The emphasis of this chapter is on the evaluation of educational programs and instructional outcomes. The evaluation of staff will be discussed in Chapter 5.

This chapter begins with a definition of evaluation and a discussion of the relationship between evaluation and decision making. A model of evaluation is presented next, which includes the following dimensions: needs assessment, program planning, formative evaluation, and summative evaluation. Each of these dimensions is then discussed in depth, and some specific evaluative tools and techniques which pertain to each of them are described in some detail. The model of evaluation presented is then related to the IPM. The chapter concludes with brief highlights of the principal's roles in evaluation for effective educational decision making.

The generalized model of evaluation which is presented in this chapter addresses a range of educational programs, from those which operate at the level of the individual student to those which encompass the entire district. Though many of the suggestions incorporated into this chapter involve district level decisions, the principal, who is responsible for program improvement in his or her building, must be aware of and influence those districtwide needs as they affect the educational programs of the building. Therefore, it is important that the principal have an in-depth understanding of decision making and evaluation at the district level as well as the building, unit, and individual student levels.

A DEFINITION OF EVALUATION

The term evaluation brings to mind a range of possible synonyms such as measurement, assessment, and judgment, to name a few. Evaluation has taken on a variety of meanings over the past several years. Definitions have emphasized the measurement and testing process (Thorndike and Hagen 1961), values and professional judgments (Phillips 1968), or variance between performance and specified objectives (Mager 1972, Krathwohl 1964, Popham and Baker 1970). More recently, expanded definitions of evaluation have been presented which deal in a more direct way with the intimate relationship which exists between evaluation and decision making (Stufflebeam 1971, Alkin 1969). Educational decisions are best made in the light of reliable and valid information. To be useful in decision making, information must be available, presented in sufficient amounts and types, at reasonable costs, in appropriate forms, and within the time constraints imposed by the decision process. Evaluation, in the context of educational decision making, is related to the presentation of information to decision makers.

The relationship between information and decision making provides a basis for defining educational evaluation as:

- Identifying important decisions to be made,
- Determining what information is most useful in making the decisions,
- Arranging to secure the required data,
- Summarizing the data in a form useful in making the decisions,
- Arranging for the timely delivery of appropriate information to the decision maker, and
- Assessing the utility of the information in the decision-making process.

The first major process in this definition involves the identification of important decisions to be made. Later in this chapter a model is presented which categorizes major decisions in the evaluation process. It is the responsibility of the decision maker to determine which decisions must be made, and it is essential that the decision area be defined sufficiently in order to assess the relevance of the information provided.

The importance of a decision is influenced by the perceptions of the decision maker. Stimuli reaching the decision maker are filtered through a perceptual screen composed of the physiological, attitudinal, intellectual, and value characteristics of the decision maker (Lipham 1974). For example, a decision maker whose value orientation stresses the importance of the 3 Rs might well decide on budgetary priorities which favor mathematics when faced with competing requests from mathematics and music. Understanding of the decision process, be it one's own decisions or decisions made by others, is dependent upon consideration of the factors included in the decision maker's perceptual screen.

In determining which information is most useful, the second process in the definition of evaluation, one must focus not only on the decision itself, but also on the factors within the educational systems which may be influenced by or which may influence the decision alternatives. Each alternative should be displayed, along with its probable impact on factors directly and indirectly related to the decision area, but which exist within the social and political context which surrounds the decision. Such alternatives may have either positive or negative impact. For example, if the problem concerns balancing ethnic distributions between elementary attendance areas, it may have partial "solutions" in either busing or redistricting. These two alternatives presumably could lead to the same degree of effectiveness in "solving" the problem, but have differing impacts on the community. These peripheral effects may be considered as consequences (functional or dysfunctional) and should be weighed to the extent possible, along with the other more direct consequences of the alternatives. Such estimates of potential consequences as may be determined ought to be presented for each decision alternative.

Since all information desired or required in making a decision is not likely to be directly available within the system, mechanisms must be developed for collecting the data. Some decisions will require unique and unanticipated types of information but, to the extent possible, systematic data collection procedures should be established to capture important data elements on an ongoing basis. Management information systems, be they automated or manual, can be quite helpful in improving the quality of information available and in reducing the time required in retrieving it.

A caution must be expressed relative to the burden which such data collection networks can place on an organization, especially an individual school. Each data element placed in such a system imposes a cost on the system in terms of collecting, storing, updating, and retrieving it. Care must be taken to specify for inclusion in such systems only those data elements which are viewed as having high value for decision making. Costs of collecting additional information, not already available, must also be weighed against their value in the making of a decision. The cost may not always be directly in dollars; it may be an indirect social or political cost. For example, information passed from one principal to another may leave the expectation that information desired by the other principal will be provided if requested.

Raw data, such as the responses of individual parents to a questionnaire, may be of little value in decision making. To be most useful, information must be available in the form which assists directly in identifying and defining problems, providing alternative solutions, and weighing the consequences of alternatives. Knowledge of the decision maker's ability to process information may be of value, since some individuals prefer and are better able to utilize information presented in written formats, some in graphic formats, and others in oral reports. It is not only the message which is important, but also the media through which it is transmitted and presented to the decision maker. Important in the consideration of the reliability and validity of information are the concepts of information source and mode of transmittal. Source refers to the origin of information. Different sources of information result in differing levels of credibility. It is also true that some modes of information transmittal tend to be more accurate than other modes. For example, information derived from a comment overheard from a teacher known to exaggerate probably would not be as reliable in decision making as that which resulted from a carefully prepared report of the Instructional Improvement Committee. Here, an informal verbal report (comment) may also be contrasted with a written formal report as a mode of transmittal.

Since information which is presented after the decision is made is of little value, such as receiving a justification for additional instructional materials after the school budget has been presented or allocated, the entire decision-making process is dependent on the timeliness of the data presented. Again, management information systems can greatly facilitate the timely display of information and ensure its availability as required.

The last process in the definition of evaluation is that of assessing the utility of information presented. Information formats, or the ways in which information is presented, types, and amounts can be adjusted to maximize their value in decision making. Procedures can be refined to improve information flow from collection to presentation, and definition of decision areas can be adjusted to specify informational requirements precisely. Such assessment is essential to improving the evaluation process.

The definition of evaluation presented is intended to be quite general and is directed toward the evaluation of educational programs rather than staff personnel. Examples of educational programs include an instructional program undertaken by an individual child, an instructional program, such as reading, undertaken by a group of students, the development of instructional materials, an inservice training program for teachers, or the implementation of a multiunit school organization. Programs consume resources of the organization and are directed toward the accomplishment of pre-stated objectives.

Programmatic changes within an organization take place in terms of four interacting variables: tasks, structures, people, and technology (Leavitt 1965). The tasks of an organization refer to the organization's goals. Structural variables include the system of authority, roles, work flow, and communication which characterize the organization. The people variable includes those individuals involved in the change program. Technology includes the problem-solving inventions, computers, audiovisual equipment and other machines. Primary goals in educational programs are directed toward change in student groups, the organization's clientele. While this is the primary focus, programs could also be directed toward change in any of the other dimensions, that is in the educational tasks such as a new environmental education program; structures, such as the implementation of the multiunit school; people, such as an inservice program for teachers; or technology such as initiating a computer-managed instruction program.

A MODEL OF EVALUATION

The model of systematic evaluation of educational programs developed at the UCLA Center for the Study of Evaluation emphasizes the relationship between evaluation and decision making. (See Figure 4.1.) This model includes the following dimensions.

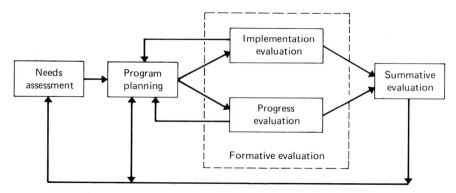

Fig. 4.1 Model of program evaluation. Adapted from M. C. Alkin 1969. Evaluation theory and development. *U.C.L.A. Evaluation Comment* **2** (October) 3.

- Needs assessment
- Program planning
- Formative evaluation
- Summative evaluation

These four evaluation dimensions are each associated with a corresponding decision domain and each includes the six processes mentioned earlier in the definition of evaluation.

Needs assessment is directed toward the identification of priority needs of the system, and the establishment of goals and objectives for an educational program. In program planning, alternative solutions for reaching these goals and objectives are weighed and the alternative program which appears most likely to achieve the desired outcomes is selected for implementation. As the selected program alternative is being implemented, its progress is monitored and changes are made in program implementation which are required to better meet the needs specified; this process is called formative evaluation. Lastly, summative evaluation involves a comparison of actual program outcomes to desired outcomes as specified in program goals and objectives and an assessment of the extent to which program results can be generalized to other educational settings.

Each of the four dimensions included in the model of program evaluation will be discussed in detail in the sections which follow.

Needs Assessment

Needs assessment includes making decisions which identify school or individual student needs, establishing a priority among needs, and specifying the objectives which must be fulfilled in order to meet the identified needs. Identification of needs typically begins with a comparison of existing states within the system with those existing in another system or with expectations which are held for the system. There are two types of evaluation which apply to needs assessment: contingency evaluation and congruence evaluation (Stufflebeam, *et al.* 1971). In contingency evaluation the principal may seek to identify situations existing in other schools which could assist in improving the school's programs. Also included in this mode of assessment are community attitude and value surveys, ideas derived from reviewing new programs as reported in the professional literature, through brainstorming retreats, and other channels. For example, a community survey may reflect the parents' desire to have greater involvement in the educational program of the school. This indicated need would then suggest that the school find ways of satisfying this desire. Contingency evaluation also includes assessments relative to predicted future trends in technology, population, political positions, social attitudes and values, and economic status. Contingency evaluation may raise "if-then" questions. For example, if the population ceases to increase, then how much must the present system be changed to adjust to this change in growth rate? Answers to such questions provide the context for the contingency mode of needs assessment.

Congruence evaluation relates general goals to the measured states of performance. This evaluation mode stresses the need for systematic monitoring of the extent to which system goals and values are being accurately reflected in the educational program. For example, information such as the difference between district and national norms on standardized tests in reading or mathematics might suggest the need for program improvements. If a school staff believes that the content of a standardized test accurately reflects the objectives of the school's program, and a negative discrepancy exists, then they might review the current program. Additional examples of discrepancies between existing conditions and expectations which might suggest a need for change would be a high or increasing rate of student dropout, absenteeism, or drug usage, or a decrease in teacher morale.

Methods of needs assessment.   A needs assessment may utilize many sources of information, such as staff and community problem identification sessions, staff community or student surveys, a review of current literature on research and development on instructional materials, visits to other school districts, forecasting of social trends, or ongoing data collection on the status of the system itself. It is also possible that needs suggestive of program change may be indicated by legislation. An example of this latter circumstance is found in recent legislation in many states which mandates procedures to be followed in providing services to students with special educational needs.

Methods of needs assessment which are invaluable tools for the IGE principal include: (1) structured surveys, (2) standardized tests and other measures, and (3) the nominal group process.

1. *The Structured Survey.* Surveys of attitudes and values of staff, students, and the community can provide the educational decision maker with valuable information for needs assessment. Surveys might include either or both questionnaire or interview formats. Chapter 6 includes a discussion of in-depth interviews. Questions to be included in a survey should be carefully prepared to ensure that they will provide the information desired in assessing need in a particular program area. Respondents to needs assessment surveys are generally asked to supply information concerning their perceptions of the actual state of a system or their views as to the ideal state of the system, or perhaps both.

As an example of a questionnaire which might be incorporated in a survey to obtain a general assessment of program priorities for an elementary school program, a modification of the Task of Public Educational Opinionnaire references might be used (See Table 4.1). In this procedure, respondents (e.g., parents, staff, administrators, citizens) are asked to sort the sixteen items into seven categories according to their view of what should be emphasized in the school's elementary program. After the data are collected, averages of the assigned priorities can be computed for each task to determine the relative emphasis placed upon each by the respondent group. It may also be useful to ask respondents to sort the set of tasks again, according to their feelings as to what tasks the educational program is actually emphasizing at the present time. Then comparisons can be drawn between what respondents feel ought to be emphasized and what they feel is actually being emphasized.

Structured, comprehensive surveys require careful attention to the detail of instrument design, data collection (particularly if interviewing is included), sampling of respondents, data analysis, and data presentation. Frequently, it may be wise to utilize a knowledgeable consultant in the design and conduct of such surveys.

2. *Standardized and Criterion-referenced Tests.* A distinction may be made between two major types of tests: standardized tests and criterion-referenced tests. Standardized tests are designed to discriminate among respondents with the intent of ordering those respondents according to the construct being measured, such as mathematics achievement. Examples of standardized tests include the Iowa Tests of Basic Skills, the Stanford Achievement Tests, Differential Aptitude Tests, and the Self-observation Scales. These tests are usually quite general, in that they cover a broad range of educational objectives. While standardized tests may be useful in reviewing educational needs of the school or district, they are generally not suitable for needs assessment on the individual student level relative to a

Table 4.1 Tasks of the Elementary School

1. Gain a foundation of facts as a basis for knowledge.
2. Develop skills in reading, writing, and arithmetic.
3. Learn how to weigh facts as the basis for conclusions.
4. Develop a desire for learning, now and in the future.
5. Learn how to respect and get along with people with whom we work and live.
6. Understand and practice democratic ideas and ideals.
7. Understand and respect people from different cultural and religious backgrounds.
8. Learn about the relationship between humans and their environment.
9. Practice and understand the ideas of health and safety.
10. Develop a feeling of self-respect and self-worth.
11. Develop moral character and a sense of right and wrong.
12. Appreciate culture and beauty in the world.
13. Develop an awareness of careers and the world of work.
14. Understand and develop the skills required for homemaking and home maintenance.
15. Learn how to be a good manager of money, property, and resources.
16. Learn how to use leisure time.

Adapted from Lawrence W. Downey 1960. *The Task of Public Education.* Chicago: Midwest Administration Center, University of Chicago, by the Board of Education, Worth School District No. 127, Worth, Illinois, 1973.

specific instructional program. A well-developed standardized test, meaning a test having reliability and validity which supports its use and one having content which covers constructs of interest to an educational community, can provide information useful in assessing educational needs. Such information usually is provided relative to a normative reference, other schools, other districts, or a national average. These results must be weighed in balance with the importance of the area measured to the educational community.

Criterion-referenced tests, tests which focus directly on the objectives (criteria) of an instructional program, are useful in assessing the instructional needs of individual students. Pretests or placement tests of a criterion-referenced nature provide information to instructional decision makers which is useful in determining which objectives in the instructional program the student has or has not achieved. Placement tests may cover several objectives within an instructional program and may be useful in "placing" a student within that program, while pretests usually focus on a small number of objectives, frequently on a single objective only. While both criterion-referenced pretests and placement tests may be used to assist in the identification of instructional need, a variety of additional information would be necessary to provide a complete picture of need; such additional information might include assessments of student motivation and learning style.

Many of the comments regarding testing and measurement presented in this section apply equally well to summative evaluation, since it is at that time that a determination is made as to whether or not the identified needs have been met. Standardized and criterion-referenced tests may be used for this purpose as well, and a further discussion of testing is included in the section on summative evaluation.

3. *The Nominal Group Process.* A third needs-assessment technique, called the nominal group process, is very useful in identifying existing or potential problems within a school and in establishing priorities among them (Delbecq and Van deVen 1971, pp. 466–492). The nominal group process follows a set of specific procedures. First, the person in charge must be certain that the room and material arrangements are appropriate for conducting the sessions. The room and tables should be large enough to seat six to ten participants comfortably and with privacy. Since it is difficult for one coordinator to work effectively with more than three groups (tables), an additional coordinator is necessary if the total number of participants exceeds 30. Materials required for each table include a flip chart (at the end of each table), 3″ × 5″ cards, two or three different colored felt tip pens, masking tape, and pencils.

In the nominal group process it is very important that an appropriate question be posed to serve as the stimulus to which the participants will respond. Since this question is central in the process, it must be clearly and concisely stated to present a comprehensive view of the problem to be explored. For example, the following question might be presented: "What are the personal and organizational barriers which prevent the optimal implementation of a program of Individually Guided Education in your school?" Note that since this question separates the subjective, personal barriers from the structured, organizational barriers, it would lead to quite complete responses. The formulated question is placed at the top of a response sheet.

When the participants arrive, they are assigned to tables of heterogeneous groups. To establish rapport with participants, the purpose of the session should be clarified and their commitment and cooperation sought. It should be emphasized that the session is for identifying problems rather than solving them, and that unrelated conversation is both undesirable and dysfunctional.

The form with the basic question on it is then distributed, the question is read aloud, and specific instructions are given to *list* responses in a few words each. It is also helpful to provide at least one exemplary response. Each participant should respond to the question in writing, quietly listing the barriers that come to mind. Early finishers should be encouraged to reflect more deeply on the question. The coordinator should assertively ensure that the silence is maintained for the duration of this activity (usually 15–20 minutes). This nominal activity is continued until most of the participants have ceased to add to their lists. It is best if the responses are short and to the point, since later they will be listed individually on the flip chart.

A recorder for the group is required for the remainder of the activities. If there is only one table, then the coordinator may serve as the recorder; otherwise, the coordinator should appoint as recorder a serious, well-organized individual at each table. The recorder is instructed to proceed around the table, requiring each participant to read one item from the problem list. This listing activity should be continued until all problems have been written legibly on the flip chart with the felt pen. The recorder must list each problem as it is read by the participant and should not attempt to redefine, categorize, or clarify any statement as it is being written. Moreover, the recorder, with support of the coordinator, should prohibit discussion of the items as they are listed. As one sheet of paper on the flip chart becomes filled, it should be removed and placed on the wall where all participants can see it. The purpose of this activity, which usually takes about 30 minutes, is to list all identified problems as expediently as possible.

Identifying and listing problems in the manner outlined provides considerable ensurance that highly verbal individuals, holders of status positions, or informal group leaders will not dominate the problem-identification process. In this way the concerns of each participant are given equal attention.

The next step in the process is designed to ensure that all participants understand the meaning of each problem which has been listed. At this juncture, the recorder should discourage discussion aimed at collapsing similar categories. Instead the focus is on clarifying each problem statement. This usually takes about 15 minutes.

To obtain an initial assessment of group priorities relative to the problems listed, a voting procedure is used. A variety of voting strategies may be utilized but, as one approach, seven $3'' \times 5''$ cards may be given to each participant to use as ballots. Then, each participant writes the numbers of the seven listed items which the participant feels to be of greatest priority— one item to a card. No attempt is made in this procedure to assign priority rankings to the seven items. These ballots are then collected and the participants given a brief break. During the break, the recorder tallies the ballots and notes the total number of votes next to each item on the flip chart pages. (It is helpful to use a different colored marker for these tallies.)

When the groups return, each group discusses its listed rankings. Participants may wish to explain why they voted for a particular item which others in the group did not consider to be important. Similar items may be collapsed, but the recorder should ensure that consensus is reached quickly on decisions to collapse (perhaps using a show of hands) rather than allowing extended discussion. It is better to have similar items on a list than to consume several minutes debating differences or collapsing items perceived as dissimilar. If desired, additional items may be added at this time. With careful moderation the ranking process can be completed within 15–30 minutes.

A new set of rankings is now requested of participants. Again, several voting procedures can be utilized, but as one approach, five 3″ × 5″ cards may be given to each participant, and all are instructed to identify the five problem statements on the list which they feel to be of greatest importance, writing the number of these items, one to a card. Then, each participant is asked to rank order the five items, from the most important (5) to the least important (1). Item numbers may be circled to differentiate them from rank. The cards are collected, and weighted tallies are computed by totaling the rankings for each item. Participants may, but need not, remain during the second tallying, since the needs assessment data collection is now completed. The materials should be collected and appreciation expressed to the participants. If participants leave prior to the final tallying, summaries of the results should be provided to them.

The nominal group process, then, is a structured technique which is designed to elicit problems and to discover the priorities assigned to them. It is a viable program-planning technique—particularly when combined with that of problem solution groups which will be discussed in Chapter 6.

These three needs-assessment procedures are illustrative of structured approaches to data collection. Naturally, many other methodologies exist, some of which are quite different from the examples given and some of which are modifications of those presented. Frequently, informal observations suggest needs which exist within a system and it is not always possible for the decision maker to have formal needs-assessment information available. The premise here, however, is that decision making will be improved in accordance with the quantity of information available and utilized in the decision-making process.

In needs assessment, the information is collected and presented in a format so that the decision maker can identify and assign priorities among system needs. Further, the information must provide a basis for the specification of goals and objectives for a new or modified program.

Statement of goals and objectives.   Priority needs for the educational program are translated into goals and objectives. Goals describe states or behaviors that units such as a school or district will attempt to achieve, while objectives refer to specific skills, behaviors, or outcomes which the program will achieve. Goals are general and broad in scope and usually of longer range than objectives. Objectives then are more focused and shorter range from goals. For example, a goal of an educational program may be to have students learn how to read, while an objective might be for students to understand rhyming elements in words. Since the difference between goals and objectives is a matter of degree rather than kind, the terms are frequently used synonymously in common usage.

Measurable objectives may be distinguished from goals, in that measurable objectives refer to specific program outcomes which are to be achieved as well as the evidence which will be accepted as sufficient for demonstrating achievement of the outcome. In instructional programs, measurable objectives are frequently referred to as instructional objectives. Unfortunately a variety of terms are used synonymously for measurable objectives; for example, performance objectives and behavioral objectives. No attempt will be made to distinguish among these terms here. An example of a measurable objective, which appears in the Wisconsin Design for Reading Skill Development (Otto and Askov 1972):

> given a word, the child selects a rhyming word based on structure (e.g., pan, man, and fan are from the same word family); or supplies a real or nonsense rhyming word based on structure.

An additional example of a measurable objective related to the program goal, to improve home-school relations through parental understanding of the basic concepts of a program of Individually Guided Education, is:

> following experience in a simulated program of Individually Guided Education, 80 percent of the parents participating in the program will score at least 90 percent on the IGE concepts test (Quilling 1971).

Another type of objective important to program evaluation is the process objective. Process objectives refer to tasks or activities which must be accomplished in order to fulfill the objectives of the program. Process objectives are not measurable in that specific criteria levels are not set and also in that they do not represent specific project outcomes, but it is possible to determine whether the process has been completed. Process objectives may be dependent on a program plan; that is, process objectives generally cannot be formulated until a specific program plan has been selected for implementation. Process objectives would, then, not be formulated until the end of the program-planning process.

The formulation of program objectives is a crucial step in the process of program evaluation since the remaining processes of program planning, formative evaluation and summative evaluation, are designed in accordance with the specified objectives. Needs assessment, then, is the important first step in program evaluation and is concerned with providing information which will assist in the identification and establishment of priority needs as objectives to be accomplished.

Program Planning

Program planning begins with the objectives specified as a part of needs assessment. Potentially, many different programs may be found which meet the requirements of a given set of objectives; these programs are weighed and the alternative best expected to succeed is selected, subject to the constraints imposed by the availability of resources. The program-planning process ends with the development of the formative and summative evaluation designs and the implementation of the selected program.

Program-planning evaluation also includes supplying information pertaining to the existence of alternative plans. Once alternative plans are specified, the process involves supplying comparative information relative to the merits of each of the identified alternatives. Information provided should include comparisons on the basis of human, financial, and material resource utilization, and of the probabilities of each alternative for success. On the basis of the information provided, a decision is formulated concerning how to allocate resources in meeting system goals.

The range of alternatives available to the decision maker for meeting identified needs is not limited to existing programs. It is possible that an entirely new approach is called for and the IIC or other groups are established to plan and develop a program to meet the needs of the school. For example, a needs assessment may suggest that a new science program, which includes concepts in ecology, be implemented in the school. A review of available programs in this area may reveal that no program exists which is consistent with the schoolwide objectives or compatible with the IPM. The IIC of the school may then decide to develop such a program.

In program planning a useful distinction can be made among three types of change settings (Stufflebeam, *et al.* 1971, pp. 220–228). In the first setting, the amount of change is small but a great amount of information is available relative to the change. As a result, little evaluation is required.

The second setting is characterized when both the degree of change and the amount of available information is small. The expenditure of considerable resources usually is not justified under these conditions, so an incremental approach may be taken. As in the example above, the IIC may wish to approach a new curricular area, such as ecology, in the context of the Instructional Programming Model. Little in the way of instructional materials, instructional activities, or measurable objectives may be available. The staff may begin with whatever materials are available, examine them to identify existing limitations, then modify and improve the program. Specific program objectives and plans for implementation would be formulated, and the modified program would then be implemented. Up to this point, little in the way of formal consideration of alternatives, their costs, or probable results has taken place.

Contrasted with the previous example is the third type of setting where program planning takes place in the innovative change setting. This type of program planning is characterized by a major change, undertaken with limited available information. If, for example, the implementation of the new program in the area of ecology were to be considered districtwide, this would constitute a change of greater magnitude than if such a change were taking place at the level of the I & R Unit. Under the conditions of a major, districtwide revision in programs, considerable investment in program-planning evaluation would be justified. Identification of alternatives existing both within and outside the district would probably be done by the SPC or other groups. The alternatives would be weighed on the basis of their strengths and weaknesses and, if the alternatives were considered inadequate, then a committee might be established to develop a new program to meet the defined district needs. Consultants might be used to provide input and otherwise assist in the developmental effort. If the process is of sufficient complexity and utility, a planning or developmental proposal might be generated to secure funds from sources outside the district. It is also possible that it would be determined at the point of program planning that an effective plan could not be formulated and that a reordering of need priorities should take place. In the innovative change setting the need for information is great, hence the need for evaluation is also great.

Methods of program planning.   Three methodologies are particularly useful to the principal in program planning: (1) network analysis, (2) the Delphi procedure, and (3) a group process model. In addition, the use of consultants in program planning is also considered.

1. *Network analysis.* Basic elements in network analysis include activities, events, times, costs, and responsibilities. Both Critical Path Methodology (CPM) and Program Evaluation Review Technique (PERT) are based on fundamental concepts of network analysis. Activities are the building blocks of a program and consume time and resources, while events mark the beginning and ending points of activities. Responsibility for each activity is fixed with an individual or group. A network of activities and events may be constructed which graphically displays interrelationships existing among activities in a program.

Network analysis is a tool which allows decision makers to simulate the steps in the completion of a program prior to undertaking a project. It also provides time and cost estimates for the program and allows for monitoring the progress of the program during implementation, and further, it permits the project manager to assess the impact of deviation from time estimates on the completion dates of the program. The activities in a network may be viewed as process objectives necessary to the completion of the program.

2. *The Delphi procedure.* Another methodology which may be used both in needs assessment and program planning is called the Delphi procedure. This procedure may be used to elicit assessments of the status of the system from a group of respondents and is most helpful when attempting to gain information about probable future events when little information is currently available.

Initially, a question is formulated which focuses the scope of the study. For example, the following question may be used: "What are the major problems which would be encountered in implementing IGE in Jefferson Elementary School?" Selected as respondents would be persons who could be expected to know about the problem area. In this example, principals and teachers who had been involved in IGE implementation, state IGE coordinators, and people who have worked on the design and development of IGE might be included as experts to respond to the question. These respondent experts receive the question(s), generally through the mail; their responses are summarized with the frequencies of similar responses tallied. Then, the summarized responses are mailed again to the experts who are asked to examine the list, delete items believed to be of no importance, modify items, add new items, and comment to clarify their views. This second review is again summarized, with points of disagreement noted, and again returned to the experts. The process may continue until the coordinator of the procedure is satisfied with the level of agreement attained and the comprehensiveness of responses. In later cycles, rating scales allowing for judgments of degree of importance can be used to assist in tallying the results.

3. *The program planning model.* This group process, which may be used in conjunction with the nominal group process discussed earlier, includes four phases: knowledge exploration, priority development, program development, and program evaluation (Delbecq and Van de Ven 1971). The knowledge-exploration phase involves experts from both within and outside of the system. The experts are placed into small groups and, through a structured process, consider alternative solutions to achieving the objectives posed from a needs assessment. The process attempts to integrate existing resources and new approaches to meeting the objectives in a single program alternative.

The priority development phase allows program needs and the solution suggested to be reviewed by participants in the preceding processes as well as by system administrators. Specialists in program development utilize the input from the preceding phases to develop a specific program proposal. This recommended proposal is reviewed and approved in the final phase, program evaluation, by representative participants from all of the earlier phases, including the needs-assessment phase. This group process model, then, is directed not only at developing sound programs but at building group consensus as well.

Consultants are frequently used in program planning since they can be helpful in identifying and modifying existing program alternatives or in working with a school staff to develop new program alternatives. To maximize the use of consultants, the contracting school should consider the following recommendations:

1. Carefully identify the domain in which information is required, so that a consultant may be identified and selected who is an expert in the area and who can provide the desired information. Ask for work samples or talk with other school staffs with whom the consultants have worked.

2. Inform the consultant beforehand of the exact work to be performed and the expectations which are held for the consultant's visit, allowing the consultant to prepare in advance for the visit. Send the consultant relevant material for review.

3. Plan in advance for the consultant's visit. Schedule the consultant's time in order to make maximum use of it.

4. Be certain to arrange plans for a summary of the consultant's visit. This may be accomplished through a debriefing with the staff at the end of the visit, or through a report written by the consultant at the conclusion or shortly after the visit. This summary may be used to provide feedback to the IIC or the I & R Unit.

A structured approach to the use of a consultant's time will bring a greater return for the investment; this is true whether the consultant is from the central office or an extraorganizational agency. Both the Delphi and the group process models are structured procedures which allow for the input of expert opinion.

Product evaluation.   Program planning frequently involves the evaluation of currently available educational materials. Programs aimed at the development of such materials would follow the steps involved in the total evaluation model presented in this chapter. The evaluation of educational products by the consumer, however, is a topic which is appropriately considered as a part of program planning. A committee of the Association for Supervision and Curriculum Development posed a list of questions which point to important considerations in the selection of new educational projects and products. Some of these questions are summarized in the following section.

Issues Related to Assessing New Projects and Their Effect on Learners *

Types of Learners

Are the materials clearly designed for a particular group—for fast, average, slow learners? for a particular age level? Do project materials vary sufficiently to benefit learners who have different cognitive styles (e.g., inquirers and noninquirers, those who work well with symbols and those who work well with concrete objects)?

Effects on Learners

What effect might the new program have on the anxiety levels of learners? What opportunities do learners have to strengthen their intellectual independence? To what extent are learners encouraged to be creative? Are such behaviors restricted by the project materials or services? As a result of the new program, are the pupils likely to become more excited about learning than they have been previously? Are learners encouraged to develop facility with a variety of materials and approaches to learning? What attitudes and values might learners acquire through the project. What kinds of behaviors—cognitive, affective, psychomotor— are learners encouraged to exhibit?

Stability of Student Groups

How will student turnover affect the success of the project? What special arrangements must be made for students who transfer into the school? What prerequisites are required if they are to participate in the new project?

Issues Related to Assessment
Adequacy of Data

Do we have initial data on learners—their achievement, their motivation, their personalities? Do we have initial data on teachers—their strategies, their motivation, their knowledge, their personalities? Do we

---

*   Ammons and Gilchrist in Leeper 1965, pp. 19–20.

have these data at many stages during the implementation of the project? Would a model assist us in making a continuing assessment? For example:

Time 1 (initial appraisal)	During a Project	Time 2 (final appraisal)
Set up instruments to assess	Observers analyze the strategies of students, teachers	Set up instruments to assess

achievement
students' personality
    motivation
		achievement
		students' personality
		    motivation

	Assessors analyze materials and their effect on teachers and learners	

satisfaction
teachers' strategies
    knowledge
		satisfaction
		teachers' strategies
		    knowledge

What happens to learners as people and to learners as learners as a result of the project? What happens to teachers as people and to teachers as teachers? Do changes justify the time and funds expended?

Answers to each of these questions should be carefully formulated after a review of program needs and in the light of staff attitudes, values, and abilities. In addition to the questions posed above, new products also need to be considered relative to their cost: the initial cost of purchase, the cost of maintaining the program (material replacement), and the cost of implementing the program including required inservice programs.

Program planning should result in a comprehensive design for program implementation. The plan should demonstrate the means by which the needs identified in systems assessment will be met. Program requirements, in terms of human, material, and financial resources, should be specified and the procedures to be utilized in carrying out the program should be defined. Within the broader context of the overall objectives to be met by the program, process objectives should be formulated. A time line should be established so that it can be determined if progress toward the major objectives is being achieved. A very important component of this evaluation phase is the development of the evaluation design to be carried out in the formative and summative evaluations which follow.

Formative Evaluation

Formative evaluation of educational programs includes two major components which are called implementation evaluation and progress evaluation. Implementation evaluation provides the decision maker with information on the extent to which the program's structural characteristics such as personnel, materials, physical space, or equipment are being utilized according to the program plan developed in the previous phase of the evaluation model. Programs involve input from a variety of resources such as the human resources of teachers and students. Implementation evaluation might ask the question: Are the teachers involved in the project trained to the extent and in the areas of specialization prescribed in the program plan? The program, for example, might involve students with special educational needs, such as the partially sighted, and require teachers with special training in working with students with visual handicaps. Implementation evaluation would assess the degree to which the teachers met the required training and experience levels. Some programs are designed for certain populations of students, such as the emotionally disturbed or the disadvantaged. Implementation evaluation would assess the degree to which these students were or were not involved in the program. In the same way consideration would be given to the availability of material and financial resources and to the program's utilization of physical space.

In addition to being concerned with the availability of all resources, implementation evaluation deals with the way in which these resources are combined to carry out the program. The program plan specifies that certain activities are to take place. For example, the IPM indicates that the instructional program ought to include periodic assessment of the attainment of individualized learning objectives. If, in fact, this periodic assessment is not taking place, the IPM is not being appropriately implemented.

On the basis of the information resulting from this evaluation, decisions are made concerning program modification. If the program plan is not being properly implemented, either changes in the program should be considered to bring the program into accordance with the plan, or a decision should be reached to modify the plan. If the deviation from the program plan is extreme and sufficient changes cannot be made in the program to correct the implementation, the program may be cancelled, a new program implemented, or a reassessment of goal priorities may take place.

A well-formulated plan which includes the specification of the activities to be conducted, their sequencing as well as their costs, will greatly facilitate the conduct of implementation evaluation. The methodology of network analysis introduced as a part of the discussion of program planning is a tool which will assist the project manager in the review of program implementation. As presented earlier, network analysis not only provides a time line for evaluation of program implementation but also provides a mechanism for determining the implications of deviations from the program plan on the completion of the program.

Progress evaluation.   Taking place at the same time, and closely associated with the decision areas of implementation evaluation, is progress evaluation. The concern of this aspect of formative evaluation is the extent to which the program is moving toward the effective realization of specified program outcomes. Questions such as the following might be asked: Is the program developing the behaviors specified as objectives in the program? Are the process objectives included in the program plan being met? Process objectives may be stated in terms of structural components and, as such, would be considered within the domain of implementation evaluation; process objectives may also be stated so as to relate directly to outcomes of the program. For example, the following process objective might be formulated: within the first three weeks of the program, 90 percent of the students participating in the program will have mastered at least one instructional objective.

Progress evaluation is not concerned only with assessment relative to formally stated process objectives. Those persons responsible for the conduct of the program are presumably in a good position to note the continuing progress of the program and to make judgments or provide information concerning that progress. If a student is not making progress toward mastery of an objective because the instructional approach utilizes manipulatives and the student does not possess the motor skill development to manipulate the instructional materials, then an alternative instructional procedure should be found. In the case of an instructional program, teacher observations, the examination of work samples, and interim quizzes will provide useful feedback in assessing student progress in the program.

Progress evaluation should also include unanticipated factors which may occur in the conduct of the program and which are not directly related to program objectives, but which nonetheless may have an impact on the participants in the program. Both positive and negative factors are of potential importance. Unanticipated negative factors, such as the inability of two teachers assigned to the same I & R Unit to work effectively together, may call for immediate remedial action.

Unanticipated positive factors can be formally integrated into the program. The program plan might be modified to enhance these contributions. If the program is to be repeated at some point in the future, then unanticipated positive factors could be important in program planning by adding to the list of benefits resulting from this program alternative.

Both the implementation and progress components of formative evaluation are concerned with decisions related to positive program modification in the event that the program is not being implemented according to plan or is not moving effectively toward meeting the objectives prescribed in the plan. While both of these evaluation components may be characterized by the formal assessment of program status relative to process objectives, they are also characterized by a less formal approach wherein evaluators and/or program participants monitor the program and provide feedback to the decision maker on problems encountered in the conduct of the program. This informal aspect is in contrast to the more structured approach characteristic of summative evaluation to be discussed in the next section.

Summative Evaluation

Most educational programs are bound within a time frame—frequently that imposed by the school year or school semester. At some point an overall assessment of the program outcomes is desirable. The question is asked: To what extent did the program meet the overall objectives prescribed for it? On the basis of information provided during the summative evaluation, decisions are made as to whether or not to continue using the program in the present setting, or to expand the program to additional I & R Units or to additional schools. ". . . the role of the evaluator in summative evaluation is to provide the decision maker with information that will enable him to make decisions about the program as a whole and its potential generalizability to other situations" (Alkin 1969). For example, the effects of a compensatory education program operating within a school would be compared to the objectives specified for the program, in order to determine the extent to which these objectives were met and to consider the likelihood of these effects being transportable to other schools and districts.

In an instructional setting, such as exists in IGE, summative evaluation is concerned with whether or not the instructional objectives related to a particular sequence of instructional activities have been met. In this case a final assessment is made prior to beginning a new set of instructional activities. These new instructional activities may focus on the original objectives in the event of nonmastery, or on a new objective in the event of mastery. (This is not to suggest that a student ought to continue attempting to attain the same objective until it is ultimately met. In some instances it is best to skip over the objective and return to it at some later time.) Summative evaluation in this example then carries the connotation of final judgment relative to the instructional objectives under consideration. An expanded notion of summative evaluation includes what is referred to as evaluative research; that is, an attempt to relate the programmatic activities to the program outcome in a cause-and-effect relationship. Studies which are directed toward the comparison of two instructional approaches for teaching the same objectives are included in the category of evaluative research and therefore summative evaluation. Evaluative research not only attempts to determine if one instructional approach is better than another but also seeks to determine why it is better.

The design of summative evaluation tends to be more formalized than that of formative evaluation. It attempts to enforce rigid controls and precise measurement. Formative evaluation and summative evaluation are sometimes in competition with each other, particularly in the case of evaluative research. Summative evaluation seeks to look at the program as a whole under controlled conditions. Formative evaluation is, as noted, interventionist in nature and seeks to modify the program as problems are identified; this process interferes with the degree of control. Due to the importance of the individuals involved in the programs, generally students, it is felt that programs cannot be allowed to continue unmodified if they are not progressing satisfactorily toward the specified goals; this compromises the experimental control of evaluative research. Generally, however, if the program is planned carefully and carried out according to plan, the required adjustments are small and corresponding effects on the experimental control are small. These adjustments must, however, be considered in the interpretations of information collected during summative evaluation.

The design of a summative evaluation cannot be delayed until the completion of the program under study. As was indicated in the section on program planning, the evaluation design should be formulated during the program-planning phase. The informational requirements of summative evaluation must be foreseen at this earlier point.

In the last few years, the view has been presented that both summative and formative evaluation should become more goal free (Scriven 1967, pp. 39–83). Evaluation which is focused directly on program objectives will tend to overlook unanticipated consequences of the program. This concern of goal-free evaluation is one which is reflected in the definition of progress evaluation presented earlier. Proponents of goal-free evaluation feel that evaluation should attempt to reflect the true nature of the program and not focus only on previously specified objectives or upon that which is most easily measured (Stake 1972, pp. 1–2).

Evaluation design and methods.   Of importance in summative evaluation, and of particular importance in evaluation research, are considerations of measurement or instrumentation, study design, sampling of participants, and data analysis. Instruments are utilized to collect the raw data required in summative evaluation and are designed to operationalize the outcomes expressed in the program objectives. As is the case in assessing the value of all measurement instruments, the validity and reliability of these measures are of great importance.

Validity, or the extent to which a measure actually measures what it is supposed to measure, is a basic concern of all measurement. This is true of "criterion-referenced" measurement as well as "norm-referenced" measurement, although evaluative research most frequently utilizes "norm-referenced" instruments. The collection of items which make up a measurement instrument should be representative of the construct being measured. For example, a valid measure of mathematics achievement would contain items or problems appropriate to the objectives of the instructional programs, and such that the collection of all items included on the test would be representative of all of the items or problems which could have been included to measure the construct.

Reliability is also a fundamental property of measurement. It is concerned with the extent to which a measurement instrument is stable or consistent. Reliability may be viewed as the extent to which two measures of the same object or person agree, or the correlation between an initial testing and a retesting. Another way of viewing the reliability of a measure is through the extent to which the several items which make up the measure are correlated. Each of these items presumably measures the same construct and therefore the items ought to be highly intercorrelated or internally consistent. Reliability estimates are usually published in manuals for standardized tests, and can and should be assessed for locally prepared tests. The reliability of measures based upon work samples or observational data is difficult to assess and frequently lower than that of paper-and-pencil tests.

In evaluative research, experimental control is essential. Most of the research conducted on educational processes cannot be carried out in a carefully controlled laboratory environment. This is not to say that we cannot, through other mechanisms, provide sufficient control to draw valid conclusions. Considerably more controlled experimentation could be conducted in school settings than is presently being done. The field of experimental design considers ways of organizing program participants and data collection so as to account for certain factors (errors) which may influence the results of a study. An example of an experimental design is the pretest-posttest control group design. In this design, two groups of program participants are randomly selected and a pretest related to the program objectives is given. One group of participants, the experimental group, receives the benefits of the planned program, while the second group, the control group, does not participate in the program. A variation of this design includes two experimental groups with differing programs for each. In either design, the study concludes with a posttest. The logic of the design implies that any difference existing between the groups at posttest which did not exist at pretest is a result of the intervening program. Any influences external to the program would have influenced both the experimental group and the control group in similar ways, so that the difference between the posttest scores would not evidence the influence of these factors.

Evaluative research is frequently conducted with the hope that the results may be generalized to a larger group of individuals. This question of generality is in part dependent upon the extent to which the participants in the evaluative research program are representative of this larger population; it is in response to this concern that random sampling and, in the case of experimental design, random assignment to groups are utilized. Strictly speaking, one would not legitimately be able to generalize the results of a study to a group larger than the one from which the actual programs participants were selected. Inferences drawn to larger groups (extended population) are dependent on the degree of similarity between the program participants and the members of the larger group. To illustrate the point, one would probably not wish to generalize results of a program conducted in an emotionally disturbed student population to a nonemotionally disturbed student population, nor the conclusions derived from a program for the gifted student to a regular student group. On the other hand one might be tempted to cautiously generalize the results of a study conducted in one student group to another student group of a similar type.

Data analysis in evaluative research generally considers changes which take place from pretest to posttest or differences which exist between the experimental group and the control group. While many different statistical methods exist which could be used in these cases, perhaps the most frequently encountered and useful are analysis of variance and the t-tests. Analysis of variance is suited to identifying differences which may exist between two or more groups or the same group on two or more testings. The t-test is a similar statistic which is useful in exploring differences between two, but not more than two, groups.

Valid inferences in evaluative research result from carefully conceptualized instrumentation, experimental design, samples, and data analysis. Schools conducting large scale research efforts may wish to consider the involvement of consultants to assist in the design of the summative evaluation.

Summative evaluation is concerned with the extent to which program objectives are achieved. When it is of value to know specifically whether one method is better than another method or that a particular result was caused by the program, as in evaluative research, the consideration of research design, sampling, and statistical analysis become crucial. In any event summative evaluation is concerned with the valid and reliable measurement of program outcomes.

Criterion-referenced testing in summative evaluation. As discussed in the earlier section on needs assessment, criterion-referenced tests are designed so as to allow for the direct assessment of whether or not specific program objectives (criteria) have been achieved. These tests are most useful in making decisions about the effects of instruction on individual students (Katzenmeyer, in press). These tests may be available as an integral part of a commercial curricular package, or they may be those developed by the staff of an I & R Unit. They may be paper-and-pencil tests or they may require other overt behaviors. When tests are used, each student is measured under identical conditions of test administration and each should be made aware that measurement is taking place—the intention being that of eliciting maximum performance.

Paper-and-pencil tests require students to respond to items by identifying or generating a correct answer. Some teachers feel that there are disadvantages to extensive pencil-and-paper tests, particularly because of pupil fears of failure. Certainly there are children whose capabilities are not revealed by written tests, but children who have known IGE only accept such measurement without qualms. When older students hold misconceptions or memories of the misuse of tests, teachers should take a positive approach to testing and reason with students about its purpose. Pencil-and-paper tests are very useful tools for creating an efficient data-based framework for instructional decision making.

Commercially prepared tests that require behaviors other than paper-and-pencil performance are also popular in IGE schools, particularly where aides are available to work directly with students. These are commonly called performance tests. Tests of this type clearly specify the tasks that the student is to perform, and under what conditions, as well as defining the behavioral criteria expected. To standardize the test administration, and to preserve the test tasks for later use, written directions are often provided. Performance tests are well suited to a variety of manipulative and motor tasks, as well as those requiring an oral response. For this reason, they are very commonly included in perceptual-motor programs.

Teachers also use a type of performance test when they ask for verbal responses from students in individual or group discussion, such as "$2 \times 4 =$ what?" or "How far is it to the moon?" This is an indispensable feedback mechanism for keeping students and teachers informed of instructional progress—as well as providing the opportunity for immediate reinforcement. When used for making individual instructional decisions, however, the process must be carefully planned. Questions must be constructed to reflect accurately and completely the objective being measured, and each student should have the opportunity to respond to enough questions so that the student's level of performance on the objective is fairly represented. Since verbal questioning provides no record of the student's performance, a simple checklist of items and responses can profitably be employed.

To reiterate, tests developed as part of a curricular package will generally reflect the objectives of that curriculum and thus will usually be valid for students whose instructional programs contain elements of the program. However, a curricular package should always be reviewed critically before adoption for evidence that the tests have been used successfully with comparable students. Reliability estimates should also be given for these instruments and should be reviewed carefully. While tests may be costly and demanding of staff and student time, it is a reasonable investment to obtain good instruments, thereby saving the effort required for local test development.

When developing tests, one must be sure that objectives are clearly spelled out and that the test reflects all aspects of the objectives. Enough behaviors should be included to ensure reliability—the number of behaviors needed depending on the breadth of the objective. For even the narrowest of objectives, two to three items should be used, while broader objectives should include ten or more items.

Work samples are another means of assessing performance. Such samples may be written work, oral presentations, or other products such as art work. Assignments given by the teacher—workbook pages, work sheets, or creative reports—can serve to test a student's mastery of an objective, thereby eliminating the need for a specifically developed test. Despite the ready availability of work samples, thought must be given to the content so that the relationship between the objective and the measurement is preserved. For example, some tasks may not relate to the objective, and the teacher may omit these in determining whether mastery of the objective has been attained; for example, the teacher may ignore spelling errors in a creative writing assignment. In several areas of the curriculum, work samples are frequently used such as letter formation in handwriting.

Observation has a special role in IGE schools. Objective-based observation is a preplanned, organized kind of measurement that the teacher (rarely the aide) undertakes unobstrusively. For example, in measuring a student's motivation for independent reading, the teacher might devise and use a checklist to observe typical performance. Since observation is often a lengthy process, it usually is used only when it is the best means of measurement. It often takes days to rate specific behaviors of a number of children, unless the classroom situation is contrived so that the incidence of the behavior is higher than usual. As an example of how an instance could be structured for observing independent reading habits and attitudes, the teacher might deliberately plan short assignments in the various subject matters so that children do have free time to reveal their preference for reading. The problem of seeing the infrequent behavior when it happens is somewhat alleviated by having all members of the I & R Unit be on the lookout for the behavior. The unit meeting is an ideal setting in which to organize the observations and compare the results. In some cases, the collective observations are quite different from those of a single teacher. Since observation is often subjective, confidence in the measurement increases when there are several observers.

Summary of the Evaluation Model

Evaluation is the process of identifying important decision areas, determining what information is most useful to decision makers involved in making the decision, arranging for mechanisms to collect the required data, summarizing the data in a form which is useful in making the decisions, arranging for the timely delivery of appropriate information to the decision maker, and assessing the utility of the information in the decision-making process. The following processes are included in program evaluation.

1. Needs assessment—The collection of information required in the identification of program needs within the unit, school or district, the establishment of priorities among identified needs and the translation of priority needs into objectives to be accomplished.

2. Program planning—The collection of information required in the translation of objectives into a program plan for meeting those objectives and the design of formative and summative evaluation procedures to provide information concerning program progress and outcome.

3. Formative evaluation—The collection of information required in the ongoing assessment of program implementation and progress, in order to ensure accomplishment of program objectives.

4. Summative evaluation—The collection of information required in the assessment of program outcomes relative to program objectives and in the certification of outcomes for generalizing to other populations.

THE EVALUATION MODEL AND THE INSTRUCTIONAL PROGRAMMING MODEL

A close parallel exists between components of the Instructional Programming Model and the evaluation model presented in this chapter. This relationship is illustrated in Figure 4.2. Following the establishment of a general set of objectives for an instructional program, a needs assessment takes place in which preassessments, past achievements, and personality and learning style of the child are analyzed or diagnosed in an attempt to determine the educational needs of that child, and this needs assessment results in the specification of instructional objectives for the student.

Program planning includes a determination of the various instruction strategies which appear to be possible ways of meeting the instructional objectives resulting from the needs assessment. These approaches may differ in terms of level of presentation, media used, size of instructional group, etc. With consideration of individualized factors related to the student involved as well as resource availability, a single instructional alternative is selected which is believed to be best for meeting that child's need. The

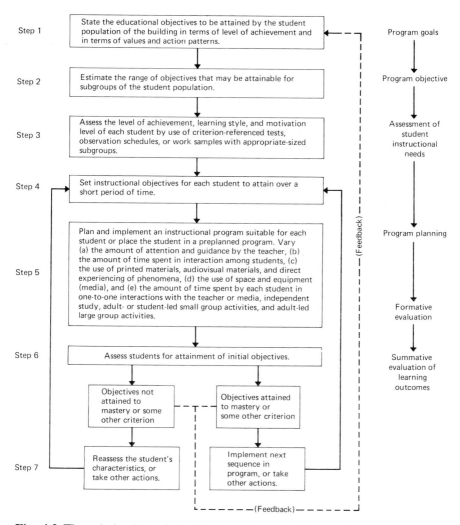

Fig. 4.2 The relationship of the IPM to the evaluation model. Adapted from H. J. Klausmeier, M. R. Quilling, J. S. Sorenson, R. S. Way, and G. R. Glasrud 1971. *Individually guided education and the multiunit school: guidelines for implementation*, p. 19. Madison, Wisc.: Wisconsin Research and Development Center for Cognitive Learning.

decision involved in program planning in this case is the selection of an appropriate instructional activity or sequence of activities, while the role of evaluation is to provide the decision maker, in this case most likely the teacher, with information related to individual characteristics of the child and the resource implications of the alternative instructional activities. The identification of other students with similar educational needs existing at that time within the unit could also be viewed as an evaluative function, relative to the decision concerned with the formation of instructional groupings.

Following the selection of an instructional strategy, the instructional process begins. While instruction is ongoing, the teacher conducts formative (implementation and progress) evaluation. As the teacher views the instructional process, he or she assesses factors such as whether or not the required instructional materials are available for use at appropriate times, whether or not the student is in school attendance on a particular day and is working on the instructional activity and, most importantly, whether or not the student appears to be moving toward mastery of the instructional objective. The teacher is also in a position to observe unanticipated consequences of the child's involvement with the identified instructional objective. In the event that the student, for one reason or another, is not progressing toward mastery of the objective, or if serious dysfunctional consequences are noted, the teachers may choose to alter the instructional activity or decide on a new one.

Summative evaluation occurs, in this example, when it is decided to determine whether or not the instructional objective has been mastered. A postassessment takes place and the determination pertaining to mastery is made. The resulting information, then, serves as input to the subsequent needs assessment and the evaluation and instructional processes begin again.

THE PRINCIPAL'S ROLES IN EDUCATIONAL EVALUATION

Analysis of the principal's roles in evaluation may be approached through analysis of decision making at the school level. The thrust of this chapter has emphasized the intimate relationship between decision making and evaluation as related to educational programs. As a decision maker, both independently or in group settings, the principal must have adequate evaluative information in order to define the decision area, identify decision alternatives, and compare the decision alternatives.

The principal as a decision maker must learn to define as precisely as possible requisite informational needs, those modes of presentation which are most desirable, and the time constraints which surround the problem area. The principal is intimately involved in such program-related decisions as identifying priority needs for staff development programs, selecting equipment and materials which best meet the needs of the school, and determining whether or not present instructional programs are effective. Each of these decisions is best made in the light of appropriate evaluative information. The principal, then, is a consumer of evaluative information.

As an evaluator, the principal might be called on to design the program evaluation as well as to carry it out. If a needs assessment is to be conducted in a school's community, it may well be the principal who plans the survey to collect the data, collects and analyzes the data, and works with the IIC in order to identify and define priorities among needs. As another example, the principal may be asked to assist in designing evaluative research for a program which an I & R Unit is contemplating. The unit staff may feel that they have a better way to approach the teaching of a particular objective and request that the principal assist in designing a study to obtain evidence which would help them make a decision about the value of the new instructional approach.

A third role the principal often fulfills in relation to the evaluation process is that of being an expert in a program area by virtue of the position held or past education or experience. The principal may well be called upon to supply appropriate information to other decision makers, such as the SPC, the school superintendent, or the board of education. In needs assessment, for example, the principal may participate in a nominal group process or respond to a questionnaire in a school survey. The principal also may suggest alternative programs which might respond to an identified need. Additionally, the principal may be asked to supply such comparative information through a process such as the Delphi procedure. Again, the principal may carry out this role at the same time that he or she fulfills other demanding role responsibilities.

Finally, it often is the principal who must decide that the need for evaluation is of such magnitude that help must be obtained from individuals and agencies in the extraorganizational facilitative environment, such as State or Regional IGE Coordinating Councils. At this point the principal must work closely with outside consultants on evaluation as described earlier.

SUMMARY

This chapter has emphasized evaluation as a process which provides valid, reliable, and timely information for use in making effective educational decisions. First, evaluation was defined and discussed as it related to decision making where decision making was defined as a rational process wherein awareness of a problematic state, influenced by information and values, is reduced to competing alternatives among which a choice is made based upon perceived outcomes (Lipham 1974). Next, the relationship between evaluation and decision making was shown which emphasizes the following dimensions: needs assessment, program planning, formative evaluation, and summative evaluation.

A major section of the chapter described numerous techniques that are useful to the IGE principal. In assessing educational needs these tools included structured surveys, tests and other measures, and the nominal group process. In program planning, network analysis, the Delphi technique, and the program-planning model were cited as helpful. Formative evaluation, consisting of implementation and progress evaluation, was defined as consisting of formal and informal mechanisms for obtaining the information required in the ongoing assessment of program objectives. Summative evaluation was considered in terms of the extent to which program outcomes fulfilled the objectives which had been specified for the program. Also discussed was evaluative research wherein the intent is to identify cause and effect relationships between program processes and program outcomes.

The concluding section of the chapter highlighted four major role responsibilities of the principal in the evaluation for effective decision making in IGE schools.

REFERENCES

Alkin, M. C. 1969. Evaluation theory and development. *UCLA Evaluation Comment* **2** (October).

Ammons, M., and R. S. Gilchrist 1965. Study questions related to assessing new projects and their effect on learning. In R. R. Leeper (ed.), *Assessing and using curriculum content*. Washington, D.C.: Association for Supervision and Curriculum Development.

Delbecq, A. L., and A. H. Van deVen 1971. A group process model for problem identification and program planning. *Journal of Applied Behavioral Science* **7**.

Katzenmeyer, C. Measurement in IGE. In press. In H. J. Klausmeier, R. A. Rossmiller, and M. Saily (eds.), *Individually guided elementary education: concepts and practices*.

Krathwohl, D. R. 1964. Taxonomy of educational objectives—its use in curriculum building. In C. M. Lindvall (ed.), *Defining educational objectives*. Pittsburgh: Regional Commission on Educational Coordination and Learning, Research and Development Center, University of Pittsburgh.

Leavitt, H. J. 1965. Applied organizational change in industry: structural, technological, and humanistic approaches. In J. G. March (ed.), *Handbook of organization*. Chicago: Rand McNally.

Lipham, J. M. 1974. Improving the decision-making skills of the principal. In J. A. Culbertson, C. Henson, and R. Morrison (eds.), *Performance objectives for school principals*. Berkeley, Calif.: McCutchan.

Mager, R. F. 1962. *Preparing instructional objectives*. Palo Alto, Calif.: Fearon.

Otto, W., and E. N. Askov 1973. *Wisconsin design for reading skill development: rationale and guidelines*. Minneapolis: National Computer Systems.

Phillips, R. C. 1968. *Evaluation in education*. Columbus, Ohio: Merrill.

Popham, W. J., and E. L. Baker 1970. *Systematic instruction.* Englewood Cliffs, N.J.: Prentice-Hall.

Quilling, M. 1971. *IGE concepts test, form 1 and form 2.* Madison, Wisc.: Wisconsin Research and Development Center for Cognitive Learning.

Scriven, M. 1967. *The methodology of evaluation.* A.E.R.A. Monograph Series on Evaluation I. Chicago: Rand McNally.

Stake, R. E., 1972. Focus or portrayal? *Evaluation and Measurement Newsletter* **14** (May).

Stufflebeam, D. L., *et al.* 1971. *Educational evaluation and decision making.* Itasca, Ill.: Peacock.

Thorndike, R. L., and E. Hagen 1961. *Measurement and evaluation in psychology and education.* New York: Wiley.

5
Developing Staff Personnel

James M. Lipham
Albert M. Holmquist
Kenneth W. Wright

Objectives

After reading this chapter, the reader will be able:

- To comprehend the nature of the school as a social system.
- To understand the IGE principal's role in recruiting, selecting, assigning and orienting staff.
- To identify the major components of an inservice improvement program for IGE staff.
- To apply appropriate procedures in the evaluation of staff performance in the IGE school.
- To recognize that the leadership behavior of the principal affects staff involvement, interaction, effectiveness, and morale.

An adequate program of staff development is absolutely necessary if IGE is to be implemented effectively. The principal, as the leader of the staff, must provide dynamic direction to the staff development program to ensure that each member of the staff possesses the understandings, skills, and attitudes required for effective performance in the IGE school.

Staff personnel relationships are the central concern of social systems theory which introduces this chapter. Since the quality of the instructional program depends directly on the quality of the staff, the major portion of this chapter is devoted to the principal's leadership role in the following major staff personnel functions: recruitment, selection, and assignment of staff; orientation of staff; inservice training and improvement of staff; and evaluation of staff performance. Concurrently reported are recent research and promising practices regarding role responsibilities and relationships; interpersonal relations; and organizational climate, motivation, and morale in IGE multiunit schools. Throughout the chapter, techniques are offered for improving the principal's competency in developing staff personnel, since the principal's responsibilities in this domain may be shared but not delegated.

THE IGE SCHOOL AS A SOCIAL SYSTEM *

In terms of social systems theory, the school may be conceived as a social system consisting of two major dimensions that are independent and at the same time interactive. The first is the normative or nomothetic dimension, consisting of the institutional roles and expectations designed to accomplish the goals of the school (cf. Getzels and Guba 1957, pp. 423–424, Getzels and Thelen 1960, pp. 53–62). Roles, representing dynamic aspects of positions, offices, or statuses within the school, are complementary or interlocking and in the IGE school are quite flexible. Roles are defined in terms of role expectations which are the normative rights and duties of a role incumbent—principal, unit leader, teacher, student, etc. When the role incumbent puts these rights and duties into effect he is performing his role. The extent to which the behavior of a role incumbent is congruent with the expectations held for that role is the measure that is used in evaluating effectiveness.

The second basic dimension of a social system is the personal or idiographic dimension, consisting of the individual personalities with their unique abilities, interests, and need-dispositions. The IGE school places particular emphasis on this dimension which is concerned with accomplish-

---

*   Portions of this section are drawn from J. W. Getzels, J. M. Lipham, and R. F. Campbell 1968. *Educational administration as a social process,* New York, Harper & Row, and from J. M. Lipham and J. A. Hoeh, Jr. 1974. *The principalship: foundations and functions,* New York: Harper & Row.

ment of the goals of the individual. Each person in the school stamps the role he occupies with his own personality which is defined as the dynamic organization of the need-dispositions within the individual that determine his unique interaction with the school environment. These needs, as Maslow (1954, p. 107) has stated, are organized hierarchically and patterned horizontally in terms of greater or less priority or potency, so that the satisfaction of a lower order need, such as survival, affects the activation of a higher order need, such as self-actualization. The extent to which the behavior of the individual is congruent with his unique pattern of need-dispositions is a measure of efficiency.

Social behavior within the school may be understood as deriving simultaneously from the normative and the personal dimensions. Behavior in a social system is a function of the interaction between a given institutional role, defined by the expectations attaching to it, and the personality of a particular role incumbent, defined by his need-dispositions. That is, social behavior results from an individual's attempts to cope, in ways consistent with his own patterns of needs and dispositions, with an environment composed of patterns of expectations for his behavior. The extent to which the demands of the organizational role and the requirements of the individual personality are congruent is a measure of satisfaction—the role "suits" or "fits" the individual, and conversely.

The institution and the individual are of course embedded in a cultural milieu which conditions and shapes both the institutional roles and the individual personalities and thereby influences social behavior. The culture may be described in terms of its prevailing ethos and values. A value is defined as "a conception, explicit or implicit, distinctive of an individual or characteristic of a group, of the desirable which influences the selection from available modes, means, and ends of action" (Kluckhohn, et al. 1951, p. 395). The principal must be aware not only of the basic values held by the community, the staff, and the students but also of the educational values which bear directly on the school and the individuals within it.

The operational model in Figure 5.1 shows the interrelationships of the normative, personal, and cultural dimensions which are the primary determinants of social behavior in the school. This model is particularly useful to the principal in understanding, predicting, and perhaps ameliorating the major types of actual and potential conflict in the school: cultural values-institutional expectations conflict, role conflict, role-personality conflict, and personality conflict. The first conflict is that which may exist in basic value orientations between and among various individuals and groups. Chapter 6, dealing with home-school-community relations, shows how the values held by citizens, parents, and others impinge directly on the educational expectations for the IGE school. The second type of conflict, treated previously in Chapter 2, is that of role conflict—lack of complementarity between and among the expectations held for the various organizational

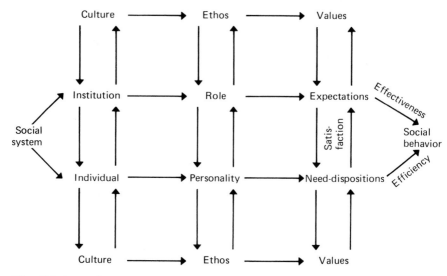

Fig. 5.1 Operational model of major dimensions of social behavior. Adapted from J. W. Getzels 1963. Conflict and role behavior in the educational setting. In W. W. Charters, Jr., and N. L. Gage (eds.), *Readings in the social psychology of education*, p. 312. Boston: Allyn and Bacon.

roles—principal, unit leaders, teachers, students, and others. The third type of conflict, particularly relevant to staff personnel relationships, is between the normative and the personal dimensions—role-personality conflict. Since the administration of the school inevitably entails the fulfillment of both institutional role expectations and individual need-dispositions, it is a unique function of the principal to integrate the expectations of the organization and the dispositions of the individual in a way that is simultaneously productive for the organization and satisfying for the individual. A fourth and final type of conflict with which the model deals is that of personality conflict—disagreements within and among the staff. Interpersonal conflicts are perhaps the most debilitating of all; they must be resolved if satisfaction, belongingness, and morale within the staff are to be enhanced.

In performing the staff personnel function the principal must pay attention to these salient elements: the interaction of *role* and *personality* in a context of *value*. This interaction is particularly prominent in the recruitment, selection, and assignment of staff.

RECRUITMENT, SELECTION, AND ASSIGNMENT OF STAFF

Central to the personnel function of any school is the identification of professionally qualified personnel who possess the requisite values, abilities, attitudes, and needs to contribute significantly to the realization of organizational goals while at the same time feeling that they are attaining their individual goals. The recruitment and selection functions deal particularly with obtaining new staff, whereas the assignment function concerns all of the staff—both experienced staff who must fulfill new roles when changing to an IGE school and inexperienced staff who must be added subsequently.

Recruitment of IGE Staff

The recruitment function is concerned with establishing a pool of potentially acceptable candidates to fulfill the differentiated roles required in the school that has implemented IGE. In performing this function, the principal initially must assess and articulate the nature of the prevailing values within the community, within the school, and between the school and community so that prospective candidates have a realistic appraisal of the working environment. Because in many school districts the supply of teachers has outpaced the current demand, there is perhaps less of a tendency than previously to engage in "hard sell" recruitment practices. Concomitantly, prospective candidates may tend to minimize or overlook basic differences in values which both underlie and influence behavior. The principal must see to it that recruitment materials and vacancy announcements portray accurately the school's community.

Another major activity of the principal in staff recruitment is to synthesize and describe the major objectives and activities of the school so that they may be communicated to and understood by prospective candidates. These objectives and activities may be abstracted from the schoolwide objectives developed by the IIC and then abstracted and included with vacancy announcements. "IGE in 111th Street School," "Lake Johanna's Educational Program," "Learning Together at Maine," and hundreds of similar exemplary materials have been found to be useful not only in recruiting teachers but also in providing others with an initial understanding of the objectives and activities of the IGE school.

Within the system of IGE, the principal's responsibilities in recruitment are increased considerably by the nature of the multiunit organizational structure. Earlier, in Chapter 2, it was shown that ideally an intern or practice teacher should be assigned to work in each I & R Unit in the school. As Paul's study (1974, p. 304) of IGE multiunit elementary schools in three states revealed, student teachers not only contribute significantly to the staffing needs and instructional capability of the school but they also serve as a primary means for linking the school with the teacher education institutions—the colleges and universities which provide the pool of certifiable candidates. In this regard, many of the IGE principals in Paul's study were heard to comment as follows: "I'm only sorry that I can't keep all of this semester's student teachers," "Two of our teachers and one of our unit leaders did their student teaching here," and "I keep the best ones!" In such situations, recruitment obviously merges with the selection process.

Selection of IGE Staff

Just as some responsibilities for staff recruitment are shared with the central office, so also is the responsibility for staff appointment frequently legislatively mandated to the board of education. Operationally, however, the selection of staff for new or existing roles within the school is the prerogative of the principal. In selecting staff, the principal and unit leader must first assess the role demands within the organization and then select from the pool of qualified candidates those whose personal qualities are congruent with the expectations for particular roles.

In the staff selection process, it is absolutely essential to specify clearly the major duties and responsibilities for each vacant position. Two complementary approaches to describing the position vacancy may be followed simultaneously, the sociological approach and the psychological approach. The sociological approach, which draws heavily on organizational theory, delineates the major duties of each complementary organizational role in the IGE multiunit school. Operating within this structure, the principal will need to meet with the IIC to determine precisely the functional demands of each new or vacant position. In this process, questions such as the following are typically raised, answered, and incorporated in the position description: "In which curricular subjects do we need additional depth?" "In which instructional grouping pattern do we need particular skills?" and "In which diagnostic, evaluative, or motivational techniques do we need help?" The resulting vacancy announcement is more likely to match the qualified individual with the specific role than the traditional principal's plea, "Send me a third grade teacher!"

Just as it is helpful to use the sociological approach, which describes the requisite behaviors in terms of major role expectations, so also is it valuable to utilize a psychological approach, which describes the position vacancy in terms of the perceived personalistic syndrome desired of applicants. In the psychological approach, questions such as the following, within affirmative action guidelines, are raised in the IIC: "What preferred age, sex, race, or other variables would ensure appropriate staff balance?" "What differing value patterns or educational philosophies should be represented?" and "What interests, abilities, and attitudes should the new staff member possess?" Whether explicitly expressed or informally surmised, such variables inevitably influence the selection process.

One caution concerning the psychological approach to staff selection should be noted. The principal and present staff should guard against the natural tendency to staff the school with "our kind of teacher." Despite the potential for possible conflict, often it is staff diversity, rather than homogeneity, which should be stressed. The total absence of conflict in the school can lead to homeostasis which is just as debilitating as the chaos created by severe conflict.

The second phase of the staff selection process involves those activities necessary for reaching consensus on which candidate from among the applicants will be offered a contract. In this phase the principal first screens the papers, recommendations, transcripts, and credentials of applicants and eliminates those with obvious deficiencies. Then, in many IGE schools the principal actively involves the unit leaders and other professional staff members in interviewing the final candidates. In some IGE schools, parents and community representatives participate in the staff selection process. The finalists may also spend the greater part of a working day being interviewed and observing in the unit and the school. Although unanticipated or last-minute vacancies may preclude such activities during the summer, it is quite common for the available unit leaders and teachers to come to the school and interview candidates. In this regard, for example, an IGE principal in Minnesota recently commented as follows:

> You wouldn't believe it! We only had one vacancy to fill this year, but on six different occasions the teachers in that unit came in to help select a replacement. That decision was so critical to them! Then, we spent another full morning before we finally agreed on whom to choose. Now, it's working out beautifully because they have a colleague they can work with. In retrospect, that one staff vacancy was a godsend.

Although practices vary, in many IGE schools the IIC actively participates in selecting members of each unit—teachers, aides, etc. Obviously, the committee must be directly involved in selecting unit leaders and other schoolwide professional personnel, such as materials center directors, resource teachers, and special area teachers. In most IGE schools, moreover, the unit leaders are involved in screening and selecting the nonprofessional staff—school secretaries, custodians, aides, and others whose assignments are critical to the success of the school.

Assignment of IGE Staff

For new or replacement staff, the assignment process follows logically and systematically from the recruitment and selection processes. For experienced staff, however, their assignment or reassignment to the differentiated roles required in the system of IGE poses unique problems for the principal in making both intraschool assignments and interschool transfers.

The basic purpose of the intraschool assignment process is to ensure increasing convergence of the principal's and the teacher's perceptions of the teaching assignment with the teacher's values, attitudes, and need-dispositions. The schematic in Figure 5.2 depicts the dynamics of the staff selection and assignment processes. In this model, based on social systems theory, the three essential components to be considered are as follows: the principal's perceptions of the teaching assignment (point A in the diagram);

the teacher's perceptions of the teaching assignment (point B); and the teacher's values, abilities, and need-dispositions as an individual (point C). Line AB represents agreement between the principal and the teacher about the major expectations of the role; line AC represents the principal's visualization of the degree of congruence between the organizational role and the personality of the teacher; and line BC represents the teacher's perceived estimate of role-personality congruence. The area of triangle ABC represents the degree of convergence of these variables at Time 1, the selection interviews. The dotted lines, AA′, BB′, and CC′, represent joint exploration and communication in subsequent conferences between the principal and the teacher concerning both the mutual expectations held for the teaching assignment and the perceptions of the teacher as a person. Ideally, these variables will converge during the assignment process (represented by the smaller area of triangle A′B′C′) to enhance the role-personality relationship for the teacher.

In IGE schools, a dynamic similar to the relationship between the principal and the teacher exists between and among the teacher and all other personnel of the I & R Unit. In making staff assignments, therefore, openness of communication must be maintained to permit consideration of

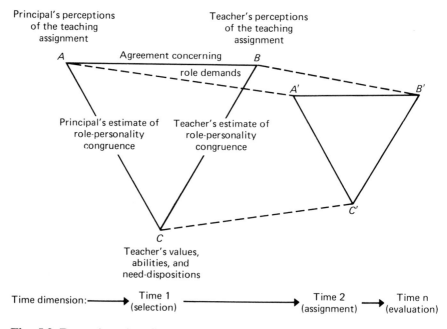

Fig. 5.2 Dynamics of staff selection and assignment processes. Adapted from J. M. Lipham and J. A. Hoeh, Jr. 1974, *The principalship: foundations and functions.* New York: Harper & Row, p. 243.

all relevant role and personality elements. After the assignment is made, the role-personality relationship should continue to converge, facilitating the development of a satisfying relationship between the demands of the organization and the needs of the staff member. Assessment of this relationship subsequently serves as a basis for the staff evaluation program.

Despite systematic and conscientious attention to staff assignment, it sometimes becomes evident that expectations, perceptions, and needs do not converge and that reassignments should be made. Several positive causes could be cited. Through additional training, for example, a teacher may develop particular skills needed throughout the school and thereby become a resource specialist to more than one Instruction and Research Unit. Through experience, for instance, a teacher may develop a particular preference for working with either older or younger students and seek transfer to another unit. As many IGE principals will attest, it is not uncommon for teacher aides or instructional secretaries to obtain certification and become unit teachers. A major strength of IGE is that the system of differentiated staffing facilitates intraschool assignment and reassignment processes.

The principal must be particularly sensitive to the negative indicators which call for reassignment, since often those who are directly affected are quite reluctant to share their disagreements, disappointments, or frustrations with others—particularly with the principal who must pass official judgments on the effectiveness of role performance. Reassignment to correct for role, role-personality, or interpersonal conflicts is a delicate matter and should be consummated only after extended consultation with the staff member involved and with others who may be affected. Although the authority for intraschool transfers rests with the principal, the IGE principal will need to consult closely and carefully with the I & R Units on reassignments affecting their operations and with the IIC on reassignments affecting the total school,

Many examples of intraschool reassignment could be cited since, in a sense, the day-to-day instructional programming decisions made at the I & R Unit level significantly alter staff assignments, activities, and behaviors. In the IGE school, however, it often is necessary for the principal to monitor such matters as overspecialization, equity of teaching load, balance in supervisory responsibilities, and other duties which are variable, rather than fixed as in the traditional school.

The need for reassignment is not limited to role responsibilities. The principal must be aware of and sensitive to the personal needs and dispositions of each staff member, since personality differences are perhaps the most frequent cause of conflict within the school. Such conflicts can be exacerbated in the IGE school because of the close and continuous interpersonal involvement of the staff in planning, implementing, and evaluating mutual behaviors of the staff and students. By contrast with the traditional school where the idiosyncratic behavior of the teacher can be concealed behind the classroom door, ideally there are no isolates in the IGE school.

In preventing or ameliorating personality conflict, the principal may find an early study of teaching teams conducted by Gilberts (1961) to be instructive. He found that some teachers preferred a team teaching arrangemen over a self-contained classroom arrangement because of the greater opportunities provided them to meet their basic personality needs for inclusion and interaction with others. Moreover, interpersonal compatibility was found to be a prime determinant of the relative success or failure of teaching teams.

The findings of Gilberts were recently corroborated by Evers (1974) who examined the relationship between interpersonal compatibility and effectiveness of I & R Units in IGE multiunit elementary schools. To the staff members in a randomly selected sample of 163 Instruction and Research Units in IGE schools in 12 states, she administered a personality measure of one's needs to control and to be controlled, to include others and to be included, and to give and to receive attention and affection, obtaining therefrom a measure of compatibility between and among the members of each unit (Schutz 1958). The *I & R Unit Effectiveness Questionnaire* was similarly administered to obtain a measure of the extent to which each unit was effective in achieving the 50 performance objectives identified as responsibilities of units. The results were straightforward, confirming the basic hypothesis: "The interpersonal compatibility between and among the staff of the Instructional and Research Unit contributed significantly to the variance in the effectiveness of the instructional program" (Evers 1974, p. 114).

As indicated in Chapter 2, interpersonal staff relations are particularly significant in the decision concerning who is to be appointed unit leader. Reassignments to and from this position are particularly critical to continued staff productivity and morale. In some IGE schools, the principal may need to correct the misperception that the unit-leader position is an intermediate supervisory position between the principal and the unit teachers. In so doing, the principal will need to maintain frequent contact with unit staffs, both collectively and individually. In this regard, the comment made by an IGE principal in Illinois pinpoints the problem she faced in reassigning a unit leader:

> Somehow, despite our best intentions, it just didn't work out. After six months of continually and endlessly working with the Alpha unit—attending meetings, reviewing plans, helping them group and regroup, and even transferring an aide—it just didn't click. The unit leader was torn and frustrated, and we were too. She really wanted to quit, but she didn't want to give up and she certainly didn't want to leave the unit.

Finally, about midyear, we all sat down together and said, "Look, something's got to give!" We talked another teacher in the unit into taking it. It's still not the smoothest operation in the world, but we're getting there!

Interschool transfers often pose even greater problems for the principal, not simply because of district transfer policies, master contracts, and tenure regulations, but because of value, status, and personality conflicts, real or imagined, surrounding the transfer process. An interschool transfer should be made only if it is fairly certain that the effectiveness and efficiency of the teacher will be enhanced. Reassignment is no panacea for inadequate potential or ineffective performance. The principal who passes on unsatisfactory staff members to colleagues in other schools is guilty of unprofessional conduct. Teacher-initiated requests for transfer pose less serious issues, and obviously could be granted for a host of legitimate professional and personal reasons.

Since the system of IGE is designed as an alternative system of schooling, it was originally envisioned that staff transfers to more traditional schools within a district would be a frequently exercised, viable option. Somewhat surprisingly, however, many traditionally oriented teachers have chosen to stay in IGE schools. Principals' comments concerning this phenomenon vary widely:

> We had three teachers I thought we'd lose for sure, but they stayed on and are still some of the best people in the place. By the time a new idea gets past them, all the wrinkles are out of it!
>
> We have one die-hard who probably should have left, but he didn't. It's hard on anybody's ego to bail out—makes it look like you're opposed to anything new. Maybe he stayed on just to make life miserable for the rest of us.
>
> We only lost one teacher when we went IGE, but surprisingly she came back the next year. She'd have problems anywhere—but at least here we understand.
>
> Since we were the last school in the district to change to IGE they had no place else to go, so if it'll work with our crew, it'll work anywhere!

Regardless of whether a staff member is being reassigned or initially assigned, the principal must coordinate the personnel orientation program.

ORIENTATION OF STAFF

In orienting the staff to the IGE school, the principal's activities will vary, depending on whether or not the orientation process is that which is necessary for new staff members entering a school already having a viable IGE program, or that which is required for all of the existing staff of a school which is beginning to implement the system of IGE.

Orientation of New Staff

The orientation of new staff members begins with the recruitment process and extends throughout that employee's affiliation with the school. The purpose of the orientation program is to increase the new staff member's understanding of the values, attitudes, and expectations held by the administration, colleagues, students, and the community.

In many school systems it is customary to conduct a one- or two-day orientation program for all teachers and other personnel new to the district. Although a frequent complaint is that such sessions bombard one with more information than can readily be assimilated, their purpose is to familiarize the staff generally with system goals, policies, rules, and regulations. Basically, however, the orientation function is the responsibility of the principal and the unit leaders, and, in IGE schools, is effectively consummated in the Instructional and Research Units.

The present staff should be sensitive to the needs of new staff members. In IGE schools, the unit leaders share actively in the orientation process. In some schools, particularly large ones, the formalized appointment of a "helping colleague" is utilized to acquaint the new staff members with operational guidelines and expectations. Sometimes parents' associations or advisory committees conduct activities designed to help new staff gain insight into the community's expectations, as well as its professional and educational resources. In other schools, student groups meet informally with new staff to increase their understanding of the students' attitudes, interests, and perspectives on the community and the school. The objective of these activities is to foster a spirit of mutual understanding and acceptance so necessary for successful integration and identification with the school.

Orientation of the Total Staff to IGE

Howes recently completed a comprehensive study to determine which factors are related to the successful implementation of IGE in elementary schools (Howes 1974). To collect data for the study, she designed and distributed descriptive organizational change questionnaires to a sample of over 2000 unit teachers, unit leaders, principals, district coordinators, and superintendents in IGE multiunit schools and school districts throughout the United States. Based on theories of educational change, the instrument ascertained which organizational and personal variables are critical at each stage in the change process: awareness, commitment, changeover, refinement, and renewal. She discovered, "Probably the most important part of the change process is the presentation of information about the change to organizational members, since orientation to the change program leads to an individual's initial acceptance or rejection of the change." (Howes 1974, p. 391)

To set up an "adequate" orientation program to ensure positive acceptance of the change to IGE one must, according to the respondents of Howes, give attention to the following six factors:

1. Time must be set aside for the proper introduction of the change. Formal awareness conferences, orientation workshops, exchange visits, and staff seminars need to be planned and organized for the orientation phase and afterwards.

2. The change (IGE) must be packaged and presented so that it is easily understood, easily referenced and related to performance results in other similar organizations, and easily seen as possessing specific operational objectives. If this is done properly, the relative advantage of the change program (the single most important attribute of a change's acceptance) can be visible.

3. The supportive services and resources available to the change effort must be identified, confirmed, and obtained, so that users of the change will see that their efforts in the change process will be supported.

4. The acceptance and support of the users' immediate supervisor for the change program and change process must be acknowledged and proclaimed so that the users of the change will be inclined to undertake the change effort (since their supervisor seems to be interested in their doing so).

5. The requirements for each individual during the change process and the necessary changes in each individual's role after the program is installed must be described. These factors relate to the second most important attribute affecting the acceptance of a change—whether individuals perceive that it will be realistically easy to install the change program and relatively unthreatening to their roles afterwards.

6. The specific roles and relationships of the users, administrators, support personnel, and agents of change must be clearly and specifically described for each individual involved in the change process and change program. If this happens, all individuals will know what to expect during the process of changing, what they will be accountable for in the change program, and how they are to relate to others during and after the change activity (Howes 1974, pp. 391–393).

Although not all of the above factors can be dealt with simultaneously, the principal contemplating change to IGE would be well advised to plan carefully the activities designed to orient the staff to IGE, since initial impressions about the program are so critical. Many have gained an initial understanding of IGE concepts and practices through attending a one-day awareness conference. Such conferences may be sponsored by the Wisconsin

Research and Development Center, state departments of education, intermediate service agencies, school districts, and teacher education institutions. The primary purpose of the one-day awareness conference is to give school district decision makers enough information to enable them to decide whether to adopt IGE. Information is also provided relative to required school district commitments and opportunities for additional inservice in order to make the changeover. Activities during the conference typically include the viewing of films which give an overview of the components of IGE and the presentation and discussion of the major role changes required by IGE. If the changeover to IGE is to be initiated by August or September of a school year, school personnel need sufficient lead time to make the necessary decisions and to allocate resources. Experience has shown that attendance at an awareness conference in October or November of the preceding year gives school district personnel sufficient lead time.

"After some of us went to the awareness conference, we organized a safari," a successful IGE principal recently commented. "Breaking the faculty into groups of three or four, I arranged for each group to visit a different IGE school already in operation." Having each group investigate a different set of questions and subsequently sharing the answers with the rest of the faculty is a common procedure. By focusing on specific IGE components and subsequently attempting to answer faculty questions about their findings, the group members can become the school's "experts" on at least one aspect of IGE. This is often more satisfactory than attempting initially to understand all dimensions of IGE simultaneously.

Providing the staff with professional articles, newsletters, and publications about IGE; encouraging attendance at professional meetings; and inviting professionals knowledgeable about IGE to visit the school and meet with the staff are other orientation activities that constitute the initial pre-entry training in IGE. They merge and overlap with subsequent staff improvement activities designed to equip the school staff to assume effectively new and expanded roles, once the decision is made to implement the system of IGE.

Concerning the critical commitment phase, wherein the decision to adopt IGE must be made, the principal of an urban school which was the first in Los Angeles to inaugurate IGE recently reflected:

> The busiest time in all my life was between the time that I attended an IGE awareness conference at the R & D Center until we got things going here. I'll never forget how utterly helpless and alone I felt on that cold, bleak day in Madison on my ride back to the airport—particularly in the face of all I knew that had to be done. And I thought to myself, "Now what have you gotten yourself into?" And then I said, "Something good, I think."

> So I came back and read, and talked, and worked, and wheedled, and scratched, till finally I got the teachers and parents with me.
>
> It's fun, now—and much easier. Kids are learning, teachers are working, parents are smiling, and now four of our schools are IGE, and the district office is quite proud of us. Don't tell me it can't be done!

In securing the necessary approvals, cooperation, and commitment the principal of a school in a medium-sized school district in Minnesota admonished:

> Be sure to take a board member or two along to the awareness conference. We were fortunate; we had three board members and three principals to go. So we "ganged up" on the superintendent and he said, "Okay." Getting him to appoint the SPC was still another matter. He balked for a while but, would you believe, they now even have a modest budget of their own to allocate for special things.

Concerning the commitment to adopt IGE in a small district, an Illinois school superintendent reported:

> We did it backwards, I guess. After I learned something about IGE I looked around and asked, "If you really wanted to change things around here, who would you involve?" So I took a couple of board members, the elementary principals, the PTA presidents, and some crackerjack teachers to an awareness conference and we formed our SPC right then and there! Most of them are still on it.

Whichever approach is utilized, during the commitment phase the principal must secure the cooperation of the school board, the superintendent and central office staff, the teachers' organization, and parent and community groups. Continuing attention must then be paid to further development of the staff improvement program.

IMPROVEMENT OF STAFF

The staff-improvement program includes all of those activities designed to enhance the understandings, skills, attitudes, and resultant role behaviors of each staff member. Staff-improvement programs typically build on preservice preparatory programs by providing additional inservice training to update knowledge and to change behavior. Until such time as IGE concepts and practices are incorporated into preservice preparatory programs for principals, unit leaders, and teachers, however, a heavy training responsibility rests at the local level. In meeting this responsibility it is useful for the principal first to understand how the system of IGE facilitates staff improvement and next to develop a staff-improvement program for implementing IGE.

IGE and Staff Improvement

Within the system of IGE, systematic attention is paid to involvement in decision making, interpersonal interaction, role flexibility, communication channels, and supportive resources, all of which are basic to the staff-improvement program. Regarding involvement in decision making, Howes's study revealed that each person must be adequately involved if that individual is subsequently to make the extra effort required in the change process (Howes 1974, p. 395). In contrast to traditional staff-development programs in which those distant from the classroom select the topics, resources, and activities to be pursued, the system of IGE involves the local staff in planning for both theoretical and practical training activities which have direct impact on instruction. As a major educational change, moreover, IGE precludes the typical "grab-bag" training approach—stabbing at a crisis here, jumping on a bandwagon there—used in some school districts.

Regarding staff interaction, a primary reason for the failure of many traditional staff-development programs is the relative isolation of the teacher who is engaged in attempts to improve. By contrast, in IGE the roles are so integrated that contacts with the initiators, implementors, facilitators, and users of the change are frequent and continuous, providing immediate evaluative feedback. The feeling, "We're all in this together!" is quite different from that which exists when one is trying all alone to initiate a change.

Concerning role flexibility, creative and varied instructional approaches are encouraged and sustained in the IGE school. Somewhat surprisingly, within this environment principals report that such unanticipated freedom has tended to stimulate even the most tradition-oriented teacher to change, as follows:

> I couldn't believe it! Here was a teacher who had never skipped a page in the teacher's manual for a day in her life saying, "Come see how our materials are working!"

Concerning communication, the principal must see to it that in addition to lateral communication, the upward, downward, and outward communication channels are all used freely and frequently to inform others about progress and to involve them appropriately in the change process. Feedback in response to unique processes, events, and issues is particularly important; it should be recorded and reported to the appropriate planning groups (in IGE, the SPC or IIC) which must deal with the solutions to problems.

Regarding resources for the change program, Howes's respondents stressed that such supportive services as resource personnel, materials and equipment, time for meetings, and other expressions of institutional commitment are essential to the success of the change to IGE (Howes 1974, p.

393). Availability of support services is particularly critical in the orientation phase wherein personal investiture and identification with the program may be tentative and less internalized by those at the operational level than in later stages of the implementation process. Normally, the school district commits its resources by entering into a written agreement with an implementation agency which initially assists the principal and the staff to assume their new roles and responsibilities. In this regard, several IGE staff-improvement techniques are viable.

IGE Staff-improvement Techniques

In terms of social systems theory, the IGE staff-improvement program focuses initially on the normative dimension—changes in roles and relationship required by IGE. Since not all staffs are equally ready to engage in major change, however, some of the inservice activities may also need to deal with the interpersonal and value dimensions of behavior.

The principal–unit leader workshop. Principals and prospective unit leaders from schools deciding to implement IGE are expected to participate in a three-day workshop that provides instruction regarding IGE roles, relationships, concepts, and practices. At the conclusion of this workshop, participants should be able to:

1. Describe the organizational structure of the multiunit school.
2. Identify the roles of the various personnel in the multiunit school.
3. Explain the elements and processes of the IPM.
4. Outline the installation of the multiunit organization and IGE in their building.
5. Plan and conduct inservice programs for their entire building staff (Klausmeier, *et al.* 1974, pp. 47–48).

These objectives are achieved through first assessing the needs of participants and then formulating various kinds of groups to meet those needs. Topics which are addressed include:

- Instructional Programming in IGE
- MUS–E—Roles and Responsibilities
- The Multiunit School—Its Organization and Operations
- Grouping Patterns
- Educational Objectives
- Assessment in IGE
- Use of Auxiliary and Special Area Personnel
- Grouping Students for Instruction

- Logistics of Implementation—Organization of Instructional Materials
- Logistics of Implementation—Curriculum, Staff, and Pupil Scheduling
- Managing Pupil Progress—Record Keeping
- Reporting Pupil Progress
- Impact of Teaming

The principal and unit leaders from each school also have an opportunity to meet as an IIC to accomplish the following:

1. Develop two or three alternative designs for organizing all children in the school (K–6) into multiage units.
2. Evaluate each design considering the instructional staff in terms of subject matter strengths, teaching style and special talents, and also considering the abilities of teacher aides or instructional secretaries.
3. Choose the most appropriate design.
4. Begin assigning staff to units.
5. Arrange daily and weekly schedules to allow planning time for unit and IIC meetings during the school day.
6. Evaluate the present utilization of space in the building and assign space to each unit.
7. Discuss ways in which performance objectives will be utilized in planning and self-evaluation.
8. Decide on the curriculum area(s) in which IGE will be developed.
9. Develop a role description for each type of staff member.
10. Prepare a draft of a three- to five-day inservice program to be conducted with the entire staff.
11. Prepare plans to obtain paraprofessional assistance on a paid basis, and/or alternative plans to obtain paraprofessional assistance if not available on a paid basis.

The preentry workshop.   Prior to the opening of school, those who participated in the principal–unit leader workshop are able to conduct the three- to five-day inservice workshop that starts the development program for the total building. This preentry workshop provides an introduction to the concepts of IGE and involves the entire staff in the adoption of program objectives, defining staff roles, and developing operational procedures.

The introductory phase is designed to provide a perspective from which to view the commitment to IGE. Specific concepts the staff is expected to master are:

- Organization and operations in the multiunit school
- Instructional objectives
- Assessment in IGE
- Grouping patterns
- Roles and responsibilities in the multiunit school
- Instructional programming for individual students

Upon completion of the preliminary activities, the staff should have a conceptual base from which to build the program, roles, and procedures for their particular school.

The IIC next presents the objectives of the educational program, outlines the staff roles developed in the principal–unit leader workshop, and engages the staff in discussing objectives and roles in order to approve and/or revise them. It is imperative that each staff role be defined in writing. If all staff members understand the roles assumed in the IGE organization and the relationship of their roles to this organization, then there will be an increase in the competency base and more effective communication channels will develop.

Finally, each unit will prepare for the opening of school by developing effective, flexible, unit operational procedures for:

- Scheduling—daily, weekly
- Student grouping
- Assessment
- Unit staff specialization
- Procedures for reporting pupil progress
- Management of student progress
- Materials and equipment—use and storage
- Student orientation
- Planning time for: unit, unit leader, and unit members

First-year inservice activities.   After the school has begun to implement IGE, the staff will need assistance in dealing with a variety of implementation problems. The principal, unit leaders, and teachers are expected to do their planning in a new organizational setting. Learning how to work together in newly defined roles requires time for adjustments to be made. In addition, the concepts inherent in the Instructional Programming Model require teachers and unit leaders to plan and carry out instruction in a manner quite different from before. To respond to this situation, a regular schedule of inservice days should be established. Two half-days per semester is considered the bare minimum. The less well prepared the school staff is to begin implementing IGE, the greater the amount of inservice effort required during the changeover year.

Although topics for the inservice days may vary widely, some principals have found the nominal group process useful during the period from September to November when diverse and unanticipated problems may be encountered during the changeover to IGE (Delbecq and Van deVen 1971, pp. 466–492). This process is a means whereby the staff can identify and give priorities to problems and issues throughout the school. At this stage it may also be valuable to have parents involved, as well. The nominal group process ensures that every individual's opinion is taken into account, that common meanings are ascribed to the problem statements, and that the problems commonly felt to be most important are shared and ranked. This process depersonalizes and legitimizes complaints, bringing them into the open where they can be dispassionately discussed and plans can be made to begin solving problems having highest priority. Some potential issues which may be identified include:

- The level of total staff commitment to IGE.
- Information and skills for differentiated staffing in the multiunit school.
- Information and skills for team building.
- Practical information and skills concerning grouping, record keeping, scheduling, use of the physical structure, and conferencing with students and parents.
- Materials for orienting students, parents, and the community to IGE.
- Procedures and skills for including special area personnel in IGE.
- Adequate preparation for leadership roles in IGE.
- Activities and materials for providing for the wide variety of individual needs of the students.

Once the problems have been identified and given priorities, task forces can be assigned to gather information regarding the probable sources of issues and to develop alternative solutions to them. In so doing, the principal will need to become thoroughly familiar with printed and audiovisual materials and exercises designed to improve the skills of teachers and unit leaders in the IGE multiunit school. Training materials concerning the subject fields of reading, mathematics, science, social studies, and concerning the unit leader's role in building team skills provide a meaningful and realistic basis for a viable inservice staff-development program. Examples are *The teacher and individually guided education, Child development and individually guided education, Evaluation of instruction in individually guided education, Objective-based reading, Individually guided mathematics, Individually guided science, Individually guided social studies,* and *The unit leader and individually guided education,* all published by Addison-Wesley, Reading, Mass. Films, filmstrips, and instructor's guides accompany all the materials.

To the fullest extent possible, inservice activities should utilize consultants as external sources of information. The principal may wish to arrange for an outside IGE consultant to spend two or three days in the school, examining instructional plans, visiting in the units, talking with teachers and students, interviewing parents or community leaders, and briefly visiting with central office staff. At the end of the second or third day, an inservice meeting could be devoted to the consultant's working with the staff to identify and review priority problems and to suggest means to overcome them. The consultant should prepare a report of the findings to serve as a basis for further refinement of the program. Obviously, the selection of the consultant is extremely important, since that person must be able to interact with the staff to create a felt need for change and to establish directions for future growth. This combination of the internal cooperative planning environment of the MUS–E organization with the external sources of information and assistance contributes to the school's self-renewing capabilities.

As in the awareness phase, on-site visits to observe other IGE schools in operation is particularly productive during the changeover year. Interschool visits may be either ad hoc or regularly scheduled. This inservice activity is especially crucial during the early period of implementation as school staffs make the transition from knowledge of the IGE concepts and principles to actually doing it themselves. The schools being visited should be informed as to specific aspects of IGE to be observed, and time should be provided for informal or formal discussions between the two staffs. Subsequently, meetings for sharing observations with the units or the total staff is inservice time well spent.

Refinement activities.   Refinement of concepts and practices is required to improve IGE. Activities in the refinement phase are focused on role, personality, and value concerns which require both the development of new skills and the acquisition of new attitudes. Certain of these activities are conducted at the individual school level; others, in colleges and universities.

One of the most basic role changes required by IGE is from that of individual autonomy to shared responsibility in decision making. Some principals, therefore, have found it productive to devote inservice time to techniques of group decision making and problem solving. Decision-making workshops using case analysis, role playing, and simulation exercises are quite useful for introducing the staff to the advantages, disadvantages, and processes of group decision making and for helping develop decision-making skills. In addition, several tools and techniques, such as the Decision Involvement Index, may be used to analyze the decision points and decision structure of the school, as well as subsequently to change the nature and extent of staff involvement in the decision-making processes of the school (Lipham 1974, pp. 83–111, and Wright 1976).

Communication workshops, utilizing prepared exercises and activities, can often be led by the principal or another staff member at low expense and high gain to the school (cf. ERNSTSPIEL 1972). These programs may be successfully utilized at either the unit or the total school level and serve not only to chart and analyze communication networks, but also to improve and enhance the clarity and continuity of information flow. Summarizing one school's experience with a communications workshop, an IGE principal recently stated:

> We went the whole route of twenty communication exercises, including the individual assignments.
>
> At first, it seemed dysfunctional and too time consuming. Everybody became so self-conscious of what he or she was saying that we were analyzing our analyses.
>
> But, believe me, it really works! Now there's little distortion around this place. When we say something we mean it. We also understand it.

As indicated earlier, personality relationships are equally as significant as role relationships within the school, since interpersonal compatibility bears a direct relationship to unit effectiveness (Evers 1974, p. 114). The trust, understanding, and feeling unit members hold for each other can be enhanced through a variety of human development programs. The film, *Making Unit Meetings Effective,* (Reading, Mass.: Addison-Wesley, 1976), is particularly useful for building team skills. Professionally conducted workshops in human relations have been used with varying degrees of success in IGE schools. In addition, the principal should encourage informal and impromptu social interaction. For example, a friendly challenge from one unit to another to a volleyball game may do more to develop compatibility than any formally directed human development program. A combination of formal and informal approaches may be needed to produce open and sincere human understanding and interaction.

Just as role and personality factors are important, so also must the value orientations of each member of the staff be considered. Since individual values underlie and influence not only behavior but also the evaluation of that behavior, the principals would do well to make explicit their own and other staff members' basic and educational values. Several brief exercises in value clarification may serve as the basis for concentrated in-service programs (Raths *et al.* 1966).

Numerous other local inservice training activities are helpful during the refinement and renewal phases of implementation, some examples of which follow:

- Have unit leaders or unit teachers observe and critique the work of other units.
- Request unit members to critique their own unit's operations.
- Videotape an instructional activity and let the unit as a whole critique the behavior.
- Prepare detailed role descriptions for staff and critique them.
- Have each member record and report the percentage of time spent on each role task during a week.
- Analyze all IIC and I & R Unit meetings for discrepancies between that which was planned and that which was implemented.
- Exchange teach, having each member work in a different I & R Unit.
- Exchange roles for a day among the principal, unit leaders, and unit teachers.
- Prepare and present to visitors the highlights of the school's program.
- Sponsor a regional or state IGE meeting at the school.

Inservice training activities conducted by colleges and universities are becoming increasingly available. This kind of opportunity typically is offered in at least two ways. One kind of experience is a short intensive institute from one to four weeks in length. Another is a course continued over a period of a semester or more. The former may be offered in the summer, and the latter may be offered during the school year through evening sessions. Either may be offered with school district inservice or college credit. Such experiences should focus on problems encountered in IGE schools and will be conducted, therefore, for experienced IGE personnel including staff teachers, unit leaders, and principals. Sometimes, however, staff members of schools expecting to change to IGE the following year will enroll in such courses.

The institute is designed to improve the understandings and skills of personnel in IGE schools, and may concentrate on any or all of the components of IGE, including the Instructional Programming Model, evaluation and assessment, interaction skills, motivation, school-home-community relations, and each of many curriculum areas. In summary, these refinement activities focus on skill building, problem solving, exchanging ideas, and gathering new information from various sources.

A prototypic sequence of inservice activities that has been demonstrated to be successful for implementing IGE was shown earlier in Chapter 2,

Figure 2.2. Since the activities listed are only the essential minimum, several suggestions have been made whereby the principal and the IIC may augment and supplement the activities at the operational level of the school. The following guidelines (Klausmeier *et al.* 1974, p. 51) may be helpful in planning each of the major activities:

1. State the rationale for the activity.
2. Identify the target audience and specify eligibility and selection criteria.
3. Formulate objectives of the activity in terms of the expected behaviors of the participants.
4. Determine in advance the methods and processes to be used through consulting with participants.
5. Prepare a detailed schedule of events.
6. Inform the participants of any postactivity commitments to be made, e.g., follow-up reports.
7. Secure participant commitment to the activity.
8. Identify the resources needed for the activity, including consultants, local personnel, equipment, materials, space, etc.
9. Attend carefully to logistical concerns, such as checking all spaces and equipment before their actual use, having supplies and materials in readiness, etc.
10. Prepare the assessment and evaluation instruments and procedures in advance, but be ready to improvise.

After Step 10, the activity is conducted and evaluated in terms of behavioral change in the staff.

EVALUATION OF STAFF

Staff evaluation is a function which includes the processes of gathering and using information to make decisions about staff competence as a basis for subsequently improving that performance. Included in this broad view of staff evaluation are considerations of (1) an enumeration of reasons for evaluation, (2) a definition of evaluation, (3) a description of who is involved in the evaluative process, (4) a consideration of the junctures at which evaluative information should be collected and utilized, and (5) a discussion of some exemplary evaluative activities.

Why Evaluate?

Reasons for evaluation are set forth clearly and succinctly here to emphasize their importance:

1. To reinforce and improve performance

2. To determine goals and roles for units and the school

3. To determining new goals and establish roles for individual teachers

4. To formulate criteria for hiring new personnel

5. To clarify and enhance mutual role expectations

6. To monitor progress toward goals

7. To stimulate a conscious concern of self

8. To encourage self-evaluation

9. To foster improved morale

10. To aid in crisis management

11. To serve as a basis for contract renewal

12. To dismiss an incompetent staff member

An NEA survey (1964) showed that 93 percent of the teachers surveyed favored undertaking an evaluation for the purpose of improving one's teaching competency. With perhaps the exception of a summative decision to dismiss a poor staff member, all of the reasons above for conducting an evaluation are aimed at improved teaching competence. Each of these reasons is incorporated into the definition of staff evaluation.

What Is Staff Evaluation?

Just as the purpose of evaluating learning is to help the students learn better, so also is the purpose of staff evaluation to help the staff become more effective and efficient. Staff evaluation typically includes observations of teacher behavior, measures of teaching outcomes, ratings of the attributes of the teacher, and measures of schoolwide behavioral characteristics.

Observations of teacher behavior are designed to obtain, record, summarize, and interpret the extent to which a teacher's role performance fulfills the expectations held for the role. In the IGE school, teachers within a unit work closely together, each contributing to the functioning of the unit and the entire school. They perform at a professional level, particularly in planning and decision making with other members of the unit. They work closely with many children and with other members in the unit in research activities, in preservice and inservice teacher education, and even in the staff evaluation process. Measures of teacher behavior in these activities provide a major source of information for evaluation, but the primary focus should be on the teacher-student relationship in the instructional process.

Large numbers of categorical schemata have been developed for observing the teaching process (A. Simon and Boyer 1970). Several of these classificatory tools divide teacher behavior into such categories as types of teacher talk (accepts feelings, praises, accepts student ideas, asks questions, lectures, gives directions, criticizes), and student talk (responds, initiates). Although these categories are explicit, their cause and effect relationship with achievement has yet to be demonstrated (McNeil and Popham 1973, p. 221). Such observations, therefore, are only one source of information for the evaluation of teacher performance.

There does not now exist, nor is there likely to be developed in the future, any common criteria against which the effectiveness of the teaching-learning process can be assessed. Frequently, such judgments are erroneously based on gain in student achievement—failing to take into account such basic and valid criteria as random assignment of teachers and pupils, multiple measures of performance, operational definition of terms, or even the prior learning of students—all of which are needed to make the chained assumption between teaching behavior and student gain. Such chaining, confusing means and ends and inferring cause and effect, is probably less likely in the IGE school, however, since a variety of assessment procedures, including criterion-referenced tests, are used.

Within the IGE school, continuous mutual judgments are rendered concerning the effectiveness of the teaching process—particularly in Step 6 of the IPM. If students have failed to attain the objectives, the entire instructional sequence is examined, including the behavior of the teacher. In a sense, the objectives of the student or group of students become the objectives of the teacher, and the reasons for their nonattainment may be mutually explored by the I & R Unit staff. Such exploration, of itself, is diagnostic and may lead to subsequent change, not only in the objectives themselves, but also in teaching approaches, grouping patterns, pacing of instruction, equipment or materials, and other variables during the next instructional sequence.

In terms of the personal dimension, the personality attributes of the teacher, such as discretion, tact, sense of humor, voice, punctuality, temperament, personal grooming, emotional stability, and attitude toward criticism, are still commonly used to evaluate staff (McNeil and Popham 1974, p. 223). These characteristics are typically rated on an "acceptable–unacceptable," "satisfactory–needs improvement", or similar Likert-type scales. Glaring problems with such scales include the lack of clarity in the definitions of terms, the halo effect wherein a high rating on one attribute may encourage a high rating on others, the common assumption that the variables are linear, and the typical view that the integral points on the rating scale are equal. The result is misleading comparisons of teachers with arbitrary standards or with one another. Moreover, these ratings often reveal as much about the rater as about the rated, since scores of the same teacher by separate evaluators are often disparate.

After three decades of research on teacher effectiveness, Barr concluded that no particular constellation of personalistic variables was systematically predictive of effective teaching behavior (Barr 1955). Instead, the following were important: commonality of objectives, agreement on purposes, similarity in values, frequency of staff interaction, attitudes toward the administration, and staff morale. Hopefully, these variables are maximized in the IGE school.

To gain insight into the behavior of the individual teacher, comparisons with some overall characteristics of the organization are instructive. The major organizational components of morale, shown in Figure 5.3, include rationality, identification, and belongingness. In the IGE school, teacher participation in goal setting is increased, as goals for pupils, units, and the whole school are conjointly formulated. Hence the goals to be attained are rational in terms of the roles designed to achieve them—"Our program makes sense!" In the IGE school, teacher participation in goal setting also increases the congruence between a teacher's personal needs and the system goals, resulting in a greater degree of teacher identification with the school—"Knock my school, and you knock me!" Moreover, teacher participation in goal and role setting increases the congruence between a teacher's personal needs and the role expectations for that teacher, resulting in a greater sense of belongingness—"I like it here!" High morale, then, results from increased rationality, identification, and belongingness among the staff of the school.

Since staff behavior in one school may vary quite drastically from that in another, a measure of "what the school looks like" and "how it feels" to work in a particular school may help in the evaluation of teacher behavior. Halpin, starting from the observation that organizational climate can be construed as the organizational "personality" of a school, developed an instrument to measure the organizational climate of schools (Halpin and Croft 1963). Teachers are asked to respond on a continuum from "rarely occurs" to "very frequently occurs" their reaction to statements such as.

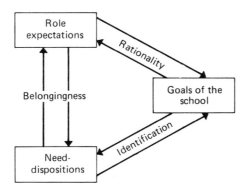

Fig. 5.3 The dimension of morale. Adapted from J. W. Getzels and E. G. Guba, Social behavior and the administrative process, *School Review,* **65** (1957): 436.

1. There is considerable laughter when teachers gather informally.
2. Teachers ramble when they talk in faculty meetings.
3. The principal sets an example by working hard.
4. Faculty meetings are organized according to a tight agenda.
5. The teachers accomplish their work with great vim, vigor, and pleasure (Halpin and Croft 1963, pp. 30–31).

From these items four factors were identified which were descriptive of the behavior of the teachers: disengagement, hindrance, esprit, and intimacy. The four factors identified as descriptive of the principal's behavior included: aloofness, production emphasis, thrust, and consideration. Combining these factors resulted in prototypic descriptions of six organizational climates: open, autonomous, controlled, familiar, paternal, and closed. Since the objectives of IGE are compatible with the description of the open climate, individual teachers' contributions toward reaching these objectives can be evaluated in light of the degree of openness among the staff of the school.

Who Evaluates?

Many persons, including teachers, unit leaders, students, parents, and consultants, may aid the principal in the staff evaluation process in various ways. Concerning the staff evaluation conference, the principal of an exemplary IGE school in Minnesota recently stated:

> In our school, evaluation is a mutual thing—we all evaluate each other. I wouldn't think of sitting down with a whole bunch of information about a teacher unless that person had equally powerful data about me! Before I tell them how to improve, they tell me!

Individually or in concert with the principal, personnel may collect information; set goals, objectives, and programs; develop role expectations; and conceive staff-development programs. Information should be gathered by those closest to the actual behavior being observed, as well as from other sources to cross-check perceptual differences. The process of setting goals, objectives, and expectations, and that of staff development and evaluation should involve maximal input from those who function within IGE guidelines.

Final decisions in the evaluative process which label staff competence are the responsibility of the principal and cannot be delegated. In the extreme case, for example, the principal may need to defend in court the decision to nonrenew a teacher. Conflicts in which goals cannot be agreed upon or on which a compromise cannot be reached must be adjudicated by the principal to the best of his or her ability based on the relevant data. These types of situations should become a rarity in the IGE school, due

to mutual goal setting and the decentralization of most decisions with ensuing consensus. When consensus cannot be reached, however, the principal
cannot escape the ultimate responsibility for finalizing a staff evaluation. The
unit leader is not a supervisor or administrator and should have no formal
or final evaluation responsibilities (Klausmeier *et al.* 1971, p. 42). Teachers
almost unanimously agree that in the end the principal is responsible for
staff evaluation (NEA 1964).

When to Evaluate

The principal's perceptions of the staff are everchanging; informal impressions are continually gained. Evaluation of a more formal nature, however, should be conducted on a scheduled basis. From the initial job interview through termination of employment, evaluation should be a continuous
as well as a summative process. Formal evaluation must occur at frequent
intervals and at critical points in time. Perceptual congruence between the
teacher and the principal in summative evaluations will be facilitated by this
continuous evaluation. Conflict is less likely when the summative evaluation
results from a systematic process.

When are some typical times evaluation might occur? Self-evaluation
by teachers may occur continuously as well as summatively and should be
encouraged by the principal. Timetables for accomplishment of short- and
long-term goals may set some dates. Teacher or principal requests, or the
occurrence of some critical incident suggest additional times. Evaluation at
critical stages of IGE implementation may be profitable. Contractual agree-
ments also determine timing.

Before school opens each year, or very early in the year, the principal
should meet with each teacher and jointly set short- and long-term personal
and professional goals for that teacher. Such conferences should take
into account the goals and objectives of the other teachers in the unit, and
the principal should determine the extent to which organizational and
individual goals are compatible and complementary. Given the increased
interaction among teachers in the IGE school, it may even be impossible to
evaluate most teachers without in part evaluating others. Goals which all
teachers in a unit or school are to meet should be set by the affected group.
These goals can be included as a part of rating checklists, levels of pupil
performance, observation measures, or other staff-performance indicators,
such as organizational climate and morale. A definite timetable must be set
up to monitor progress toward the achievement of goals. Evaluation dates
should be agreed upon mutually. Agreement might also be reached that
additional evaluations may be made at the request of either party at any
time. An evaluation is especially important whenever the teacher asks for
it, since acknowledgment of a problem is a first essential step toward
changing that teacher's behavior. A request for evaluation in the absence

of any particular problem also may be an unconscious plea for recognition of a "job well done." Principals, given their busy days, may easily put aside such requests under favorable circumstances, but positive reinforcement may turn out to be as rewarding for the principal as for the teacher. An evaluation should occur at the principal's discretion also, since he or she may perceive factors about a teacher's behavior needing immediate change which may not be apparent to that teacher.

Evaluation should also occur reasonably soon after a critical incident among the staff, such as a personality conflict or a dispute about teaching roles. The evaluation of each individual's behavior in the incident may then serve as a basis for new goals and roles for each individual so that the possibility of a repeat incident will be alleviated. Even so, not all conflict can be avoided; some conflict may be necessary to articulate problems and to set new goals and role expectations.

Evaluation might also occur at critical stages of IGE implementation. In the awareness stage, teachers naturally ask, "What kind of changes will I have to make if we implement IGE?" It is necessary to know what baseline behaviors exist before answers can be given. Personnel evaluation forms a large part of that description.

In the changeover year when teachers are coping with mastering all of the components of IGE and even writing their own role descriptions, all will need to recognize that these goals and roles determine the behavior for each individual in the school. It is from such goal and role statements, however, that evaluative instruments specific to individual IGE schools can be constructed.

In the refinement and renewal phases, instructional programs and teaching methods will change and new teachers may be brought in to replace those who leave. In the case of staff turnover, a composite evaluation of the individuals remaining in the unit and the school will give direction as to the type of person needed to complement the remaining staff. This evaluation will, in turn, form some of the goals and role expectations for the new teacher. As indicated earlier, these are a primary consideration during the employment and selection processes.

Summative staff evaluation in most school districts is mandatory. Decisions on contract renewal usually require competency evaluations by a specific date. Traditional summative evaluation, which may be required by district policy or contractual agreement, occurs from once or twice per year for beginning teachers to perhaps only once every three years for those on tenure. Checklists and rating forms used for these evaluations may attempt to portray evaluation as a continuous process by requiring the principals to note the number of times or dates they observed the teacher. Checklists and rating forms usually fail, however, to provide any mechanism for the use of these observations or relate the number and timing of evaluations to the need for them. Such checklists can be useful only for determining competency in a broad time perspective. Recommendations for teachers' credential files also require summative evaluations and should be completed at the end of each year to avoid recall problems at a later date. Goal and role setting for the individual, an entire unit, and the entire school is facilitated if evaluations are conscientiously completed at regularly scheduled intervals.

How to Evaluate

Several modes of staff evaluation may be used in IGE to focus on the teacher as an individual, the teacher in the unit, and the teacher in the school. Checklists are frequently used for individual evaluation; formal and informal observations typically relate to behavior in the unit; and formal measures of morale, motivation, and organizational climate are often used to focus on behavior in the entire school. Regardless of the instrument used, care must be taken to avoid such pitfalls as "one-shot" evaluation, use of arbitrary standards, and overreliance on one person's perceptions.

Checklists. Since many districts are committed to the use of checklists, several suggestions to improve these measures and adapt them to IGE schools may be offered. Creating or clarifying definitions of terms, including adding performance criteria, makes an excellent topic for an inservice program at the unit or school level. Consensus concerning exactly what is being evaluated will encourage teachers to participate in collecting information. The ensuing discussions concerning one another's competence will also be conducted in a more professional and expert manner. Devising a system of checklist data collection should: ensure completion of ratings by the teacher, superordinates, and subordinates; include a procedure for compiling these ratings across evaluators; and set forth a method for resolving conflicting ratings.

Items specific to the roles and responsibilities of IGE unit leaders and staff teachers as set forth in the *IGE Implementation guidelines* (Klausmeier *et al.* 1971, pp. 89–126), and selected listings of specific tasks for IIC and I & R Units are more fully elaborated in *Evaluation procedure for use with multiunit elementary school personnel* (Morrow *et al.* 1969, pp. 22–39). Items listed for the unit leader are derived from the responsibilities of the IIC. The principal may also be partially evaluated on these criteria. Items listed for the staff teacher are derived from the responsibilities of the unit. All criteria listed for staff teachers are also applicable to unit leaders. A sampling of items which might be included (with operational definitions and behavioral performance criteria to be determined by the individual IGE school) follows.

	Unit Leader	*Staff Teacher*
Instructional programming	▪ participates in development of general objectives for the area selected for IGE implementation ▪ participates in development of criterion-referenced tests and instructional objectives for the subject matter area above ▪ plans across units	▪ carries out responsibilities for IGE planning tasks ▪ carries out preassessment, record keeping, regrouping
Organizational operations	▪ contributes to IIC agenda ▪ contributes to brainstorming sessions ▪ ensures several kinds of unit meetings (e.g., goal setting, grouping, evaluational) are regularly held	▪ contributes to unit agenda ▪ appropriately utilizes aides ▪ develops expertise in some curricular area
Staff development	▪ plans an inservice program ▪ conducts evaluation of inservice program	▪ participates in staff-development program ▪ participates in evaluation of staff-development program
Home-school-community relations	▪ conducts evaluation of home-school-community relations program	▪ reports student progress to parents in a manner that reflects the IGE program

After checklists are administered, they should be discussed by the teacher and the principal or within the unit if this is viewed as desirable by the staff. This conference should focus on identifying areas of needed improvement and devising strategies for achieving change. Particular attention should be paid to low areas on the evaluations. If general weaknesses are identifiable within a unit or a school, the implications for the staff development are obvious. Repeated use of the checklist scales over time can serve as an indicator of change and growth in competency. Teacher change is also a partial evaluation of the staff-improvement program. This entire process becomes cyclical and interactive over time as the staff improves, as staff turnover occurs, and as the IGE program becomes fully implemented.

Observation.   Observation is a valuable means for gathering information about a variety of teaching and other behaviors. Observations relevant to teacher evaluation may be collected in a variety of situations, be recorded in several ways, and focus on different types of interactions.

Most structured observations of teacher behavior focus on teacher-pupil interaction in the instructional setting. Other teacher behavior, such as the amount of time the teacher spends on various activities or the nature of interpersonal relations, can be gathered in unit or other meetings, in the teachers' lounge, or elsewhere in the school. Knowledge of informal relationships, according to H. A. Simon (1957, p. 148), gives the evaluator insights into the more formal relationships which are being observed and recorded. Some potential observable informal relationships include awareness of which teachers sit together in the lounge, group together in hallways, attend the same functions, ride together in car pools, or participate in similar interest, activity, or community groups outside the school. In addition to noting the positive nature of such relationships, the principal should be on the lookout for negative interactions, such as avoidance of one another or outright personality clashes.

Data to document the quality of the teacher's behavior in meeting formal expectations can be collected by using any of several observational measures of the teaching process. Many systems exist for codifying observations of teaching. A valuable compilation of these instruments, *Mirrors for behavior* (A. Simon and Boyer 1970), includes instruments and guidelines for collecting information in both the cognitive and affective domains. Several of these instruments may be modified to fit the individual school. An excellent inservice program would consist of comparing several forms and developing an observational system unique to the school.

In designing an observational system several questions should be addressed: What should be observed? How should observations be recorded? What procedures should be used to try to ensure the accuracy of the observation? Who should be observed? Where should the observation take place? What is the behavioral act that will be recorded? What act initiated that act? What appears to be the reason for the act? Toward whom is the behavior directed? How long did the act last? How frequent was the act? What happened after the act? To what use will the observations be put? Answers to these questions should yield a category system having clarity, comprehensiveness, and utility.

The observational-rating system can be used in a variety of ways. Unit teachers can observe one another, with the unit leader and principal also serving as observers. Teachers may first want to videotape their instruction for self-analysis. Group analysis at the unit level, a typical IGE procedure, may precede direct involvement of the principal and unit leaders.

Preceding each actual use of an observational instrument, the teacher and the observer should hold a preobservational conference to clarify objectives of the teaching, exchange information about the students, and discuss other information pertinent to the observation. Desired outcomes should be listed on the form. During data collection the observer should stress what is heard and seen, rather than attempt to make inferences in order to fit behavior to a category. Immediately following the observation, or as soon as feasible thereafter, a conference should be held to analyze the results. Analysis should focus on the actual obtained results versus the desired preobservation goals. From the differences, new teaching strategies can be derived to improve instruction, the primary aim of observation.

There are several common problems associated with the use of any observational system focusing on classroom behavior. One is observer effect. The presence of the observer in the classroom may promote atypical behavior from both the teacher and the students. This effect is usually negated over time as more and more observers enter classrooms. As the staff of any IGE school will attest, observers are so common that their presence is often ignored. It also may be difficult for the freshman observer actually to sit back, observe, and not interact with students—particularly in IGE schools where individual students will often make inquiries of the observer. Some observation schedules may even be constructed so that pupils themselves can complete the ratings.

A second problem with the observational system is that of interobserver reliability. Clarity of definitions and practice in the use of the instrument can usually increase agreement among observers. The comparison of individual ratings of a videotape by the unit and the principal is an excellent technique to reduce perceptual differences.

Care must be taken to sample teaching behavior over time, as well as in a variety of instructional settings and curricular fields, since these factors may cause teacher behavior to vary. Since the IGE teacher will also be utilizing several types of grouping patterns, the observational systems will also have to be adaptable.

A common misuse of category-rating systems is the description of a high frequency of one type of behavior as somehow being "good" and labeling other results as "bad." Instead, goodness or badness of instruction should relate to the difference between the actual results and intended goals set in the preobservational conference.

Can observational-rating scales then be used to evaluate the total effectiveness of the teacher? While these instruments are most useful for describing the teaching act, their relationship to changes in student growth still has not been clearly demonstrated (McNeil and Popham 1973, p. 221.)

Hence, it is often necessary to obtain formal global measures of staff behavior.

Formal measures.   Measures of the characteristics of an entire organization provide data which may help interpret information already gathered about the individual teacher. Instruments developed by the Wisconsin Research and Development Center for Cognitive Learning, and standard measures of organizational structure may be used to examine overall characteristics such as morale, motivation, and climate. Although studies of organizational variables have been conducted in many schools, the central issue relevant to staff evaluation remains, "What is the nature of the morale and climate in schools that have successfully implemented IGE?" The results of two studies which examined this question are particularly enlightening.

A recent definitive study of staff morale in IGE as compared with non-IGE schools was conducted by Herrick (1974). The unit of analysis consisted of multiunit and nonmultiunit schools in Wisconsin which employed ten or more staff members during 1971–1972. The population consisted of schools which had implemented IGE and those that had not implemented IGE. A total of 34 multiunit and 38 nonmultiunit schools participated; a random sample of fifteen teachers from each school provided the data. Organizational structure was defined in terms of the axiomatic theory of organization (Hage 1965, pp. 289–320). School means of complexity, centralization, formalization, and stratification, along with school size, were used to describe the organizational structure of the schools. Teacher motivation was defined in terms of the organization's reward system measured by expectancy theory. Expectancy theory states that motivation or effort to perform is a multiplicative function of the probability of receiving a particular reward and the importance of the reward to the individual.

Hypotheses were formulated and data were gathered to answer the following questions: "Is the level of teacher motivation in IGE multiunit schools significantly different from that in non-IGE multiunit schools?" and "Is there any significant relationship between such organizational variables as complexity, centralization of decision making, and stratification and a teacher's motivation to perform? Some of the major findings were as follows:

- Multiunit schools were less centralized, less stratified, and had more highly motivated teachers than did nonmultiunit schools.

- Organizational complexity was a significant predictor of teacher motivation in nonmultiunit schools but not in multiunit schools.

- Centralization of decision making was a significant predictor of teacher motivation in both multiunit and nonmultiunit schools.

- Stratification was a significant predictor of teacher motivation in both multiunit and nonmultiunit schools.

Concerning these findings, Herrick (1974, pp. 30–31) concluded, "Administrators interested in developing higher levels of teacher motivation should make every effort to involve teachers in the decision-making process."

A recently reported study of 35 IGE schools conducted by Kelly (1974, p. 570) also revealed that there was a significant decrease in the extent to which the overall institutional environment was "closed" in successful IGE schools. He concluded,

> Since the IGE model seeks to emphasize development of both students and staff within an "open" environment, the conclusion is that implementation of the IGE model will, for teachers, foster the development of its intended outcomes.

SUMMARY

In this chapter the principal's leadership role in the staff personnel functions of recruitment, selection, assignment, orientation, inservice training improvement, and evaluation was described in terms of the interactive role, personality, and values dimensions of social systems theory. The principal's responsibilities in recruitment were described as assessing and articulating prevailing values so that recruitment materials and vacancy announcements accurately portray the school community to potential candidates. Selection of staff was viewed as achieving maximal congruence between the major role responsibilities for the position vacancy with the qualifications of candidates as viewed through a consensus of professionals in the school. The dynamic of the staff selection and assignment process was depicted as that of increasing role-personality compatibility. The orientation of new staff to an existent IGE school and the orientation of total staff to IGE emphasized the need for a systematic series of activities to ensure positive acceptance of change.

Factors basic to a staff-improvement program—involvement in decision making, interpersonal interaction, role flexibility, communication channels, and supportive resources—suggested several unique IGE staff-improvement techniques. A prototypic sequence of IGE inservice training activities was presented with elaboration on the principal-unit leader workshop, the preschool workshop, first-year inservice activities, and concentrated inservice activities to enhance the understandings, skills, abilities, and resultant role behavior of each IGE staff member.

Evaluation was defined as the effort to determine the extent to which the behavior of the staff is organizationally effective and individually efficient. The involvement of staff in evaluation, the timing and rationale for evaluation, and suggested procedures for evaluation, including checklists, observation instruments, and measures of school climate, were suggested for use by the principal in evaluating staff performance. Results of research studies based on social systems theory were cited to show the relationship between evaluation and staff morale.

REFERENCES

Barr, A. S. *et al.* 1965. Measurement and prediction of teacher effectiveness. *Review of Educational Research* **25** (June).

Delbecq, A. L., and A. H. Van deVen 1971. A group process model for problem identification and program planning. *Journal of Applied Behavioral Science* **7.**

ERNSTSPIEL 1972. Center for the Advanced Study of Educational Administration, Eugene, Ore.: University of Oregon.

Evers, N. A. 1974. *An analysis of the relationship between the effectiveness of the multiunit elementary school's instruction and research unit and interpersonal behaviors.* Technical report no. 298. Madison, Wisc.: Wisconsin Research and Development Center for Cognitive Learning.

Getzels, J. W., and E. G. Guba 1957. Social behavior and the administrative process. *School Review* **65.**

————, J. M. Lipham, and R. F. Campbell 1968. *Educational administration as a social process.* New York: Harper & Row.

————, and H. A. Thelen 1960. The classroom as a unique social system. In N. B. Henry (ed.), *The dynamics of instructional groups.* Chicago: National Society for the Study of Education, University of Chicago.

Gilberts, R. D. 1961. *The interpersonal characteristics of teaching teams.* Doctoral dissertation, University of Wisconsin–Madison.

Hage, J. 1965. An axiomatic theory of organizations. *Administrative Science Quarterly* (December).

Halpin, A. W., and D. B. Croft 1963. *The organizational climate of schools.* Chicago: Midwest Administration Center, University of Chicago.

Herrick, H. S. 1974. *The relationship of organizational structure to teacher motivation in multiunit and nonmultiunit schools.* Technical report No. 322. Madison, Wisc.: Wisconsin Research and Development Center for Cognitive Learning.

Howes, N. J. 1974. *Change factors related to the institutionalization of the multiunit elementary school.* Technical report No. 319. Madison, Wisc.: Wisconsin Research and Development Center for Cognitive Learning.

Kelly, E. A. 1974. Implementing the IGE model: impact on teachers. *Phi Delta Kappan* **60** (April).

Klausmeier, H. J., J. E. Walter, and L. J. Lins 1974. *Manual for starting and maintaining state IGE networks.* Madison, Wisc.: University of Wisconsin/ Sears-Roebuck Foundation IGE Teacher Education Project.

————, M. R. Quilling, J. S. Sorenson, R. S. Way, and G. R. Glasrud 1971. *Individually guided education and the multiunit elementary school: guidelines for implementation.* Madison, Wisc.: Wisconsin Research and Development Center for Cognitive Learning.

Kluckhohn, C., *et al.* 1951. Values and value orientations in the theory of action. In T. Parsons and E. A. Shils (eds.), *Toward a general theory of action.* Cambridge, Mass.: Harvard University Press.

Lipham, J. M., and J. A. Hoeh, Jr. 1974. *The principalship: foundations and functions.* New York: Harper & Row.

———— 1974. Improving the decision-making skills of the principal. In J. A. Culbertson, C. Henson, and R. Morrison (eds.), *Performance objectives for school principals.* Berkeley, Calif.: McCutchan.

Maslow, A. H. 1954. *Motivation and personality.* New York: Harper & Row.

McNeil, J. D., and W. J. Popham 1973. The assessment of teacher competence. In R. M. W. Travers (ed.), *Second handbook of research on teaching.* Chicago: Rand McNally.

Morrow, R., J. Sorenson, and G. Glasrud 1969. *Evaluation procedures for use with multiunit elementary school personnel.* Madison, Wisc.: Wisconsin Research and Development Center for Cognitive Learning.

National Education Association (NEA), Research Division 1964. *Evaluation of classroom teachers, research report 1964—R13.* Washington, D.C.

Paul, D. A. 1974. *The diffusion of an innovation through interorganizational linkages.* Doctoral dissertation, University of Wisconsin–Madison. Technical report No. 308. Madison, Wisc.: Wisconsin Research and Development Center for Cognitive Learning.

Raths, L. E., M. Harrison, and S. B. Simon 1966. *Values and teaching: working with values in the classroom.* Columbus, Ohio: Merrill.

Schutz, W. C. 1968. *FIRO: a three-dimensional theory of interpersonal behavior.* New York: Holt, Rinehart and Winston.

Simon, A., and E. G. Boyer (eds.) 1970. *Mirrors for behavior I–XIV: an anthology of observation instruments.* Philadelphia: Research for Better Schools.

Simon, H. A. *Administrative behavior.* New York: Macmillan.

Wright, K. W. 1976. *Development of an instrument to measure real and ideal decision structure and involvement in IGE schools.* Doctoral dissertation, University of Wisconsin–Madison.

6
Improving Home-School-Community Relations

B. Dean Bowles
Marvin J. Fruth

Objectives

After reading this chapter, the reader will be able:

- To understand the general goals of a home-school-community relations program in an IGE school.
- To identify the major principles of an effective home-school-community relations program.
- To understand the political context of home-school-community relations.
- To recognize the primary interaction patterns of the IGE school with the community.
- To illustrate the major concepts and competencies necessary for an effective home-school-community relations program.

Public education is no better than the public's understanding of the school. There are three general goals of a home-school-community relations program for increasing public understanding of the IGE school:

1. To make the IGE staff more aware of and responsive to the educational expectations and available resources of the community, parents, and students;

2. To make the community, parents, and students more aware of and responsive to the requisites of the instructional program as implemented in IGE; and

3. To identify and utilize ways and means of actively involving both staff and community in the awareness, commitment, changeover, refinement, and renewal phases of implementing IGE in the school.

To achieve these goals, the staff must be actively and effectively involved in the school community. Moreover, means must be found whereby the principal, unit leaders, and staff of IGE schools can involve the various subpublics in both policy development and important operational decisions which will contribute to the effective implementation of IGE. This involvement should begin during the awareness and commitment phases of the implementation of IGE and continue through the changeover and refinement phases in order that IGE can truly become a self-renewing system.

The principal plays a key role in the home-school-community relations program of an IGE school for several reasons. First, the principal is responsible for the leadership of the IIC, the paramount decision-making body in the school. In this capacity, the principal not only interacts with and provides input from the entire school community but also coordinates the home-school-community relations activities of the several I & R Units. Second, the principal fulfills a critical role in communicating and articulating the policies and practices of the IGE school to the Systemwide Program Committee, the central office, and the Board of Education. In short, the principal is responsible for providing effective leadership and is a liaison among three particularly important groups in the home-school-community relations program—the school staff, the central office, and the school board. Third, while the home-school-community relations program requires the active involvement of all professional staff of an IGE school, certain activities in this domain cannot be delegated; they must be performed by the principal. Finally, the IGE school requires economic, political, organizational, and moral support from its various subpublics to function effectively. The principal is in an excellent position to secure that support. The IGE school program is visible to virtually all subpublics. Because of this visibility the various subpublics in the school community such as the Board of Education, Systemwide Program Committee, central office, I & R Units, teachers, students, parents, and the general citizenry not only look to the principal for leadership but also hold the principal both organizationally and personally accountable for the effectiveness of the school.

This chapter deals with the home-school-community relations program for an IGE school and the role of the principal in ensuring that the program functions effectively. The chapter is organized into six major sections. The first section sets forth several principles about home-school-community relations which bear on the role responsibilities of the principal. The second section elaborates on the political context of home-school-community relations. The third section discusses the primary interaction patterns expected in the home-school-community relations program of an IGE school. Specific concepts and competencies of the principal in pursuing an effective home-school-community relations program are systematically explored in the fourth section. The link between home-school-community relations and the instructional program is briefly examined in the fifth section. Finally, section six illustrates several analysis, communication, involvement, and resolution activities of the home-school-community relations program for the principal of the IGE school.

PRINCIPLES OF HOME-SCHOOL-COMMUNITY RELATIONS

There are several underlying principles of an effective home-school-community relations program. First, it must be recognized that good home-school-community relations involve much more than the effective use of media. That is not to say that effective utilization of communication media—newspaper, TV, radio, and newsletters—is not a part of good home-school community relations. However, some principals have stressed media to the exclusion of other mechanisms for home-school-community relations and have thought of media as the total operationalization of a good home-school-community relations program. In short, the intelligent use of media is a necessary ingredient, but is not a sufficient home-school-community relations program.

If the instructional and organizational changes associated with IGE are to be implemented effectively, their benefits must be tangible and visible to the various subpublics in the school community. This means that principals are expected to involve subpublics early in the implementation process and to present information clearly and in terms that the various subpublics can understand. At present, the benefits of facilitative environments, the Instructional Programming Model, and the multiunit organization are probably neither tangible nor visible to most subpublics of the school community. They want answers to such questions as: "Will my child be a better reader as a result of IGE?" "How much say should children have in what they will do and learn?" "What will happen to my child if she has several teachers?" "Does IGE provide both the needed structure and flexibility for effective learning?" Answers should be provided in concrete and specific terms that parents and other community members can understand.

An effective program of home-school-community relations involves working very closely with parents. Examples of this include parent volunteers working in the school, observations by parents, home visits by staff, and parent participation and involvement in making educational policies and operational decisions which affect the instructional program and school life of their children. Such participation will enhance the school program. Principals will have to expand the current "open-door" policy and adopt a "go-out-the-door" policy in relating to the school community.

The staff of the school must avail themselves of the educational resources of the community. In many IGE schools it has been found that these resources not only enhance student learning but also expand the knowledge of the staff concerning the community. Such knowledge of the community includes, but is not necessarily restricted to, the influence of political and social factors on the instructional program. The IGE school staff also should internalize an inclusive and elastic concept of community. Educators have too long held to a "we–they" or "friends of education–foes of education" orientation. Similarly, some educators see only the subpublics "outside" the school building as being the community when perhaps the most effective groups are right in the schools—the students and the staff. Typically the concept "community" is limited to those involved directly in education. It should include not only students and staff but also nonparent adults, senior citizens, and other subpublics. Unfortunately, in some districts educational affairs are considered in isolation from community affairs and municipal issues.

As a corollary to the concept of an inclusive and elastic concept of community, the IGE staff should be aware that the most important subpublic in any home-school-community relations program is that of the students. Often taken for granted, students not only are the purpose for which schools exist but also are the most consistently influential subpublic with which the school deals. Students continually communicate their perceptions about school to adults, particularly parents, and this is their parents' primary source of information about teachers, instruction, and the school in general. Moreover, this information applies to the primary student as well as to the adolescent. This fact has long- as well as short-range home-school-community relations implications because students bring many of the perceptions and experiences about school which were learned in childhood into their adult experience. In short, the premier efforts of the principal and staff in any home-school-community relations program should be focused on the students.

The staff of the IGE school should try to avoid the typical "crisis-management" orientation of most home-school-community relations programs. All too frequently, programs in home-school-community relations respond only to crises, and are otherwise passive and impotent rather than active and preventative. The notion that involvement in home-school-community relations is necessary only when the school is confronted with a crisis is debilitating to an effective home-school-community relations program. Typically, schools anxiously mobilize the community shortly before a critical bond election; comfortably "committeeize" such problems as pupil-reporting systems; stress building programs in the media; and crudely confront racial incidents in an attempt to manage crises. Schools do and should, of course, react to such crises both swiftly and effectively. However, an effective program of home-school-community relations is more than crisis management; it is an ongoing, interactive, and meaningful relationship among the home, school, and community. In this regard, a noteworthy axiom is that the best program of home-school-community relations is fostered and maintained in times of tranquility rather than in times of torment.

The idea that the home-school-community relations program is equivalent with an advisory committee is another limiting view. Study groups, community advisory committees, ad hoc parental committees, and similar mechanisms are, of course, excellent involvement strategies. Principals must be able to delegate and use committees effectively, but all too often they follow the maxim, "If in doubt, appoint a committee." "Buzz-grouping" or "committeeizing" problems and plans is no substitute for a total program of home-school-community relations. The advisory committee is only one tool in the home-school-community relations program.

The IGE principal, in leading the development of a home-school-community relations program, must recognize that interest, participation, and stakes in the policies and practices of the schools are no longer limited to the cadre of professional employees and a handful of involved and interested parents. Home-school-community relations require communication and involvement with many more subpublics today than was the case several years ago. For a variety of reasons, many subpublics which were once mute or disorganized concerning school affairs now act collectively and voice their demands persistently. For example, ethnic and racial minorities, women's groups, students, organized teachers, and many other special interest groups were not heard from many years ago. Now, however, the best home-school-community relations practices are required to (1) build these groups into the equation of operations; (2) adapt and adopt new and more effective means of communication; (3) seek authentic involvement of these subpublics in the alternatives impinging on the critical decisions affecting both policy and practice; and (4) develop means to resolve actual or potential conflict among the school, home, and the newly organized and enfranchised subpublics.

Finally, it must be realized that educators do not hold a monopoly on the expertise about educational philosophy policy and practices. The educational system and current affairs have succeeded in developing people, who even if they do not have requisite expertise about educational matters, know how to get it, or failing that, know at least which questions to ask. Principals developing home-school-community relations programs must deal with better informed, more knowledgeable, and more sophisticated subpublics than in the past.

THE POLITICAL CONTEXT OF
HOME-SCHOOL-COMMUNITY RELATIONS

Principals in IGE schools need to understand fully the political context of an effective home-school-community relations program. The political process encompasses two principal functions:

1. The resolution of actual and potential conflict in the school community and among its various subpublics, and

2. The allocation through both policy and practice of scarce economic resources, the choice among differing social values, and the distribution of unequal political power to various educational objectives for the benefit of the several subpublics.

The political objective of any effective home-school-community relations program is the resolution of both manifest and latent conflict among the various subpublics which may be associated with policy decisions or administrative practices which determine (1) the use of available, scarce resources; (2) the value choices to be made regarding the educational program; and (3) the locus of power in the educational enterprise. In this context, principals and IGE school personnel are aware that many of the concepts and practices associated with IGE are inherently political. Nongradedness, differentiated staffing, shared decision making, criterion-referenced assessment, and resource reallocation all contribute to actual or potential conflict among various subpublics within a school community. For example, in what proportion should an IGE school allocate its resources for paraprofessionals, teachers, and materials? Who is involved in shared decision making—unit leaders, unit teachers, paraprofessionals, and parents? Can the decisions of a unit stand relatively plenary or are they subject to easy veto? Should mainstreaming of special education children be practiced within IGE units? Is differentiated staffing a management or union concern? Does individualized instruction mean more, or less, competition; more, or less, cooperation? What values do various subpublics place on competition and cooperation? The crucial functions of resolving manifest or latent conflict, allocating resources, choosing values, and distributing power are largely political.

One may logically conclude that an effective home-school-community relations program is good, practical politics. In this context, politics is not of the national, partisan variety, but of the type which determines the nature of the community in which people live, the sort of schools provided, and the kind of educational program conducted. Hence, all of the media, committee structures, community analysis techniques, modes of communication, and involvement activities are but means to accomplish the twin objectives of (1) the resolution of conflict, and (2) the allocation of resources, the choice of values, and the distribution of power. Principals bear the burden of responsibility for the politics involved in implementing IGE. If principals are to fulfill this responsibility effectively, they must understand (1) the primary interaction patterns in the home-school-community; (2) the critical concepts and competencies in an effective program of home-school-community relations; and (3) the implications of home-school-community relations for instructional programming.

PRIMARY INTERACTION PATTERNS
IN THE HOME-SCHOOL-COMMUNITY

The Home-School-Community Relations Model for IGE Implementation in Figure 6.1 includes two major dimensions: primary interaction patterns, and concepts and competencies. The concepts and competencies will be treated in the next section of this chapter. Primary interaction patterns in the home-school-community of the IGE school are set forth here. As may be observed in Figure 6.1, home-school-community relations are simultaneously operative at four interdependent levels. Each level represents an aspect of community and school interaction which ultimately influences the kind and quality of the instructional program in the IGE school. More specifically, the primary interaction patterns are between the child and the teacher, the home and the unit leader and staff, the school community and the principal and IIC, and the district community and the administration and SPC. Although these interaction patterns are most prevalent in actual practice, there may be frequent, even persistent, home-school-community interactions across the stated primary patterns.

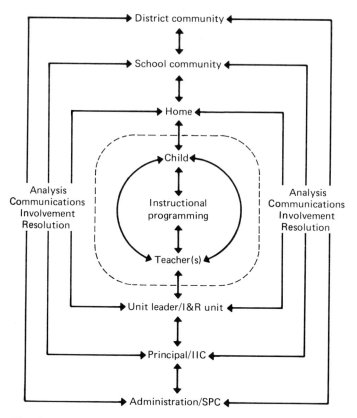

Fig. 6.1 Home-community-school relations in the IGE school. Taken from B. D. Bowles, M. J. Fruth, and J. E. Kim 1975. *Home-school-community relations: the state of the art.* Theoretical paper. Madison, Wisc.: Wisconsin Research and Development Center for Cognitive Learning.

District Community-administration/SPC

The outer ring in Figure 6.1 represents the larger school district. In the final analysis, the community controls the school through its willingness to expend power and resources on programs which mirror its values and interests. Interactions at this level are customarily between school boards, administrators, the SPC, teachers' associations, community influentials, and the like. While the district community and school board/SPC interactions are critical to the combined support of individual schools especially as they relate to budgetary matters, this chapter focuses on the primary interaction patterns at the school level and on the role of the principal in facilitating those interactions.

School Community-principal/IIC

A community establishes schools to meet the needs of both society and its children, and the subpublics in each attendance area have certain expectations as to how these needs are to be best met. If the values held by the community are communicated to the staff and the staff is responsive to these expectations, then the community is more likely to use its power and resources to support the values represented by the instructional program. Conversely, if the staff does not satisfactorily accommodate to the expectations of the community, then the community is certainly less likely to continue its full support and will either withdraw resources—witness the fate of many bond referenda—or will use its power to reallocate resources or to replace the staff with personnel who will accomplish the tasks expected in a manner acceptable to the demands of the community. The staff expectations for the community are that it will furnish the resources and support to implement the instructional program. Although the principal and staff have power in their expertise and the capability to withdraw their services if they do not receive adequate support, staff members are ultimately agents of the community and must either accommodate to community demands or change them.

Open and clear channels of communication must be maintained in order to optimize the instructional program. The message for those who would implement an instructional improvement is that the benefits and rewards of an innovation must be within the tolerance of community expectations. The principal plays a crucial role in identifying these expectations, in the short run, and in expanding them, in the long run. Thus, under the guidance of the principal and the IIC, the school and its community influence each other, as the process continually recycles.

Home-Unit Leader/I & R Unit

The focus here is on one specific sector of the community, namely the parents, who have expectations for the school which are quite specific. Often these expectations are influenced by their own children's situation and, therefore, are less objective than those held by the wider community. Parents also have a great and direct effect on the input of each child into the instructional program. Because of this intense interest in both the objectives of instruction and the means for achieving the objectives, parents generally are one of the most influential school-related groups and may have considerable impact on community awareness and educational policymaking within the larger community.

Because of the many changes required to implement IGE, parents must be presented with a clear picture of the cognitive, affective, and psychomotor development of their children and the procedures used in promoting

such development. This responsibility belongs to the unit leaders and the
I & R Units. From the point of view of the unit staff, the reality of the
intense family influence on children elucidates the necessity of parental inputs. The unit leader and unit staff must understand the home truly to
understand the child. Moreover, they depend on the home to support their
instructional programs for individual students.

Child-Teacher

At the center of Figure 6.1, the teacher utilizes the IPM to monitor the
learning program of each student. As the figure shows, the child's family
and community ties influence the student's attitudes, abilities, and skills.
Each teacher's understanding of these influences, as well as awareness of
the available resources in the home and the community, provide the teacher
with maximal operational input, thereby increasing each child's potential
for maximal operational output. This inner level of the model of home-
school-community relations is further discussed in section four of this
chapter.

CONCEPTS AND COMPETENCIES
OF THE PRINCIPAL AND STAFF

Four concepts and competencies must be developed in order to establish
and maintain an effective home-school-community relations program for
the implementation of IGE: analysis, communication, involvement, and
resolution. Both the principal and unit leaders must focus considerably on
communication and involvement. These concepts and competencies relate
to reporting pupil progress; conducting parent conferences; and utilizing
parent volunteers, paraprofessionals, aides, and student teachers. The principal and unit leaders, as members of the IIC, set and interpret school
policy and practices to staff, students, and parents through open, two-way
communication. The principal has two additional duties. First, the principal must ensure continuing and systematic analysis of the school community
in terms of subpublics, issues, and potential conflict. Second, the principal
must often initiate and frequently become involved in resolving actual or
potential conflict within the school community. While the four concepts and
competencies of analysis, communication, involvement, and resolution are
frequently interdependent, each can be analyzed separately.

Analysis

Analysis entails three distinct functions. First, it requires that the principal
identify the issues and issue elements. Second, it demands that the principal
identify the participant individuals and subpublics. Third, and finally, the

principal must associate the identified issues and issue elements with the participant individuals and subpublics so that some plan for communications, involvement, and resolution of conflict can be enhanced.

Issue identification.   There are several ways in which issues can be identified. The most obvious is the customary "on-the-job sense" of the practitioner. The principal who knows there is "something in the wind" when some aspect of IGE is being implemented has an intuitive grasp of possible issues. While this is certainly the most effortless way to know the issues, it is not always reliable, since the principal may be isolated from the source of issues for any number of reasons, among them: (1) newness in the community, (2) being outside of the customary lines of communication in the community, (3) the issues being incipient and having not reached the institutional or governmental stage, and (4) factionalism in the community which sometimes causes a principal identified with one faction to be outside the mainstream of communication about issues emanating from another faction. "On-the-job sense" tends only to detect the most vocal issues.

A second means of identifying issues is the use of a systematic survey. Such a survey could use the mails or volunteer interviewers, or it can be done informally at conferences depending on the objectives, sophistication, percentage of response, and quality of response desired. Utilization of this method is recommended in order to assess periodically the demise or emergence of issues in a school community. Its utility comes from its relatively objective format and from the fact that the periodic surveys can "catch changes over time."

A third common means of identifying issues involves in-depth, open-ended interviews with persons in the school community. (See subsequent sections of this chapter for a detailed discussion of the in-depth, open-ended interview.) The advantage of this method is that the in-depth interviews provide some flesh on the skeleton of response whereas the survey method provides a range of issues but little explanation. An in-depth interview not only can clarify issues but also suggest several courses of action for resolution of the issues, as well as persons to involve in resolving the issues. Moreover, the in-depth interview, when done periodically and without crisis attending it, creates little concern and is, in itself, a tremendously effective home-school-community relations technique.

A fourth means of identifying issues in a community is to employ some planned, participatory group dynamic process (Delbecq and Van deVen 1971, pp. 466–492). Participatory techniques have the advantage not only of identifying issues but also of developing priorities among them, as well as consideration of their resolution. A properly selected community group can set priorities and simultaneously begin working toward issue resolution.

Issue identification means more than the simple cataloging of topical concerns. If the identification of issues is to be effective in a home-school-community relations program, then the issues must be scrutinized for their component elements. Hence, the larger issue, for example, "discipline" in an IGE school, may have several elements. Some may understand the "discipline problem" to be one of "noise"; to others the problem may be one of "movement"; to still others it might be "unevenness of punishment for whites and blacks"; to still others it might be the lack of a "command presence" of teachers. Yet the "discipline" problem can neither be completely understood nor adequately resolved unless and until the principal can know what the individuals and groups mean by "discipline." "On-the-job sense" and surveys are less adequate than in-depth interviews and participatory techniques in isolating and analyzing the basic elements of an issue.

Identification of participant subpublics.   Participant subpublics include both individuals and groups, whether informal or organized, who are active or whom one could anticipate being active on a particular issue. There are three recognized means for identifying participants in a home-school-community relations program.

The first is the "role-position" technique. Role position is the simple process of identifying participants from their formal roles or positions in the community. For example, a participant is assumed to be one who is in a position or role to exercise influence, such as the superintendent, the parent-teacher organization president, a banker, a board member, etc. This method both assumes and ascribes an interest and influence to holders of status positions in the school community. Although this approach may be a useful starting point, it possesses certain flaws, because neither an interest in participating nor influence in controlling the resolution of an issue in a school-community necessarily follow from one's formal roles or positional status.

A second method for identifying participants is the reputational technique (Hunter 1953). This technique determines participant interest and influence by saying: "Name the persons whom you know are interested and influential in the affairs of our school community." If done systematically, the principal might start with a list of perhaps a hundred persons and then proceed to ask each of them the same question. That step might reduce the list to twenty-five frequently nominated persons. The process could be repeated with the twenty-five, perhaps yielding ten frequently nominated persons. The process might then be repeated with these ten, and so forth. The result is a pyramid of interested and influential persons with a few of reputed great interest and influence. One disadvantage of the reputational approach is that a pyramid always results whether one exists in reality or not; it may be perceived but not real. Another disadvantage is that it is difficult to associate the nominated people with the issues. The chief advantage is that the reputational technique can be done quickly and easily to identify people for subsequent in-depth interviews and "issue analysis."

A third technique for identifying participants is the "issue analysis" method (Dahl 1966). This technique requires that interviews be obtained with a number of persons. During the course of interviews, past issues are identified and the history or story of those issues explored. The respondent is asked to identify participants simultaneously with a discussion of the issues. Those persons identified with issues are assumed to be those with a continued interest and influence in school-community affairs. Disadvantages are that the technique is neither quick nor easy. Moreover, it relies heavily on history, and what may have been the case in the past may not be so today. Advantages are that respondents are less reluctant to discuss people in conjunction with past events than they are when associated with current affairs, and that this method identifies persons who do not necessarily occupy formal roles or positions.

Subpublic participants and issues.   The next step in conducting an analysis of the school community is to associate the participants with the issues and issue elements. It is very important that this step be taken because the processes of communication, involvement, and resolution are meaningless unless this association is made. After all, communication has to be to someone about something; involvement has to include someone for some purpose, and resolution requires that actual or potential conflict be resolved between two or more participant subpublics relative to specific issues. Moreover, participants have an interest in a school community relative to specific issues and issue elements. Their interest is not abstract and disassociated from the real political questions of allocating resources, values, and power or resolving manifest or latent conflict. The association of participants with issue elements will reveal the "stakes" which various parties have in the resolution of an issue.

"Stakes" is the direct, immediate association of an issue element with the individual participant or group making the demand. For example, for the issue of "open space" schools, individual A may demand "strict discipline and control"; group B may seek "a return to physically structured classrooms." Simultaneously, group C may demand wider, freer utilization of the open space, and individual D may want some structured space as an alternative for some children. While the issue, broadly conceived, is "open space," the issue elements or demands are linked or associated with the various participant individuals and groups. This linking or associating elements and demands with participants is the identification of "stakes." The final objective of analysis is understanding "stakes" because communication and resolution are both difficult if not impossible without this form of analysis.

We may take an illustrative issue and its several elements and develop a matrix which shows the stakes associated with the process of resolution. One IGE school was undergoing tremendous community pressure on a variety of issues. It was charged by the "Basic Education Group" that the open-concept building was creating an atmosphere of permissiveness (Issue 1). Another group in the community criticized the poor discipline in the school (Issue 2). The reading program was said not to "get at the fundamentals" (Issue 3). The individual learning stations were labeled as the source of discipline problems (Issue 2a). There were other charges in the general attack to return the school to more traditional ways. In this case, the principal and unit leaders undertook holding thirty interviews with citizens. The interviews averaged two hours each and explored the whole array of home-school-community problems, including "IGE problems." Participants were identified by using the issue analysis technique. After the issues were identified in the interviews, interviewers pressed for the issue elements. This is what they discovered. First, concerning permissiveness (Issue 1), it was learned that this issue was only symbolically associated with the building design; the real culprit issue element in Issue 1 was the change to a new reporting system (it was only coincidental that the new building came when As, Bs, and Cs went). Issue 2 was also not what it seemed, but also associated with the new parent-teacher conferences which no longer included a "citizenship" grade, as had the old report card. The reading program (Issue 3) was found, on in-depth issue analysis in the interviews not to be questioned at all. The only element at stake in this instance was the anxiety expressed by parents that their children "were no longer getting a normative evaluation as they did with the old report card." The high quality of the reading program was praised—much to the surprise of the interviewers. The teaching stations and discipline issues also proved to be a report card problem. There were also other issues associated with the school program which will not be elaborated upon here.

With this information, the IIC resolved the issues by (1) incorporating some aspects (normative elements) of the old reporting system, (2) retaining all other aspects of the newly adopted reporting system, and (3) changing nothing else in the IGE program. IGE in this school is now moving ahead due to the home-school-community relations program brought about through effective techniques of analysis and resolution. By contrast, the school had lost a principal, and several unit leaders had returned to staff-teaching positions in the three years prior because of their inability to handle such "hot" issues as "permissiveness," and "poor discipline."

Communication

Both the media (the means of communication) and the message (the substance of the communication) are vital. The influences of home, community, and school on the student have the potential to be supportive or inhibitive of learning. To maximize learning, communications must be open and clear, so that the media and the message are compatible. Communications have both form and direction; they may be written, verbal, or non-verbal. Nonverbal cues sometimes belie the comment to a parent, "Jimmy is doing just fine." This section focuses on several concepts of communication in which the principal must be competent: one-way/two-way communication, communication style, vehicles for communication, conditions for effective communication, and quality of the message.

One-way/two-way communication.* Regarding direction of communication, communication must be two-way, (school $\longleftrightarrow$ home), rather than one-way, (school $\longrightarrow$ home), for several reasons. What are the advantages and disadvantages of one-way and two-way communication?

One-way communication has generally been found (1) to be faster and more orderly, (2) to lack accuracy, (3) to be more enjoyable for the sender, (4) to be more frustrating for the receiver, (5) to place responsibility for understanding on the listener, (6) to treat all listeners as having the same physical and mental capabilities, (7) to cause the communicator who receives no feedback to interpret this as if it were positive feedback, and (8) to force the listener to greater concentration. Thus, some reasons for using one-way communication are to maintain orderliness and control, to communicate messages which are simple and concise, to speed up the communication process, to hide mistakes or to maintain ambiguity, to scapegoat others for sender mistakes and ambiguities, and to divide members of a group.

Two-way communication, on the other hand, (1) is slower, (2) is less orderly, (3) is more accurate, (4) is more enjoyable for the receiver, (5) is less enjoyable for senders due to the realization of their oversights and mistakes, (6) places responsibility on the receiver to seek clarification and on communicators to clarify, (7) forces the communicators to pace themselves to the slowest listener, and (8) allows one listener to receive additional cues from the questions of other listeners. Some reasons for using two-way communication are to increase accuracy of communication, to ensure that the intentions and nuances are understood, and to increase participation and satisfaction. Therefore, if time is limited and the message is simple, one should probably use one-way communication. On the other hand, if there is available time, if the message and its nuances are complex, and if there is a desire for improving satisfaction and group cohesiveness, two-way communication is absolutely essential.

Communication style. In terms of communication style, the concepts and principles discussed above are relevant here as well; however, there are

---

*   The material in this section was taken from F. C. Thiemann and C. S. Bumbarger 1971. *One-way and Two-way Communication Exercise Book.* In ERNSTSPIEL, Casea's Task Group Development Series, Eugene, Ore.: University of Oregon.

some primary concerns that are particularly important in the one-to-one relationship between principals and various subpublics.

Communication initiated by principals or teachers, whether vocal or written, should begin on a positive or neutral note. Even if the message in some way reflects a failure of the child, positive human relations require that the initial communication be positive; they can continue on negative as well as positive dimensions. Contact between school and parent should not focus only on negative behavior.

Communication should be made in language that is clear and sufficiently explicit to convey what is meant. In communicating with parents and others, educators should avoid pedagogical concepts, meaningless mnemonics, or technical terms. At the same time, one must beware of "talking down" to others. Some parents avoid contact with educators because of cross-cultural conflict; language is an essential factor in many of these instances.

Vehicles for communication.   The vehicles for staff-parent and principal-community program communication are another area of concern. Four modes of communication are: face-to-face, telephone conversations, written notes, and mass media techniques. Research has demonstrated that the most effective means of getting a message across is through face-to-face interaction, and the next most effective means, the use of the telephone. However, schools for the most part use mass media and written messages—the least effective techniques. In choosing the most appropriate vehicle, there should be a consideration of the degree of importance of the message, the time available for communication, the complexity of the message, and the specific receiver of the message. Failure to consider such variables will result in using vehicles of communication that are dysfunctional to an effective home-school-community relations program.

Conditions for effective communications.   Apart from the primary concerns of one-way/two-way communications, communications style, and vehicles for communication, another important concern for effective communication between principal and community subpublics is that of the conditions under which communication is conducted. Where face-to-face interaction is required, the conditions to be considered are time, location, and quality control.

Face-to-face communication should occur at the reasonable convenience of the parent—not solely as a result of the principal's schedule. This is not to suggest that instructional or planning time is to be taken from the principal, unit leader, teacher, or students, but that alternatives and contingencies should be available to meet parents at their convenience. Provisions may sometimes have to be made for released time to allow school personnel to meet with parents at their mutual convenience. The time should also be sufficient to allow full analysis, communication, and resolution of issues, as well as to reach agreement on a plan of action for the subsequent resolution of the problems or concerns.

The location of principal-parent communication is also important. Here is a good opportunity to exercise the "go-out-the-door" policy and meet the parents on their ground, rather than simply always meeting at the school. Occasionally, some parents may not wish to have school personnel come to the home. In any event, a place should be set aside where parents and the principal can interact in an environment free of disturbances and conducive to productive conversation and effective communication.

A final consideration concerning the conditions for effective communication is whether the nature of the communication is public or private. While the communication between a principal and parent is public in the sense of contributing to the effective education of the student, principals need to develop a sharpened sense of that which is strictly confidential (given to the principal alone), that which is professionally sound and required for effective functioning of the school relative to the student in question (given to the principal for sharing with other staff members of the school for the benefit of the child), and that which is extraneous information. Long-term as well as communitywide communications require the development of trust between principals and parents as to the relative confidentiality and professional use of their shared communications. Perceived violations of trust on the part of the principal quickly terminate any potential for ongoing, long-term, communitywide communications on a professionally sound and candid basis. Indeed, the breakdown of trust by a principal can build a suspicion of all educators who deal with the school community. In sum, principals must be professional, socially sensitive, intellectually honest, and mature in their professional and social behavior.

Quality of the message.   Finally, the quality of the message, whether verbal or written, ought to reach a standard that will ensure communication. Too often a note is written hastily and sent to parents containing insufficient information, some mistakes (technical or factual), and entirely too much information. While a conversational and extemporaneous quality ought to permeate verbal communications between principals and parents, these qualities ought not to be understood as synonymous with "playing it by ear" or lack of preparation as to information base and objectives, style, and conditions. Principals ought to keep communications factual, being based on anecdotal and other records, not just opinion. They also should plan their communication to avoid the problem of creating conflict, on the one hand, and consuming time, on the other.

In short, principals must become quite conscious of the factors contributing to effective communications and must utilize them effectively when communicating with parents and other subpublics.

Involvement

Although communication is a form of involvement, in the present context involvement means the active participation of the several subpublics in various aspects of analysis, communication, and actual or potential conflict resolution. The outcome is expected to be an improved instructional program. Involvement can include activities planned and organized by the principal and the IIC, such as meetings of the parent-teacher organization, back-to-school nights, volunteer programs, or other structured processes. Planned, structured involvement is defined as that which the principal has some reasonable degree of predictability on the course of events and control over the agenda of issue and/or participant subpublics. Involvement also includes unplanned and spontaneous interactions between parent and principal, confrontations wherein parent groups control the agenda, unannounced visits, or brainstorming and problem-solving sessions growing out of structured group processes. An unplanned, unstructured involvement is one in which the principal has relatively little control over the agenda or participants, and even less predictability about the ultimate course of events. It should be emphasized once again that since all subpublics in the school community have stakes in IGE, they should be appropriately involved as early as the commitment phase in the implementation of IGE.

Principals must necessarily reflect on which kinds of activities provide effective communication between the home, school, and community. Five activities customarily used in IGE schools are as follows: (1) home visits, (2) parent visits to the school, (3) parent conferences, (4) use of parent volunteers, and (5) parent representation on the I & R Units and the IIC. While certain of these activities are customarily conducted by the unit leaders and teachers, the principal not only must initiate effective communications practices, but also monitor the units to ensure that effective practices are indeed implemented.

Regarding home visits, dates and times must be at the option of the parent; a written message or phone call should precede each visit; the interaction should begin on a positive note; the visitor must perceive accurately the values and expectations of parents; and finally the visitor should avoid overstaying the welcome. Access to the home is based on the assumption that parents and educators are working cooperatively for the benefit of the child. Often the invitation to visit is initiated by the student. Frequently, members of the staff, such as the nurse or social worker, will have direct contact with the parent and access can come through such persons.

Parent visits to the school are a particularly productive form of staff-parent interaction. Apart from considerations of time and place discussed earlier, it is important that parental expectations, parental input, teachers' expectations for the role of the parent, and the general responsibility of the school be considered in scheduling parental visits. Frequently, the presence of an aide during a visit is an effective means of relieving anxieties and linking the common interests of staff and parents. For all parental visits, whether one-to-one, small group, or large gathering, a formal or informal plan for the meeting is a must. In practice, there usually is an agenda for large-group sessions, but too often in one-to-one encounters, the agenda is left to chance. Finally, the parent and the staff should have the benefit of a two-way debriefing period to reach closure at the end of the visit.

Many of the same concerns expressed for home and school visits also pertain to parent conferences. It is important to have an agenda, mutually agreed upon objectives, and an opportunity for two-way communication. In many cases, the student may be present as an active participant in the conference, making it very important that previous positive interactions have occurred. In some schools, more than one staff member of the unit meets with the parent; in others, only the "homeroom" teacher. Parents also may have a preference in this regard. The important thing is that the staff member has comprehensive data and supportive information about the individual child. Nothing is more destructive to the philosophy and practice of IGE than to have a staff member say, "I really don't know much about that. It is Mrs. Smith's area." An honest parental query might be, "Then why isn't Mrs. Smith here?" The concern, "Nobody knows anything about my child," must be rendered void.

Many parents and some teachers are apprehensive about conferences. An analysis of the neighborhood and previous communication either in large groups, by phone or written messages will add rapport to the conference, as will matters already mentioned, such as privacy, candor, and a sensible choice of time and location. These are crucial to the resolution of potential conflicts between the school and the home.

A fourth activity suggested is the use of parents or other citizens as volunteers in the instructional program. Such involvement can be clerical and passive, perhaps having volunteers listen to children read, or active participation in the instructional process. Volunteering for active interaction is frequently met with trepidation by both volunteers and teachers. Such fear is likely a function of lack of previous interaction, a fear of the unknown, and a result of being placed in a highly vulnerable environment. However, once the decision is made to recruit and utilize parents and citizens as volunteers, there are several considerations. First, the volunteer is participating on the school's terms and is bound by the policies, objectives, and procedures set forth by the school. Second, volunteers should not be thrown into situations they cannot handle or be asked to give more time than they have. Third, the purpose of an activity is not only to involve volunteers in routine tasks but to make the role diversified enough to maintain volunteer interest. It may take a special, schoolwide, inservice program to train volunteers to go from a passive to an active role.

A fifth suggestion is to enlist parent involvement in meetings and activities of the I & R Units, the IIC, and the SPC. The extent of such participation can range from serving as casual observers to that of permanent membership. Obviously, the role expectations of parent representatives must be clarified and internalized, since these groups inevitably deal with sensitive matters, such as staff performance and individual student achievement.

Implicit in the aforementioned suggestions is the assumption that when parents and other citizens become involved, the students benefit directly. Then, the parents of children in IGE schools, parents of children in other schools, parents of preschool and secondary school students, as well as nonparents in the community will likely perceive IGE as viable and will support its implementation.

Issue Resolution

The fourth basic concept is that of issue resolution. The processes of analysis, communication, and involvement are used in resolving actual or potential conflict, allocating resources, choosing values, and distributing power. Again, such resolution is an objective of the home-school-community relations program. Since there are several modes for resolving issues, the principal should be competent in judging when to employ which mode and should be skilled in implementing the chosen mode. The four modes of resolution are (1) the rational decision process, (2) persuasion, (3) bargaining, and (4) power play. The basic modes have been adapted from J. S. March and Herbert Simon, *Organizations.* New York: Wiley, 1963. The interpretation, however, is the responsibility of the authors.

Rational decision process.   The rational decision process is described in typical textbooks on administration as "decision making." Rational decision processes assume that the goals which participant subpublics have at stake are the same or mutually shared. In such instances, the participants can work together to achieve their common objectives. This form of resolution is most amenable to the usual communications, committees, group processes, and involvement mechanisms.

Persuasion.   Persuasion is used when the goals which participant subpublics have at issue are different, but the differences are *changeable*. That is, the participants enter into the process of resolution with differences but the differences are not sufficiently intense or so firmly held but that evidence, argumentation, and rhetoric will suffice to change the goals of one of the participants to coincide with the objectives of the other. In this instance, the participants employ both reason and emotion to alter the stakes of the other participant. When that is accomplished, the party which changed feels comfortable and adopts the objectives of the other participant.

Bargaining.   Bargaining is employed when the goals which participants have at issue are both *different* and *not changeable* but *negotiable*. Bargaining assumes that there will be no persuasion of either participant to the objectives of the other, and that the parties can negotiate so that one participant can gain one goal and lose another, and that the other participant can also gain or lose. Hence, bargaining involves a *quid pro quo* where both parties can gain, and lose too, but neither is brought to adopt the objectives of the other, as in the case of persuasion. By contrast with rational decision processes and persuasion, bargaining is a conflict and not a consensus, mode of resolution. The stakes and the risk tend to be greater and, because an accommodation on common objectives cannot be reached, it will always be in the interest of the participants to seek new, more advantageous *quid pro quos* as the participants' self-interests would dictate and as their power will allow.

Power play.   Power play is employed when the goals which participants have at issue are not only *different* but the goals are also *not changeable* and *not negotiable*. It is a case where neither persuasion nor bargaining are useful means of resolution, and one participant must prevail in his goal over the other participant due solely to his power advantage. Needless to say, the use of power play does not necessitate a great deal of involvement— only a raw exercise of power. Power play results in a loser and a winner and considerable residual animosity on the part of the loser toward the winner—animosity which can always return to disrupt the pacificity of the system.

In implementing IGE, the principal may employ several modes to resolve home-school-community relations problems. To reiterate, the principal must be able to analyze issues properly, communicate effectively, involve others appropriately, and utilize the best mode for resolution—rational decision making, persuasion, bargaining, or power-play techniques, as the situation dictates.

HOME-SCHOOL-COMMUNITY RELATIONS AND INSTRUCTIONAL PROGRAMMING

The Instructional Programming Model, described earlier in Chapter 3, assumes an understanding of the students which can only be gained through comprehensive knowledge and appreciation of the home and community as they impinge upon the students. One cannot, for example, "state the educational objectives to be attained by the student population . . ." (Step 1) or "assess the level of achievement, learning style, and motivational level of each student . . ." (Step 3) without an understanding of the student's home conditions. If, as in Step 6a of the IPM "The objectives were not attained," what form should reprogramming and reassessment take?

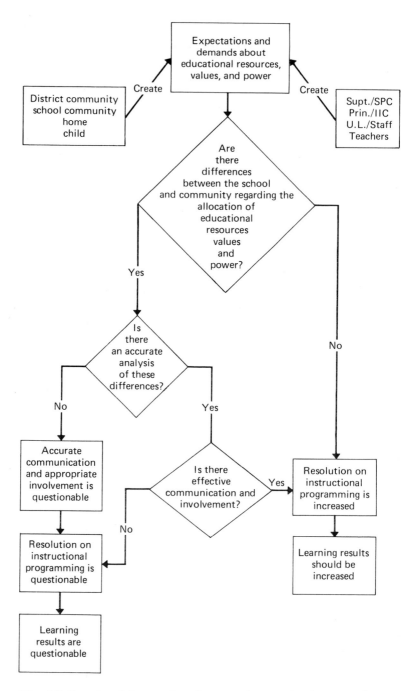

Fig. 6.2 Functional interactions between home-school-community relations and instructional programming.

Figure 6.2 presents the major concepts of the Home-school-community Relations Model in a functional flowchart and relates them to the IPM. The top row of rectangles is merely an abbreviated version of the primary interactors specified in Figure 6.1. A major assumption which underlies this flowchart is that learning outcomes will be increased if there is agreement among the major participants within the school community on the allocation of resources, choice of values, and distribution of power regarding educational issues. As shown in Figure 6.2, in instances where differences occur, where there is an accurate analysis of what those differences are, and where there is effective communication and involvement of the major participants, then conflict on instructional programming is more likely to be resolved, and learning outcomes should be improved. Inaccurate analysis, inaccurate communication, or inappropriate involvement of the major participants will affect the instructional program adversely.

COMMUNICATION AND INVOLVEMENT ACTIVITIES OF PRINCIPALS

This section describes some exemplary activities which IGE principals can use to improve home-school-community relations through better analysis, communication, involvement, and resolution. Some of the activities were identified in a series of case studies on home-school-community relations conducted by the Wisconsin Research and Development Center (Miles *et al.* in press); others were contributed by principals, unit leaders, and teachers in IGE schools across the nation.

In-depth Interviews as an Analysis Activity

The use of in-depth interviews to analyze school community has proven quite successful. This technique possesses a number of virtues. First, it provides the opportunity for an informal, positive, and noncrisis contact with community subpublics. Second, it is an effective means of communications regardless of any other objectives for which it might be used simultaneously. Third, the interviews identify the important subpublics and issues in the school community both historically and currently. Fourth, the technique can suggest mechanisms for the resolution of actual or potential conflict growing out of the issues and among the subpublics identified during the course of the interviews. Fifth, interviews have proven to be a successful training ground for interpersonal communication with a variety of subpublics, using their agenda, at their designated time, and usually on their territory. Sixth, a relatively thorough analysis of an elementary school attendance area can be accomplished with perhaps twenty, and normally no more than thirty-five interviews. Finally, this technique can be executed with a minimal investment in inservice training for interviewing and analysis.

Customarily, the principal, the IIC, the staff and parents can be trained for interviewing in two to three hours without a practicum and about five to six hours with a practicum. The real advantage of this technique is that with some experience, the original interviewers can train subsequent interviewers. Hence, the in-depth interview technique possesses the potential for utilizing the critical concepts and competencies discussed earlier, analysis, communication, involvement, and resolution.

Setting the objectives of the interviews.   The in-depth interview technique can be used during times of crisis, as well as during periods of tranquility. When used in crisis situations, the customary objectives are to determine: (1) which subpublics have an interest in the outcome of issues; (2) what are the issues that precipitate the crisis; (3) what are the associations or links of the various subpublics with the issues; and (4) what are possible alternative mechanisms for resolving the conflict? Hence, when in-depth interviews are used for crisis management, the ultimate objective is to gain information which will contribute to the resolution of a particular set of issues.

On the other hand, when the in-depth interview technique is used in the absence of crisis, the emphasis on resolution is a minor objective. In these cases, the objectives are generally those of (1) identification of any and all significant subpublics, rather than those associated with particular past events or controversies; (2) identification of the wide range of issues, problems, and concerns, both past and present; and (3) association of subpublics with issues.

The illustrations of the in-depth interview technique in this section assume that the process will take place during times of tranquility rather than times of crisis. It also may be assumed that the primary objective is to find out about the "home-school-community relations program." The objective could be as broad as "the success of the school" or perhaps as narrow as "reading achievement." Experience has shown that relatively narrow objectives prove less fruitful than broadly defined objectives. Moreover, restrictive topics inevitably emerge as "issues" when broad-range objectives are explored, but rarely will real problems or "other" issues emerge if the topic is narrowly defined. Hence, a focus as broad as the "home-school-community relations program" will usually stimulate general concerns, as well as specific issues, such as "grading," "reading," and "discipline."

The focus on "home-school-community relations" is also a good one for the initial venture into in-depth interviewing, because it normally provides easy, justifiable access to people in the school community. For example, it is easier for a principal to explain an interest in getting the opinion of various subpublics on the question of school-community relations than it is on other topics. Moreover, a focus on home-school-community relations is often perceived as an effort, in itself, to improve relationships.

The interview schedule.   Physically, the interview schedule can be as small as a 5″ by 8″ card with questions or stimulus words on it, or it can be an elaborate schedule with space available for recording responses.

Although open-ended, in-depth interviews may not follow a programmed script, a sample interview schedule follows:

Sample In-depth Interview Schedule

1. Name of respondent _____

   Address _____

   Telephone number _____

2. Introduction of interviewer and statement of purposes and uses

   a. Who is the interviewer? What is the relationship of the interviewer to the school community?

   b. Objectives of the interview: To discuss the home-school-community relations of _____ School with its community and to obtain opinions on means to improve the more positive aspects and eliminate the more negative aspects.

   c. How was the respondent's name selected?

   d. Confidentiality: How will the data be used? Who will have access to the interview data? Is there to be a report? Who will have access to it? Will there be anonymity for respondents?

3. Biographical data on the respondent

   a. Personal data: How long in the community? How long in the school? Educational background?

   b. Family data: How many children? In what schools? Names, grades and ages of children? What has been their experience generally in school?

   c. Please describe your relationship with _____ School, particularly as it has related to your child(ren), _____, _____, and _____, and the home-school-commu-

nity relationships you and your child or children have experienced at
_____ School.

4. What are the more positive aspects of school-community relations with
   respect to _____ School and the community it serves?

   Negative aspects?

5. What are some of the issues, concerns, or problems regarding school-
   community relations between _____ School and its community?

   Are there other issues, concerns, or problems?

   Are there other people who feel as you do about these issues, problems,
   and concerns?

6. Who are some of the people or groups who are most interested, knowledgeable, and concerned about school-community relations?
   How do they feel about the issues, concerns, or problems enumerated
   above?

7. Are there any other issues, problems, or concerns which you have not
   identified? people and groups?

8. Are there any problems in home-school-community relations regarding
   the following school practices?

   a. Discipline

   b. Reading   Are there other people or
                                 groups who feel as you do
   c. Report cards   about these problems,
                                 issues, or concerns?
   d. Transportation

   e. Other

9. It would appear from our discussion that Mr. _____ and
   Ms. _____ are quite knowledgeable about _____
   School and its school-community relations program. I don't know them
   very well; I am wondering whether you would be willing to call them
   and provide reference for me so that I could talk to them, or maybe

write them or, if there is some inconvenience in that, if you would allow
me to use your name in reference when I call them.

10. May I call on you again if I find that I require more information or
    that my information is incomplete on certain items?

11. Thanks.

12. (Write a letter of thanks soon after the interview.)

The data obtained in Item 1 are obviously necessary for coding. The
purpose of Item 2 is to set the respondent at ease, anticipate and answer
most of the questions regarding "Who?", "Why?", and "How?" This
section should be designed to answer all questions candidly and parsimoni-
ously; it is not detailed. The reason for Item 3 is to obtain biographical
data to personalize relationships with the school. Item 4 elicits negative or
positive reactions regarding home-school-community relations. Items 5, 6,
and 7 identify issues in home-school-community relations and link them
with subpublics. Item 8 is the checklist question; here specific issues or
problems of interest to the interviewer can be probed. It is important that
this question come after and not before the voluntary nomination of issues
and subpublics contained in Items 5–7. Item 9 seeks the assistance of the
respondent in obtaining another interview or in contacting or referencing
the interviewer to the next respondent. Item 10 guarantees that should the
interviewer require additional information, a return visit will be easier. Items
11 and 12 provide customary courtesies which, unfortunately, are too often
forgotten.

The respondent sample.   Typically, the attendance area of an elementary
school of 300–1000 students can be adequately analyzed with approximately thirty interviews. The following procedure has proven highly successful in choosing respondents. The principal and the IIC should first nominate
about seven knowledgeable, influential people associated with the school.
The parents, including parent-teacher organization officials, should nominate about seven respondents using the same criteria. Seven respondents
should then be chosen randomly from the school files, representing a
range of grades in the school. The other nine will be determined from
nominations obtained in the course of the first interviews from references
secured from the answers to Item 9. Of course, additional nominations
should always be obtained in the possibility that some of those identified are
unable or unwilling to participate.

The training of interviewers.   Three to five interviewers can adequately conduct the approximately thirty interviews. In some situations this has frequently included several principals cooperating to help analyze each other's school communities. In the more typical situation, the staff of an elementary school does the job, sometimes with the help of selected parent volunteers. The necessary training can be accomplished in as short as two and one-half hours; satisfactory results have been obtained using several short sessions. The training sessions deal with the objectives of the in-depth interviews, framing of a common instrument, rehearsing the lines of questioning, and demonstrating interview techniques with one or more persons doing the interviewing, followed by critique. A list of Dos and Don'ts should be reviewed including, but not limited to, the following:

- Maintain and record the time reference of the respondent. Try to get times, dates, years. If not specifics, obtain *befores* and *afters*. Don't let any issues of people pass in the interview without placing in a time reference. Sometimes it will be necessary to interrupt the respondent for this information.

- Names must be obtained. There should not be a single pronoun used without the interviewer noting the referent or securing the specific name. This includes the generic "they" as well.

- All issues need to be operationalized into their elements. For example, when discipline is brought up by the respondent, the interviewer needs to say, "What do you mean by discipline?" Then ask for illustrations.

- All people and groups must have their association and attitudes toward the issues explored as fully as possible. Do not let either people or issues become disassociated from each other. When people are mentioned, encourage the respondent to associate them with issues, and vice versa.

- Save the interviewer's favorite people, groups, and issues for the checklist at the end. Let the respondents nominate their agenda of people and issues; don't force the respondents to react to the interviewers agenda.

- Don't use a tape recorder.

- Don't exchange information obtained in one interview with the respondent in another interview, even if asked.

- Do answer all inquiries about the interviewer, the objectives, and how the data will be used; don't be so verbose and elaborate that the interviewer raises more questions and "red flags" than can be answered.

- Don't intervene in the philosophical, sentimental, or value systems of the respondent by either disagreeing or agreeing.
- Reconstruct the entire interview verbatim as soon after the interview as possible. Don't delay putting scratch notes into decipherable order.

Finally, the means of access and courtesies of exit are emphasized. The in-depth interview process can be a great boon to school-community relations if access is handled properly and thanks given sincerely. Since a well-trained interviewer will require about two hours for the interview, it is necessary to make preliminary calls. Customarily, a letter to the prospective respondent is mailed indicating how the respondent was chosen, asking the respondent's assistance, and stating that the interviewer will be telephoning to determine the best time and place for the interview. When this telephone call is made, the two-hour time block should be emphasized, and the interview should be scheduled at the time convenient to the respondent, even if it is outside normal working hours. Next, the place convenient for the interviewee should be determined—avoiding the school unless the respondent insists.

At the conclusion of the training sessions, the trainer should briefly review what will happen at the debriefing sessions and the types of data and objectives that will be most useful in explaining home-school-community relations. Finally, the trainer stresses the ethics of confidentiality of data. While much of the data will be openly discussed among the interviewers during the debriefing sessions, the interviewers are reminded that some of the data were not intended for direct attribution, but were provided only for the ears of the interviewer. In short, gossip stops when the interview begins.

Making sense of the data. The trainer should return and help make sense of the data at the debriefing sessions. These sessions obtain the best results when the discussion leader asks one of the interviewers for the most critical issue nominated in the course of the interview. Those data are placed on a chalkboard and the leader then encourages all other interviewers to respond to that issue—indicating names associated with the issues, attitudes and dispositions toward the issues, linkages among the individuals or groups relative to the issues, operational definitions of the issues, and some specific examples. The result should be several issues which are identified, defined, and exampled with notations of distinctive differences in definition of issues and examples provided by different sets of respondent subpublics.

Next, another interviewer is asked to group people and their associated organizations according to their disposition toward the various issues. The result should be a sociometric-type chart indicating the groups, their interrelationships, and interactions. Finally, the discussion leader should seek out possible alternative solutions and mechanisms for the resolution of actual or potential conflict concerning each of the nominated issues. The overall outcomes are: (1) a set of issues which become the IGE principal's list of home-school-community relations priorities to resolve; (2) individuals or groups of people who might be used in further school-community relations activities and in the resolution of actual or potential conflict in the community; and (3) recommended (by respondents) means and mechanisms for resolving conflict concerning the key nominated issues.

Communication Activities

A number of communication activities have proven successful in the home-school-community relations programs of IGE schools. This section describes four mechanisms which can be readily utilized by principals.

The local press.   Certain principles and practices of successfully working with newspapers are basic. Several IGE schools have followed most of these principles and practices and have developed an excellent relationship with the local newspaper—so much so that the successful implementation of IGE can be in large measure attributed to general public support of IGE growing out of newspaper coverage. We may consider an outstanding example, the Darlington Elementary Schools, Darlington, Wisconsin.

The first step taken by the principal was to hold unit leaders and teachers responsible for reporting specific events and activities to the local press. Specifically, the principal encouraged the reporting of tangible, visible, and successful unit activities. Teachers responsible for special activities (art, music, and physical education) also reported on their special events and programs. District and schoolwide policies and programs were the unique province of the principal and the IIC, as was the responsibility of coordinating and "spreading out" press coverage of the school.

The second effort of the principal was to have all the staff—usually in groups of five—visit the offices of the newspaper, meet the education editor, and have good give-and-take sessions on what the newspaper was and was not capable of doing. These interactions overcame staff reluctance to work closely with the people at the newspaper, including telephoning when something newsworthy was to take place in the unit, writing brief press releases, or providing pictures to highlight IGE activities.

The third operational activity was to provide pictures for all news releases. This required that a camera (one was donated by the parent-teacher organization) be available when the newspaper could not send out a photographer. Annually taken pictures of all staff members and children were also placed on file with the newspaper.

The fourth step was to ensure that newspaper personnel were on the invitation list to all school activities. In many instances, the customary invitations to school affairs were followed by special telephone and personal invitations.

Fifth, the upper intermediate I & R Units developed and published their own school newspaper four times a year. The newspaper allowed the units to have a small group learn the production process at the newspaper. This same group subsequently served as a small cadre of reporters who developed stories about the school as a part of their language arts activities; their products appeared in both the community paper and school newspaper.

Finally, the staff aggressively provided articles and pictures to the newspaper; they did not wait for the newspaper to come to them. The effective outcome of these practices was an estimated average of at least five column inches of coverage, plus pictures, for this IGE elementary school every week. Frequently, there was broad coverage of important school events. Three or four times a year the newspaper featured some special aspect of the IGE program with full page coverage.

Newsletters.   The use of a monthly, biweekly, or, in some cases, a weekly newsletter is a communication activity often used in IGE schools. For example, in one IGE school, the Beattie Elementary School in Fort Collins, Colorado, the monthly newsletter is coordinated by the parent-teacher organization. Parents come to the staff for material, then write the stories, edit the copy, and distribute the newsletter throughout the school community. The newsletter chronicles meetings and events and alerts parents to future meetings, activities, and programs. It also gives the principal and the IIC an opportunity to communicate with a large audience about present concerns and future plans.

In another IGE school, the Jefferson Elementary School in Pueblo, Colorado, the monthly newsletter is a major responsibility of the principal. In this instance, the principal seeks out the information and assumes the responsibility for the preparation and distribution of the newsletter. In this case, the principal uses the newsletter to keep constantly in tune with the activities of the I & R Units. Parental reactions to the newsletter were uniformly laudatory: "It's my number one way of finding out what is happening at school," and "I would really miss it if it were discontinued."

Parents' handbook.   In many IGE schools, as for example, in the Franklin Sherman Elementary School of McLean, Virginia, a handbook for parents is revised annually and distributed widely. Such handbooks are often written by the principal in collaboration with the IIC, unit staffs, and parents. As one handbook says, "It covers about as much information about policy and local customs as we can think of, so that you and the children will be at home in your school." It also provides information on a number of ways parents might be involved in the school, among them:

1. Parents are welcome: Join us for lunch any day. Just let us know in the morning;

2. Visiting school classes: Make your date through the school office. A classroom observation may be arranged at any time after mid-September;

3. Parent coffees: Parent coffees with the principal, unit leaders, and teachers will be held monthly on the first Wednesday of the month at 9:30 A.M. Come and talk about what we are doing, tell us what you are thinking about, your ideas, your suggestions, your concerns—and your good comments, too;

4. Join the volunteer aide program: We need you at school! Whatever your time or talents, share them with us. There is no finer reward than working with children. If you have special talents, we'd love to have you share them with us. Please let us know. You can contribute to a much richer program for the children.

Informal coffee meetings.   In many IGE schools, informal coffee meetings are held with parents. In the Beattie Elementary School, Fort Collins, Colorado, the principal initiated a kaffeeklatsch program at school for "first-year" IGE parents. This principal asks ten or twelve parents to come to coffee on Thursday morning to discuss schoolwide problems and programs. The parents then spend the remainder of the morning visiting with their children for instruction, and then staying for lunch. For second-year parents, the principal held informal coffees in homes, rather than at school. The principal asked the parents to serve as hosts, assisted them in determining whom to invite, set initial agenda, and then announced the semester's schedule in the monthly newsletter.

What was the net result of the kaffeeklatsch program? First-year parents were definitely enthusiastic about having an opportunity to "get their hands on IGE" and "get a feeling about what was going on in the school." The program also created a cadre of informed parents who had actually been in the school and could report information factually. In addition, the program also served as a ventilation device for those who might have questions about programs or policies.

Involvement Activities

Parent-teacher organizations, parent advisory boards, and volunteer programs are useful mechanisms for achieving meaningful and active parent and citizen involvement in the program of the school.

Parent-teacher organizations. Parent-teacher organizations are vital in many IGE schools. For example, in one IGE school the parent-teacher organization is the vehicle for obtaining parent representation on the IIC and to the I & R Units. The result is that the parent representatives are full participants, offering invaluable insight into the operation of the school, issues in the community, and the expectations of the various subpublics. The formal inclusion of parents in the operating structure of an IGE school provides firsthand, reality-based input from the community.

In another IGE school, the parent-teacher organization is systematically oriented to solving current issues facing the school. The principal and the IIC stimulate participation, discussion, and action concerning the current and prospective issues confronting the school. Specifically, the principal helps the parent-teacher organization to identify issues and problems, establish priorities, and create task forces to attack each problem. Task forces are scheduled in phases, to permit a systematic solution of problems. For example, one parent-teacher task force may be identifying issues; another, defining issues; another, setting priorities; and still another, implementing solutions. The cycle is continuous, keeping many persons working systematically on priority tasks.

Membership in the parent-teacher organization must always be open. Moreover, task force memberships should be available "for one more member." Such efforts have assured a continued representative, legitimate involvement of the community in several IGE schools.

Parent advisory boards. In some communities, parent advisory boards have been mandated by board of education policy to function as mini-boards of education, to act as means of communication, and to serve as buffers between the central office/Systemwide Program Committee and the school/Instructional Improvement Committee. The Beattie Elementary School in Fort Collins, Colorado, formed its parent advisory board through the initiative of the principal. The principal sent out letters to all families outlining his concern for organized parental involvement. A meeting was announced for all interested parties to attend. At the meeting, a parent-teacher organization was organized for general communications, fund-raising, and social activities, and a parent advisory board of eleven members was elected (nine directly elected, one parent-teacher organization official, and the principal). The mandate given the parent advisory board was to assist in the task of formulating school policy on an advisory basis. Parent advisory councils are also capable of playing an advocate's role before the board of education when the interests and programs of the school are at stake. Of course, they muster considerable talent and human resources to tackle topics of importance to the implementation of IGE.

Volunteer aide programs.   An important distinction must be drawn between the expectations of parents with children in school and others who participate in volunteer aide programs whether paid or unpaid, whether full-time or part-time. Research has shown that parents with children in school expect their job assignments and duties to place them in frequent interaction with the teachers of their children. Put differently, job satisfaction on the part of participant parents and overall success of the volunteer aide program depends on parental contact with teachers far more than any other factor. Many of those who volunteer as aides have internalized the norm, "It is the job of the teachers to teach without 'interference' from parents." Although the volunteers viewed certain parent-initiated activities as "interference," they found volunteer participation to be both satisfactory and legitimate. The operational conclusion is forthright: In coordinating the volunteer program, principals of IGE schools would be well advised to assign parent volunteers so that they can interact frequently and meaningfully with the teachers of their children.

Resolution

This section sets forth two mechanisms utilized in IGE schools for the resolution of actual or potential conflict: the nominal group process/problem-solution groups, and the use of block parents.

Problem-solution groups.   As indicated earlier in Chapter 4, the nominal group process is useful for identifying and assigning priorities to issues to be resolved. Problem-solution groups consisting of participants in the nominal group process (Delbecq and Van deVen 1971), may be used to resolve the issues. To be effective such groups should follow certain structural and procedural guidelines. If twenty-five persons participated in the nominal group process, for example, this number would then be broken down into five groups of five persons each, called problem-solution groups. Each of the five groups should proportionally represent such factions or divergent subpublics as may exist.

Each of the five problem-solution groups is then given one of the problems or issues of top priority which resulted from the nominal group process. The problem-solution groups then work on one distinct issue for perhaps an hour. During that time the groups must define the problem more precisely, illustrate the nature of the problem through examples, and, most importantly, begin to offer solutions to the problem. In IGE schools, the principal and unit leaders initially chair the groups. The task of each group is to suggest as many separate and distinct solutions as possible and seek total consensus on the definition of the problem and proposed solutions or courses of action.

It is unlikely that all the solutions will be proposed or consensus reached by the end of an hour. Even so, a representative of the first problem-solution group is asked to take the report of his or her group and move physically to the second problem solution group (a representative from group two moves to group three; from group three to group four; from group four to group five, and from group five moves to group one). Then, the representatives present the problem definition and proposed solutions to these new groups which are asked to modify the definition of the problem and offer additional solutions, modify solutions offered by the previous group, or eliminate previously suggested solutions, and gain consensus. The second work period typically takes half an hour. When the half-hour is concluded, the same initial representative from group one who had spent the half-hour with group two now moves to group three (group two representative moves to four, group three to five, and group four to one, and group five to two). The process is repeated, except now the time is shortened to fifteen minutes. The rotations are repeated at fifteen minute intervals until there is consensus on all problem definitions and proposed solutions by everyone in all groups. Normally, this process takes several rounds to obtain satisfactory problem definitions and efficacious solutions.

Whereas the nominal group process is an excellent vehicle for identifying and rank-ordering problems, problem-solution groups are an excellent mechanism for clarifying and redefining problems, rationally generating and examining alternative solutions, forcing agreement on problem definitions, and achieving consensus on solutions—which courses of action to follow. The nominal group process and problem solution groups may be used with staff, students, or parents or combination of any subpublics, depending on the groups, issues, and desired outcomes (Bowles and Fruth 1975).

Block parent program.   Some IGE principals have developed an effective communication and crisis management technique called the Block Parent Program. In one IGE school a pyramidal communication network was formed whereby when needed two parents from each I & R Unit would contact five other parents, those five would contact another five, and so on, until all parents would be quickly and effectively contacted. Subsequently, the system was expanded to include nonparent adults. The result was that in the matter of a few hours all citizens were assured of relatively accurate and timely information. In times of manifest conflict the Block Parent communications network proved to be extremely effective. Similar communications networks have been used to generate support for the local IGE school, pass bond referenda, and lobby in support of favorable state legislation. Such a system requires an excellent parent-teacher organization or volunteer program, an annual survey of participant parents and interested citizens, a natural selection of responsible parents near the top of the communications pyramid, and periodic usage, so that the system does not atrophy.

SUMMARY

This chapter first identified the goals of the home-school-community relations program as those which make the staff of an IGE school more aware of and effective in its work with the school community, make the community more aware of and effective in its work with the school, and identify means for encouraging the implementation of IGE by the appropriate involvement of the staff, parents, and other subpublics in the community.

Next, several operational assumptions about home-school-community relations were set forth for the principal, including the belief that home-school-community relations is, in the final analysis, a political process operating within a complex and interactive social system consisting of the home, the school, and the community. A primary objective of the home-school-community relations program was stated as the resolution of actual or potential conflict over the allocation of scarce resources, differing values, and unequal distribution and exercise of authority and power.

Then, a two-part model of home-school-community relations was set forth. This model defined Primary Interaction Patterns as being between the school-community and the principal/IIC, the home and the unit leader/I & R Unit, and the child and the teachers. The second major dimension of the model included the following concepts and competencies: analysis, communication, involvement, and resolution. A flowchart traced the major functional interactions between home-school-community relations and instructional programming for the individual student.

The chapter concluded with a description of several exemplary tools and techniques for improving home-school-community relations through better analysis, communication, involvement, and resolution. These included: conducting in-depth interviews; working with the local press; publishing school newsletters and handbooks; meeting in coffee groups; working with parent-teacher organizations and parent advisory committees; utilizing volunteer aides; conducting problem-solution group meetings; and using block parent programs. Throughout, it was shown how the quality of the principal's leadership in utilizing each of the techniques is crucial to the success of the home-school-community relations program.

REFERENCES

Bowles, B. D., and M. J. Fruth 1975. *Problem solution groups.* Mimeographed, 3 pp. Madison, Wisc.: Department of Educational Administration, University of Wisconsin—Madison.

Dahl, R. A. 1966. *Who governs? democracy and power in an American city.* New Haven: Yale University Press.

Delbecq, A. L., and A. H. Van deVen 1971. A group process model for problem identification and program planning. *Journal of Applied Behavioral Science* **7**.

Hunter, F. 1953. *Community power structure: a study of decision makers.* Chapel Hill, N.C.: University of North Carolina Press.

March, J. S., and H. Simon 1963. *Organizations.* New York: Wiley.

Miles, W. R., B. D. Bowles, and M. J. Fruth 1975. *Casebook on home-school-community relations programs and activities and the implementation of IGE.* Madison, Wisc.: Wisconsin Research and Development Center for Cognitive Learning.

Thiemann, F. C., and C. S. Bumbarger 1971. *One-way and two-way communication exercise book.* ERNSTSPIEL, Casea's Task Group Development Series, Eugene, Ore.: University of Oregon.

7

Managing Financial and Physical Resources

Richard A. Rossmiller
James M. Lipham
Joseph J. Marinelli

Objectives

After reading this chapter, the reader will be able:

- To understand the relationship between economics and education.
- To recognize the relationship between environmental effects and learning processes.
- To understand the relationship between school resources and educational outputs.
- To comprehend how the components of IGE may be utilized to maximize student learning.
- To comprehend the unique aspects of providing resources in IGE schools.
- To comprehend the different cost configurations in IGE schools.

IGE makes it easier for a school staff to maximize productivity and satisfy demands for accountability. To achieve the full potential of IGE, however, the principal, unit leaders, and teachers must be able to capitalize on those unique IGE characteristics which facilitate the efficient use of all of the resources which they can draw upon to create the best possible learning environment for students.

In this chapter, a brief discussion of economics and education introduces consideration of the link between learning and the appropriate use of human and material resources. To clarify the relationship, a conceptual framework is presented which links resources, the instructional process, and learning outcomes. This framework portrays the various elements of a school as an educational system in dynamic interplay as that system strives to realize the goals set for the school. After each element is defined, it is shown how emerging systems concepts of program analysis and cost-effectiveness analysis are useful to the principal and the staff in managing resources.

Next in the chapter it is shown how each component of IGE helps maximize the use of resources. Particular attention is paid to the uniqueness of the budget-making process and the utilization of personnel, materials and equipment, and the physical plant in IGE schools.

School districts interested in implementing IGE are naturally concerned with its relative cost compared with other forms of schooling. The chapter concludes by citing the results of two recent research studies which illuminate this issue.

ECONOMICS AND EDUCATION

Although philosophical linkages between education and economics can be traced to Adam Smith, the growing interest in the economic aspects of education during the past decade is based less on theoretical than on practical grounds. Three reasons for this growing interest can be identified: (1) the realization that education is one of our largest industries and one of the chief employers of highly skilled personnel, (2) the recognition that education may influence significantly employment and income opportunities and thus affect the distribution of income and wealth in society, and (3) the recent emphasis on economic growth and development in which education plays an important role as the provider of skilled personnel (O'Donoghue 1971, p. 1).

With respect to the economic magnitude of education, during 1972–73 a total of $89.5 billion was spent by educational institutions in the United States and an estimated 6.4 million persons were employed by these institutions. Public elementary and secondary schools alone expended $57.3 billion and employed over three million persons (NEA 1973). The size of the school age population is the major determinant of demand for services of teachers and other highly trained professional personnel. When students are included, well over one-fourth of the population of the United States is directly or indirectly engaged in the educational enterprise.

Concerning the influence of education on wealth and economic growth, economists, following the lead of Schultz (1963, pp. x–xi), became interested in the concept of human capital, for they found that not all economic growth could be explained by land (natural resources), labor (human services), and capital (means of production) alone. It was found that well over half of the total economic growth for the postwar years in most western countries could not be accounted for by these traditional factors of production, and education was one of the most likely candidates put forth to claim the honors. The view that education is a form of human capital is based on the notion that skills and knowledge possessed by people are in fact resources, and that the skills and knowledge possessed by people are a very important part of the capital available to any society. Although there is considerable debate over the extent to which formal education influences economic growth, it is generally believed to be a significant factor.

A question of great importance to society is whether or not the resources allocated to education are being used efficiently. To answer questions about efficiency one must be able to specify what resources are needed, and in what quantity and in what combination with other resources, to produce a desired level of knowledge, skills, or behavior specified as the desired outcome of instruction. Educators are confronted with such questions as: Do differences in resources lead to different educational outcomes? What school characteristics, configurations, and programs lead to differences in outcomes? What impact do schools have on students? Methodologically adequate research evidence is difficult to find, since schools are not ideal natural "laboratories" in which one can manipulate organizational features, such as the distribution and utilization of resources, the composition of the student body, the placement of students into programs, the methods of instruction and evaluation, or the operational objectives of school programs. Despite these difficulties, however, educators cannot avoid the question of whether or not the resources at their disposal are being allocated in the most effective way.

Numerous studies have attempted to relate levels of resource input to the results of schooling, typically using some measure of student achievement. For example, some researchers have found a statistically significant relationship between the teacher's verbal ability and student achievement in language arts. Other researchers have found that the teacher's educational training and experience correlate positively with student achievement, as does the overall student-teacher ratio. School facilities, as measured by such variables as size, age, use, and availability of equipment and materials, also have been shown to affect student achievement. A significant relationship between instructional expenditure per pupil and student achievement has consistently been found.

Aspects of the general educational environment which bear upon the student are also worthy of mention. Studies have revealed that the student's mental ability, educational background, aspiration, interests, attitudes, and self-concept are related to the student's success in school. In addition to the attributes of students themselves, progress in school also has shown high correlations with family income, value of family dwelling, and parental occupation.

An awareness of the linkages between characteristics of students, teachers, the school, and its environment with student learning outcomes is necessary if the school is to deliver the best combination of human and material resources to its students in an IGE setting. One way to understand these linkages is to build a conceptual framework which depicts some of the important linkages.

A CONCEPTUAL FRAMEWORK LINKING SCHOOL RESOURCES AND EDUCATIONAL OUTCOMES

A model which portrays a school as a system provides a useful framework for viewing the process of allocating resources. The framework shown in Figure 7.1 is equally useful for viewing a unit, a school, a district, or even a state as an educational system. This framework portrays the linkage of the resources the school obtains from its external environment to the edu-

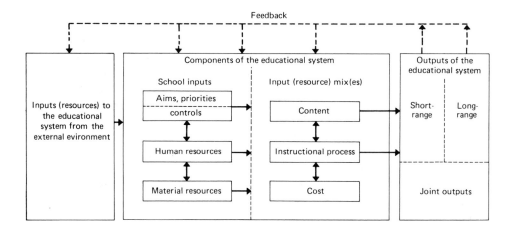

Fig. 7.1 Model of the school as a system.

cational process which occurs in the school to a set of outputs which represent the outcomes (or outputs) of the educational process. Feedback ties the outcomes to both the educational process and the resource inputs so that changes can be made either to modify the process or change the inputs in order to accomplish the objectives established for the school. First, each major element of the conceptual framework is described. Then, it is shown how the model can be applied through the use of program analysis and cost-effectiveness tools and techniques.

The System Elements

In linking school resources to educational outcomes one must consider the following basic elements: the resources from the external environment, the inputs of the school, the resource input mix, the outputs of the school, and feedback to the system.

Resources from the external environment.   Schools serve many purposes. While most people agree that the major function of schools is to educate students, views of what constitutes education are by no means identical. In short, various subpublics hold differing expectations for the schools. Regardless of the expectations held for them, however, all schools must work within a set of constraints imposed by the resources made available to them.

Schools obtain resources from the communities they serve, from the state, and from the nation. They are expected to use these resources to produce "educated" students. The nature and amount of the resources made available to the school and the way these resources are used will significantly influence the nature of the education which students receive.

The resources the school obtains from its external environment are very important. These resources (or inputs) consist of students, teachers, money, buildings, buses, books, food, and all of the other human and material resources needed to operate the school. The single most important input to the school from its external environment is students. Research has shown that the attitudes, values, knowledge, and skills possessed by pupils when they enter school significantly influence the nature of the educational process and the results of that process. The Coleman Report (1966), for example, indicated that environmental factors were more significant predictors of pupil achievement than were school factors. If the principal, the IIC, and the I & R Units are to utilize resources efficiently, they must be very familiar with the community the school serves and must be able to tailor the educational process to meet the needs of students. Schools whose students come from disadvantaged backgrounds will need to provide different types of educational experiences than are provided in schools whose students come from advantaged backgrounds. A school does not exist in a vacuum; it exists to serve an identifiable school community. The educational processes and outcomes of the school are heavily influenced by the nature of the community it serves, the pupils who attend the school, and the expectations of its clientele.

Another important input to the school from the external environment is money (or fiscal resources). Money is needed to pay for the human and material resources required to operate the school's educational program. The level of fiscal resources available to the school will depend to a large extent upon the community in which it is located and will be influenced by state and federal policies concerning the financing of education. The school budget is one of the most important constraints within which the staff of a school must operate. Most IGE schools, for example, operate with about the same per pupil cost and budgetary constraints as do all other schools in a given district. Commenting on problems in this domain, a principal in an urban IGE school said:

> One of the biggest battles we ever had around here was when we wanted to use our textbook allocation for some supplemental enrichment kits and filmstrips. It almost takes an act of God to get that line item of the budget changed in this district.

A third resource which the school obtains from the external environment is knowledge about the educational process and how it can function most efficiently. The principal and staff of an IGE school are expected to utilize this knowledge in organizing the educational program, selecting appropriate learning activities, and managing the resources made available to the school.

The inputs of the school.   The word "school" as used in this section is interchangeable with I & R Unit if one wishes to focus on a segment smaller than the school, or with school district if one wishes to focus on a segment larger than the individual school. As shown in Figure 7.1, a second important component of an educational system is the school itself. A school has three broad categories of resources with which to work: material resources, human resources, and the aims, priorities, and controls which have been established for the school.

Material resources include all of the physical supplies and equipment provided for use in the school. The largest material resource is the school building itself. In addition, there are such things as textbooks, library books, desks, maps, globes, and all of the other learning aids and equipment which are available for students and teachers to use in the instructional process.

Human resources fall into two major categories—the children who are students in the school and the adults who make up the school staff. By far the most important resource are the children who attend the school. They are the only reason for existence of the school in the first place, since without students there would be no need for the other resources. The background and characteristics of students will significantly affect the learning activities and objectives of the school.

Also important are the adults employed by the school—the administrators, unit leaders, teachers, librarians, reading specialists, counselors, and other professional personnel, as well as the aides, secretaries, cooks, custodians, bus drivers, and other persons needed to operate the school plant and support the educational program. As indicated in Chapter 5, a major task of the principal is to recruit and organize the staff in such a way as to maximize achievement of the school's objectives. The principal and the IIC, for example, must balance the potential contributions and cost of a teacher aide or instructional secretary against those of an additional teacher. The principal must consider the professional strengths and personal characteristics of existing staff members when recruiting to fill vacancies and must try to identify the professional qualifications and personal characteristics of persons who will best meet the needs of the students in the school. Needs for specialists in areas such as counseling, health services, and other specialized services must also be weighed so that proper staff balance is maintained. Since about 80 percent of a school's operating budget typically goes to pay the salaries of employees, the importance of the staffing decisions made by the principal and the IIC is apparent.

The aims, priorities, and controls established for the school are also important considerations. Aims and priorities are established by the community through its board of education, and by the state through its legislature and administrative agencies. Controls consist of rules developed within the school, rules and regulations adopted by the board of education, and state statutes. They may take such forms as a specified pupil/teacher ratio as a result of a negotiated agreement, a specified length of school year established by state statutes, or an allocation per pupil for supplies and expenses established by the board of education.

The aims established for a school by its clientele must be translated into educational objectives by the principal and staff. The relative importance of the various objectives serves to identify priorities for use of the resources which are available. The principal and staff must try to achieve the goals and objectives established for the school with the resources at their disposal and within the limits established by controls on operating policy imposed by the state or the community through its elected representatives.

The resource input mix.   The principal and the school staff have the job of taking the human and material resources made available to the school and, in the context of the aims, priorities, and controls established for the school, identifying the combination of resources most likely to achieve the school's objectives. It is at this stage that the resources made available to the school are translated into an educational program. For the total school, the principal and the IIC are concerned with both the content of the program and the instructional processes employed in conducting the program. Instructional objectives must be specified for each unit and each curricular area. Decisions must be made concerning the number of I & R Units to be established, the amount of time to be allocated to various elements of the school curriculum, the instructional materials which will be required for each unit's activities, the grouping patterns which are needed to enable pupils to make continuous progress in each subject matter area, and how the space within the building should be utilized. The principal will share responsibility for many of these decisions with the IIC and may delegate responsibility for some of them to the I & R Units. The principal and the IIC must also identify the supportive services needed to carry out the program efficiently and make sure that these services are available at the proper time and in the proper amount.

It is at this stage of the resource allocation process that the success or failure of the educational program will be determined. Regardless of the amount and nature of the resources made available to them, the principal and staff must utilize them in ways which enable students to achieve maximum educational gains. At this point, the professional competence of the principal as an educational leader and manager is put to the acid test, as is highlighted by the following comment of an IGE principal in the Minneapolis area:

> It burns me up when citizens, parents, and even consultants come in and say "Why don't you do this?" or "Why can't we have that?" Yet every time it costs money. They must think I'm a magician who can just pull things out of thin air. Discretionary funds in this district are zero, period. Instead, it's a balancing act, always weighing the advantages and disadvantages of one thing against another.

The outputs of the school.   The third major component of the educational systems model shown in Figure 7.1 is identified as the output of the educational system, i.e., the outcomes of the educational process. It is convenient to divide the results of the educational process into three parts: (1) the immediate or short-term outcomes, (2) the long-range outcomes and (3) the joint outcomes, i.e., incidental outcomes inextricably associated with the operation of the system. The results of the educational process are compared, in one way or another, with the objectives established for the system to assess the effectiveness of the educational process as well as to assess the system's efficiency. (In contemporary educational terminology, formative and summative evaluations are made of the system.) Such evaluations provide feedback which let the principal and the staff of each unit know how well the system is doing. Based on this feedback, corrective action may be taken or current practice may be continued.

The immediate or short-range outcomes of the educational process may be expressed in many ways. They may, for example, take the form of cognitive, affective, or psychomotor achievement; possession of basic knowledge; display of intellectual or manual skills; display of powers of reasoning and criticism; demonstration of values, attitudes and motivation; exhibition of powers of creativity and innovation; expression of a sense of cultural appreciation; demonstration of a sense of social responsibility; display of understanding of the modern world; or demonstration of ability to learn independently. Some of these outcomes may be measured by achievement tests or tests of basic knowledge; others can be demonstrated by performance skills; and still others are best assessed through anecdotal records and observations.

The long-range outcomes of the educational process are embodied in individuals better equipped to serve themselves and society as individuals and family members, as workers in a productive economy, as leaders and innovators, as contributors to culture, and as participating citizens. The contribution of the school to the long-range outcomes of the educational process is much more difficult to determine than are the immediate and short-range outcomes. Although many social institutions are involved in the educational process and influence an individual's ability to function in society, it is clear that the school plays a significant role. The indicators of long-range outcomes are much more ambiguous than are those for the immediate and short-range outcomes. Indicators of the long-range outputs may be such items of information as participation in governmental and social activities, voting behavior, work records, and similar proxy measures of a personally satisfying and socially useful life.

Joint outcomes of the educational system may be thought of as the unintended outcomes of the educational process. They occur whether or not they are sought. They are similar in this respect to the change in land values when a highway is built or odors are produced by a paper mill. One joint output of the educational process, for example, is staff morale. Although higher or lower staff morale often is not a primary objective of the educational process, staff morale will surely be affected in the process. And just as the smoke produced by a factory may require attention if it becomes obnoxious, so may staff morale require the specific attention of the principal and the IIC if it becomes seriously impaired.

Feedback to the system.   The fourth major component of the educational system represented in Figure 7.1 is identified as feedback. Feedback provides the self-correcting mechanism for the system—it functions as the system's governor. Feedback is the result of evaluation, i.e., a comparison of achievement with objectives. Evaluation goes on continuously whether or not it is planned by the school. If, for example, a number of students fail to learn to read, then their parents will soon make this known to the school and corrective action will be expected. Ideally, the IIC and the unit staffs will continually monitor the progress of the educational program and will modify the educational process when the need for change is indicated by evaluative and feedback processes. It is through evaluation and feedback that resource allocations are altered or modified to achieve a better match between objectives and results.

UTILIZING IGE TO MAXIMIZE RESOURCES

No principal has an easy task these days and the principal in an IGE school is no exception. Every school principal is challenged to utilize efficiently the resources made available to the school. The IGE principal, however, must work more actively to involve other members of the staff in decision making through the IIC and I & R Units, must maintain a close working relationship with all members of the staff, and must monitor progress so that necessary changes can be made in a timely fashion. The principal's responsibility for managing efficiently the school's resources is not reduced in multiunit schools; in fact, it is much greater than in traditionally organized schools. Each of the seven components of IGE has implications for the principal's job of allocating resources in ways which maximize achievement by pupils of the instructional objectives which have been established.

As discussed in Chapter 2, the multiunit organization characteristic of IGE schools is a well-designed plan for organizing the instructional staff of the school to facilitate the tailoring of instruction to the needs of individual students. At the unit level, the I & R Unit is an organizational structure which enables the staff to plan, conduct, and evaluate, on an individual student basis, the instructional program of the school. It also facilitates continuous on-the-job development of its members, permits the members of the professional staff to teach in the areas of their greatest strength, and encourages a free flow of information among them. The unit structure was designed specifically to help improve the effectiveness and efficiency of each member of the professional staff. Thus, the I & R Unit can be one of the principal's most important assets in managing resources. For example, the multiunit arrangement lends itself easily to differentiated staffing, thus enabling teachers to concentrate on the things they do best. As one IGE principal in Massachusetts said:

> The great thing about the unit arrangement is that I can capitalize on the strengths of the staff, not the weaknesses. Miss X is superb in language arts but doesn't really enjoy teaching math. Miss Y is just about the opposite. By having them as members of one unit, they can do the things they like best and do best. The kids benefit, and so does the staff!

The differentiation of roles and responsibilities within the multiunit organization also encourages efficiency in the use of materials. Unnecessary duplication of supplies and equipment is avoided by coordinating its use within and among the units in the school. Teachers are able to specialize in the tasks of planning, instructing, and evaluating according to their capabilities and interests. For example, some members of the unit may be especially effective in small group or large group instruction and they can specialize in these areas. Others may be very creative in developing materials for use in the instructional program or skilled in working with individual pupils on special problems. The multiunit organization permits them to specialize in those instructional tasks which they do best and enjoy most. It also permits teachers to concentrate on instructional tasks by utilizing teacher aides or instructional secretaries to handle routine nonteaching duties.

The IIC provides a vehicle for coordinating the activities of the various I & R Units so that continuity is achieved in all curricular areas. Working with the principal, the unit leaders arrange for the use of facilities, equipment, and materials so that duplication and overlap are avoided. If the IIC is functioning as it should, the instructional space within the building will be utilized more efficiently than in traditionally organized schools. Unnecessary duplication of instructional equipment will be avoided, and the use of supplies and equipment will be coordinated. As chairman of the committee, the principal is the person most directly responsible for "making it go." The value of a smoothly functioning IIC is evident from the following comment by an IGE principal in California:

> It's hard to believe how much of a load the IIC has taken off my back! I used to have to coordinate the use of one gym and library by each of the individual classes and even schedule use of the projectors. Now with the unit leaders working with me to coordinate activities, I never have to worry about such things. Instead, I can spend my time working to improve instruction.

As was shown in Chapter 3, the Instructional Programming Model provides a plan for achievement of instructional objectives by tailoring instruction to accommodate the individual differences among students. This model provides a workable way to individualize instruction and thus to achieve greater efficiency in the use of educational resources by enabling each child to progress continuously according to his own skills and abilities in each curricular area. Students are not required to waste time studying material they already have mastered; they can move ahead and take on additional educational tasks based on an individualized program of learning objectives.

If instructional programming is to be fully successful, however, the school must have a plan for measurement and evaluation which enables the unit staff to easily monitor each student's progress. If students are to achieve maximum progress, the instructional program designed for them must be tailored to take advantage of their specific characteristics—their strengths and weaknesses. A workable plan for measurement and evaluation which enables teachers to determine each student's present status in a curricular area, to develop an individualized program of study for the student, and to assess regularly the student's progress so that necessary modifications and adjustments can be made is essential if truly individualized instruction is to become a reality.

If the Instructional Programming Model is to be effective, curricular materials suited for use on an individualized basis are essential. For example, the Wisconsin Research and Development Center for Cognitive Learning has developed commercially available instructional materials in reading and mathematics which incorporate the sequence specified by the instructional programming model. Any instructional materials can be utilized so long as they lend themselves to individualized instruction tailored to suit a student's particular requirements. The development or modification of curricular materials which facilitate individualized instruction for pupils is one of the difficult challenges confronting teachers, and one of the most time consuming. The principal and the IIC must take into account the need for appropriate instructional materials and provide adequate time for planning and developing material to fill the gaps.

The importance of the guidance provided by the IPM is illustrated by the following comments by the principal of an IGE school in Ohio:

> We always have prided ourselves that we were paying attention to the individual needs of the children who attend this school. Until we adopted IGE and became familiar with the IPM, though, we never did have a co-ordinated approach. The IPM gives us a clear and easily understandable blueprint to follow. We still have a way to go, but we are coming much closer to really individualizing instruction than we did in our pre-IGE days. The IPM pinpoints where our resources and energy are most needed.

The community served by the school is an important factor in shaping both the objectives of the school's educational program and the characteristics of its students. Effective involvement of the community in school affairs is necessary to generate the support and encouragement of parents and other adults whose attitudes weigh heavily on pupil motivation and learning. Equally important is the need for members of the school staff to be aware of the potential instructional resources in the community and to know something about the expectations held for the school by parents and others. Home-school-community relations are not one-way streets. Interaction is required between teachers, parents, and the community at large in order to establish appropriate goals and objectives for the instructional program to tailor the instructional program to the individual needs and interests of pupils. The community often is a rich source of instructional resources which can be drawn upon by I & R Units. As an IGE principal in South Carolina observed:

> We never before realized what a rich source of help we had right under our noses. We have been able to greatly expand our store of instructional material (and talent) with hardly any increase in our budget—and believe me that's important in these days of tight budgets! We found parents who were willing to come in and help us with specific topics, an unbelievable number of slides and films which we can borrow, retired persons and mothers who are happy to donate a few hours a week to serve as aides, just to mention only a few. Best of all, people who get involved with the school know what we are trying to do and have become our most ardent supporters.

IGE is a developing system which by no means has all the answers. Research and development of IGE at local, state, and national levels must be continued. Additional curricular materials must be developed or adapted and additional refinement of the multiunit organization is needed to adapt it to the widely varying conditions which exist in the many school districts of the United States. The problems of measurement and assessment are far from solved, and continuing research is needed to provide the instruments necessary for assessing individual student progress, as well as for assessing the effectiveness of instructional programs. While IGE is a promising alternative form of schooling, continuing research and development are necessary if schools are to achieve the potential inherent in IGE.

PROVIDING RESOURCES FOR IGE

It should be apparent from the preceding discussion that when properly implemented, IGE makes it possible to increase the productivity of the resources made available to the school. However, the process of providing those resources in IGE schools poses some unique considerations for the budget-making process, the utilization of personnel, materials and equipment, and physical facilities.

The Budget-making Process in IGE

In traditionally organized schools the principal prepares the budget and the teacher typically is relegated to the role of only providing information and making requests. In the IGE school, the principal shares responsibility for preparation of the budget with the IIC, unit leaders, and unit teachers. The school budget is a fiscal interpretation of the school's educational program. In IGE schools it is important that the budget be a product of shared decision making involving those persons who are most knowledgeable about the school's program and who can help translate that program into a budget document.

In IGE schools each teacher is involved in planning, carrying out, and evaluating the unit's instructional program. Teachers work together to develop and clarify instructional objectives, and to design and implement instructional programs which enable each child to make continuous progress. The unit leader coordinates the activities of the unit and, as a member of the IIC, works with the principal to develop schoolwide objectives, plans staff development activities, and coordinates the use of facilities, equipment, and materials. Within this structure, the procedures and processes involved in budget planning and development flow logically from the instructional unit to the school and district levels.

Preparation of the school budget should follow a sequence of events in which the proposed educational program is related to the resources which will be needed to carry out the program and then translated to fiscal requirements in the budget document. In this approach to budget preparation an educational plan is projected into a budget document with cost estimates extending over a time span of three to five years. Budget development in this context involves defining the educational program and the delivery system through which the program is provided for students, determining the resources that the program will require, and converting the resource requirements into estimated program costs. The principal must take the lead in acquainting unit leaders with this approach and must work closely with them in order to build a sound and defensible educational plan and tentative budget for the school. In short, the development of a budget involves (1) determining the school's educational goals and objectives, (2) determining the mix of resources which characterizes the program or delivery system needed to reach those goals and objectives, and (3) translating those resources requirements into fiscal requirements.

At the unit level, the unit staff is continually assessing the needs of each pupil and evaluating each pupil's progress. The results of this assessment and evaluation are, in turn, translated into an instructional program for that pupil. The program requires the availability of resources which only the staff of the unit is in a position to decide. Therefore, the unit leader, working with unit teachers, needs to prepare a tentative budget for the unit which reflects the needs of all pupils. These unit budgets provide the focus for budget deliberations of the IIC.

With regard to the educational systems model shown in Figure 7.1, the IIC must identify and specify the content of the instructional program, must determine the instructional processes which will be used, and must determine the required supportive services. Once these three components of the total resource requirements are specified, then the costs associated with them can be estimated. If the program is currently in operation, the inventory of anticipated materials, equipment, supplies, etc., which will be carried over and available for use in the following year can be matched with the resources required and the additional amounts needed can be determined. The resources which will be required each year are determined by comparing the progress of each pupil with the objectives established for the pupil and to the overall program objectives of the unit. Each unit leader should be asked to prepare a unit budget proposal based on documented evidence of need following the guidelines above. The care and effort spent in defining the program (or resource input mix) will be reflected directly in the accuracy of the cost projections.

At the district level, the principal will be hard put to defend the school budget without a sound justification based on clearly stated educational goals, a plan to accomplish those goals, and a reasonably accurate expenditure projection. That IGE provides a framework for achieving more accurate and effective budgeting has been recognized by school boards and superintendents. Although the individual school's allocation of resources ultimately is determined by the superintendent, central office, and school board, the shared decision-making characteristics of IGE should produce supporting information which makes the job of the superintendent and board easier. In IGE, budgeting is a cooperative effort involving the principal, unit leaders and unit teachers, thus helping to ensure that the school's budget accurately portrays the kind and level of resources needed to accomplish the goals and objectives established for and by the students.

Although the planning of new programs, projects, and curricular changes is a continuous activity, a specific schedule should be established for each school year which permits the intensive work of budget preparation to be accomplished early enough to resolve problems originating at the unit level which have implications at the school and district levels. Shared decision making is the watchword in the budgeting process. The principal initiates and monitors the process; the IIC prepares the school's educational objectives and plan and helps convert that plan into a budget document; the units identify specific requirements.

If a new program is to be implemented, its acquisition or start-up cost can be projected using categories such as the following (Curtis 1971, pp. 134–137):

- Program Implementation—The direct cost of those activities required to implement a specific program on an operational basis.
- Equipment—The cost of the equipment and furniture necessary to the program.
- Materials—The materials needed to begin operation of the educational program, e.g., textbooks, workbooks, initial stocks of paper, and supplies.
- Preservice Training—The training provided to the teachers or other instructional personnel before the start of the program.

All programs, whether new or ongoing, will include operational cost categories such as the following (Curtis 1971, p. 136):

- Salaries—The salary of the staff required by the instructional program, including employees benefits.
- Inservice Training—The training provided the staff during the course of the program, including both maintenance of capability and improvement.
- Materials and supplies—The consumable materials and supplies for the program.
- Equipment—The replacement of equipment because of normal wear and tear, as well as costs to maintain equipment.
- Facilities operation and maintenance—The operation and maintenance of additional or special facilities required for the program.
- Contracted services—Any special contracted services not provided for in other programs, e.g., computer time or special telephone charges.
- Media services—The expenditures for audiovisual equipment and services.
- Transportation—Transportation required for field trips taken as part of the instructional program.

Effort expended during the budget-making process is time well spent, since the resulting budget document serves as an operational guide for the utilization of resources.

Utilization of Resources in IGE Schools

Just as the budget-making process is unique in IGE schools, there are also some unique practical procedures and guidelines for the utilization of resources in the IGE school. These relate to staff personnel, materials and equipment, and the school plant.

Staff personnel.   The principal must keep in mind that the school staff represents a set of human resources. It is important that the time and talents of the staff be used efficiently, since typically 80 percent of a school's annual budget goes to pay for staff salaries and fringe benefits. Coupled with the fact that of all of the resources devoted to education the teacher has the greatest impact on a child's learning, it is obvious why proper staff utilization is of great importance.

The organizational structure for IGE provides a mechanism for helping achieve maximum effectiveness in the use of personnel. This structure facilitates a division of labor that enables the unit teacher who is best qualified to direct instruction in a particular subject to do so with support from other unit members. Staff teachers can specialize in the various curricular areas and instructional tasks according to each one's capabilities and interests. This approach should improve both their instructional effectiveness and their personal satisfaction. Not only are the talents of staff members better utilized, but the shared decision making which characterizes IGE helps ensure that decisions about the use of resources will be valid.

As emphasized throughout Chapter 5, staff development activities are especially critical to the success of IGE. The principal and the IIC must plan and provide inservice activities for the staff which will help them develop a clear understanding of the roles of the principal, unit leaders, unit teachers, aides, volunteers, and others. Without a clear understanding of one's responsibilities in IGE there are likely to be misunderstandings and conflicts which will divert attention from instructional tasks and thus reduce effectiveness.

Special attention must be paid to the task of properly integrating specialists—for example, teachers of art, music, and physical education, and teachers of handicapped children—in the IGE school. The multiunit school organization is ideally suited for mainstreaming handicapped children in regular classes with supplementary support provided by a resource room teacher. When this approach is used, the I & R Unit includes as one of its members a teacher with special training in the education of handicapped children. The unit might also include a teacher who specializes in art, music, physical education, or specialists in these subjects might form a separate unit for planning purposes. If the latter course is followed, it is important that the specialist's unit interact frequently with the I & R Units to ensure close coordination and articulation with the instructional program in each unit. Again, the IIC must take the lead in making sure that all instructional resources are utilized in a coordinated manner.

Whenever interaction between members of a school staff is close and frequent, as is the case in the IGE school, the possibility of interrole and/or interpersonal conflict among staff members is greatly increased. The individual teacher's domain is altered in IGE, since teachers share space, students, materials, and equipment with their colleagues in the same and other units rather than being isolated in self-contained classrooms. Teachers accustomed to traditional status differentiations where seniority is rewarded and where instructional equipment and materials are viewed as prized possessions of individual teachers, rather than resources to be shared with other teachers, may find it difficult to change when IGE is implemented. Teachers must also understand that a unit's share of the school budget should be based on demonstrated needs, not on an equal allocation to each I & R Unit. Achieving equity between units does not imply that an equal amount of funds must be allocated to each unit each year. Instead, long-range planning in a spirit of cooperation, rather than competition, is essential. In some schools, it may be necessary to introduce staff-development programs which reinforce sharing and how to share, as well as caring and how to care.

Learning aids: materials and equipment. The principal has a significant role to play in securing, selecting, purchasing, utilizing, and maintaining learning aids, materials and equipment. An IGE school, like any other school, needs a wide range of instructional materials and resources. The principal, working in concert with the IIC, is responsible for obtaining materials and scheduling the use of space and equipment for all units (Klausmeier *et al.* 1971, pp. 34–36, 39). It is helpful to follow a systems approach in planning, and a good beginning point is a complete survey to identify existing resources. This information may then be matched against the needed facilities, equipment, supplies, and instructional materials to determine what additional items are needed. The following are among the items typically inventoried:

Materials	*Equipment*
Textbooks and reference books	Projectors
Magazines and newspapers	Tape recorders
Filmstrips and motion pictures	Record players
Records, audiotapes, and cassettes	Earphones
Models, maps, and learning kits	Learning machines
	Study carrels

Application of the IGE IPM emphasizes the importance of careful selection from among the wide array of commercially available instructional materials. Teachers must be provided with information concerning the instructional materials which are available. Sources of materials include: educational publishers, free and/or inexpensive materials, community resources, and teacher-made materials.

If a program package such as the *Wisconsin Design for Reading Skill Development* (WDRSD) is adopted, it provides guidelines for identifying, selecting, and using instructional materials. Included in the WDRSD program is a Teacher's Resource File for the Word Attack, Study Skills, and Comprehension elements of the Design. *The Teacher's Resource File: Word Attack,* for example, includes 39 folders of materials, with separate folders provided for most of the 45 skills/objectives. Commercial materials appropriate for teaching a given skill are identified, and related teacher-directed activities and procedures are also suggested.

But commercial materials represent only a small part of the vast array of potentially useful material. Teachers' resource files should be augmented in each school and keyed to the appropriate objectives by the teachers who use them. Materials included in textbooks, teachers' manuals, skill texts, and other supplementary materials should be examined and keyed to learning objectives. Coordination by the IIC is needed to avoid excessive duplication as the school staff builds the file of instructional aids. There should not be a series of collected resource files of published materials restricted to given levels and stored in different locations; rather, a master collection that is centrally located and accessible to all teachers is more efficient and much less costly.

In many IGE schools, the principal and the IIC have devoted a good bit of attention to the development of specific guidelines for evaluating instructional materials; in some schools this activity has served as the basis for a complete staff development program. Several guidelines have been suggested by Sowards and Scobey (1968, pp. 374–408) for evaluating instructional materials. The materials selected should:

- Be designed to achieve the purposes and objectives of the program.
- Be appropriate to specific learning situations.
- Provide valid content for learning.
- Be appropriate to the individual differences of learners.
- Represent variety in kind and function.
- Foster active participation on the part of the learner.
- Provide cooperative learning, help children recognize and accept both individual and group research responsibilities, and develop problem-solving skills.
- Approach high standards of mechanical excellence, attractiveness, and utility.

Several IGE schools systematically obtain and utilize free and/or inexpensive materials. Questions such as the following can serve as standards for evaluating such materials:

- Is the agency which produced the materials clearly shown?
- Are reputable and authoritative sources cited?
- Is the date of publication recent and the information current?
- Have the materials been favorably (or unfavorably) reviewed in standard guides?
- Do the materials promote special interests without due regard for objectivity?
- Would any community mores and values be offended by the materials?
- Can the materials be easily incorporated into the school's resource file?
- Does use of the materials obligate the school in any way?

Not to be overlooked as an inexpensive source of instructional materials and resource personnel is the community which the school serves. Usable as sources for learning experiences are local libraries, museums, industries, governmental agencies, hospitals, service organizations, and the like. Valuable published materials are also found in census reports, industrial and other organizational reports, brochures, pamphlets, pictures, and films. Again, such materials should be indexed as a valuable part of the school resource file, as should the names of citizens with special expertise they are willing to share. IGE schools characterized by a systematic program of home-school-community relations frequently utilize a wide range of community resources to enrich and extend the school's instructional program. The varied patterns of instructional grouping characteristic of IGE foster the effective and efficient use of resource persons in situations ranging from large group presentations to individual tutoring. With regard to the use of community resource persons, an IGE principal in South Carolina recently commented:

> People are coming and going in and out of this place all the time. In addition to you visitors today, we have enrichment "classes" in knitting, guitar playing, and great works of art. That farmer over there is helping the unit get ready for a trip to his dairy. The high school students you see are an enthusiastic bunch of future teachers listening to children read.
>
> Sometimes the best help comes from where you least expect it, so we keep a file for future use on how well each activity goes.

Interviews with IGE principals reveal several distinctive features of IGE with respect to the purchase, utilization, and maintenance of instructional resources. In IGE schools, a lower percentage of the budget typically is spent for textbooks than is the case in conventional schools. Whereas in the school with self-contained classrooms each child typically is provided a text for each academic area, in IGE schools a smaller number of textbooks may be adequate for an entire I & R Unit, or even for the total school, since textbooks are often shared among units. On the other hand, a higher than usual expenditure for teacher-made learning materials and assessment devices is required in IGE schools in order to implement the Instructional Programming Model. Since audiovisual materials and equipment are in great demand in IGE schools, they are likely to require more frequent repair and replacement than in traditional schools. In this regard, it is wise to arrange for inservice training in the use of such equipment to reduce the frequency of repairs or replacements. In summary, IGE school budgets are likely to reflect fewer textbook purchases, higher expenditures for consumable materials, and higher costs for repair and replacement of equipment. Overall, such costs probably will even out. Such differential costs, however, underlie the importance of allowing the principal to exercise discretion in allocating and transferring funds within and among budgetary categories.

The school plant.   The Council of Educational Facility Planners, stressing the significance of the school building, stated:

> Depending upon its design characteristics, a school building will tend to encourage or to inhibit certain instructional programs, instructional methods, patterns of student and staff interaction, patterns of neighborhood organizations, and patterns of cost for operation and for construction. Depending upon its design characteristics, a school building will unquestionably influence school organization and staffing (Theodores 1968, p. 5).

Concerning the design characteristics of IGE schools, Klausmeier and others (1971, p. 9) suggested:

> The school building is constructed or remodeled to facilitate IGE practices. Pods of varying shapes and sizes in recently constructed buildings accommodate 75 to 150 children and permit one-to-one, small group, class size, and total unit activities. Older buildings are remodeled so that there is one large instructional materials center (IMC) that accommodates 90 intermediate-age children and another that accommodates at least 60 primary-age children in a school of about 600 enrollment. Audiovisual materials and equipment, and other instructional aids, are available in the IMC. Noisy and vigorous activities, such as music, and physical education, are conducted in a large space.

Attesting to the organizational demands on school plant space are the following questions to which an IGE principal must respond:

- Is the total space available adequate for the number of students to be accommodated?
- Are there adequate teaching stations for each certified member of the unit?
- Are the stations on the same floor and adjacent to each other, or nearly so?
- Are one or two of the stations sufficiently large so that groups can meet simultaneously?
- Does the typical daily pattern provide for a teacher to teach more than one group?
- Are large spaces such as the instructional learning centers or library, all-purpose room, or gymnasium, available for use by all units?
- Is space available for use by nonprofessional staff members? (Klausmeier *et al.* 1971, p. 36.)

To investigate the relationship between school plant characteristics and the effectiveness of IGE practices, Strand (1974) studied twelve IGE schools housed in both traditional and open-type school plants. From an

architect's point of view, he analyzed on-site the specific design characteristics, including total space, deployment of space, and illumination, thermal,
sonic, and service features of each instructional area in each school plant.
From an educator's point of view, he obtained through interviews with
principals, unit leaders, teachers, and instructional aides their evaluations
of the extent to which each feature of the building design facilitated or
impeded instructional activities in each grouping mode, ranging from large
group to one-to-one instruction. Several of the findings have important implications for the principal's role in educational facility planning and utilization.

With regard to how IGE staffs utilized existing space within their
schools to accommodate the functions of each learning mode, Strand (1974,
p. 170) found that with sufficient commitment and desire on the part of
teaching staffs, IGE could be successfully implemented and the learning
modes accommodated in school plants irrespective of design features—
whether open or traditional. Obviously, the attitudes, ingenuity, and
resourcefulness of the staff are critical. Respondents exhibited a definite
feeling of pride when they identified a space typically considered inappropriate for instructional use as accommodating the functions of a learning
mode. This sense of achievement seemed to have motivated all I & R Units
within the facility to view space in a "different light."

That I & R Units become competitive for space was also amply
demonstrated. For example, one unit, having "confiscated" a former storage
room for unit-planning activities, was regarded by other units as being
somewhat selfish for having appropriated this space, and guidelines were
being worked out by the IIC for sharing it. In traditional schools, such extensive use of space within a school plant would have suggested extreme
overcrowding. In summary, the multifunctional use of space becomes the
normal mode of operation in a school plant where IGE is operational. It
can be anticipated that each and every space in a multiunit IGE school will
be viewed by the instructional staff in terms of the potential for accommodating the activities of some grouping pattern or learning mode.

Concerning the amount of instructional space needed, pupil density
within a school plant will considerably influence grouping patterns of pupils,
organization schemes for units, and pupil activities in IGE programs. A
conventional classroom usually has twenty-five to thirty square feet of
floor space per child and a capacity of approximately twenty-five or thirty
pupils. In the conventional classroom one teacher typically interacts with a
small group of children while the remaining students are engaged in "quiet"
seat work. The teacher has a controlled learning environment. Consider that
same classroom in IGE. Those pupils previously engaged in seat work are
now actively involved in two or more small groups within the same space;
some of these same students may be engaged in independent study, or
participating in one-to-one learning activities. The tranquility of the

conventional classroom and the "controlled" learning environment have disappeared. This "drives out" teachers and pupils to seek quiet spaces in other areas. Where are such spaces to come from? It is safe to conclude that, when appropriately implemented, IGE increases the need for additional net square feet per pupil of appropriate space, as contrasted with conventional schools.

Strand (1974, p. 166) found that primary teachers, to a far greater extent than intermediate teachers, regarded the distance from their classroom areas to instructional resource centers to be restrictive. The desire of those working with primary-age pupils to have a separate instructional resource center deployed adjacent to their units was commonly stated. Primary teachers were reluctant to send their pupils to distant spaces for independent study, especially in school plants with large pupil enrollments. Also, the greater the distance from the kindergarten areas to the primary units, the fewer were the opportunities for kindergarten students to become integrated into unit activities. The reluctance on the part of kindergarten teachers to use the instructional resource center and to participate in primary unit activities was only reinforced as the travel distance between spaces increased for kindergarten students.

Although centrally located instructional resource centers existed, in many schools they were inadequate. Greater space allocations for instructional resource centers are justified in IGE schools. Also, if the instructional resource center is to accommodate expanded independent study opportunities for pupils, consideration must be given to restricting the activities of other learning modes in the instructional resource center. In several schools, respondents were quick to note that existing walls did not permit free flow to and from the classroom areas and resource center. Approximately 50 percent of the school plants analyzed did not have classroom areas deployed adjacent to or within close approximation of the instructional resource center. Increased pupil traffic, therefore, contributed to higher sound levels. This was especially acute where the instructional spaces for a given I & R Unit were deployed on different levels within the building.

Concerning space as a restriction on learning activities, Strand (1974, p. 164) found independent study, one-to-one, and small group learning modes to be most often restricted in both conventional and open-space plants. The fact that a multitude of spaces not always designed for instructional purposes must be utilized to activate the learning modes in IGE contributed to this restriction, particularly with respect to size and shape of space. In several schools, shape of space was restrictive of a teacher's vision sweep or sight lines of students, even in open-space schools. Frequently, respondents stated that the degree to which they were able to schedule small or one-to-one study groups was simply dependent on how many places were available.

Strand (1974, p. 174) found that pupil density, space allocations, space deployment, use of space, and building materials all contributed to a less than appropriate sonic environment in IGE schools. Of the three energy sources investigated, the sonic environment was identified in both types of school plants as the greatest restriction to each of the IGE learning modes. Increased sound levels are generated by the operational practices in IGE schools. Any manner in which the sonic environment might be improved in a school plant merits consideration. Carpeting, drapes, and similar controls become more of a necessity than a luxury.

Irrespective of school plant design—traditional or open—the amount of net square feet of available space per pupil will influence instructional effectiveness to a great degree. The potential for activation of all IGE learning modes undoubtedly will increase in proportion to square foot allocations per pupil in a school plant which exceeds the standards expressed in conventional formulas. Current decreases in elementary school enrollments may contribute to increased space allocations in a few schools. Districts having several elementary schools may also wish to consider the transfer of pupils to balance space allocations per pupil.

To achieve greater efficiency in the use of school plant resources, the principal and the IIC should place greater emphasis on the inventory of space within a school plant. All spaces should be analyzed with respect to the possible accommodation of the respective learning modes. Spaces may be diagrammed on paper by outlining the space and then planning the space arrangement to show various utilization practices. Teachers will show an increased awareness of school plant characteristics and their relation to IGE learning modes when they participate actively in an inventory of each space.

Schools changing to IGE probably should delay major remodeling and furniture purchases until a brief trial period is spent in the existing facility with the new organizational and instructional process in operation. The removal of walls, for example, may not always be in the best interests of the program. Space utilization also will be enhanced if furniture is provided which permits flexibility and facilitates grouping and regrouping of pupils during the school day. Proper furnishings should permit a variety of learning stations within one space. Consideration of the characteristics of a particular activity, for example, the generation of sound, will reduce the potential for conflict within a space with multiple learning stations.

A final injunction concerning the rate of implementation of IGE was stated by Strand (1974, p. 174), "The IGE school would be well advised in terms of school plant characteristics and space utilization to 'go completely IGE'." He found demands on the school facility to be greatly increased to accommodate the multiplicity of diverse functions in IGE schools. Such demands were exacerbated when spaces must also continue to accommodate conventional instructional groupings and processes. For example, placement of furniture, equipment, and materials, while appropriate for one block of time, becomes a restriction for the next period of the school day. A custodian in one such school summarized the situation aptly: "It's move this, move that, every hour, every day. You can say one thing about our school—'It really moves!' "

THE COST OF IGE

School districts contemplating the move to IGE must be able to answer two questions: How much does IGE cost? How does that cost compare with the cost of other forms of schooling? Two recent studies provide some answers to these questions.

From a study of IGE schools throughout the nation, Evers drew the following conclusions about the first-year costs of implementing IGE (Evers 1973, pp. 34–36):

1. The majority of the schools reported no increase or decrease in expenditures related to vandalism and pupil absenteeism.
2. The majority of the schools reported no change in the number of certified teachers, central office personnel, special teachers, substitute teachers, paid student teachers, or custodians who were employed.
3. The majority of the schools reported a greater number of paid paraprofessionals; the median increase was four.
4. Disregarding normal salary increments, the majority of the schools reported no increase or decrease in expenditures for salaries of unit leaders, certified teachers, paid paraprofessionals, substitute teachers, special teachers, central office personnel, paid student teachers and custodians.
5. The majority of the schools reported higher expenditures for inservice materials; the median reported increase was $250.
6. The majority of the schools reported higher expenditures for workshops and conferences; the median reported increase was $500.
7. The majority of the schools reported no increase or decrease in expenditures for consultant services.
8. The majority of the schools reported no increase or decrease in expenditures for instructional materials and equipment.
9. The majority of the schools reported they were able to use materials and equipment more efficiently.
10. The majority of the schools reported no increase or decrease in expenditures for school plant and furnishings.

A second study conducted by Boardman and Hudson (1973) examined both IGE start-up (first-year implementation) and ongoing (second-year) costs, using seven cost categories and thirty cost factors. With respect to staff development, there was a substantial start-up cost and little continuation cost. The typical IGE school encountered start-up costs of $4738 for preservice and $1805 for inservice staff development. Expenditures for inservice materials were high, but costs for visitations, consultants, and professional books were nonexistent or insignificant. Additional expenses for instructional personnel were attributable to a more extensive use of aides (approximately $7900) and the additional stipends (averaging $300) paid unit leaders. The data did not reveal expenditures over and above those made prior to implementing IGE for instructional materials and equipment for either classrooms or the resource center/library. No increase in administrative costs was identified, although the utilization of clerical and volunteer aides in IGE may have absorbed such additional costs. A report of "no expenditure" on facilities for IGE programs did not mean that improvements had not occurred, but did reflect the opinion of school officials that any building changes or new furnishings would have been provided regardless of the type of instructional program used.

What implications may be drawn from these studies concerning the preparation of a budget for an IGE school? Certainly the cost variance reported between schools indicates that costs reflect unique local needs and conditions. Schools that are already employing paraprofessionals and have an ample supply of instructional materials will experience relatively few additional costs. Schools that are operating on a meager budget undoubtedly will need to spend more money if they are to implement IGE successfully. It is clear, however, that the IGE school budget should include sufficient funds for paraprofessionals, a preservice and inservice staff development program, and salary supplements for unit leaders. The unit leader has additional responsibilities and additional time commitments that fully justify an additional salary increment. The budget must also cover the cost of instructional materials needed to individualize instruction, for example, books, audiovisual materials, assessment instruments, and other materials needed to provide diverse learning activities for the pupils in each unit.

SUMMARY

This chapter, introduced by a basic view of economics and education, was concerned with the role of the principal and the staff in making efficient use of resources in IGE schools. The allocation of resources was viewed in terms of a conceptual framework which delineated the major inputs, processes, outputs, and feedback of the school as a dynamic system. Within this framework the utility of program analysis and cost-effectiveness was shown.

Next, it was indicated how each basic component of IGE enhances the resource input mix, organizational structure, educational processes, and evaluative outcomes. Since the budget-making process is somewhat unique in IGE schools, some specific processes and guidelines were suggested for estimating cost categories in building the budget.

The appropriate utilization of resources includes attention to staff personnel, materials and equipment, and the school plant. Since the subject of staff personnel previously was treated extensively in Chapter 5, particular emphasis was placed in this chapter on inventorying, obtaining, and sharing instructional materials and equipment. Utilization of the school plant directed attention to how the size, shape, deployment, and service features of school buildings facilitate or impede the several instructional modes of IGE in both conventional and open-space plants.

In the concluding section of the chapter, recent research was cited which shows that except for certain minimal start-up costs, IGE compares favorably in cost with other forms of schooling.

REFERENCES

Boardman, G. R., and C. C. Hudson 1973. *Development of a cost analysis model which schools may use to determine budget needs for implementing individually guided education.* Lincoln, Neb.: Teachers College, University of Nebraska.

Coleman, J. S. *et al.* 1966. *Equality of educational opportunity.* Washington, D.C.: U.S. Government Printing Office.

Curtis, W. H. (Project Director) 1971. *Educational resources management system.* Chicago Research Corporation, Association of School Business Officials.

Evers, N. A. 1973. *IGE/MUS–E first-year implementation cost survey.* Technical Report No. 256. Madison, Wisc.: Wisconsin Research and Development Center for Cognitive Learning.

Klausmeier, H. J., M. R. Quilling, J. S. Sorenson, R. S. Way, and G. R. Glasrud 1971. *Individually guided education and the multiunit elementary school: guidelines for implementation.* Madison, Wisc.: Wisconsin Research and Development Center for Cognitive Learning.

National Education Association (NEA), Research Division 1973. *Financial status of the public schools.* Washington, D.C.

O'Donoghue, M. 1971. *Economic dimensions in education.* Chicago: Aldine-Atherton.

Schultz, T. W. 1963. *The economic value of education.* New York: Columbia University Press.

Sowards, G. W. and M. Scobey 1968. *The changing curriculum and the elementary teacher.* Belmont, Calif.: Wadsworth.

Strand, G. A. 1974. *Relationship of school plant characteristics to components of individually guided education programs in Wisconsin.* Unpublished doctoral dissertation, University of Wisconsin—Madison.

Theodores, J. L. 1968. *Crisis in planning.* Columbus, Ohio: Council of Educational Facility Planners.

8

Strengthening Facilitative Environments

Douglas A. Paul
James M. Lipham

Objectives

After reading this chapter, the reader will be able:

- To recognize four alternative strategies for educational change.
- To describe facilitative environments for IGE at local, regional, state, and national levels.
- To understand the role of the principal in working with the IGE networks.
- To describe the relationships of persons and agencies concerned with implementing IGE.
- To identify the leadership role of the principal in implementing IGE as a planned educational change.

The principal as an agent of change must understand the dynamics of planned educational change and must strengthen the supportive and facilitative environment for change. The component of facilitative environments in IGE consists of the requisite personnel, material, and resources in two categories: intraorganizational relationships and extraorganizational relationships. Previous chapters have dealt largely with intraorganizational variables—the multiunit school organization which is the facilitative environment for change at the local school and school district level. This chapter focuses on the extraorganizational facilitative environment—the linkages and relationships which should be established and maintained between the local school district and the larger environment including other school systems, the state education agency, teacher education institutions, and other groups which share in the implementation of IGE.

A brief treatment of the need for educational change introduces this chapter in which four alternative change strategies are defined. A major part of the chapter is devoted to describing the system of extraorganizational facilitative relationships among the individuals, agencies, and groups involved and concerned with installing and refining the system of IGE. Research is also cited in this section which shows how the system of facilitative environments can be utilized to enhance the capability of local schools in implementing IGE.

The chapter concludes with several guidelines and suggestions whereby the principal can provide leadership in implementing IGE as a planned educational change.

THE NEED FOR PLANNED CHANGE

A major concern in education is the need for translating theory and research into viable and beneficial educational programs. The promise of timely and efficient diffusion of research findings from their source to their users establishes the need for planned change. Local schools may not be aware of the need for change or may not know how to manage change, which is one reason for including facilitative environments as a component of IGE.

Change should be instituted so that (1) the integrity of the change is protected; (2) the change is suited to the conditions in the school; (3) the conflict over the change is resolved; (4) the change results in improved performance; and (5) the consideration of future change is heightened (Maguire 1970, p. 3). The need for planned change arises not only from the limited capabilities of local schools to become aware of and to manage planned change. It also derives from the broader need for translating new theory, knowledge, and techniques into improved role competence. There is a close relationship between the utilization of educational research developments, on the one hand, and improved educational practice, on the other. Planned change may be viewed in terms of the research-practice relationship, and IGE as a product of theory, research, and development.

The Research-practice Relationship

The question of the relevance and application of educational research has been voiced by many sectors of the educational community. The need exists for accelerating and improving the research-practice continuum. In this regard, Carter (1966) emphasized:

> Traditionally it has been assumed that there is a fairly smooth sequence from research through a developmental phase to the utilization of research results. Evidence shows that this sequence is seldom followed in actual practice and that special efforts must be made to assure that the results of research are applied.

The link between inventor and user is probably one of the weakest interfaces in our contemporary educational system (Rogers and Svenning 1969, p. 5). Three causes for the gaps between research developments and administrative practice which serve as barriers to change are: (1) the lack of effective communication between researchers and school administrators, (2) the lack of psychological linkages between administrators' knowledge and their actions, and (3) the lack of connection between the practitioner's action repertoire and the requirements of the situation (Schmuck 1967, pp. 8–11).

The underlying concern for linking inventors of educational techniques and programs with the school staff is the belief that education can and must be improved. One means for improving education is the establishment of mechanisms for translating theory and research into developed programs and, in turn, translating these developments into practice. The need for narrowing the research-practice gap is overriding, and it serves as the basis for the five-phase implementation strategy of IGE—awareness, commitment, changeover, refinement, and renewal.

IGE: A Product of Theory and Practice

IGE as an alternative form of schooling with its seven components originated during the period 1966 through 1968 as a product of four closely related sets of activities: analysis of the educational practices of a few elementary schools in four school districts of Wisconsin, identification of undesirable conditions in those schools that hindered the improvement of educational practices, elimination of the undesirable conditions in the schools as described earlier in Chapter 1 of this book, and replacing them with conditions as embodied in such components of IGE as the multiunit school organization and instructional programming for the individual student.

These activities, in turn, were part of the continuing cooperative problem solving activities of the IGE conceptualizers of the Wisconsin Research and Development Center and school personnel, including the superintendents and other central office personnel of the school districts, and the principals, unit leaders, and teachers of the participating elementary schools (Klausmeier 1975). In 1968, formal research and related theorizing regarding the various facets of IGE began in IGE schools (Pellegrin 1971) and since then concepts, relationships, and procedures from one or more of the following strategies of planned change have been applied by different persons and groups to IGE at the national, state, and local levels: (1) social interaction; (2) problem solver; (3) research, development, and diffusion; and (4) linkage perspectives.

Concerning the social interaction view, for example, the importance of interpersonal relationships and peer group support is one basis for the creation of the interlocking network structure in the facilitative environments component. This strategy also relates to recognition of the problems associated with age-graded instruction, self-contained classrooms, homogeneous teaching roles, and minimal interlocking of staff effort which is particularly treated during the awareness phase of the implementation process.

Staff training for the new roles and behaviors needed to solve problems is also a critical ingredient of the IGE implementation effort. These two needs, problem clarification and staff capability, are major ingredients of the problem-solver strategy.

The research, development, and diffusion strategy focuses on interorganizational relationships among universities, regional centers, state education agencies, teacher education institutions, and local educational agencies. This change strategy emphasizes the orderly translation of research and development into practice.

The emphasis on interlocking organizational and group relationships to facilitate implementation is emphasized in the linkage strategy. By creating a proper mix of face-to-face contact, training, and consulting activities at a mutually agreeable frequency, external agencies and school-related groups are able to sustain facilitative environments for the implementation of IGE in local schools.

Because principals and unit leaders have a critical role in the process of changing to IGE, they must be knowledgeable about widely practiced strategies of planned change, appropriate uses of each strategy, strengths and weaknesses of the strategies, and alternative ways in which the change process can be carried out. Therefore, the next section deals with the four strategies for change with particular attention to how a principal might utilize each strategy.

STRATEGIES FOR PLANNED CHANGE

Difficulties associated with implementing a complex instructional and organizational concept like IGE may be made more understandable and manageable by examining the four strategies of planned change: (1) social interaction; (2) problem solver; (3) research, development, and diffusion; and (4) linkage.

Social Interaction Strategy

The social interaction strategy emphasizes the effects of influence patterns and communication in the change process. The principal should be aware of the patterns of influence and communication which affect the decision to adopt IGE. Research has shown that opinion leaders such as the principal are very influential and instrumental, particularly in stages of awareness and adoption of IGE (Goodridge 1975). Understanding of the innovation on the part of the principal provides a base for initiating and managing planned change.

According to the social interaction perspective, there are five major phases through which an individual or group progresses in the change process: (1) awareness of an innovation which may create a "need" for the innovation, (2) interest in the innovation which results in actively seeking information concerning its viability and utility, (3) evaluation of the innovation by judging its efficacy vis-à-vis present practice, (4) trial of the innovation which involves implementation on a small scale, and (5) adoption of the innovation which results in its continued use (Rogers 1962, p. 81). Within this view, the social interaction between the potential adopter and significant reference groups is the major source of communication concerning the innovation.

The essential feature of the social interaction approach is being aware of the sources of information about an innovation. Personal versus impersonal sources of information and influence are key distinctions in the social interaction process. For example, impersonal sources of information may be effective at the awareness and information-seeking stage of the social interaction strategy, while personal sources may be more effective at the later stages of evaluation, trial, and adoption. Consequently, the principal may read an article about IGE and then discuss the idea with the superintendent, central office personnel, or teachers. As more information is gathered, and if a trial seems possible, then personal sources of information are usually sought. This might include obtaining information from other principals or visiting an IGE school. The individual who first learns about IGE and passes the information along to other members is considered an opinion leader. Within the social network of the school, opinion leaders play a key role in influencing others and contributing to the diffusion and acceptance of innovations.

The initial research responsible for the social interaction approach emanated from the field of rural sociology and the study of the adoption of new agricultural products by farmers. Subsequent research in education has also shown social interaction and personal influence to be the key variables in the adoption of educational innovations (Carlson 1965). Personal versus impersonal sources of information and influence are key distinctions in the social interaction view of planned change.

Problem-solver Perspective

In contrast to the social interaction perspective, which portrays the potential user of an innovation as part of a social influence network, this strategy focuses on the difference between that which exists and that which is desired. It views the user of an innovation as a client to be helped in a collaborative setting. It emphasizes the design of solutions to solve unique problems and the training of local staff to solve future problems. The need for clarifying problems in education and the importance of tangibly illustrating how IGE can help to solve these problems is a critical role of the principal. Progress in moving through the implementation phases will be facilitated by acknowledgment of a felt need, on the one hand, and by understanding of how IGE will reduce the need, on the other.

A seven-stage model of change which focuses on the deliberate search for solutions to identified school problems has been developed. These seven stages are as follows (cf. Lewin 1952, pp. 459–473, and Lippett, *et al.* 1958, pp. 130):

1. Developing a need for change
2. Establishing relationships with outside sources
3. Diagnosing the problem
4. Examining alternative goals and establishing plans of action
5. Transforming plans into change efforts
6. Generalizing and stabilizing the change
7. Achieving a terminal relationship

The first step in the model, developing a need for change, includes problem awareness, desire for change, and desire for external help. Establishing a relationship with an outside source is step two of the model. This step is crucial since a collaborative relationship between an outside change agent and the personnel of the school is the basis for the problem-solver strategy. In IGE, the outside source might be personnel in a regional or state education agency or a teacher education institution. The success or failure of almost any change project depends heavily upon the quality and the workability of the relationship between the change agent and the client (school) system.

It is in the first two steps that the problem-solver strategy distinguishes itself from the social interaction strategy. In the problem-solver strategy, the motivation for change comes from identification of a problem and a subsequent desire for external help to solve the problem. In the social interaction strategy, a preexisting innovation is transmitted through information channels regardless of the documented needs of the school.

The third, fourth, and fifth stages of the model deal with diagnosing the problem, examining alternative goals and establishing plans of action, and transforming plans into change efforts. The diagnosis stage provides a basis to suggest alternative solutions to the problem. At the fourth stage, the client or school may wish to pilot test the alternative solution in order to minimize future failure and evaluate the effectiveness of the solution. The fifth stage of transforming the best solution into action or implementation is the critical point in the change strategy. Continuous monitoring of the change is suggested in order to minimize premature discontinuance and in order to adjust the plan to unforeseen conditions. Input for these stages might come from a variety of educational agencies, the central office of the school system, or teacher education institutions.

The last two stages of the problem-solver strategy include generalizing and stabilizing the change and achieving a terminal relationship. In order to stabilize the change it is necessary to provide structural support and rewards for the client (school) system. Structural support includes a new or revised organizational configuration consistent with the change, and rewards include tangible benefits which accrue to the staff. In IGE, the multiunit organization within the school system and the state network linking the local system to a variety of support agencies in the state provide this stability.

The last stage, terminating the external change agent relationship, is based on the tendency for a school to feel dependent on the outside resource. New skills and role competencies needed to maintain and refine the change must be developed within the client system of the school. When the school is confident in making the change, the relationship with the outside change agent can be terminated. However, since IGE is a dynamic concept that is constantly being refined, the relationships with the national Association for Individually Guided Education, state networks, regional networks, and other agencies should not be terminated, even though the demand for input may diminish as the change stabilizes in a school.

The seven problem-solving stages furnish a conceptual scheme for perceiving, analyzing, and planning the change process. There are also a number of important distinctions implied by this problem-solver strategy. Initially, the school must be self-motivated in order to facilitate the mutual relationship with the change agent. Without self-motivation the school cannot successfully progress through the logically interrelated stages of the problem-solver strategy. However, the source of the motivation also may come from the change agent. This means that a school's change to IGE might be initiated by school personnel or by outside sources such as the state or regional education agency or teacher education institution.

There is a need to distinguish between the premature adoption of solutions which may not correspond to the problem, and the tendency to establish committees which may never act on the problem. This need is somewhat related to the issue of school capability. Much time and energy must be devoted to training the school staff in the use of a major planned change. Learning the new roles and techniques associated with the change is critical. If ignored, it will eventually lead to the failure and discontinuance of the change. As indicated in Chapter 5, in IGE, a strong, in-depth inservice program is necessary to prepare principals, unit leaders, and teachers for the new and altered roles they will assume.

A recent study which involved the problem-solver strategy of change and the implementation of IGE was conducted by Smith (1972). She found that a change-agent-intervention strategy, characteristic of the problem-solver approach, lacked sufficient emphasis on (1) clarifying the innovation; (2) increasing motivation; and (3) facilitating the development of internal capability for establishing new roles, procedures, and goals associated with the innovation. The lack of problem identification and the failure to establish mechanisms for monitoring and refining an innovation were two causes for the unsuccessful implementation of change. It should be stressed that a short-range view of change will inevitably lead to failure of an innovation. This is particularly important with respect to IGE which is a long-term, comprehensive, and complex change. It is necessary, therefore, for the principal and the unit leader to understand the need for continuous feedback concerning the effectiveness of the change. By not taking a long-range view of the change process, the staff may unknowingly thwart the successful implementation of IGE.

Although the seven-stage model has received considerable attention and has many proponents in the field of education, there are a number of difficulties in the approach which the principal and unit leader, and other staff members should understand. For example, awareness of a problem, desire to solve the problem, and a search for external help depend on the individual's ability to identify problems, the attitude that the problem can be solved, and the assumption that outside change agents can help solve the problem. Many schools have neither the capability to identify complex educational problems, nor the determination to solve them. Moreover, outside change agents, such as personnel from state or regional educational agencies or teacher education institutions, are sometimes viewed by practitioners as impractical or "too theoretical."

Research, Development, and Diffusion Strategy

This strategy is based on an interorganizational view of change. Here, the unit of analysis is the organization, as opposed to the individual in the two previous strategies. The major implications of this strategy for the role of the principal revolve around the basic need for closing the gap between research and practice, on the one hand, and the need for understanding the interorganizational relationships involved, on the other. This strategy of change is first discussed in terms of its four main stages—research, development, diffusion, and adoption. Then, some assumptions and critical components are reviewed.

The research strategy considers the receiver of new ideas and practices initially as passive. It differs from the social interaction perspective in that the change process is viewed from an earlier point in time, i.e., at the research stage. It also differs from the problem-solver strategy. Instead of focusing on school needs, it emphasizes the predetermined solution to problems, and centers on closing the gap between research and practice.

The research stage includes depicting, relating, conceptualizing, and testing without concern for practical application. In this regard, it has been asserted that the researcher "needs to be free from pressures for immediate payoff" (Guba 1967, p. 8). The development stage where problems are identified, and solutions are invented, packaged, and field tested logically follows the research stage. The importance of maintaining a distinction between research, the discovery of new ideas, and development, the solution to problems, is stressed. In the developmental stage, "It is this activity, and not research, which is at the heart of change, for while research may make change possible, it is development that actually produces an innovation that may be adopted." (Guba 1966, p. 12)

The first two stages, research and development, assume that there are a variety of problems common to most schools and that solutions to these problems can be prepackaged for delivery. It should be noted, however, that when developers become aware of the needs and problems of local schools they are then able to design relevant innovations. The balance between prepackaged solutions to general problems, on the one hand, and solutions to unique individual school problems (problem-solver approach), on the other hand, is a critical issue in the research perspective.

The diffusion stage as described by Guba (1967, pp. 42–43), includes telling, showing, helping, involving, training, and intervening. It is directed toward "building awareness and understanding of an innovation and causing practitioners to consider its features with a view to possible application." Guba focuses on three critical issues: (1) the identification of problems the innovation is designed to solve; (2) the creation of demonstration centers in order to increase credibility and provide the practitioner an opportunity to determine whether the solution fits the problem; and (3) the training of staffs to train other teachers. All of these issues have been dealt with in IGE.

Making clear the problems that the innovation is designed to solve minimizes false expectations and helps to solve specific problems. The importance of problem identification at the diffusion stage is also related to the need for balance between prepackaged and unique solutions at the development stage. Credibility may be favorably influenced by demonstration centers—in the case of IGE, smoothly functioning IGE schools—but it is also related to the relevancy of the innovation with respect to the problems recognized by the potential adopting system and the system's perception of the researcher.

The research, development, and diffusion strategy recognizes the need for training principals, unit leaders, and teachers to facilitate the adoption of an innovation. However, training typically is not a primary focus or role of the researcher. This is in contrast to the problem-solver perspective which is directed toward training in order to increase the capability of clients or schools to solve recurring problems. Oftentimes, practitioners do not distinguish between the role of the researcher and the role of the problem solver.

Adoption, the fourth stage, includes trial, installation, and institutionalization. The trial component of the adoption stage assumes that variations in local characteristics may modify the universal advantages of the innovation. The installation aspect assumes that modifying, training, equipping, and organizing are necessary prerequisites of institutionalization. The institutionalization aspect assumes that assimilation and acceptance will follow over time. The adoption stage of the research approach places the initiative on extraorganizational systems which are responsible for encouraging and supporting the target system throughout the adoption stage. The degree of external intervention, involvement, and support is the primary focus and a critical issue in the research, development, and diffusion perspective. Within this view it is assumed that as the adopting system progresses toward the institutionalization and refinement of an innovation, elaborate help must be provided by an outside enabling agency. In IGE, the outside agency might be the regional, state, multistate, or national network.

Linkage Strategy

The linkage strategy to planned change also emphasizes the need for structured interaction between sources and users of knowledge. Linkage agents facilitate interorganizational cooperation and communication. Since the principal is in a position to encourage or discourage interorganizational interaction, the principal must understand and appreciate the role of linkage agents, the need for regular training and consulting on a face-to-face basis, as well as the short-term inconveniences and the long-term benefits of working with internal and external agencies, groups, and individuals.

The seven stages of the linkage approach are as follows (Havelock 1971):

1. Linkage, which signifies the degree of interpersonal connection and mutual communicative relations among two or more parties
2. Structure, which signifies the systematic organization and coordination of elements within the research-utilization continuum
3. Openness, which signifies readiness to give and to receive new information
4. Capacity, which includes factors related to a broad range of human, fiscal, and political resources
5. Reward, which represents positive reinforcement going to members of the systems involved in the research-utilization continuum
6. Proximity, which signifies physical accessibility
7. Synergy, which is a combined action of forces organized toward adoption of an innovation

The significance of the linkage strategy is, in part, centered on the introduction of organizational concepts within the seven-stage model. However, in order to understand the eclectic nature of the linkage strategy, references will be made to the social interaction; problem-solver; and research, development, and diffusion strategies.

The social interaction strategy emphasizes the importance of the social relations network, the potential adopter within the network, the strengths of informal personal contact and the effect of group norms. These have been integrated into the linkage approach. The factors of linkage, reward, proximity, and synergy are related in that (1) linkage corresponds to interconnections within the social relations network, (2) reward corresponds to the reinforcing effect of meeting group norms, (3) proximity corresponds to informal contact, and (4) synergy is related to the overall repetition of social contact within the social system network.

The problem-solver strategy is also related to factors within the linkage strategy. The problem-solver approach emphasizes the mutual collaboration between change agents and practitioners, the awareness of the problem to be solved by the practitioner, and the capability of the practitioner to solve recurring problems. These three factors correspond to the linkage factors of openness (willingness to enter into collaborative relationships with external agents), reward (sense of accomplishment resulting from solving a problem), and capacity (the resources within and the capability of the user system).

The research, development, and diffusion strategy, which in part stresses the need for an orderly transition from research to use, is also related to two factors within the linkage strategy. The factor of linkage is concerned with the need for connecting the producers of new knowledge with systems that need and can use the knowledge. The factor of structure stresses the need for a coordinated and systematic approach to the process of knowledge utilization.

The linkage strategy, although receiving minimal empirical or descriptive verification, has focused attention on the major concept of linkage. Chase (1970, p. 320) commented on the need for linking sources and users of knowledge as follows:

> The building of organizational links to facilitate the flow of knowledge into educational practice is going forward slowly but persistently. Education not only suffers from inadequate knowledge-producing resources, but also from the lack of closely linked agencies for moving knowledge through essential processes and phases to widespread and effective use.

The relationships among linkage, structure, and capability on the diffusion of IGE in three states were explored in a recent study by Paul (1974). Interviews conducted with personnel from the Wisconsin Research and Development Center, state education agencies, teacher education institutions, and IGE schools revealed that linkage between organizations possessing knowledge of IGE and capable of assisting local school personnel was an effective means for diffusing IGE. Frequent face-to-face contact and frequent training activities were found to be conducive to complete implementation of IGE. Teacher education institution personnel played a major role in the linkage effort by visiting schools and providing inservice and preservice instruction. In addition, student teachers assigned to the I & R Units in IGE schools not only served to enhance considerably the instructional capability of the school, but also served as a significant link between the school and the teacher education institution.

The greatest value of the linkage approach is its recognition of organizational variables as predictors of the adoption of an innovation. The interorganizational theme of the linkage strategy provides a basis for the national and state-regional-local networks which constitute the extraorganizational facilitative environment for IGE.

EXTRAORGANIZATIONAL FACILITATIVE ENVIRONMENT FOR IGE

The extraorganizational facilitative environment which has been established for the diffusion of IGE includes national and state-regional-local networks. The principal engaged in the process of implementing IGE as a planned change should appreciate the structure and function of the networks in order to utilize them effectively.

The National Network

The Association for Individually Guided Education (AIGE) was established in response to the need for improving the nationwide implementation of IGE.

A structural system of interlocking members provides the basis for the AIGE, a nonprofit association founded in 1973. As may be seen in Figure 8.1, the organization of the AIGE consists of three interconnected hierarchical levels to facilitate the diffusion, implementation, and refinement of IGE.

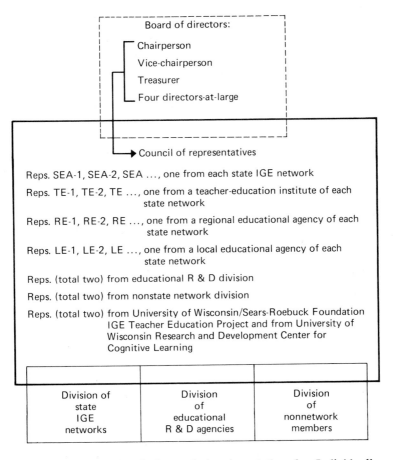

Fig. 8.1 Organizational chart of the Association for Individually Guided Education (AIGE). From H. J. Klausmeier, J. E. Walter, and L. J. Lins 1974. *Manual for starting and maintaining state IGE networks,* Madison, Wisc.: University of Wisconsin/Sears-Roebuck Foundation IGE Teacher Education Project.

The role of the Association is centered upon the need for a coordinated and systematic approach for implementing IGE. The structure of the Association was designed to heighten communication, cooperation, and participation. The trilevel arrangement, with interlocking communication links, allows for communication between the Board of Directors, The Council of Representatives, and the three divisions. The Division of State IGE Networks corresponds to the state-regional-local IGE Coordinating Council discussed in the following section. The Division of Educational Research and Development Agencies incorporates representatives from research and development centers concerned and interested in IGE. The Division of Nonnetwork Members allows for representation from the University of Wisconsin/Sears-Roebuck Foundation IGE Teacher Education Project and from the Wisconsin Research and Development Center.

The Council of Representatives, the second hierarchical level, consists of four representatives from each state network and two representatives each from the Division of Educational Research and Development agencies and the Division of Nonnetwork Members. The third hierarchical level consists of seven members elected by the Council of Representatives.

Each level of the Association is represented in each succeeding level. This joint membership feature not only promotes communication and coordination, but also provides for conflict resolution. Communication is heightened since a representative from one level may interact on a face-to-face basis with members at the next level. Coordination and cooperation are maintained since duplication of effort can be reduced and sharing of expertise can be increased. Resolving conflicts concerning the roles, responsibilities, and obligations of the Divisions, Council, and Directors is facilitated by the interlocking membership structure. By resolving conflicts early, the Association will be able to devote its full energies toward expanding and improving IGE throughout the nation.

State-regional-local Networks

State-regional-local networks were created to serve as the structural means for channeling feedback, promoting collaborative interaction, and stimulating cooperation among state education agency, teacher education institution, intermediate education agency, and local education agency personnel. The two new structures in this network are the State IGE Coordinating Council and the Regional IGE Coordinating Council. The structure of the state-regional-local network is shown in Figure 8.2.

The AIGE at the national level is linked with the state network through the Division of State IGE Networks, on the one hand, and the State IGE Coordinating Council on the other. Consequently, a complete system of interlocking arrangements has been designed to channel the concerns, problems, and issues related to IGE upward and to funnel the programs,

Reps. SEA-1, SEA-2, SEA-3, ... of state education agency, including IGE coordinator	Reps. *TE-1, TE-2, TE-3,* ... of teacher education institutions of state	Reps. SPC-1, SPC-2, SPC-3, ... of SPCS of state

SEA-1 *TE-1*			SEA-2 *TE-2*			SEA-3 *TE-3*		
SPC-1	SPC ...	SPC ...	SPC-2	SPC ...	SPC ...	SPC-3	SPC ...	SPC ...
SPC of school district 1 of region 1	SPC of school district 2 of region 1	SPC of school district 3 of region 1	SPC of school district 1 of region 2	SPC of school district 2 of region 2	SPC of school district 3 of region 2	SPC of school district 1 of region 3	SPC of school district 2 of region 3	SPC of school district 3 of region 3

- - - - - - - State IGE coordinating council (SICC)
————— Regional IGE coordinating council (RICC)
————— Systemwide program committees (SPC)

Fig. 8.2 Organizational arrangement of a state-regional-local IGE network. From H. J. Klausmeier, J. E. Walter, and L. J. Lins 1974. *Manual for starting and maintaining state IGE networks,* Madison, Wisc.: University of Wisconsin/ Sears-Roebuck Foundation IGE Teacher Education Project.

opportunities, and information from the Board of Directors of the National Association downward.

As with the national Association, each state network consists of three interlocking hierarchical levels: the State IGE Coordinating Council, the Regional IGE Coordinating Councils, and the Systemwide Program Committees (SPC). The SPC at the school district level provides the foundation upon which the Regional and State Councils rest. As indicated in Chapter 2, the SPC is the local facilitative network composed of each IGE school in a district. Here, the concerns, problems, and plans involving the IGE schools of a district are presented, discussed, solved, and evaluated.

Issues which transcend local school district boundaries are addressed by the Regional IGE Coordinating Council. The Regional Council is a facilitative network which considers concerns, problems, and plans affecting two or more school districts in the region. Depending on the structure of education in each state, the Regional Council is composed of comparable geographical regions incorporating at least one teacher education institution which serves the schools in that region. In addition to the teacher education representatives, one of which serves on the State Council, there is also a member from the state education agency. If the state has intermediate educational service agencies, then they are also represented on the Regional and State Councils. Each SPC in the region is represented on the Regional Council and it is recommended that at least one of these be a unit leader or teacher. Thus, the structure provides for interlocking membership from the level of the I & R Unit to regional, state, and national levels.

The third hierarchical level of the state-regional-local network system is the State IGE Coordinating Council. Issues which transcend regional boundaries, concerns involving two or more Regional Councils, and problems of a statewide nature are presented, discussed, and evaluated by the State Council. Representation on this Council includes: one or more members from the state education agency; one intermediate education agency member from each Regional Council; one teacher educator from each Regional Council; and one SPC member from each Regional Council. The full-time state IGE coordinator, usually affiliated with the state education agency, is also a member of the State Council. Criteria for membership of state education agency personnel include: (1) responsibility for a statewide educational program; (2) authority to recommend new or revised programs; and (3) fulfilling a role concerned with program development, teacher education, or elementary or secondary school programs. Criteria for representatives of teacher education institutions include responsibilities for: (1) inservice to local schools, (2) preservice IGE teacher education, and (3) graduate programs for school principals or unit leaders.

The functions of the state-regional-local network include indexing needs, developing programs to meet needs, implementing programs, and evaluating programs. Concomitantly, effective channels of communication between and among the three hierarchical levels must be maintained to minimize duplication and maximize coordination. The interlocking membership structure is designed toward this end. The interdependence of the State Councils and the need for interstate cooperation is given expression in the national AIGE. Consequently, a complete chain of representation spanning local, regional, state, and national perspectives has been designed to facilitate awareness, commitment, changeover, refinement, and renewal of IGE.

The Need for Interconnected Networks

The series of IGE networks is based on the need for sharing and cooperating between and among the local school, regional education agency, teacher education institution, state education agency, and research center personnel. Three studies have focused on the problems involved with the nationwide implementation of IGE. These studies provide insight into the scope and complexity of educational change on the one hand, and the need for extraorganizational facilitative networks, on the other.

The United States Office of Education commissioned the Educational Testing Service to conduct a nationwide study on the effectiveness of the installation of the multiunit organizational component in first-year IGE schools (Ironside 1972, pp. 14–18). The two phases of the study included interviews, visits, and questionnaires involving over 250 schools in ten states during the 1971–72 school year and a follow-up study involving over 90 schools during the fall of 1972. Several findings from the first phase of the study pointed to the need for national, state, regional, and local networks. This study found (1) diverse definitions among principals concerning the initial adoption procedures; (2) a lack of clarity in implementation guidelines; (3) minimal resources available for adopting IGE oriented curricula; (4) wide variations in the installation activities among states, districts, schools, and units; (5) wide variations in the extent of training (preservice and inservice) given principals and their staff; and (6) a wide range of attitudes expressed by school staffs toward IGE.

Additional findings related to the need for a series of facilitative networks. Principals, for example, felt frustrated during the initial stages of implementation over having to search for personnel capable of assisting in the difficult task of installing IGE. Added to the plight of principals was the frustration of teachers who felt that they had received inadequate preparation. As a result of the difficulties faced by principals and teachers, the actual implementation of some of the major components of IGE was not achieved by all schools.

The second phase of the study was designed to determine the extent of continuance and/or strengthening of IGE in a sample of the schools studied the previous year. Several of the findings relate to the need for facilitative networks. For example, "a considerable need for technical assistance was expressed, as much among the earlier installing schools as among the 1972–73 group, across a large number of topics" (Ironside 1973, p. 5). The national, state, regional, and local networks were subsequently created to provide technical assistance to principals and teachers.

Reinforcing the need for external assistance are the findings of a descriptive study of four multiunit schools reported by Packard (1973) and conducted in Wisconsin during 1972. Exhaustion, personnel turnover, difficulties in implementing the multiunit organization, and lack of external assistance after the first year were found to be related to premature implementation closure. Fear of making mistakes also contributed to the adoption of identical procedures by I & R Units (Packard 1974, pp. 127–129). These findings indicate that technical assistance is needed to support, encourage, revitalize, and renew the staff.

The processes of interorganizational interaction was the focus of a descriptive study of IGE conducted in three states by Paul (1974). The relationships between and among the Wisconsin Research and Development Center, state education agencies, teacher education institutions, and local IGE schools were explored and described. This study also concluded that facilitative networks are needed to help train IGE staff, to ensure proper implementation, and to provide support and encouragement. Teacher education institutions, through the supervision of student teachers, were found to be effective sources of support. Mutual understanding and agreement between the teacher educators and IGE principals concerning the extent and nature of assistance contributed to a mutually beneficial relationship.

Figure 8.3 illustrates the linkage relationships among the resource system (the Wisconsin Research and Development Center), the mediating system (state education agencies and teacher education institutions), and the user system (local IGE schools). In this diagram, the direction of the arrows refers to interaction (one-way and two-way) while the density of the arrows refers to the frequency and amount of interaction. The schematic shows that (1) teacher education institutions were actively involved, that

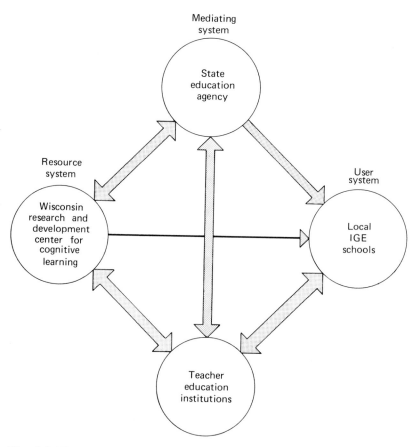

Fig. 8.3 The linkage relationships among resource, mediating, and user systems.

(2) state education agencies were moderately involved, and that (3) the Research and Development Center was the least involved in direct contact with local schools. Since the teacher education institutions are geographically dispersed throughout the country, they have the advantage of proximity with schools wishing to implement IGE. The broad responsibilities and the larger client population of state education agencies constrains their potential for frequent maintenance and refinement activities with multiunit schools. The Wisconsin Research and Development Center involvement at the national level with over 2000 IGE schools is clearly limited in the extent and kind of direct services it can provide to individual schools. To enhance effective implementation of IGE, each agency must give attention to its role in improving the linkages. In addition, several specific problems were pinpointed, among them being that university personnel were often too theoretical, that state agency personnel were spread too thinly, and that teacher training personnel often disrupted the daily routine in some I & R Units. The system of extraorganizational facilitative environments was designed, therefore, not only to increase the quantity of interaction, but also to enhance the quality of interaction among agencies concerned with implementing IGE.

THE PRINCIPAL'S ROLE IN PLANNED CHANGE

The principal as a linkage agent must be able to utilize the strategies of planned change in strengthening the extraorganizational facilitative environment for IGE. The role of the principal vis-à-vis the national Association and the state-regional-local networks, although broadly defined, is critical to the effective implementation of IGE. Initiating and maintaining communication, cooperation, and interaction between the school and the networks is a primary responsibility of the principal. Attending network meetings and channeling information to and from the networks and the IIC may require considerable time but the outcomes are well worth the effort. The linkage perspective of change stresses the need for a collaborative relationship between the sources and the users of knowledge. The principal, as a user of IGE, must establish mutually beneficial relationships with extraorganizational resources. The networks provide a means whereby the principal can initiate and maintain these relationships.

In the SPC the principal can interact with other principals, the superintendent or designee, central office consultants, unit leaders, teachers, and community representatives. In so doing, the principal is able to learn new ideas from other IGE principals, communicate concerns from the school that involve the district, help plan districtwide inservice activities, help revise policies, and secure financial resources for the IGE at the school. It is important that principals be able to discern districtwide issues, problems, and concerns and provide input to their solution. Similarly, in working with regional and state committees the principal can initiate, maintain, and refine relationships with the teacher education institution, state education agency, and intermediate educational agency. These three organizations represent knowledge resources which should be harnessed to facilitate the implementation of IGE.

Understanding the concepts and relationships of extraorganizational linkage, clarifying the roles of linkage agents and systems, maintaining a training and consulting orientation, ensuring that interaction is face-to-face, and establishing mutually agreeable frequencies of interaction are important responsibilities of the principal. Since the function of linking the school to outside resources is a relatively new practice, it may conflict with past traditions of isolation or autonomy. Concomitantly, the principal should understand the dynamics, difficulties, and significance of extraorganizational linkages. By understanding the concepts and relationships involved, the principal will be better prepared to cope with the unforeseen consequences of extraorganizational linkage.

The principal should work to clarify the role of each organization in the linkage chain, particularly that of the local school. Ambiguous or assumed roles will result in frustration, dissatisfaction, and conflict. The relationship between the outside organization and the school must be made explicit—what will be done, how will it be done, and when will it be done—and delineated as clearly as possible before major programs and activities are initiated.

In relationships with extraorganizational personnel, the principal also should stress the training and consulting relationship. Too often, the difficult and time-consuming tasks of relearning roles and developing new skills are presumed by merely disseminating information without regard for "putting it into practice." The principal must insist on an effective training orientation on the part of outside consultants. Conversely, the principal has a responsibility to communicate information which provides a reality base for relearning on the part of the consultant.

The principal also must see to it that a majority of linking experiences are conducted on a face-to-face basis. The advantage of direct, personal contact is that two-way communication is facilitated, feedback between sender and receiver is immediate, and clarity of the message is enhanced. Face-to-face contact and two-way communication are worth the time and effort.

Establishing a mutually agreeable frequency of interaction with the extraorganizational resource is also a responsibility of the principal. There must be role agreement between the principal and the linkage agent concerning the frequency of interaction. Frequent visits by the outside resource may create a feeling of intrusion, whereas too few visits may lead to feelings of neglect. In establishing a mutually agreeable level of interaction the principal should take into account not only the needs of the staff, but also the responsibilities of the linkage agent.

Just as the school may benefit from the network structure, so also does it have an important contribution to make to the larger profession. Experienced IGE principals, unit leaders, and unit teachers may share, through the network structure, their knowledge and experiences with new and other IGE school personnel. Specialized knowledge may be made available to a wider audience, thereby obviating the need for each school to rediscover proven techniques and procedures.

The principal has a central role in implementing IGE. The principal is the linkage agent between the networks, the central office, and the community, on the one hand, and the unit leaders and unit teachers, on the other. The degree to which the developed research product of IGE is adopted and established within the school, the degree to which outside enabling groups enter into a collaborative relationship with the staff of the school, and the degree to which the community is involved with and committed to IGE are the responsibility of the principal and the IIC. Consequently, the principal contributes directly and actively to the need for planned change and to bridging the research-practice gap in education- -both important outcomes of planned change.

SUMMARY

The need for planned change was first discussed with attention being directed toward the gap between the developments of research and their use in schools. To provide the conceptual base whereby the principal can strengthen and utilize the facilitative extraorganizational environment for IGE, four strategies of planned educational change were first described: social interaction; problem solver; research, development, and diffusion; and linkage perspectives of change. The social interaction approach emphasizes communication channels and influence patterns. The problem-solver approach emphasizes the design of solutions to solve unique problems, as well as the training of local staff to solve future problems. The research, development, and diffusion approach emphasizes the interagency relationships and dynamics involved in closing the gap between research and practice. The linkage approach emphasizes the need for linkage structures to facilitate cooperation and communication in sharing resources to implement change effectively at national, state, regional, and local levels.

Next, IGE as a planned educational change was discussed with particular attention being directed toward the role and structure of the national Association for IGE, and the state-regional-local networks. The Association and networks were shown to be potentially powerful forces for improving the implementation of IGE. Research was cited to show the need for and importance of working with the networks, and some guidelines were traced for the principal in doing so.

The major outcome of planned change is that of narrowing the gap between research and practice. The understandings, skills, and competencies required of the principal were shown to be of central importance in utilizing research and development to implement IGE effectively.

REFERENCES

Carlson, R. O. 1965. *Adoption of educational innovations.* Eugene, Ore.: Center for the Advanced Study of Educational Administration, University of Oregon.

Carter, L. F. 1966. *From research to development to use.* Santa Monica, Calif.: System Development Corporation, Report N. SP-2332, January, ERIC Document Resume, ED 026 741.

Chase, F. S. 1970. R & D in the remodeling of education. *Phi Delta Kappan* **51** (February).

Goodridge, C. G. 1975. *Factors that influence the decision to adopt an educational innovation, IGE.* Doctoral dissertation, University of Wisconsin—Madison.

Guba, E. G. 1967. *Development, diffusion, and evaluation.* Bloomington, Ind.: National Institute for the Study of Educational Change.

————, 1968. Development, diffusion, and evaluation. In T. L. Eidell and J. M. Kitchel (eds.), *Knowledge production and utilization in educational administration.* Columbus, Ohio: University Council for Educational Administration, and Eugene, Ore. Center for the Advanced Study of Educational Administration.

————, 1966. *The change continuum and its relation to the Illinois plan for program development for gifted children.* Paper delivered to a conference on educational change, Urbana, Illinois. ED 011403.

Havelock, R. G. 1971. *Planning for innovation through dissemination and utilization of knowledge.* Ann Arbor, Mich.: Center for Research on Utilization of Scientific Knowledge.

Ironside, R. A. 1973. *The 1971–72 nationwide installation of the multiunit IGE model for elementary schools,* Vol. I. Princeton: Educational Testing Service.

Klausmeier, H. J., J. E. Walter, and L. J. Lins 1974. *Manual for starting and maintaining state IGE networks.* Madison, Wisc.: University of Wisconsin/Sears-Roebuck Foundation IGE Teacher Education Project.

Lewin, K. 1952. Group decision and social change. In G. E. Swanson (ed.), *Readings in social psychology.* New York: Holt, Rinehart and Winston.

Lippitt, R., J. Watson, and B. Westley 1958. *The dynamics of planned change.* New York: Harcourt.

Maguire, L. M. 1970. *Observations and analysis of the literature on change.* Philadelphia Research on Better Schools.

Packard, J. S. 1973. Changing to a multiunit school. In W. W. Charters, Jr. et al. (eds.). *Contrasts in the process of planned change of the school's instructional organization.* Eugene, Ore.: Center for the Advanced Study of Educational Administration, University of Oregon.

Paul, D. A. 1974. *The diffusion of an innovation through interorganizational linkages.* Technical report No. 308. Madison, Wisc.: Wisconsin Research and Development Center for Cognitive Learning.

Rogers, E. M. 1962. *Diffusion of innovations.* New York: Glencoe.

————, and L. Svenning 1969. *Change in small schools.* University Park, N.M.: New Mexico State University. ERIC Clearinghouse on Rural Education and Small Schools.

Schmuck, R. 1967. *Social psychological factors in knowledge utilization as applied to educational administration.* Paper presented at the University Council for Educational Administration Career Development Seminar, October, Portland, Ore.: University of Oregon.

Smith, M. A. 1972. *A comparison of two elementary schools involved in a major organizational change: or you win a few, you lose a few.* Doctoral dissertation, University of Oregon.

Stufflebeam, D. L., et al. 1971. *Educational evaluation and decision making.* Itasca, Ill.: Peacock.

Walter, J. E. 1973. *The relationship of organizational structure to organizational adaptiveness in elementary schools.* Technical report No. 226. Madison, Wisc.: Wisconsin Research and Development Center for Cognitive Learning.

9

IGE as a Self-Renewing System

James M. Lipham
Herbert J. Klausmeier

Objectives

After reading this chapter, the reader will be able:

■ To understand the dynamic aspects of IGE as a self-renewing system.

■ To identify possible refinements related to each of the seven components of IGE.

■ To recognize that the principal is a key figure in implementing IGE.

■ To identify several means for the principal's continued professional growth and development in IGE concepts and practices.

The dynamic system of IGE continues to undergo refinement and renewal as its seven components are tested in the crucible of practice in schools throughout the nation. Already, during its first decade, several substantive changes have emerged, others have been suggested, and undoubtedly others are yet to be conceptualized.

In attempting to chart some directions of a dynamic, changing system, there is the obvious danger that the particular dimensions documented will quickly become dated. Even so, this brief chapter will suggest some possible refinements in each component in the current configuration of IGE. Particular attention will be given to the continuously emerging role of the principal in implementing IGE, including the task of leading the building staff in self-renewal activities. The chapter concludes with a consideration of some general competencies required of the IGE principal, as well as some suggestions for further professional development and self-renewal.

FUTURE CHANGES IN THE COMPONENTS

Certain changes, expressed in terms of current concerns, may be needed in each of the following seven basic components of IGE: the multiunit organizational structure, instructional programming for the individual student, evaluation for educational decision making, curricular materials, home-school-community relations, intra- and extraorganizational facilitative environments, and continuing research and development.

The Multiunit Organizational Structure

Evidence from current research and practice reveals that the multiunit form of organizational structure is a powerful means for bringing the human and material resources of the school to bear directly upon improvement of education.* Schools where the structure has been implemented appropriately

---

*   Cf. R. G. Nelson, *An analysis of the relationship of the multiunit school organization structure and individually guided education to the learning climate of pupils,* Technical Report No. 213, 1972; K. B. Smith, *An analysis of the relationship between effectiveness of the multiunit elementary school's instructional improvement committee and interpersonal and leader behaviors,* Technical Report No. 230, 1972; J. E. Walter, *The relationship of organizational structure to teacher motivation in multiunit and nonmultiunit elementary schools,* Technical Report No. 322, 1974; T. J. Sheridan, *Perceived role and effectiveness of the unit leader in conducting unit functions,* Technical Report No. 318, 1974; N. A. Evers, *An analysis of the relationship between the effectiveness of the multiunit elementary school's instruction and research unit and interpersonal behaviors,* Technical Report No. 298, 1974; and G. W. Gramenz, *Relationship of principal leader behavior and organizational structure of the IGE/MUS–E to I & R unit effectiveness,* Technical Report No. 320, 1974. All published by the Wisconsin Research and Development Center, University of Wisconsin—Madison.

report substantial gains in organizational effectiveness, individual efficiency, and group morale of teachers, students, parents, and other subpublics of the school. The new role of unit leader and the new structures of the IIC and the I & R Units have served to maximize staff leadership, interpersonal communication and coordination, participation in decision making, and improved role performance.

While these desirable conditions are prevalent in IGE schools of 350 to above 700 enrollment, two interrelated problems will require continuous attention: first, the membership of the IIC, and second, the size of this group and its related ability to function as a group. Concerning membership, the possible inclusion of special teachers of art, music, and physical education, teachers of children with learning and other disabilities, and the director of the instructional materials center must be considered in terms of effects on the school's instructional program and also on the functioning of the committee when it increases in number. The problem is that while these persons have much to contribute to formulating the school's educational program, increasing the size of a group above seven tends to decrease its cohesiveness and problem-solving effectiveness. Similarly, IGE schools with large pupil enrollment that have more than five unit leaders, one or more assistant principals, and other persons with schoolwide responsibilities already have a very large IIC. Whether to reorganize this large committee into primary and intermediate groups, or to move in some other direction requires continuing study and experimentation.

An exploratory analysis of the membership, functions, and operation of the SPC shows considerable variation in the perceived effectiveness of this important group (Krula 1974). Undoubtedly, this is due to several situational factors, such as school district size and structure, as well as societal stresses on school systems—particularly in large urban centers. There is some evidence, moreover, that central office personnel are not perceived as in the vanguard of change (Benka 1972), and that more often than not IGE is a change for which the adoption has been initiated by principals and teachers (Goodridge 1975).

Since basic principles of organization stress the need for viable structures to span relationships between subunits and the larger organization, it seems imperative that continuing attention be directed toward clarifying the role of the SPC. Already, for example, it has been recognized that in large, urban school districts, program committees may be needed at subdistrict levels, and in such situations an additional linking mechanism, perhaps an executive committee is needed. (Schools of Los Angeles organized in this manner in 1974–75.)

In addition to the situation in large school districts a different condition occurs when many or all of the elementary schools of a smaller district become IGE and also when the secondary schools of the district start the changeover to IGE. The SPC is small and homogeneous when there are only a few elementary IGE schools; it is large when there are many. In addition, as the number of IGE schools increases, the role of the central office consultant and administrators should also change. Thus, when all the elementary schools of a district are IGE, there is no longer a need for an SPC; the SPC should be the mechanism involving all the central office staff and local school representatives.

In regard to the need for districtwide articulation of IGE it must be observed that the principal is remiss in an important leadership responsibility who does not attempt to initiate appropriate organizational structures. The basic concepts of the SPC provides opportunities for the principal to exercise leadership at the district level.

Instructional Programming for the Individual Student

The IPM, at the heart of IGE, is a sound guide for adapting instruction to the educational needs and personal characteristics of the individual student while yet meeting the objectives of education as developed in the local school and school district. Current concerns are not so much with the model as with its appropriate use—or lack of use.

In perhaps too many IGE schools instructional programming for the individual student is applied unevenly across the various curricular fields. In this regard, one is reminded of the school in which the principal and staff proudly boasted that they had "gone IGE"—only further observation revealed that programming for the individual student was limited to one hour's instruction per day in reading; in other curricular areas age-graded, group instruction was still being practiced. This is particularly ironic in that the model of instructional programming for the individual student is based on sound curricular, learning, and motivational theory; it can serve equally well in all curricular areas and in all kinds of schools as a guide for adapting instruction to the individual student.

An additional impediment to effective instructional programming for the individual student is the lack of attention given by the principal and the IIC to Steps 1 and 2—setting schoolwide objectives and establishing the range of objectives that may be attainable for subgroups of the student population. In such schools, attempts are made to start with Step 3, the assessment of each student, only to find subsequently in Step 4 that the instructional objectives set for each child may bear little relationship to major educational objectives of the school, the school district, and the state. A close examination of the model will reveal, "You can't get here (Step 1) from there (Step 4)." The principal, particularly, should lead the staff to the realization that decisions on objectives for the total school, for subgroups of students, and for individual students are nested decisions. Only then can the pitfall of having hosts of unrelated objectives be avoided. Further, each school must incorporate any district and state educational objectives into its own objectives if it expects to receive financial support from these sources. While each school develops schoolwide objectives appropriate for its student body and its community, it does not proceed independently of the district and state of which it is a part.

Finally, it is observed that many IGE principals have failed to utilize the IPM appropriately to ensure educational accountability and full use of the school's resources. In this regard, it is unfortunate that IGE is being simultaneously attacked from two opposing orientations. On the one hand, some incorrectly assert that IGE is highly unstructured and open—if not chaotic. On the other, some erroneously equate IGE with highly structured "individualized" programs in which all students use the same materials and are engaged in the same activities but merely proceed through the material at different rates until all the objectives are "mastered." IGE is neither of these, nor is it necessarily somewhere in between. In effect, in the IGE school the IPM is used as a guide for translating the vague concept of "individualized instruction" into a sound program of instructional programming for the individual student and which then in turn can be used in connection with encouraging students to be accountable for attaining specified objectives; teachers to be accountable that students attain the objectives; and administrators to be accountable for providing the conditions that make attainments accountable by teachers and students.

Perhaps the greatest deterrent to more effective programming of instruction for individual students is lack of information and skills by principals and unit leaders required to manage instruction simultaneously in several curricular areas. This book and other books in the series provide accurate information about instructional programming; also, computer management of instruction in IGE schools is under development and should markedly facilitate record keeping, assessment, and similar matters as it becomes economically feasible.

Evaluation for Educational Decision Making

The third basic component of IGE is that of evaluation for effective educational decision making. Within this domain future efforts should be addressed to reducing inconsistencies and incompatibilities between evaluation theory and decision theory, and to making available the information needed for informed decision making. In both of these areas it may well be that present practice has outrun our current conceptualizations.

There is hopeful evidence of some rapproachment between instructional evaluation theorists and organizational decision theorists in terms of conceptualizations which underlie both evaluation and decision making as rational processes (Stufflebeam, *et al.* 1971). For example, many similarities can be observed not only in the steps or stages, but also in the requisite activities, even though they may be given different names. Those who are concerned with evaluation of instruction should reexamine their prescriptive approaches to see whether or not they are relevant at school and district levels. Conversely, those concerned with decision making should focus more on decisions made by teachers and others at the workflow level—the I & R Unit in the IGE school.

Concerning the need for accurate, relevant, and timely evaluative information for use in decision making, better ways must be found to obtain, process, and summarize data needed by unit leaders and teachers in diagnosing and providing programs of instruction for the individual student. Although instructional or clerical aides can be utilized profitably to meet this need, better management and instructional information systems than wall charts, color-coded sheets, and similar data systems are demanded. Moreover, creative programs in computer-managed instruction currently being developed (Belt and Spuck 1974) will call for a substantial investment in computing facilities and trained personnel in the school of the future.

Compatible Instructional Materials

Instructional materials compatible with instructional programming for the individual student and the evaluation procedures of IGE increasingly are becoming available in many subject fields and this trend undoubtedly will continue. Several alternative programs have been published commercially in the basic fields of reading, mathematics, science, and social studies, and others are being developed in the fine arts, physical education, and environmental education.

Future concerns regarding this IGE component relate to the need for additional curriculum development and the need for specific criteria for determining the degree of compatibility between the materials produced and the system of IGE. Concerning the need for additional curriculum development, it must be acknowledged that great amounts of money are required to mount significant curriculum development projects—comparable to those that were allocated earlier in such fields as biology, physics, and mathematics. And while some may question the viability of the outcomes of such projects, there is no denying that the quickest, and perhaps most efficient, way to influence significantly what happens at the instructional level is to provide teachers with current, manageable, and useful teaching materials.

The task of developing instructional materials—except for minor modifications to meet schoolwide objectives—is probably beyond the capabilities of most local schools. In fact, professional educators can be fairly faulted for "continually reinventing the wheel" in this domain. Since federal funds for curriculum development are uncertain, increased efforts must be made by IGE schools and regional, state, and national networks to share information concerning curricular and other materials.

Concerning the need for specific criteria for judging the degree of compatibility of curricular materials with IGE, at present only some general guidelines have been developed. These must be made more specific. As an example, the advertising brochures and order forms of some publishers show "IGE" in type print larger than the title of the books, yet no information is provided concerning the extent to which the particular materials have proved effective in meeting the rates and styles of learning of carefully described target populations of students. Clearly, the need today is for materials that are suitable with students who do not profit from verbal instruction —either from reading and studying printed materials or listening to oral explanations given by teachers. Audiovisual materials and direct experiencing of objects and events are needed for these students until they can handle the verbal instruction. Also, some of these students require small group activities, tutoring, and one-to-one guidance before they can handle independent learning activities which require reading. Most IGE schools seem to have a large task ahead in providing for differences in learning styles of students.

Home-school-community Relations

A recent trend in our contemporary culture is the geometric increase in citizen participation in education at the local school level. In keeping with this trend, the system of IGE specifically provides for meaningful parental and citizen involvement at all levels in the multiunit organization. And while some may say that this is by no means unique, community involvement in IGE schools differs in quantity, and probably in quality, from that in many other settings.

A "Johnny-come-lately" development in IGE, the component of home-school-community relations is currently beset by a syndrome of sharing techniques for improving communication, and, hopefully, commitment. Needed in more IGE schools is a better understanding of the concepts of analysis, communication, involvement, and conflict resolution as described in this book.

This in no way belittles the creative approaches of many principals and unit leaders in formulating excellent programs of home-school-community relations. Rather, it is only recently that a comprehensive model of home-school-community relationships has been formulated. Similarly, the excellent practices of outstanding schools are only recently being documented. More information sharing and a greater effort by the IGE educational community in general is called for.

Facilitative Environments

The component of facilitative environments includes two sets of relationships, the intraorganizational and the extraorganizational environment. The intraorganizational environment is described by the multiunit organizational structure for IGE schools; the extraorganizational environment is concerned with the national, state, and regional networks for IGE. Pressing needs in IGE have surfaced in these domains.

Concerning the multiunit organization, the emphasis thus far in IGE has perforce been placed on the more formal aspects of defining role responsibilities, inservice training, and staff evaluation, since many organizational and structural changes were called for to "get the system going." Yet experienced IGE principals universally state that the implementation of IGE has not only increased staff effectiveness and productivity but simultaneously has stimulated group coordination, cooperation, satisfaction, motivation, and morale. Moreover, these phenomena persist, pervading the school long after the initial "halo effect" of change adoption has faded. In fact, it is through the informal processes of daily planning and working together that basic and beneficial changes in staff behavior occur. The implementation of IGE results in the continued personal and professional development of each staff member.

Regarding financial and physical resources, it is universally observed that the "age of accountability" is upon us. Increasingly, all educators are being called upon to account for the proper use of the vast material and personnel resources directed to education. In our view, the system of IGE holds promise for meeting accountability demands. Again, needed here are better conceptual views of the programming-budgeting processes which, thus far, have been difficult to cost at the instructional level. Following from this, specific procedures are needed for relating IGE practices and procedures to resource inputs, processes, and outputs. The IPM perhaps possesses potential for use in this effort.

The extraorganizational facilitative environment is concerned with mutual relationships of the local school and regional-state-national agencies, institutions, and individuals which together constitute a self-renewing system of education, preschool through higher education. We are probably at a point in our educational history when no local school can expect to become self-renewing unless it is involved in a cooperative improvement effort with the school district central office, intermediate education agency, state education agency, or teacher education institution. Similarly, teacher education institutions and state education agencies themselves cannot be very helpful to IGE schools unless they too develop a self-renewal capability. They cannot do this independently of local schools. Cooperative relationships among the educational agencies and educational institutions, such as outlined earlier in the discussion of state IGE networks and regional IGE networks, are needed. Perhaps then we can think not only about self-renewal in the context of an IGE school, or a teacher education institution, or a state education agency but also in terms of a comprehensive educational program, preschool through higher education.

Research and Development

Earlier in this book the start of IGE in 1966 was explained as an outcome of cooperative problem-solving activities by personnel of local school districts and the Wisconsin Research and Development Center for Cognitive Learning. This initial start paved the way for subsequent research regarding the entire IGE system and its various components. This kind of research is accelerating rapidly and its results are being incorporated into improved practices and higher-level conceptualizations and theories. This research, must continue if IGE is to flourish as a dynamic kind of schooling.

School personnel involved in starting the first IGE schools also called for better instructional materials, more sophisticated means of adapting instruction to individual students, better means of managing instruction, new means of working with parents, and better ways of motivating students. These expressed needs resulted in the production of staff development materials related to the various components, as well as materials for use with students. Continuing development of materials, processes, and structures is needed into the foreseeable future so that refined, second-generation products and processes become available to meet the continuously expanding and legitimate requirements of administrators, teachers, and students. The principal has a key role in working with the staff to identify additional research and development needs and to communicate these needs to appropriate personnel of the state networks and also to federally funded agencies.

The need for continuing research and development becomes apparent also from the study of the interactive linkage relationships discussed in connection with facilitative environments. To many, the system of IGE can be pointed to with pride as an effective example of building a bridge between theory and practice—with, it might be noted, quite limited resources. Moreover, it perhaps is not immodest to mention that many of the needed refinements in IGE suggested throughout this chapter are ample evidence that feedback from practitioners is also essential for refining administrative and instructional theory.

The local IGE school, and particularly the I & R Unit, is the rational locus for continuing to conduct in-school research of many varieties to enhance and improve the learning process. In the years ahead, feedback from this level of the organization is needed for testing the viability of each component of IGE, for suggesting component configurations as yet undiscovered, and for conceptualizing even better future systems of schooling.

THE SELF-RENEWING IGE PRINCIPAL

In this and previous chapters it is possible that the practicing IGE principal has been portrayed as a paragon—particularly since many times it has been stressed that the principal "absolutely must," "positively should," and "certainly ought" to do many things. Moreover, our injunctions abound with adjectives and adverbs that are probably more prescriptive than descriptive —due largely to our effort to show that IGE is a system of schooling. Thus, the principal contemplating the implementation of IGE might well ask: "How can I become better prepared to serve as an IGE principal?"

There are several means whereby the IGE principal may engage in a continuous program of professional development and self-renewal, including the professional literature, preservice and inservice programs, visits to IGE schools, and interacting with IGE networks. Studying the professional literature is a very useful means for increasing one's understanding of IGE. Persons in preservice principalship programs in college will, of course, find this means more viable than will presently practicing principals who often must read and run at the same time. Increasingly, however, general and specialized research reports, journal articles, and newsletters about IGE are becoming available.

Many colleges and universities, as well as local school systems, are providing courses, seminars, institutes, and workshops for administrators, unit leaders, and teachers in IGE schools. The self-renewing IGE principal not only will seek out such experiences, but also will serve as the stimulus for their development.

Visits to functioning IGE schools are a highly effective means of professional development and self-renewal. Firsthand observation is particularly useful at the awareness stage of implementation, since the gestalt often differs from the discrete description. In the changeover and subsequent stages of IGE implementation, it is a policy in many schools to engage in intervisitation programs.

Active participation in the SPC, Regional IGE Coordinating Council, State IGE Coordinating Council, and the national AIGE provides the principal with a continuing source of new concepts, ideas, procedures, and activities. It is through such shared relationships that the education of self and others can continually be improved.

Finally, cooperative group problem solving involving practitioners and professors has been a key factor in starting and refining IGE and remains a major form of renewal. We can move ahead only by identifying, analyzing, and solving our problems. Clearly the intellectual resources of present educational personnel are sufficient to identify and solve the problem of providing higher quality education for more students and better working conditions for teachers, principals, and other educational personnel.

SUMMARY

This brief chapter revealed the system of IGE to be dynamic, continually being refined in both theory and practice. Certain conceptual and operational changes apparent on the current scene were analyzed in relation to each of the seven components of IGE: the multiunit organizational structure, instructional programming for the individual student, evaluation for educational decision making, compatible curricular materials, home-school-community relations, facilitative environments, and continuing research and development. The chapter concluded with several suggestions for the continued professional development of the IGE principal as an agent of educational improvement.

REFERENCES

Belt, S. L., and D. W. Spuck 1974. *Computer applications in individually guided education: a computer-based system for instructional management (WISE-SIM).* Working paper No. 125. Madison, Wisc.: Wisconsin Research and Development Center for Cognitive Learning.

Benka, J. T. 1972. *The director of instruction as an agent of organizational change—individually guided education in the multiunit school.* Doctoral dissertation, University of Wisconsin—Madison.

Evers, N. A. 1974. *An analysis of the relationship between the effectiveness of the multiunit elementary school's instruction and research unit and interpersonal behaviors.* Technical report No. 298. Madison, Wisc.: Wisconsin Research and Development Center for Cognitive Learning.

Goodridge, C. G. 1975. *Factors that influence the decision to adopt an educational innovation, IGE.* Doctoral dissertation, University of Wisconsin—Madison.

Gramenz, G. W. 1974. *Relationship of the principal leader behavior and organizational structure of the IGE/MUS–E to I and R unit effectiveness.* Technical report No. 320. Madison, Wisc.: Wisconsin Research and Development Center for Cognitive Learning.

Herrick, H. S. 1974. *The relationship of organizational structure to teacher motivation in multiunit and nonmultiunit elementary schools.* Technical report No. 322. Madison, Wisc.: Wisconsin Research and Development Center for Cognitive Learning.

Krula, L. W. 1974. *The functioning and effectiveness of the systemwide policy committee as found in school systems implementing individually guided education.* Doctoral dissertation, Northern Illinois University.

Nelson, R. G. 1972. *An analysis of the relationship of the multiunit school organization structure and individually guided education to the learning climate of pupils.* Technical report No. 213. Madison, Wisc.: Wisconsin Research and Development Center for Cognitive Learning.

Sheridan, T. J. 1974. *Perceived role and effectiveness of the unit leader in conducting unit functions.* Technical report No. 318. Madison, Wisc.: Wisconsin Research and Development Center for Cognitive Learning.

Smith, K. B. 1972. *An analysis of the relationship between the effectiveness of the multiunit elementary school's instructional improvement committee and interpersonal and unit behaviors.* Technical report No. 230. Madison, Wisc.. Wisconsin Research and Development Center for Cognitive Learning.

Stufflebeam, D. L., *et al.* 1971. *Educational evaluation and decision making.* Itasca, Ill.: Peacock.

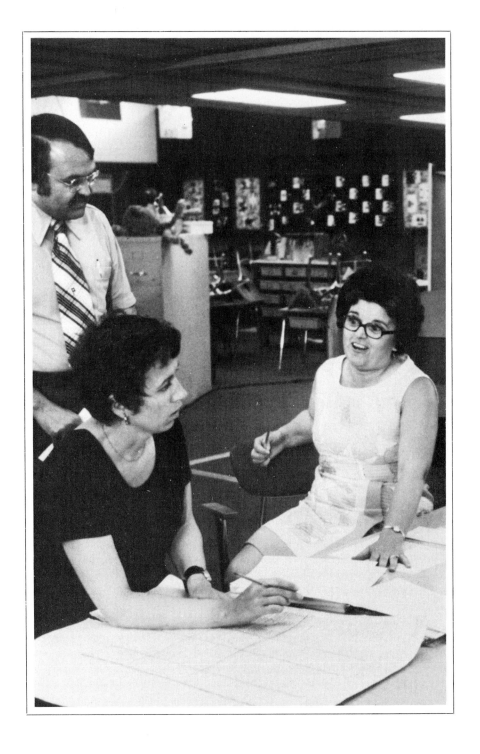

10
Case
Studies

Objectives

After reading this chapter, the reader will be able:

- To recognize key problem areas in implementing IGE.
- To understand possible origins and causes of the problems.
- To develop skills in analyzing and solving problems.
- To develop strategies for preventing serious problems from arising.
- To recognize that differential leadership and decision-making strategies are applicable in the solution of operational problems.

The effectiveness of IGE is directly related to the ability of local school personnel to identify and solve educational problems. In the cases which follow we have attempted to identify some difficult problems that an IGE principal might encounter.

The case study method of instruction has been pioneered by professors of educational administration and has been found effective in many credit courses, noncredit workshops, and independent study situations because of its flexibility. An individual may read and analyze a case independently, a small group may analyze the case, or an instructor may lead a class in the analysis. The eight cases that follow provide information that will enable persons to analyze reality-based situations and to develop greater skill in decision making in IGE schools by applying their knowledge of administration and of IGE. One can also evaluate one's own understanding of the administrative and IGE concepts presented in this book through their immediate application to an important problem area.

The cases that follow deal with difficult problems of the kind that many principals may not experience and assuredly it is hoped that no one principal will experience all of them. The cases were selected to present difficult problems because the authors feel that analyzing them and learning how either to solve them or to prevent them from becoming problems will improve principals' decision-making skills and, therefore, improve the leadership in IGE schools. Although the cases focus on particular problems and require knowledge of specific IGE concepts, the interactive effects of the problem environments and the interrelatedness of IGE are such that there are usually several alternatives, each of which if carried out will produce somewhat different results. Being able to identify possible consequences of actions before putting them into effect is a mark of effective leadership.

Thus we invite you to read and analyze the cases independently. Determine if perhaps more information might be needed in certain cases and supply the information. Also, review the concepts and principles presented in this book that may assist in the analysis and solution. Discuss your methods, information, and your conclusions with your colleagues. Be prepared to contribute to a class discussion. Recognize, too, that IGE offers great promise for improving the quality of education inasmuch as the multiunit organization and the facilitative environments permit optimum use of intellectual resources in cooperative problem solving and decision making.

Case 1
The
Big
Decision

Walter E. Krupa

The city of Benton has a population of 23,000 and is located on the southern border of the large, industrial city of Linsberg. Historically, Benton has been considered a bedroom community with most residents working in Linsberg and commuting daily. The last decade, however, has been one during which Linsberg experienced extensive industrial development to the south. Due to the growth of Linsberg, Benton finds itself gradually becoming more and more urban and, with this change, the institutions and values of a traditionally suburban community are under stress.

The Benton school system has a history of excellence and strong community support. During the past ten years, the school system has had to face the challenge of meeting the needs of a new clientele. No longer is the community homogeneous, reflecting middle-class needs and values. The influx of citizens from lower socioeconomic groups has created a student population of considerable diversity. Over the past few years, the school system has been criticized by the established Benton residents as having deteriorated in its academic standards and educational excellence. Newcomers, on the other hand, have attacked the system as being unresponsive to the particular needs of their children.

The Benton school district includes six K–6 elementary schools, one 7–8 junior high, and one 9–12 high school. Most of the school buildings reflect the traditional philosophy of a conservative community. Although the schools are well designed by standards of a decade ago, they are essentially self-contained and the facilities are somewhat limiting, considering present trends toward team teaching and individualized instruction.

As principal of the Oak Street Elementary School, Lee Peters found the past two years to be quite eventful. He was hired two years ago to start the first IGE school in Benton. Superintendent Reed was counting on IGE as the system capable of meeting the needs of the changing community.

In the first year, Lee was charged with the responsibility of preparing the Oak Street School for the changeover to IGE. This involved planning a continuous inservice program, selecting unit leaders, participating in a principal-unit leader workshop, and conducting a preopening of school workshop for the entire school faculty. The faculty under the leadership of the past principal had already been exposed to IGE awareness activities and had earlier made the commitment to implement the program.

Lee felt that his first September meeting with the faculty of the Oak Street School was relatively successful, even though it seemed obvious that an underlying concern of the professional staff was the prospect of beginning a challenging new program with an unknown quantity in the role of the principal. Subsequent planning meetings with the faculty led him to make the following observations:

- The previous principal had participated with the staff in IGE awareness activities conducted by the state department of education.
- The general knowledge level of the professional staff regarding IGE was rather low, and this lack of information had created some anxiety.
- Although none of the teachers expressed open opposition, there was good reason to believe one or two faculty members would prefer not to change the present school program.
- The selection of prospective unit leaders needed to take place before effective planning could occur.
- Although formal training for IGE was not to begin until January when the principal-unit leader workshop would be conducted, it was felt imperative that the community and professional staff be provided with enough information to enable them to make some important decisions about IGE in the Oak Street School.

Setting about the business of selecting prospective unit leaders, Lee settled on a process which included providing adequate information to the faculty regarding the role of the unit leader, asking the faculty to nominate fellow teachers for the unit leader role, interviewing all nominees, and finally selecting the unit leaders. By early October the selection process was completed and the IIC was established.

Lee and the unit leaders planned an inservice program for the Oak Street faculty which provided sufficient information prior to formal training programs. The following time line for inservice activities was developed and presented to the faculty for questions and discussion:

October: Faculty visits IGE schools, and examines IGE materials
November: IIC conducts inservice session on IGE curricular programs

December: IIC conducts inservice sessions on the multiunit school organization
January: The principal and unit leaders attend a workshop
February-June: IIC conducts monthly inservice sessions with faculty
August: Preopening of school workshop (entire staff)
September: Oak Street School implements IGE

The months of October, November, and December of last year passed quickly. The inservice activities conducted by the IIC were helpful, but many questions remained. Lee and the prospective unit leaders were anxious to participate in the principal-unit leader workshop sponsored by the state department of education. The January principal-unit leader workshop was excellent and provided a solid foundation for the IIC of the Oak Street School. Armed with new information and understandings, the principal and unit leaders felt equal to the task of training their fellow faculty members. As part of the three-day workshop, the IIC had to consider various alternative strategies for implementing IGE. After considerable planning and discussion, the IIC decided to present three possible implementation strategies to the faculty for their comments and recommendations, as follows:

I.   Strategy One, the total approach—estimated time required for implementation, one year

   1. Adopt the multiunit organization within established guidelines.

   2. Multiage and team teach in all subject areas from the outset.

   3. Utilize the instructional programming model in all skill areas from the outset.

II. Strategy Two, the organizational approach—estimated time required for implementation, three years

   1. Adopt the multiunit organization within established guidelines.

   2. Multiage and team teach in all subject areas from the outset.

   3. Utilize the instructional programming model in one subject matter area, and add other subject matter areas as staff confidence increases.

III. Strategy Three, the curricular approach—estimated time required for implementation, three years

   1. Implement the multiunit organization gradually as the instructional programming model is implemented.

   2. Multiage and team teach in one subject matter area only, initially, while maintaining age-graded, self-contained classrooms the remainder of the school day.

3. Utilize the instructional programming model in one subject matter area initially, but over a period of time expand and develop both the organization and instructional programming in a gradual process.

Superintendent Reed requested that the principal and unit leaders present a status report by April first. To meet that deadline they had to decide which implementation strategy would be most appropriate for their school. At a general faculty meeting, the participants reported on the principal-unit leader workshop experience and after presenting the three possible implementation strategies, they separated into unit level meetings. Each prospective unit was charged with the responsibility of discussing and selecting one of the three strategies.

The results of these meetings confirmed Lee's feeling that one or two faculty members were somewhat less than secure with the idea of abandoning the self-contained classroom for IGE or any other alternative system. Strategy Three, the curricular approach, was the clear-cut choice of the majority. The following comments by teachers were typical of those submitted regarding each of the three strategies considered:

I. Strategy One, the total approach

    We know of only one or two schools in the state that have successfully implemented using this approach.

    The task is overwhelming and the risk of failure too great.

    I don't think it is possible and seriously doubt anyone's claim to have done it.

II. Strategy Two, the organizational approach

    We may not be ready to work together as a team.

    Parents may object to the sudden elimination of the age-graded system.

    This approach appears reasonable, but it seems as though we would be starting at a point of no return. I'm just a little frightened.

    If we are going to implement IGE, let's not beat around the bush. This strategy appears to be the least we can do.

III. Strategy Three, the curricular approach

    A very reasonable approach that will allow the school and the community to gradually implement the new program.

    This is the route we should take. There appears to be much less chance for failure.

    I felt reluctant to try IGE, but the curricular approach is one I can live with very easily. There won't be that much change in the fall.

The majority vote to implement via the curriculum approach was no great surprise. It was the most conservative implementation strategy considered. In some respects, however, it was most difficult since it involves shifting daily from one type or organization to another in each curricular area. A few individuals were out-and-out advocates for total change, a majority was willing but extremely cautious, and a few were still silently hoping that IGE would go away.

In the April first presentation, Superintendent Reed commended the staff on their progress to date, approved the implementation strategy, and agreed to support the preservice training program required for implementation in September of the next school year. After the presentation, he asked Lee to visit his office. Superintendent Reed stated emphatically, "The success or failure of IGE at the Oak Street School has powerful implications for our entire school system. I hope that half of the elementary schools in the city will become multiunit schools within three years."

The course was set and the school year progressed to a smooth conclusion.

Prior to the opening of school in September, Lee and his unit leaders ran a five-day workshop for the entire faculty. The workshop included a review of the components of IGE, unit planning, and ironing out the details for implementing in the chosen subject matter area. They chose one of the components of the reading, and selected the *Wisconsin Design for Reading Skill Development—Word Attack* as the first area for implementation.

September was a busy month as the staff set about implementing the Word Attack program. The logistics of assessment, grouping, and record keeping proved challenging and motivating. By the end of October, "the dust had settled" and the staff exuded pride and confidence as the results of the first teaching cycles indicated success. Armed with this early success, the minority of staff members who favored a more rapid implementation process began a campaign to accelerate implementation by adding a second subject matter area. The positive experience with Word Attack was enough to convince a majority of the faculty that IGE was desirable. At a November meeting of the IIC, the unit leaders and the principal agreed to implement a second subject beginning in March.

Fortunately, the decision to add an area to the IGE operation did not require a great deal of curricular revision. During the previous school year, considerable time and effort had been spent modifying the science curriculum for IGE implementation. Science had been favored as a possible first area for implementation and it was only after considerable deliberation that the faculty decided to start with Word Attack. Word Attack was selected primarily because many other schools had started with it successfully.

With several positive months behind them they began planning in earnest. Gradually, the scheduling, assessment, grouping and record-keeping procedures began to fall into place, and the staff felt that they would meet the March first starting date. Shortly thereafter, as the implementation of science progressed, however, ominous signs began to emerge. The staff was working to capacity and the time investment was staggering. At first they dismissed the time element as a start-up factor; however, by late April they realized that no matter how much they streamlined the operation, the limit had been reached. There was no more time! Had they peaked out? Was it really possible to implement IGE totally? The prospect of adding a third subject in the fall was absolutely out of the question. Morale began to decline as the issues appeared insurmountable.

Early in May, they invited the state IGE coordinator to one of their IIC meetings and discussed their status with him. He suggested a reexamination of the school organization and seriously questioned their strategy for implementation. He further contended that it is possible to implement IGE in many subjects and provided them with the names of several schools in surrounding districts with the suggestion that they arrange visits to them.

Arrangements were made to visit three IGE schools late in May and, prior to the visits, a general faculty meeting was held to determine who from the faculty would participate in the visits and to set objectives for the visitation team. Skepticism and anxiety permeated the faculty meeting. Many who had formerly remained silent voiced their doubts and had obviously decided on the answers before the questions were asked. Eventually, the meeting settled down and the following guidelines for the visits were agreed upon:

- The visitation team will consist of the principal and one teacher or unit leader from each unit.
- The same team will conduct all three visits.
- The visitation team will report to the entire faculty on or before June seventh.
- The visitation team will be guided by the following objectives:
  a. To determine if any of the three schools have implemented the programming model in more than two subject areas. If so, report specifically the procedures, organization and resources employed to do so.
  b. To develop recommendations appropriate for consideration by the Oak Street School faculty.

In the week that followed, the members of the visiting team were selected by their respective units and a meeting of the team was held to discuss the policies governing visits to the three IGE schools involved. In each case, the visits were to start off with a presentation by the principal or unit leaders who would provide an historical overview of IGE implementation and the strategy which that particular school had adopted in implementing the program. After the introductory meetings, the visiting team would be free to move about the building to observe and talk with staff members as they desired.

The three visitations were productive; they provided some rewarding surprises. The primary objective of the visits, to reexamine strategies for implementation, was done and much more! The visiting teams accumulated ideas on scheduling, record keeping, planning techniques, use of aides, home-school-community relations, reporting, and many other areas. But most importantly, they found that all three schools had experienced similar frustrations early in their IGE implementation, but they had managed to solve most problems. The enthusiasm and pride they exhibited was infectious! All persons on the visiting team were anxious to return to their units to share ideas with the staff.

Those who made visits spent the equivalent of one-half day as a group in formulating their report to the faculty.

The following observations were unanimously cited as significant:

- All three schools were using the instructional programming model in three or more subject matter areas.
- All three schools used multiaging throughout the school day.
- All three schools were team teaching in all subjects.

The first school visited had started IGE by utilizing the same basic approach as the Oak Street School. However, in their second year they decided to change their implementation strategy from the curricular approach (adding subject matter areas and teaming accordingly) to the organizational approach (multiaging and teaming in all areas from the outset, but implementing the IPM incrementally). Lee Peters asked the principals why they had decided to change their approach. One responded as follows:

> The multiunit organization in IGE is designed to provide you with maximum flexibility in managing human and material resources. The unit has the capability to free-up individuals for planning or other tasks critical to unit operation, to change the schedule as need be and to utilize the space. It has a multitude of ways to meet the needs of youngsters. The subject-by-subject approach or curricular approach, as you call it, was not working for us. Two organizational systems existed in the building. Unit leaders were frustrated in their attempts to manage the learning program when teachers were spending 80 percent of the time isolated in their self-contained, age-graded classrooms. As long as vestiges of the old system remained, many of us were reluctant to make the full commitment needed to ensure the success of IGE. There were others who held onto self-con-

tained age-gradedness like a security blanket, perhaps hoping that IGE would eventually go away.

It created problems with the children and parents as well. Teachers were pigeonholed by grade and when we did multiage and team teach for our IGE subjects, parents were upset when their third grade child was taught by a second grade teacher. I'm glad all of that is behind us. If I were you, I would face up to multiaging and team teaching. The approach you're using can take you only so far. Then you have to make the "big decision."

The words, "big decision," were ringing in Lee's ears as he turned to the agenda item, "Recommendations for further implementation of IGE at Oak Street School."

CASE ANALYSIS

1. What further implementation time lines would you recommend for Oak Street School?

2. What does this case study suggest regarding the relationship between the multiunit organization and IGE instructional programming?

3. Devise and justify an implementation strategy other than those presented in this case.

4. How might the Oak Street School have avoided the necessity to revise their implementation strategy? As principal, what specific steps would you have taken to ensure that the initial implementation strategy would be appropriate?

Case 2

Who Should Lead the Units?

James E. Walter

"Who should lead the units?" was the question that faced Tom Jacobs as he was about to begin implementing IGE in the Monroe Elementary School. Monroe, one of two elementary schools in the Ryan Independent School District, was the only school making the changeover to IGE. Built in the 1950s, the school was a typical two-story building in excellent condition, but it was not overcrowded, having an enrollment of only 500 students. The staff included 20 classroom teachers; an instructional materials center director; one teacher each for music, art, and physical education; and five paid teacher aides. The school was well supplied with a variety of instructional materials and audiovisual equipment. In terms of facilities, size of staff, and supplies and equipment, Monroe was in a good position for making the changeover to IGE.

In late January, Tom sat at his desk pondering how he should proceed to identify the unit leaders. He had to make his decision shortly, for he and the unit leaders were scheduled to attend a principal-unit leader workshop in late February. The following September was the target date for beginning the implementation of IGE at Monroe. As he pondered over the best means for identifying the unit leaders, Tom reflected on the makeup of the district and how it had come to make the changeover to IGE.

Ryan Independent School District was created in 1964 out of four elementary districts. It is nestled between two cities of about 45,000 population each. Each city is an independent unified school district. Logan, 20 miles to the north, is primarily an industrial city in which an assembly plant of a large automobile manufacturer is located. Hyatt, 15 miles to the south, is also an industrial city in which the largest employer is a nationally known meat-packing firm. A small liberal arts college with an excellent reputation is also located in Hyatt. Both cities serve as shopping and trade centers for the farmers of the area. The residents of Ryan School District, numbering

8000, include wealthy executives, college personnel, industrial employees, small businessmen, farmers, and several families on welfare. Most of the population is Caucasian with a few blacks, Spanish-Americans, and American Indians.

The Rush River divides the district into western and eastern sectors. The western sector is the more rural of the two and, even though it contains about two-thirds of the land, has only one-fourth of the population. Because property is less expensive in the western sector, lower socioeconomic families live there. Randall, the other elementary school, is located west of the river. It is the smaller of the two with about 300 students. School records show academic achievement lower and discipline problems higher at Randall than at Monroe.

The eastern part of the district, where Monroe is located, contains most of the district's population. The residents are, for the most part, well-to-do because the executives, professors, businessmen, and factory supervisors live there. The small businesses in the district are also located to the east of the river, as are the district's middle and high schools.

In terms of its political composition, the district overlaps three townships, each with an elected town board comprising mainly persons with rural and conservative political orientations. Some community leaders, those of a liberal persuasion, had taken the initiative in 1964 to create Ryan Independent School District. The district's seven-member board of education, which had originally comprised these leaders or their candidates, had undergone some changes in recent elections. In Tom's opinion the board now comprised four members supportive of educational innovation and three who were much more conservative and who preferred to see the school district operate much as it had when they were in school.

Fiscally, the district is independent of other political entities, such as the town boards. By state law, however, it must present a recommended budget to the residents of the district who then vote on the budget and any other major proposals. Following the approval of the budget, the tax levy is set. These annual school meetings are held on the fourth Monday in July. With the conservative elements of the district gaining in political power both on the school board and at the annual school meeting, it was becoming increasingly difficult to obtain approval of the budgetary items to support innovation. Tom was thankful for the excellent condition of the building, the size of the Monroe staff, and the more than adequate supply of materials and equipment which had been approved in a more favorable and supportive era.

The district's administration was generally flexible and innovative, reflecting the interests and desires of the community leaders who had spearheaded the organization of the district in 1964. The administrative staff consisted of the superintendent, the assistant superintendent in charge of business services, the high school principal, the middle school principal, and the two elementary principals. They ranged in age from 34 to 42. Tom was the youngest. The administrators met every two months as an informal administrative team, commonly called the "cabinet," to discuss the progress of the district, to consider problems, and to develop proposals for improvements in district operations.

With the advent of IGE in Monroe, the administrators had agreed to allow teachers and unit leaders to have representatives on the "cabinet" and thus it would become the SPC.This agreement had not been reached easily. The assistant superintendent and the high and middle school principals had not been particularly enthusiastic about this change; they did not see how teachers and unit leaders could contribute much to the discussions and they were reluctant to formalize the "cabinet." Tom wondered if they were not concerned that the program committee discussions might focus too much on instructional matters and provide Monroe School with undue influence regarding its own programs. The Randall School principal, however, was in favor of the change. She saw it as an opportunity to select influential staff members who might, in turn, help other staff members and district residents see the benefits of IGE for the Randall school. The superintendent, wholeheartedly in favor of IGE, an excellent instructional leader, and supportive of shared decision making, had been influential in obtaining the agreement of the administrators to create the SPC.

Tom had been principal at Monroe for four years. He had first heard about IGE at the annual meeting of the state elementary principals' association three years ago, and since then had read about it in several professional journals and newsletters. His own interest in providing instructional leadership and in involving the staff in decision making caused him to be enthusiastic about IGE. The staff at Monroe had tried some team teaching, group planning, and various attempts at individualizing instruction. But somehow Tom and the staff had not been able to "put it all together." The superintendent had been supportive of their efforts, but unable to devote the time necessary to make things work. The more Tom learned about IGE, the more he was convinced that it was what the Monroe staff needed to help bring about the improvements they wanted in their school.

As soon as Tom felt he was knowledgeable about IGE, he approached the superintendent who also was quite interested in and somewhat informed about IGE. This conversation had occurred about a year ago. Shortly after, they heard about an IGE informational conference sponsored by the state department of public instruction and decided to attend the meeting to see if they could learn more about how they might obtain assistance in implementing IGE. After the conference, at which they learned that the department and a cooperating university could provide the necessary inservice, they began to develop strategies for informing the rest of the Monroe staff, as well as board members and district residents, about IGE. It had also been discussed at a "cabinet" meeting during which Tom found out that the Randall principal also knew about IGE, even though she felt that her staff and community were not yet ready for IGE. The other administrators thought that IGE might be a good idea to be tried in the district. They also agreed that Monroe would be the logical place to implement IGE since it was a larger school, had an adequate supply of materials and equipment, a good staff, and a community that might be more receptive. Wisely, Tom reflected, he had let the superintendent lead the discussions.

With the administrative support of the district, Tom and the superintendent proceeded to inform the Monroe staff, the board members, and community residents. They utilized the usual channels of communication in their informational efforts. The department of public instruction provided them with brochures, an introductory film, and a consultant who made presentations to the school staff and at a districtwide parent-teacher meeting. Informal coffees also were held in various parts of the district, particularly in the Monroe attendance area. Before the school year came to a close last year, most of the important audiences had been exposed to IGE. Fortunately, a newspaper from a large metropolitan area about 90 miles from the district also had carried a favorable feature article about IGE.

Tom and the superintendent had earlier agreed not to push for a "go or no-go" decision about IGE during the previous spring. As Tom reflected on that decision, he wondered about its wisdom. For at the annual school meeting last July, the issue was raised with a somewhat negative note by the conservative element in the district. It wasn't openly attacked, but comments were made about frills in education and the importance of basics. Questions about what was wrong with the way things were now and whether they were as good as in days past were asked. The superintendent pointed out that no decision had been made; that the administrators and board had only been exploring the possibility. One of the liberal members of the board and some of the residents from the west of the river commented that they were very interested and wanted to know more about the program. Luckily, should they decide to adopt IGE, Monroe would not require additional funds, although the superintendent had made some provisions in the staff development budget for teachers to attend inservice activities. Higher pay for unit leaders would still need to be considered, but undoubtedly there would be some vacancies due to retirement and, if younger teachers could be hired, then there would be no need to increase the total salary budget for Monroe. No formal action was taken, however, at the annual meeting.

When school opened in September, Tom received notice that the department of public instruction would be sponsoring a one-day awareness conference in early October. He conferred with the superintendent and they decided that not only would they attend but also that selected teachers from

Monroe, two or three board members, and a couple of interested parents would be invited. As it turned out, the teachers and the board members did attend. After the awareness conference, the superintendent and Tom decided that it was time to push for a decision. Tom took an informal poll of the staff at Monroe and found that most of the teachers were favorable. To formalize the decision, he put the matter to a vote at the October faculty meeting and while there were two or three teachers opposed (although not strenuously so), the staff decided to implement IGE the following fall. The superintendent then arranged for the consultant from the state department to make a presentation along with Tom and members of the Monroe staff at the December meeting of the board. After the presentation and some discussion both from board members and the audience, the board voted to adopt IGE on an experimental basis at Monroe School for two years.

Tom was surprised at the closeness of the vote, 4 to 3. He was not aware that some community representatives had become opposed to IGE. Perhaps they were not opposed to IGE as much as they were opposed to any change, Tom thought. One of the issues centered on the signing of an agreement between the board and the department of public instruction. Some board members felt that this was an intrusion on local autonomy. The department's consultant persuaded them that the agreement was only to ensure a basic level of quality control, and that the agreement made it possible for the school district to obtain a wide range of assistance not otherwise available. Besides, the department was not dictating that the school had to implement IGE; it was still their choice. So the board decided to go along.

"So, here I sit," Tom thought. "Finally, we're all ready to go IGE. But how do I select the unit leaders to attend the workshop with me next month?"

Tom first considered his own orientations as an educational administrator. He was vitally interested in being an instructional leader. He was not content to be "just a paper pusher and money counter." He believed in giving his staff as much involvement as possible in making educational decisions. At the same time, he had some definite ideas about what constitutes good education. Faced with a conflict, he wondered, "How can I move my ideas into action faster and at the same time not impose them upon the staff?" Tom wanted to be successful. He had been in education for thirteen years, six as a teacher and seven as a principal—the last four in Ryan Independent School District. He would like to complete his doctor's degree next year and hoped to become a superintendent, at least, by the time he was 38. He thought that he had a reputation for being an excellent administrator—at least, the superintendent had told him so when he was hired. He really wanted the program to succeed, yet letting teachers assume greater responsibility was a risky business. "What if they make some real blunders?"

he asked himself. Certainly, he was ultimately responsible and accountable for decisions made in his building. Tom said to himself:

> Well, I've been a risk taker in the past. I might as well take some risks this time. After all, I was intrigued by the multiunit organization because the teachers, unit leaders, and the principal cannot make major decisions in isolation. I can let the staff be involved extensively and still know what goes into the decisions. I can still influence the decision if it seems to me to be headed in the wrong direction. But we're not IGE yet, so how can I let them participate in selecting unit leaders? Won't the unit leaders be more responsive to those who chose them than to me? I'd like to mainstream the special education students, for example, but I know that most of the staff are not willing to do so.

Tom then turned to thinking about the staff of the school. One by one he thought about each teacher and tried to visualize how each would work out as a unit leader. The director of the instructional materials center and the special area teachers would not be candidates since they had responsibilities throughout the building. Tom had already decided that since the IGE model did not clearly make allowances for these persons, the IMC director would be a permanent member of the IIC and that the special area teachers would participate in committee meetings when the agenda included matters related to their areas. They would work as much as possible with each of the I & R Units, both in planning and in helping the teachers carry out the instruction in the special areas. He had discussed this arrangement with the staff and they had agreed that the plan would be satisfactory until they had more experience and could devise a better alternative.

In keeping with the recommendations in the IGE literature, Tom and the staff had also agreed that the school should be organized into four units of not more than five teachers and about 125 students each. Each unit would have one aide and the fifth aide would be assigned to the instructional materials center. Since it was a K–5 school, Unit A would comprise the kindergarten and less mature first grade children; Unit B, the more mature first graders and the second graders; Unit C, the third graders and about half of the fourth graders; and Unit D, the remainder of the fourth graders and the fifth graders. These were tentative arrangements which would be finalized after the workshop in February and when they had better information on the enrollment for the coming fall.

"I know what I'll do," Tom thought, "I'll go about this thing systematically, first, grouping the teachers by their tentative units; next, listing some basic information about each; and then, assigning some ratings on such basic criteria as working with children, parents, and colleagues; teaching ability; task orientation; and some essential personal qualities, such as innovativeness, maturity, organizational ability, and consideration of others."

As he worked on his chart, Tom first thought, "Say, this moves along pretty well. Having worked closely with this staff for so long, I can rate them on each of these criteria." (His chart appears on the next two pages.) On some of the variables, such as relations with staff and consideration, however, he felt that he really would like to know what the others thought. "I'd love to administer a few sociograms," he mused, "but that would be too transparent—at this juncture they'd see through that in a minute. Already, six people have told me they'd be glad to volunteer—even Alice."

Tom reexamined the criteria at the top of his chart. It was crucial, he felt, for the unit leaders to be organized and task oriented since they did not have the 20 percent of released time suggested in the IGE model, and the work must get done. At the same time, the unit leaders should be able to relate well to their staffs and, because of the concern in the community about adopting IGE, to the community and parents. He also wanted them to be innovative. He really did want to try mainstreaming the special education children. It would be nice if the unit leaders were model teachers, but in Tom's opinion it would be acceptable if they were not, so long as they were not poor teachers.

"Well, let me take it unit by unit," Tom thought. "There are several possibilities in Unit A. Anne is the teacher to whom others look for educational leadership, but Cheryl is the social leader. Both are opinion leaders. In Unit B, Sally is a leader to whom others turn for help on teaching matters, but her lack of organization would pose problems for everybody.

"In Unit C, I'd probably choose Amy, although Sue relates better to the children and the community—maybe Georgia would be better than either of them," Tom concluded. "In Unit D, Joan would probably make a good unit leader, but both Al and Alice have volunteered. Maybe some reassignments to units should be made," Tom thought. "In any event, it looks like Unit D would require a lot of help and supervision."

As Tom mulled over his chart, he returned to the nagging issue, "Why am I doing all this, except perhaps to soften the blow for some not chosen and to encourage others to serve?" He saw four possible ways the unit leaders could be selected. First, he could proceed as he had been doing, and select the unit leaders unilaterally. While initially this might involve the least risk, it certainly ran counter to his desire for staff involvement in decision making. Second, he could meet with the total staff, and throw open the issues of both assignment of staff to units and choice of unit leaders, but that might negate some earlier planning as well as reflect unfavorably on Unit D. Third, he could have the groups meet by units and let them make the decision. Undoubtedly the verbal and dominant ones would be chosen in some units. Finally, he could ask each unit to nominate two persons from which he could make the choice, but then there would be at least four people who might be hurt or disappointed.

CHARACTERISTICS

Staff member	Unit	Age	Years of Experience	Grade Now Teaching	Curriculum Area Strength	Preference for Range of Children	Group Size Preference	Relations with Children	Relations with Colleagues
Anne	A	62	40	K	K	Average	Small	Excellent	Good
Gail	A	26	5	K	K	Low	Small	Excellent	Adequate
Barb	A	46	21	1	LA	High	One-One	Good	Excellent
Cheryl	A	52	30	1	Math	Average	Small	Good	Excellent
Lynn	A	39	9	1	LA	High	Large	Good	Good
Andrea	B	26	6	1	Reading	Average	Small	Adequate	Good
Kelly	B	35	13	2	LA	Low	Small	Good	Good
Bonnie	B	42	20	2	Math	Average	Small	Good	Good
Sally	B	35	13	2	Math	Average	Large	Good	Excellent
Tina	B	34	10	2	Science	Low	One-One	Adequate	Good
Marilyn	C	33	10	3	Soc Stu	High	Class Size	Good	Poor
Sue	C	26	6	3	LA	Average	Class Size	Excellent	Excellent
Amy	C	27	5	3	Reading	High	One-One	Good	Excellent
Georgia	C	44	12	3	Math	Low	Small	Adequate	Good
Mike	C	32	8	4	Math	Average	Large	Adequate	Adequate
Leslie	D	38	16	4	LA	Average	Class Size	Good	Good
Joan	D	24	3	4	Reading	Average	Class Size	Excellent	Good
Jim	D	29	7	5	Science	High	Class Size	Good	Good
Al	D	31	12	5	Soc Stu	High	Class Size	Adequate	Good
Alice	D	55	23	5	LA	Low	Small	Good	Poor

CHARACTERISTICS

Relations with Community Parents	Principal's Assessment of Performance	Task Orientation	Orientation to Rules	Innovativeness	Maturity	Organization	Consideration of Others
Excellent	Excellent	Medium	Medium	Medium	Great	Good	High
Adequate	Good	Low	High	Medium	Acceptable	OK	Medium
Good	Good	High	Medium	Medium	Acceptable	High	Medium
Excellent	Good	Medium	Medium	Low	Medium	Good	High
Adequate	Good	Medium	Medium	Medium	Medium	Good	Low
Poor	Good	Medium	Medium	Medium	Acceptable	Good	Low
Adequate	Good	High	Medium	Low	Medium	High	Good
Good	Good	Low	Medium	High	Acceptable	Good	Medium
Excellent	Excellent	Low	Medium	Medium	Acceptable	Low	High
Good	Good	High	Medium	Medium	Low	High	Medium
Adequate	Good	Medium	Low	Medium	Acceptable	Good	Low
Good	Good	Medium	Medium	Low	Medium	Good	High
Adequate	Good	High	High	Low	Low	High	Medium
Excellent	Excellent	Low	High	Medium	Great	OK	Medium
Poor	Adequate	High	Low	Low	Low	Good	Low
Adequate	Good	Medium	Medium	High	Acceptable	Good	Medium
Good	Excellent	Medium	Medium	High	Medium	Good	Medium
Good	Good	Low	Medium	Medium	Medium	Good	Medium
Good	Good	Medium	Medium	Medium	Acceptable	Good	Medium
Good	Poor	High	Low	Medium	Acceptable	OK	Low

The principal-unit leader workshop was imminent, and the staff knew it. They also probably realized that his unwarranted delay in choosing unit leaders was becoming dysfunctional. Tom took out the registration form which was due soon. It was now 5:30 and he had to be at a father-son Cub Scout banquet at 7:00. "I'll think about it," he decided, "and take some action first thing in the morning."

That night, Tom fell into a troubled sleep.

CASE ANALYSIS

It is the next morning, and you are the principal of Monroe Elementary School.

1. How would you go about selecting the unit leaders of the school? Would you utilize Tom's four alternatives, or some other means for selecting unit leaders? Justify your choice, considering the consequences in terms of short- and long-run benefits as well as potential problems.

2. Regardless of the selection procedures used, who should be the four unit leaders? Justify your selections in terms of the idealized expectations prescribed for the unit leader's role.

Case 3

Implementing the Instructional Programming Model at Washington School

William H. Klenke
Nancy A. Evers

Washington Elementary School will be implementing IGE in the fall of the upcoming school year. It all began when the principal, Pat Jones, and several other elementary principals in the district, the curriculum director, and the superintendent of schools attended an IGE Awareness Workshop sponsored by the State IGE Coordinator last year. During this workshop Pat became very interested in implementing IGE at Washington School. This enthusiasm and a general understanding of IGE were subsequently transferred to the staff through a series of staff development meetings. Pat also invited an experienced teacher and principal from a nearby IGE school to come to Washington and talk with the staff about IGE. Following this, several of the teachers visited two IGE schools in a neighboring district.

Subsequently, the decision was made to begin the implementation of IGE in September of the following year. In preparation for this, the staff and Pat selected four unit leaders, Liz, Chuck, Bertha, and Ron. Pat and these four staff members attended a three-day, principal-unit leader staff-development workshop. As a result of that workshop, the multiunit structure was established and the following arrangements were made by the IIC and accepted by the staff:

Unit A	Unit B	Unit C
1 Unit Leader (Liz)	1 Unit Leader (Ron)	1 Unit Leader (Bertha)
4 Staff Teachers	3 Staff Teachers	5 Staff Teachers
2 Instructional Aides	2 Instructional Aides	2 Instructional Aides
1/2 Clerical Aide	1/2 Clerical Aide	1/2 Clerical Aide
1 Student Intern	1 Student Intern	1 Student Intern
123 Students	99 Students	156 Students
Ages 5–7	Ages 6–8	Ages 8–10

Unit D	*Support Staff not assigned to any specific unit*
1 Unit Leader (Chuck)	Music—2-1/2 days per week
4 Staff Teachers	Art—5 days per week
2 Instructional Aides	Physical Education—5 days per week
1/2 Clerical Aide	Corrective Reading, Speech Therapy, and
127 Students	Psychological Services are on a district basis,
Ages 9–12	serving in an on-call schedule.
1 Student Intern	

Although it is only April, the staff has made considerable progress. The IIC conducted a self-evaluation to determine the unique curricular and teaching strengths of each staff member in the school; they analyzed particular needs of students in the school's attendance area, and they conducted in-depth interviews with parents and other community leaders concerning which areas of the curriculum should be given greatest emphasis. As a result of these activities, the key decision was made selecting mathematics as the initial curricular area in which to apply the IPM, beginning in the fall. A commitment also was made by the school district central office to support the implementation of IGE at Washington School, and approval was granted for a one-week, preschool workshop in the fall and for two half-day planning sessions this April and May.

Wednesday, April 12, the students were dismissed at noon to permit the IIC and I & R Unit staffs to meet and plan. The principal, Pat, and the unit leaders, Liz, Ron, Bertha, and Chuck are now meeting as the IIC to deal with the main item on the agenda: "Develop an overall plan and time line of activities for applying the IPM in mathematics." This item already has been the focus of considerable discussion and planning in the weekly meetings of the I & R Units.

As the five members of the IIC begin to converse in the meeting room, we listen in on their deliberations:

Pat: Say, you'll probably be glad to hear that I received a call today from Mrs. Thomas, Becky's mother, and she just wanted to let me know how pleased she was with the "IGE Parent Overview" meeting we had last week. From what I've heard, it appears that the majority of our parents are supporting us in changing over to IGE.

Liz: I've been getting positive comments from parents too.

Bertha: I'm sorry for running a bit late. I was talking with my unit about individualizing in math. Jan and Lois were concerned about not having enough materials for the program.

Ron: Did you tell them not to worry because that will be part of the plan that we will outline at our meeting today?

Bertha: Yes, but I wanted to communicate their concerns anyway.

Ron: How are you Chuck, Liz? Hi, Pat!

Pat: Hi! We have a lot of things to do today so let's get started immediately. As you know, the main item on the agenda is the development of a plan that outlines the activities that will be undertaken
to apply the IPM to our first IGE curricular area, math. What we
do in math and how we do it this coming year is going to be critical
to the overall acceptance and success of IGE at Washington. That's
why our task here today is so important. We must develop a good
operational plan. I'm sure each of us has given a great deal of
thought to what is needed. When I was thinking about a way, a
strategy, to implement the IPM, I thought of the several strategies
which we heard about and discussed at the principal-unit leader
workshop. One strategy was where the IIC actually completes the
initial tasks in the IPM. A second strategy was where the IIC still
maintains that responsibility but delegates the performance of the
tasks to an ad hoc committee which is composed of teachers from
each of the units. As I said, I really debated this issue in my own
mind and therefore I would like to propose that we, the IIC, assume the responsibility for and the performance of the initial steps
in the IPM. What do you all think?

Liz: Pat, do you actually mean that *just* the IIC will be doing all the
work?

Pat: Well, yes and no! What I'm saying is that we should perform the
initial steps involved in implementing the IPM. While the IIC, all
of us, would be responsible for most of the work, I'm sure we can
call upon others for assistance. We might find it advantageous to
work with our curriculum director, outside consultants, or some
of our own staff members. So realistically Liz, while we may not
be doing everything ourselves, we will be doing the major share
of it.

Chuck: It sounds fine to me. As Pat said, we will be getting constant help
from our units to make the necessary decisions.

Pat: Let me just make sure we all understand what my recommendation
entails. Within the first three steps of the IPM, the IIC will be responsible for developing our schoolwide and our specific instructional objectives for our math program. We will also be responsible
for developing an assessment program by which the units can assess
the instructional needs of each child in relationship to the objectives. This recommendation also entails some responsibility once
the units begin implementing the program.

Liz: That's what I thought you meant. That certainly is a lot of work.
We have a school year coming to an end very shortly, a preschool
workshop to plan, a staff to inservice, and you know we still have
kids to teach!

Bertha: Come on Liz, don't worry! We are all in this together. Among all of us we can do it.

Liz: Well, you all know that math isn't my strength, but let's get on with it!

Chuck: You know, I've been thinking. What about Phil, Sarah, and Marty? They've really put a lot of work into this project already. They were really the three teachers who were influential in getting math selected as our first IGE area. I think when we get started we should make sure we involve everyone we can—the curriculum director, math supervisor, Phil, Sarah, Marty, and any other staff member who wants to be involved.

Bertha: Wait a minute Chuck! Just what do you mean? If our IIC is going to be responsible for these tasks, we have to do them in an organized fashion. We just can't have everyone involved just for the sake of being involved. What I am saying is that if we feel someone has something to definitely contribute, let's involve them, but if not, let's not waste their time—nor ours!

Pat: You both made some good points. Let's look at our time line and when we consider what has to be done, then we can determine the appropriate consultative help and teacher involvement.

Liz: I would like to suggest that some time before the second week in May we review our district curriculum policies and programs. I would also suggest that we look at our current math program in the school to determine what is applicable to IGE, in an objective sense. Finally, I would suggest that we gather as much material that relates to math objectives and programs as possible. The reason I am making these suggestions is that before we start writing our objectives and assessment materials we should have everything at hand to assist us. For example, Ron, you've been on a state committee looking at individualizing math—they must have something that will help us.

Ron: Yes, I have some objectives that were written.

Pat: I think that now we are starting to get on the right track. Liz, I hear you saying that before we start writing the objectives and assessment we should do three things. One, review and know our district curricular practices and policies, as it relates to math. Two, review our own math program. And three, gather all possible materials to help us with our tasks.

Liz: That's right. I think we have to know where we are starting from and what we have to work with.

Ron: I'd like to take those three ideas and be a little more specific. I'd like to place several activities on our time line. First I'd like to place a meeting with our curriculum director for next week. Secondly, I'd set the second week of May as the time when we would have all materials available to us so we can begin our work. That would give us about three weeks to get our objectives, at least a first draft, together for staff reaction.

Liz: What about reviewing data from our current math program? You forgot that.

Chuck: That would really be pushing it, Ron. I'm afraid we can't get things done that fast.

Ron: Excuse me, Chuck. Liz, I think we may be premature in evaluating our own math program before we have our objectives set. If we take our math program and evaluate it beforehand, we may, consciously or unconsciously, end up making our IGE program fit our current math program.

Liz: But Ron, I think that we and the parents both know that our math program needs changing. If we review our present program, it will give us a better feel for which improvements are necessary. It will identify weak spots in math, highlight the strengths, etcetera. I'd suggest we still do that before we start writing.

Chuck: That's just something else that will make our deadlines even more unrealistic. How can we get this all finished?

Bertha: Liz, I agree with both you and Ron, but in the interest of time I think we can put some of our new math program together without first formally reviewing our old program. Since we all have worked with it, I think we will sort of keep it in mind as we develop our IGE program.

Pat: Well, I think that basically we agree. Let's add to our time line two more activities. At our next IIC meeting we will meet with the curriculum director to review district policies. At our second meeting, in May, everything we need to begin our tasks will be on hand. Are there any objections to those being added?

Chuck: Yes, we just will not have time to get them done. We'd better be sure our time line is reasonable.

Pat: Thanks, Chuck. Liz, do you feel all right about not running a formal evaluation of our current math program.

Liz: Not really, but I guess it will be okay. Although I understand your reasons. I'd feel more comfortable if we did a little more evaluation.

Ron: Okay, let's take it from the second week in May. As I see our schedule of events, it will give us about two or three weeks to have something ready for staff reactions and suggestions.

Chuck: That just isn't enough time, I think . . . .

Liz: Okay, Chuck, let's pull together our thoughts and our entire time line, and then look at it to see if it is reasonable.

Chuck: Fine, then what do you see happening next?

Bertha: I'd like to be able to take to the total staff a program that outlines our schoolwide objectives and at least a summary of the topics that our short-range objectives will be built upon. We could also have some specific objectives done in certain of the areas.

Liz: I agree!

Ron: Sounds reasonable.

Pat: Okay, between the end of May and the close of school, the total staff will have an opportunity to react to our first draft. That will give us more input and help us to finalize the program.

Chuck: Let's now assume we have our objectives completed. How are we going to go about getting our assessment program together? I mean that is going to have to get done during the summer. I'm not too sure I'll have time to do much then; I've got other things planned.

Ron: I agree, that will pose a problem for all of us.

Liz: We'll just have to make some sacrifices this summer to get everything in shape for fall. We just have to understand that.

Chuck: But Liz, we *all* have other responsibilities in the summer.

Pat: Well, let's outline the tasks that have to be completed during the summer and then if we assign individual tasks it may not be so difficult and time consuming as we think.

Ron: First of all, we have to have our objectives completed so we can know the type of assessment that's needed. Let's assume that by the end of June our objectives are finished. Then, what do we have to do? I think we will have to establish some procedures for assessing where all the kids are in math, in a general sense. This will obviously have to be in relationship to our program. Then, we have to either find or write assessment items for each of our specific math objectives.

Liz: We also have to be able to keep track of all of those things we find out about the kids' math progress.

Chuck: Are you saying that we all will have to keep track of the kids the same way?

Liz: I think it would certainly help. It would keep each unit from having to make out new charts or whatever for each kid that comes into the unit.

Chuck: Well, our unit already has worked on some ways to keep track of progress. We have some pretty definite ideas as to what would work best.

Liz: Chuck, we don't even have a program yet. How can you be involved in a record-keeping system already?

Chuck: Well, you know our unit. We work hard!

Pat: With regard to this summer, we have to decide on some way to get a general overall assessment of the kids' math needs in the fall. We also have to have some measures for assessing our specific instructional objectives. And I also heard the need for a single record-keeping system.

Bertha: I'd like to add that we should also begin to organize our materials so we know what we have and what parts of the program they will apply to.

Liz: The staff can do some of that before school is out. Instead of putting everything into individual cabinets in the rooms we can begin to organize the materials in our IMC.

Chuck: But, Liz, we won't have a program set by the end of school!

Liz: At least we'll have our long-range objectives and the general topics to be included in the program. We can begin at that point.

Pat: Is that a fourth activity to be completed this summer?

Ron: Well, perhaps not. Maybe some of those things can be done during our preschool workshop.

Bertha: What do you mean, Ron?

Ron: Well, if we get our program together the staff can organize the materials then. Also, the staff could work on record-keeping devices during that time.

Chuck: That's the best idea I've heard all day. I think we, as an IIC, have to be first concerned with the most important aspect of our task, writing the objectives and developing the assessment program. The things affected by that, like the materials organization and record-keeping system, can be completed in the fall during the workshop. After all, we can't do everything!

Pat: Well, what do you all think? What can we complete during the summer?

Liz: I think we can get everything completed.

Chuck: I think if we can get the objectives and the assessment program done, that will be enough.

Bertha: I agree with Chuck, but I'd like to add a record-keeping system.

Pat: What do you think, Ron?

Ron: I agree with Bertha. If we are going to manage the assessment and maintain consistency among the units, we should take care of that task, also. I don't think it will be that difficult.

Pat: Liz, how do you feel?

Liz: Well, I guess it will have to be okay, but I still would rather that we get some of our materials organized. After all, over the summer someone will have to order the materials we need. And, now that I think of it, if we expect our staff to begin making materials, they ought to know what we have already and what we don't.

Chuck: I'm not crazy about doing everything this summer but, since I've done some work with record-keeping systems, it won't be that much more work. I'll go with doing everything this summer except organizing our materials.

Pat: Okay. On the time line then I'll add these three tasks indicating that they'll be done by the second week of August. That will give us time to consider where we are when we put our preschool workshop together.

Liz: Well, Pat, let's look at our time line and see what activities we have.

Ron: Then, let's see what each of us can do so that we can meet our time line.

CASE ANALYSIS

1. Prepare the time line agreed upon by the Instructional Improvement Committee of the Washington School. Does it include the essential activities necessary to complete the first three steps of the IPM by the beginning of the preschool workshop? Are the time allocations reasonable? What activities should be added or dropped?

2. Given the time line which was developed, prepare a chart outlining the specific subsequent responsibilities of the principal, each unit leader, and the I & R Unit staffs.

3. Critique and analyze the leadership behavior of the principal and unit leaders during this meeting in terms of instrumental, supportive, and participative leadership. Similarly, analyze the decision-making behavior of the principal and unit leaders in terms of decision content, involvement, and representation.

Case 4

How to
Help Helen

Albert M. Holmquist
James M. Lipham

Highland Elementary School implemented IGE last year. The school consists of six units, each including a unit leader, three staff teachers, a half-time aide, an intern teacher from the local college, and approximately 130 students. Last year, Helen Holmes was an intern teacher in Unit D. She was particularly strong in working with small groups and with individual students, bringing fresh insights and open ideas into the school's operation. Since she seemed to share the philosophy of the staff and received high recommendations from the college, she was offered a one-year contract. Because of the negotiated agreement with the teacher's organization, the principal is solely responsible for her evaluation. Now, Jean Adams, the principal of Highland School, must decide and recommend to the superintendent whether or not Helen will be offered a second-year contract. The superintendent will back the principal's decision, as will the Board of Education. Jean's final decision is due on February 1.

Early in September, Sue Jones, another teacher in Unit D, stopped by and said:

> The IGE preservice last week didn't do any good. We're attempting to provide instructional programs for individual students, but Helen's trying to run an open classroom as she did as an intern. She just lets those kids run wild.

Sue often simply stops by the office and drops such comments. She can spot potential problems before they become serious and is very helpful in surfacing them. Sue expressed some concern about Helen's open-classroom approach several times last year. Then, the principal responded by asking her to give Helen a chance—saying that after all she was only a student teacher —and pointed out how well individual students responded to her teaching methods.

Shortly thereafter, on September 5, the IIC met in the teachers' lounge which was adjacent to Unit D. Throughout the meeting Jean could not help but notice a high level of noise nearby, and made a mental note to review Helen's performance—and soon.

September 12

A second IIC meeting is held. Again, noise is heard. Returning to the office after lunch, the principal reexamined Helen's college evaluation checklist from last spring.

Certification: Recommended ☑

Certification: Not Recommended ☐

Evaluation Scale for All Student Teachers

Name of Teacher _____ Miss Helen Holmes _____

School ____ Highland ____ Grade or Subject ____ 4-5 ____

Purpose: The purpose of this rating scale for teachers is to promote better teaching through the evaluation and supervision of instruction and the maintenance of a high quality professional staff.

Directions: Please place a " ✓ " indicating your evaluation of this teacher in comparison to other teachers. Descriptive words are only suggestive and not intended to be all-inclusive. The rater may wish to cross out words that do not apply, underline those that do, or add descriptive phrases or words.

	Poor	Fair	Satisfactory	Strong	Exceptional

1. PERSONAL QUALITIES

A. Character ——————————————————— ✓ ———

B. Health and absenteeism
   record ———————————————————————— ✓ ——

C. Emotional
   stability ———————————— ✓ ——————————————

D. Personal
   relations ———————————————————————— ✓ ——

2. TEACHING ABILITY

A. Professional
   knowledge ———————————————————— ✓ ———

	Insufficient educational background	Adequate for ordinary needs	Well read, up to date on current knowledge in field

B. Professional
   interest ✓

| Shirks school duties | Responds, interested in regular work | Enthusiastic, makes useful contributions |

C. Assignments ✓

| No consideration for individual differences, not clear or stimulating | Satisfactory | Considers individual differences, clear, stimulating |

D. Daily
   preparation ✓

| Unplanned, slipshod | Satisfactory | Systematic, businesslike |

E. Control of
   pupils ✓

| Unable to control pupils, weak, follows rather than leads | Satisfactory for ordinary needs | Stimulates pupil self-control |

F. Techniques
   of
   teaching ✓

| Routine, unimaginative, dull, unable to meet children at their level | Satisfactory | Imaginative, stimulating |

I have observed this teacher 1, 2, 3,④ 5–10, 11–20, more than 20 times this school year. (Circle one)

Date __2 - 3 - 76__   _Jean Adams_
                              Principal

I have read this evaluation   Student Teacher

The next Monday morning the mail contains the following letter from an officer in the parent-teacher organization:

September 12, 1977

Dear Jean:

My daughter Ruth is in Unit D. She says that it is always so noisy in Miss Holmes's group that she can't get her work done. Ruth always wants to read, but the kids don't leave her alone so she can this year. Some of us parents, as you know, were afraid of this about IGE. I want you to keep it quieter so my daughter can learn. I'll drop by to visit with you further about this, if you wish.

Sincerely,

Mrs. John Frederickson

Mrs. John Frederickson

September 15

The summary of the schoolwide mathematics assessment program completed during pretesting revealed that several of the students with whom Helen worked most closely last spring semester did not reach the criterion level on many of the mathematics objectives.

October 3

Jack Fry, the supervising professor from the local college stops by to explain a type of evaluation instrument they are using with interns this year.

Teacher Talk	Accepts feelings	
	Praises	
	Accepts student ideas	
	Asks questions	
	Lectures	
	Gives directions	
	Criticizes	
Student Talk	Response	
	Initiates	
	Silence or confusion	

It is called the Interaction Analysis Scale (cf. Flanders 1966). Jack explains that one simply observes the teacher for about five minutes and puts a mark in the appropriate box every ten seconds. He leaves Jean a copy of the form:

October 12

During the principal's eight-week visits to each teacher, Jean decides to visit Helen unannounced. After about five minutes, Helen calls a skill development group to the small group area (a rug, several pillows, and two old car seats). Jean fills out the observation schedule. The small-group lesson up front is a straight, drill-type activity. There are right and wrong answers. Helen is using this approach since the IIC agreed earlier this year that pupils would have to score better in basic skills. The remainder of the area is chaotic. The noise level is so high that students in the math group have to shout their answers. A few students seem oblivious to the noise and are intent on their tasks. The majority of the other students, however, wander from one area to another, talking and engaging in horseplay. After filling out the form, Jean retreats to the quiet of the principal's office and examines the chart.

Teacher Talk	Accepts feelings	////
	Praises	̶H̶H̶ /
	Accepts student ideas	/
	Asks questions	̶H̶H̶ ̶H̶H̶ /
	Lectures	///
	Gives directions	/
	Criticizes	///
Student Talk	Response	̶H̶H̶ ̶H̶H̶ ̶H̶H̶ ̶H̶H̶ /
	Initiates	̶H̶H̶ ̶H̶H̶ //
Silence or Confusion		̶H̶H̶ ̶H̶H̶ ̶H̶H̶ ̶H̶H̶ ///

October 13

Tom Brown, another teacher in Unit D, stopped by the office to mention that he and the other teachers in the unit were trying to help Helen, particularly by handling some of the disciplinary problems that came up when she was working with a class-size group. "Increasingly," he said, "it is becoming a problem because her vision sweep seems only to include those nearest her." They had arranged some of the furniture, which seemed to help, and visited with her about the problem. She was trying desperately to improve, but he wondered how much longer the teachers could make allowances for balance in the work load, since she could not always work with small groups only.

October 15

After the IIC meeting, Jean asks Sarah Robbins, Helen's Unit Leader, to remain a moment. Jean indicates the concern about Helen's teaching—particularly the noise and confusion when she is working with larger groups.

Sarah: Yes, there is considerable noise, and we've talked with her about it. We've all made several suggestions. It just seems that she's oblivious to it—notices only what is happening right around her. Sometimes it creates extra work for all of us, having to watch our kids and hers. I know she's trying awfully hard to meet the objectives we've set. But it's beginning to affect morale in our unit.

November 1

Fred drops in. Fred is the principal of the first IGE school in the district which started implementation four years ago.

Fred: How's it going, kiddo?
Jean: Well, fine, except for one of our first-year teachers, Helen Holmes. I'm trying to help her now. I've been doing some observing and I have checked with her unit leader several times. She's trying to meet the objectives they're working on, but it's a real struggle.
Fred: Did you agree with the teacher on what you were looking for before you observed her—so you both can check specifically on what she must do to improve?

November 5

After attending a Unit D "objective-setting-for-the-next-week" meeting, Jean drops in on Helen.

Jean: Hello. You're aware that I am required to observe you several times this year before contract renewal time. When would be the best time for me to come in?
Helen: Could you come during math for a couple of days? We're working on common denominators now and should finish the topic this week. Do you know which objectives we're working on?
Jean: Yes. Will you be giving them a test when they're done?
Helen: Yes.

Jean: Unit D gave a pretest before you got that group, didn't they?

Helen: Yes.

Jean: Then we can compare where they were with what they've learned since they've been in your group.

Helen: Yes.

Jean: I'd like to also see how you accept student ideas and feelings, how you reinforce children, how you use concrete examples, and particularly how you give directions and maintain control of the group.

Helen: Afterwards, could we review what you write down, and can we talk about it?

Jean: Of course! Let's get started Monday.

November 9

Jean observes in Helen's room at the appointed time. There is only the math group there. The following notes are recorded:

Accepts student ideas— *mostly lecturing, didn't really ask for kids' ideas*

Accepts student feelings—

Method of reinforcement— *verbal, occasional smile, says "that's right" a lot*

Use of concrete examples— *only chalkboard*

Type of directions—

November 10

The notes for the next two days are almost identical, except that Helen gave fewer directions.

November 12

An emergency came up yesterday. Scotty broke his arm swinging on the door in the bathroom during Unit D's math time.

Today, there was nothing to see except the children taking the final tests. The results revealed that only 50 percent of the objectives were accomplished across the group.

November 15

In a private conference with Jean, Helen acknowledges her difficulties in teaching mathematics. Jean suggests that she talk with Miss Booth about some of her problems. Miss Booth is the math resource person for the school. Jean frees up one-half day released time for Helen and Miss Booth. During their conference Jean drops in and suggests that since Helen seems to be enjoying such success with small group reading instruction, perhaps Helen and Miss Booth could talk about small group math techniques.

November 20

In a Unit D unit meeting, Helen requests that since they are regrouping for math again, she do all small group instruction. Reluctantly, the principal agrees.

December 15

The posttests for Helen's small group show 85 percent mastery of all objectives. Obviously, she is quite pleased with the progress, but again she makes the request of the unit leader to work only with a few children when regrouping occurs.

January 8

Fred drops by with several different kinds of observation scales he has used over the years. Some can be used across teachers, others can be used across subject matter and teaching techniques of the same teacher. February first is coming up quickly, and Jean still hasn't decided about Helen's renewal. After school Jean visits Helen's room.

Jean: Helen, after the observations, you remember, we spotted areas for improvement and talked about how they could be improved. And you certainly were successful with the small math groups. I also would like to observe your large-group teaching soon.

Helen: How many times do you have to observe me? You just said I was doing fine. You never visit Tom or Sarah . . . . And what about Judy? She's trying out the open-classroom idea too, and you never go to see her?

(Judy has been in the school system 17 years. She is a primary unit leader. She has a master's degree in curriculum and spent a year's sabbatical in a British infants' school. Jean asked Helen to observe her to see how she works with all kinds of groups.)

    After several moments of uncomfortable silence on Jean's part—not knowing whether to respond in any way, wait, or go away—Sarah Robbins happens by. After a kind hello, Sarah suggests that it might be a good idea that not just Helen, but perhaps the entire unit might be observed, since they are all concerned about the progress of the children. Helen asks if Sarah, Tom, or the other teachers in the unit can also do some actual observing. Jean suggests that the next IIC meeting might be a good place to take this matter up.

IIC Meeting, mid-January

The matter of evaluation of teachers in IGE is discussed, and there is general agreement that there is no one best procedure to use. Although not discussed, everyone knows the basis for the concern in Unit D. The IIC recommends that an ad hoc committee be formed by the principal to develop a comprehensive evaluation plan especially tailored to Highland School. It is agreed, however, that hereafter all plans will be taken to unit meetings for discussion and then reviewed by the IIC before any actual use is made of them.

It's now only a week before Jean must make Helen's final evaluation. The ad hoc committee is working hard but has not yet produced a procedure which can help the principal make a final decision. To gain Helen's own perception of her teaching, Jean Adams requests Helen to help her fill out a form identical to the one used by the college.

CASE ANALYSIS

1. Critique the initial decision to offer Helen a one-year contract, in terms of the relationship between expectations held for teachers and the student teaching performance of Helen. What evaluative criteria should have been used at that time?

2. In terms of suggested procedures for evaluating IGE staff members, critique the formal and informal evaluation activities undertaken by the principal, Jean Adams.

3. Regarding the suggestion by the IIC that an Ad Hoc Committee on Staff Evaluation be formed:
   a. What criteria would you use for selecting the members?
   b. Describe the guidelines you would give the committee.
   c. What information would you present the committee?
   d. How would you implement their recommendations?

4. In terms of the information available, make a decision on the contract renewal of Helen and defend it in terms of future actions required to implement and evaluate your decision.

REFERENCES

Flanders, N. A. 1966. *Interaction analysis in the classroom.* Ann Arbor: University of Michigan.

Case 5

Johnson Is
Our School

William R. Miles

Johnson Elementary School serves three separate neighborhoods on the south side of Ramosa, a mountain city of 70,000 population. The first is Southboro, in which the school is located. Built during the past four years, this attractive area of 3–4 bedroom, ranch-style homes represents a major step outward and upward for the middle managers, skilled craftsmen, and small business people in their move from the older parts of Ramosa. The ethnic makeup of the Southboro neighborhood is approximately 90 percent white, 9 percent Spanish surnamed, and 1 percent other.

The second major neighborhood served by Johnson School is Golf Estates which is located about a mile east of Southboro. Houses in Golf Estates currently average about $10,000 higher in value than those in Southboro. The area is definitely upper-middle class, including many professors and other professionals. The population is 100 percent white. Families in Golf Estates typically drive their children to school, since many of the children also attend middle and senior high schools.

The third neighborhood served by Johnson Elementary School is King Acres, and is located high on a hill about two miles to the west of Southboro. The lots are large, ranging from two to ten acres, so that people can keep horses on their property, typically surrounded by attractive and functional fences. Although some of the original homes in the area sell for as low as those in Southboro and Golf Estates, homes have been built recently in the $100,000 range. The life-style and orientation of the 97 percent white and 3 percent Spanish surnamed leaders—doctors, lawyers, and corporation officials—who live there indicate that King Acres, indeed, is appropriately named.

The rapid burst of housing in the late 1960s had tapered off by 1970. However, there are attractive flatland areas which could be developed between the three tracts which serve Johnson School. Indeed, rumors had been circulating in the past two years that the federal housing agency had been approached about a low-income apartment complex in the flatlands. Ramosa officials never seemed to be able to substantiate the rumors; moreover, the city did not have a central school-city building planning commission through which such programs could be coordinated.

Johnson is one of the seventeen elementary schools in the Ramosa School District, now called Ramosa Joint 3 because of a merger eleven years ago with two outlying districts. In the last decade, the school population has grown from 6500 to 15,000 students. The district now includes three high schools and five middle schools and, of the seventeen elementary schools, four are one-room mountain schools. A seven-member school board serves the district. Members are nominated to represent geographic areas of Ramosa J–3 but are elected at large for four-year terms. Because board members represent an area, they are called directors of that particular area.

Jack Clarke has been the Superintendent of Schools in Ramosa for six years, replacing a man who previously held the superintendency for nine years. Clarke worked his way up through the administrative hierarchy, holding the assistant superintendency for administrative services for four years before becoming superintendent. Clark views himself as an effective communicator with community subpublics, but many citizens do not see him in this light. Parents and citizens in certain parts of the district do not trust Mr. Clarke, presumably because of what they call broken promises over mountain school closings, several building referenda, and attendance boundary changes.

Since the south side of Ramosa has experienced the greatest growth, plans were laid as early as five years ago for an elementary school to be built in Southboro. At that time, Ramosa J–3 passed a major bond issue for future building and made a definite commitment to the concept of small neighborhood elementary schools. An open-style school plant in Southboro was presented initially on the basis that it would be cheaper to build, but many parents came to like and support the open-school concept for Johnson Elementary School which was built and opened in the fall, two years ago, to accommodate a projected enrollment of 380 students.

In the spring prior to the school's opening, a group of interested parents scheduled a meeting at the central office with Superintendent Clarke, and convinced him of the need for early planning of the educational program to go into their new, open-style school. According to Judi Rikopo, parents looking for alternatives were a minority at that time, probably including twenty to thirty parents who were led by the Kellys and Cruzes from King Acres, the McDermotts and Rikopos from Southboro, and the Thompsons from Golf Estates. As Judi said, "If there hadn't been a few of us that took action, the whole school would have become bogged down in tradition." Some of the parents had visited the first IGE school in the district and liked its principal, Rob Jackson.

Principal Jackson had been the key figure in bringing IGE into the Ramosa school system. Rob, in his middle thirties and a native of Ramosa, was clearly admired by everyone as one who can get things done—a leader and motivator of people. He was certainly an energetic individual—currently serving as president of the state principals' association, and a member of many district and municipal task forces related to education. He had been instrumental in introducing IGE into his previous school, and in the formation of the Ramosa Systemwide Program Committee for IGE schools.

Perhaps as a result of the several sessions with the influential parents, Superintendent Clarke called Rob Jackson in December and offered him the Johnson School principalship, starting immediately. Jackson was somewhat surprised that he was offered the job because at times he did not get along particularly well with the superintendent, but he took it, being delegated with the prospect of planning the program for the new school, selecting the staff, and working with the community. Although the school was already being built, the superintendent involved Rob in the later stages of building planning, and he made some changes in the open-space design so that another pod could be adjoined, if future enrollment demanded it. Rob was given a free hand in getting the IGE program underway in the school.

By late spring, he had selected most of the staff and had met with them several times. During their planning, they decided to become an IGE school. Unit leaders were selected and they went to an IGE Principal-Unit Leader Workshop at a nearby resort in April. The staff met informally throughout that spring and summer, devoting many hours of hard work to program planning. A high level of staff cohesiveness developed; they even adopted a nickname, the "Johnson Joggers," since many of them arrived at school early in the morning to work at their new roles.

Everyone interviewed agreed that the opening of Johnson as an IGE school was smooth indeed. In July and August, the local newspaper ran a series of articles explaining IGE. During September and October, each I & R Unit held a series of meetings which were designed as small group informational sessions for parents. The parent unit meetings, held on different nights so that all could attend, were enthusiastically received. The staff later reported that parents were knowledgeable about education in the question and answer sessions—particularly concerning the reading program. All parents seemed to hold very high standards for their children. Throughout the first semester of implementation, Johnson School's home-school-community relations program took shape with some ten different kinds of ongoing community related programs and activities, as follows:

Activity	*Primary Responsibility*
Informal Coffees	Principal
"Introduction to Johnson Elementary School" Slide/Tape Presentation	Principal
Parent/Visitor Procedures	Office Staff
Unit Meetings with Parents	Instructional Improvement Committee (IIC)
Weekly Conferences/Report Cards	Unit Staff
Good Time Notes	Instruction and Research
Specials Unit Potpourri	Specials Unit Leader and Staff
Sports Program	Physical Education Teacher
Monthly School Newsletter	PTO Volunteer
Parent Volunteers	PTO Committee

In Ramosa J–3, Parent Advisory Councils were mandated by board of education policy to communicate and suggest policies and problems to the SPC, the administration, and the board of education. How was Johnson's Parent Advisory Committee formed? Rob Jackson sent a letter to all families in September outlining his concerns for the need to organize parental involvement. He announced a September meeting date for all interested in attending. At the September meeting, over 120 parents came and the Advisory Committee was formalized. Leaders were nominated, to include the principal, the President of the Parent-Teacher Organization, and nine parents to be elected—three from each neighborhood. It was agreed that the Advisory Committee would assist with the development of school policy and the solution of pressing problems. The leader subsequently elected came mainly from the committed group of parents who had previously exercised informal leadership in establishing the school.

At subsequent meetings, the Parent Advisory Council of Johnson School established two task forces. The first, a Task Force on Pupil Progress, was to work out a new system of reporting to parents which would replace the old report card system. The second, a Task Force on Enrollment was concerned with recommending alternatives to relieve overcrowding at Johnson School which had been built for 380 students but, with increased building throughout the attendance area, already enrolled 420 students by Christmas. Something would have to be done about the overcrowding, and soon.

The Task Force on Enrollment, with Dr. Cruz from King Acres as Chairperson, set about systematically to analyze the situation and recommend alternatives. First, an informational session was scheduled for the January program of the Parent-Teacher Organization. At this meeting, attended by over 200 people, several parental complaints were registered, including charges that youngsters sometimes could not keep track of their materials, and that they could not find places to work independently in small groups. At this meeting, the task force was urged to get the school board to begin construction immediately on the other pod to the building. The suggestions that busing of students to other schools or redrawing of attendance boundaries might relieve the situation were roundly rejected. "Johnson is our school," "They can't do this to us," and "We won't stand for it!" were among the comments made. For the first time, there was open dissension among Southboro, Golf Estates, and King Acres parents about who the school was *really* built for in the first place. Mrs. Kelly, who lived in Golf Estates complained bitterly "My children have gone to four different schools over the years, and finally we have an excellent school and they're all doing beautifully. There is no way I'm going to stand for another move!" Professor McDermott, a sociologist who also lived in Golf Acres, volunteered to join the task force to help analyze the situation. It was decided that a study would be made, including individual interviews with all heads of households in the Johnson attendance area.

As the Task Force on Enrollment continued its work, it became necessary to augment the group, not only to conduct the in-depth interviews, but also form two other groups, one to analyze current space utilization in the building, and another to reanalyze land use patterns and project realistic enrollment figures for the Johnson attendance area in the future.

In March, the subgroup on projected enrollments discovered to everyone's surprise that an area in "the flats" slightly north of King Acres and Southboro had been rezoned from light industrial to apartment-type dwellings and that preliminary plans had been approved for 250 2–3-bedroom public housing units. District officials who were contracted denied knowledge of the proposed change, stating that only after approval by several agencies would they customarily be notified. The next day the headlines of the morning paper read: "HUD Approves Johnson Area Project." Calls came pouring in from concerned citizens. Johnson parents, Enrollment Task Force members, and nonparents from the school attendance area began to ask the principal how they could determine what should be done in the wake of the HUD decision.

CASE ANALYSIS

Assume that you are Rob Jackson, Principal of Johnson Elementary School.

1. What actions will you take to assist the Task Force in dealing immediately with the manifest conflict concerning enrollment and with latent

conflicts concerning values and expectations within your school's three communities?

2. What suggestions can you and the IIC make to the SPC and the school district administration for relieving the overcrowding both immediately and in the future at Johnson School, and for building trust and understanding of school district policies, procedures, and personnel?

3. What dimensions of the actual and potential conflict are resource, power, and value issues? What can be done about each?

Case 6
Reorganization in Rock Falls

William R. Miles
Marvin J. Fruth

Rock Falls, a rural Midwestern town of 2500, is surrounded by three small farming communities, Black Creek, Yellow Springs, and Crescent. There are 1300 students in the area served by the Rock Falls School District. Schools in the district include a high school for grades 9–12; a grade school building which houses kindergarten, grades 5 and 6, and the 7–8 middle school; three outlying elementary schools; and a one-room kindergarten facility.

The educational philosophy of Rock Falls is child centered; they wish the very best for their children. In the last ten years, the district has become known as one of the most innovative in the state. The high school, for example, implemented a flexible modular schedule program six years ago, and the district was an early adopter of IGE. Throughout the district educational innovations are accepted if they are viewed as being "good for the kids."

The Rock Falls School District was unified and consolidated in the late 1950s, when the three surrounding rural school districts were merged with the Rock Falls schools. Each of these small districts, Black Creek, Yellow Springs, and Crescent had just built new four-room school facilities, The Rock Falls District took them over as a part of the district operation, as well as assuming their indebtedness. Not all of the rural people welcomed the unification with Rock Falls. The rural schools served as centers of social activity in their communities. Many of the farmers were suspicious of the "larger" district and felt a loss in autonomy.

Prior to the adoption and implementation of IGE, the four elementary schools in Rock Falls as well as the one-room rural kindergarten school were typical self-contained classroom schools. When the small farms merged with large farms in the late 1960s, many families with school-age children moved away. Also at this time, the declining birthrate caught up to Rock

Falls. Thus, one sees the dilemma: declining enrollments in each neighborhood, but relatively new schools.

The former School Superintendent, Tom Anderson, was instrumental in initiating IGE in the Rock Falls school system. According to some board members, Anderson was hired with the mandate to "shape up" the elementary schools, which he felt included the evaluation of alternatives for the elementary schools. One of those alternatives was IGE. During the 1971–1972 school year, the district's inservice theme was analysis of the elementary school situation.

Several factors led to the analysis of the elementary schools. One certainly was the bus-routing problem in filling up the rural schools, especially the Black Creek School. Children would have had to ride forty to fifty minutes each way to justify keeping the Black Creek school open. Another reason centered around a desire for innovation at the elementary school level to keep pace with changes in the high school. The superintendent prior to Mr. Anderson had left a list of district priorities, number one of which was upgrading the elementary schools.

Rock Falls' first formal contact with IGE per se came when Mr. Anderson called the State IGE coordinator. At that time, Superintendent Anderson; John Swenson, the elementary principal; and Margaret Oimoen, the elementary supervisor, were only looking at a variety of alternatives—multiaging, team teaching, and nongradedness—but IGE was chosen because it seemed to have the better aspects of each woven into it.

As discussion seemed more and more to be centered on the IGE program, two key individuals needed to be convinced, Mr. Swenson and Ms. Oimoen. Mr. Swenson was already feeling the pressure of the bus-routing problem, which was his responsibility. In order to keep neighborhood schools, he was faced with closing a classroom out in Black Creek while renting one or two classrooms from the parochial school in town. An elementary reorganization would mean new bus routes and better use of existing facilities. Ms. Oimoen eventually became convinced of the soundness of IGE, and was particularly impressed with the Wisconsin Design for Reading Skill Development program.

Late in the summer, the board of education intensified the search into alternatives for organizational patterns in the elementary schools. Representatives from the State Department of Education came to visit early in the fall with Anderson, Swenson, and Oimoen. In October, Mr. Swenson and Ms. Oimoen attended an IGE Awareness Conference. Subsequently, they also visited several IGE schools in their own and neighboring states. Swenson became sold on IGE because of its combination of organizational and instructional components. He also saw IGE as a means for eventually resolving the bus-routing problem. Ms. Oimoen viewed IGE as analogous to the one-room rural schools in which she had worked and supervised, and used that analogy when later talking with teachers and parents. She also mentioned the excellent reading materials.

School board members were kept informed periodically by Mr. Anderson concerning developments of the elementary reorganization investigation. In January, Superintendent Anderson, the president, two other board members, and an unofficial representative from Black Creek visited an IGE elementary school in a city nearby. By the end of January no formal decision had been reached to implement IGE in Rock Falls. However, Mr. Anderson definitely was orchestrating movement toward that point. He, Mr. Swenson, and two teachers attended another IGE workshop in January.

Subsequently, Anderson arranged for the state IGE coordinator to come and run a series of workshops on IGE for interested teachers in Rock Falls and surrounding districts. The workshops ran from February to May. Teachers had to pay a $25 registration fee, but they were awarded credits on the salary schedule for additional increments. Although attendance was voluntary, all of the elementary teachers in Rock Falls attended except those who were going to retire that spring.

The weekly newspaper picked up IGE as newsworthy. In February, a long article outlined IGE as an instructional program and described the inservice class and various meetings which had been attended. In March, a follow-up article on the inservice program discussed some of the teachers' activities at the workshops. An April article described the teachers' "plans for implementing an individually guided program of instruction for our elementary school youngsters."

That article also called for parent attendance at an IGE informational meeting to be held at the final inservice class in March in the middle school. The March meeting, attended by over 150 parents, began with an overview of IGE by Superintendent Anderson.

He then broke the group into small groups clustered around teachers. IGE was described as being "good for kids"; it was stressed that the students could compete better amongst themselves in an IGE setting. Continuous progress and multiage grouping were seen as analogous to competition among intellectual peers rather than age peers.

For three weeks in May the teachers at Yellow Springs School tried the organizational arrangements of being an I & R Unit. Yellow Springs was chosen from among the three outlying rural schools because it had an excellent potential unit leader, Gwen Henkel, and it had the weakest rural centeredness. Actually, Yellow Springs identified more with Rock Falls than with the local area. By the end of May, a genuine commitment to trying IGE had been made by teachers, administrators, and board members, and a "wait-and-see" posture had been taken by parents. One of the parents commented in this way: "Well, John (Swenson) and Margaret (Oimoen) are the educators; if they say it's a good program, it must be okay."

Teachers at Yellow Springs were brought in for three days of IGE preentry activity prior to the actual opening of school in the fall. Parents were invited to attend the last preentry session prior to school's opening. Yellow Springs was to open with the 90 children who would be in grades one and two. Crescent and Black Creek Elementary Schools remained essentially the same as before for that school year.

The implementation of IGE went very smoothly. The Rock Falls teachers had visited IGE schools, attended a semester-long inservice workshop, had a three-week trial period in May, and held a three-day preentry workshop prior to the opening of school. The teachers and administrators felt that by the Education Week Open House in November, parents at Yellow Springs had accepted the IGE program. The overwhelming response to why they accepted it was that their children came home happy and satisfied with school. Another possible reason for acceptance may have been that the teachers were well prepared to implement IGE and had done so successfully.

Excellent informal school-community contacts continued at Yellow Springs School throughout the fall. Parents were encouraged to visit and observe instruction. In addition, an Open House was held so that not only parents from Yellow Springs but all parents who were interested in the IGE program could attend and talk with the staff.

The Yellow Springs parents had read newspaper articles on IGE and had visited informally with school leaders Gwen Henkel, John Swenson, and Margaret Oimoen. Many of them also had attended the informational session the previous spring during which they talked in small groups with the staff. Moreover, they were included in the preentry activities so that they were fully aware of the nature of the IGE program. A decision for the Rock Falls elementary schools had been made far previous to any formal school-community contacts. However, a combination of the interpersonal contacts in the rural setting, plus a great feeling of trust in Ms. Henkel, Mr. Swenson, and Ms. Oimoen, ensured the program's acceptance.

It must be acknowledged that in the implementation of IGE in Rock Falls the hidden agenda item was that the strong neighborhood ties would be broken to achieve better school building utilization for instruction. Although this was made, John Swenson was concerned about the bus routes and knew that shifts had to be made. However, the loss of rural school identity and the fact that children might have to be bused at some distance were never publicized during the initial stages of IGE implementation.

At the end of the first year of implementation of IGE, Superintendent Anderson resigned to return to graduate school. The new school superintendent, Robert Bachman, was hired with the expectation that the implementation of IGE would continue systematically. In an August board meeting, IGE implementation was discussed with the understanding that it would be implemented at Crescent and Black Creek schools since the program had succeeded at Yellow Springs. Board members were solidly behind the IGE Program. Thomas Anderson had laid the ground work and had an implementation plan for installing IGE in all of the Rock Falls elementary schools, and subsequently in the middle school.

The weeky newspaper also continued its good coverage of the IGE program. In a February article, a meeting was announced to be held at Black Creek School to discuss "Consideration is now being given to extending the system of IGE through the fifth grade next year and to use it at Crescent and Black Creek as well." The article continued with a report of a visit to Yellow Springs, particularly citing favorable impressions about the reading program.

The decision had been made by the board of education on the recommendations of Superintendent Bachman, Mr. Swenson, and Ms. Oimoen to break the schools up into two K–3 units in Yellow Springs and Crescent, and have all the fourth and fifth graders go to Black Creek. The basis for that decision was their feelings that this would enhance the instructional program while making maximum use of building resources. Trial balloons were put up in January, 1973, by the administration and school board members about the busing and reorganization. Mr. Swenson discussed this topic informally with Black Creek residents and gained the impression of consensus among residents there.

The Black Creek School was selected as the first one in which to hold the informational meetings because the community was very active and customarily held local meetings in the school. For example, the Black Creek Mothers' Club held monthly meetings, often card parties, in the school. Teachers also attended and shared information about their children's progress—almost a monthly "report card" conference. The 4–H Club met at the school, men played basketball there, and it was open for a host of activities. The high point of the Black Creek social life was the annual spring picnic at which baseball and other games were played while the women prepared the food. The picnic was held on the final day of school, and students were released at noon to participate in the fun.

In the 1950s, the Black Creek School became the recipient of a large endowment given by a former Black Creek resident, Eric Hanson. Mr. Hanson set up a trust fund with the interest from the money being available for the Black Creek Elementary School Board of Education to spend as they saw fit. With the school consolidation process in the 1950s, the Black Creek Board of Education was absorbed into the Rock Falls Board of Education which assumed the management of the Hanson Fund. The new board, however, did allocate the Black Creek Mothers' Club some discretionary funds, usually about $1000, to spend for the school each year. In addition, any money spent out of the Hanson Fund, typically $9000 per year, was spent on improvements to the Black Creek school. Critics in Black Creek maintained that some funds usually were available for one year only and then were redistributed to other schools which subverted the intent of the Hanson Fund to improve education at Black Creek.

Implementing IGE at Black Creek School was the topic of the public meeting to be held on February 15. Superintendent Bachman opened the meeting with a few general remarks, and was followed by Mr. Swenson, Ms. Oimoen, and Ms. Henkel who described the success of the program at Yellow Springs. There were also some unofficial ambassadors—three or four sets of parents from Yellow Springs. These parents happened to include the president of the school board and also the mayor of Rock Falls. The board president spoke as a satisfied parent when asked questions at the meeting about the board's perspectives on IGE. Ms. Oimoen used an analogy comparing the multiunit school with the one-room rural school, emphasizing how much more is known now and how a better job can be done. Questions were invited from the 100 Black Creek residents in attendance.

No one was prepared for the blowup that followed. There was a persistent barrage of unfriendly questions, insinuations, and charges. One woman asked Superintendent Bachman three times what the board of education vote had been on IGE implementation and on busing/reorganization, without getting her question answered satisfactorily. Others charged that the school board should be sued for robbing the school of the Hanson funds. Another dissident claimed that the busing of children would destroy their entire community—no ball teams, no informal meetings, and even no picnic. The school board member from Black Creek was bitterly attacked. Taken aback, he even tried to appeal to the group as friends and neighbors to listen to reason. Finally, Mr. Jensen and Ms. Oimoen were able to quiet the group by focusing on educational improvement. Even so, the almost unanimous feeling at the end of the meeting was stated by one parent as follows:

> You school people, including the mayor and other bigwigs, did not come out here to discuss a "consideration of implementing IGE" as the newspaper suggested. You've already made the decision and you'll have to ram it down our throats.

After the meeting the school board member from Black Creek and the school administrators circulated during the coffee hour, attempting to smooth over some of the issues with the most vocal parents. Even so, the following comment was overheard, "Just wait until they see what's going to happen at Crescent next week."

CASE ANALYSIS

1. Analyze the conflicts in the case in terms of the power, resources, and prevailing values in Rock Falls and Black Creek.

2. Critique the plans and procedures that were used for implementing IGE in Yellow Springs, Black Creek, and the total district of Rock Falls.

3. Project solutions to the manifest conflict situation, in terms of analysis, communication, involvement, and resolution concepts and competencies.

Case 7

Building the Budget at Bayside

William H. Klenke
Joseph J. Marinelli

Bayside Elementary School is in its first year of operation as an IGE school. The school, organized into four I & R Units, has an excellent principal and unit leaders who, along with the director of the instructional materials center, serve as the IIC. Throughout the changeover year, this committee has provided very effective leadership in assessing educational needs, setting schoolwide objectives, planning instructional activities, and evaluating educational outcomes.

Prior to the changeover year, the decision was made to implement the IPM first in the area of reading. Except for the need for some additional capital outlay items for instructional equipment and for some additional instructional materials and assessment devices in reading, the program has progressed smoothly—so well, in fact, that the decision was made in January of this year to implement an individualized program of instruction in the area of mathematics, beginning next fall.

Working with the SPC, members of the IIC were instrumental in getting the district board of education to approve, in addition to the regular budget, a special allocation of $1000 for mathematics materials. It is impossible to increase this allocation further for next year. The basic budget allocations for the coming year from the school district business office were arrived at through a set formula based on student enrollment. There are no restrictions as to what the specific items can be within each category; i.e., most instructional materials and supplies can be ordered, but it is not permissible to transfer monies from one account to another unless permission is granted by the board of education. The matter of transfer of funds was brought up at a SPC meeting last year, but the members of the committee felt that it was not advisable to request the board to change the policy on the transfer of funds at this time. The Bayside budget for next year is as follows.

Budget Category	Allocation to Bayside	Guidelines for preparing unit budgets
Special allocation (materials and supplies)	$1000.00	$ 250.00
Instructional materials and supplies	2500.00	625.00
Capital outlay	500.00	125.00
AV for the school's resource center	350.00	
	$4350.00	$1000.00

Having been quite pressed last year with the issues involved in changing to a multiunit form of organization, writing schoolwide objectives in reading, and planning for the preopening of school workshop, the Instructional Improvement Committee recognized that they could give scant attention not only to the budget, but specifically to which reading materials in which amounts should be purchased during the summer. As one unit leader commented, "The budget just comes at the wrong time—if only we could be *sure* of our needs!" Even so, they did the best that they could and, during the summer, several staff members pitched in to help the principal and the IMC director review, order, and distribute equipment and materials. Throughout the fall, the staff willingly shared scarce items, but everyone on the Instructional Improvement Committee agreed, "Next year, we'll do it right!" As a consequence, a detailed inventory was completed in both reading and mathematics, and the unit leaders agreed to project tentative budget requests, not only for their units but for the IMC as well. The following are the "asking" budgets prepared by each of the units:

Unit A

Description of Item *Instructional materials and supplies*	Quantity	Unit cost	Total cost
Math Puzzles	4	$ 2.50	$ 10.00
Lotto (Addition)	6	1.00	6.00
Readings Laboratory	1	250.00	250.00
Mathboards	25	2.75	68.75
Flannel Boards and Games	4	15.00	60.00
Flash Cards (Addition)	5	.75	3.75
Flash Cards (Substraction)	5	.75	3.75
Flash Cards (Multiplication)	5	.75	3.75
Flash Cards (Division)	5	.75	3.75
Our School (Reader)	30	3.95	118.50
Math—Level 1	30	2.50	75.00
Math—Level 2	30	2.75	82.50
Reading—Book A	20	4.00	80.00
Reading—Book B	15	4.50	67.50
Singing Story Book	30	6.00	180.00

Description of Item	Quantity	Unit cost	Total cost
Instructional materials and supplies			
Our Homes (Reading)	20	$ 5.00	$100.00
Our Numbers—Book A	50	4.00	200.00
Our Numbers—Book B	50	4.15	207.50
Our Numbers—Book C	50	4.90	245.00
			$1,765.75

Capital Outlay
for Unit **A**

Cassette	3	$ 39.50	$118.50
Filmstrip Viewer	10	13.95	139.50
			$258.00

For Resource Center

Our Numbers (Transparencies)	1 set	$ 30.00	$ 30.00
Our Homes (Filmstrip)	1 set	8.50	8.50
Friendly Games (Study Prints)	1 set	10.00	10.00
Number Occupations (Study Prints)	1 set	10.00	10.00
The Library (Filmstrip)	1 set	80.00	80.00
			$138.50

Unit **B**

Lotto (Beginning Consonants)	10	$ .75	$ 7.50
Magic Alphabet (Game)	1	190.00	190.00
Scrambatic (Game)	6	3.00	18.00
Cross-tac (Game)	6	5.80	34.80
Level Z—Math Publishing	15	2.75	41.25
123 Math—Book D	40	4.00	160.00
123 Math—Book E	40	4.25	170.00
123 Math—Book F	40	5.00	200.00
The Number System	10	5.50	55.00
			$876.55

Capital Outlay
for Unit **B**

Record Player	1	$ 42.60	$ 42.60
Cassette	3	35.10	105.30
			$147.90

For Resource Center

The Metric System (F/S-Tape)	1 set	$ 67.00	$ 67.00
Number Occupations (Prints)	1 set	10.00	10.00
Maps (Filmstrip)	1	12.00	12.00
			$ 89.00

Unit **C**

Description of Item	Quantity	Unit cost	Total cost
Instructional materials and supplies			
MNO Reading Laboratory	1	$250.00	$250.00
123 Hop-tac	10	4.25	42.50
Flash Cards (Multiplication)	5	.75	3.75
Flash Cards (Division)	5	.75	3.75
Flash Cards (Fractions)	10	.75	7.50
Number Flash-O-Matic	1	95.00	95.00
S-E Book 7	30	5.00	150.00
S-E Book 8	30	5.00	150.00
S-E Book 9	30	5.00	150.00
Reading—Level 4	10	4.10	41.00
Reading—Level 7	5	5.05	25.25
Our Numbers—Book L	20	5.00	100.00
Our Numbers—Book M	10	5.00	50.00
Our Numbers—Book N	30	5.50	165.00
456 Math—Book G	5	5.25	26.25
456 Math—Book H	30	5.50	165.00
			$1,425.00

Capital Outlay
for Unit **C**

Cassettes	5	$ 35.10	$175.50
Filmstrip Viewers	10	13.95	139.50
			$315.00

For Resource Center

The World of Numbers (F/S with cassette)	1 set	$100.00	$100.00
Let's Look at Fractions (F/S with cassette)	1 set	35.00	35.00
The Slide Rule (715)	1	22.50	22.50
The Abacus (Model)	5	10.00	50.00
			$207.50

Unit **D**

Math Drill Tapes	1 set	$200.00	$200.00
Science Materials—Replacement Kit 7	2	33.50	67.50
Science Materials—Replacement Kit 11	1	3.80	3.80
Computation Skill Building—Dittos	1	8.00	8.00
Word Analysis Skills—F/S with Cassette	1	92.30	92.30
Number Skills—Cassette	1	75.00	75.00
Two Worlds: A Story—Cassette	1	5.50	5.50
The Calypso	10	3.00	30.00

Description of Item	Quantity	Unit cost	Total cost
Instructional materials and supplies			
S–B Math—Book L	5	$ 4.10	$ 20.50
W–S Math—Book 8	5	5.25	26.25
S–W Math—Book 4	5	2.90	14.50
The Math Reader	15	3.50	52.50
Reader—Book K	10	3.75	37.50
Reader—Book L	15	4.00	60.00
Reader—Book M	15	4.50	67.50
Reader—Book N	5	5.00	25.00
			$785.85

	Quantity	Unit cost	Total cost
Capital Outlay			
for Unit **D**			
The Shakesperian Classics (Cassettes)	1 set	$ 35.00	$ 35.00
The Mysterious Molecules (F/S-Cassette)	1 set	30.00	30.00
Practical Problems	1	18.00	18.00
Think Math (F/S-Cassette)	1 set	48.00	48.00
Multiplication Is Fun (Record)	1	5.50	5.50
Growing UP (F/S Cassette)	1 set	58.00	58.00
			$194.50

	Quantity	Unit cost	Total cost
For Resource Center			
Cassettes	10	$ 35.10	$351.00
Televiewer	1	590.00	590.00
F/S Viewers	5	13.95	69.75
Moveable Science Table (Laboratory)	1	350.00	350.00
			$1360.75

The IIC met to exchange and review their "rough cut" budgets. As they had feared, in all of the units, the items perceived as "necessary" exceeded budgetary constraints in one or more categories.

"Perhaps we can review our lists and consolidate them," one unit leader suggested.

"I'm not too hopeful," another replied. "Perhaps we should start all over, approaching our needs area by area, beginning with math, then reading, and so on."

"It might be possible for us to cost each objective or program" another proposed.

Other suggestions were made, including the ideas of perhaps starting with schoolwide capital outlay, or first considering schoolwide instructional items for the IMC which all could share. "Remember," the IMC director said, "this is the year we're going to do it right!"

CASE ANALYSIS

1. In terms of the budget-making process recommended for IGE schools, critique the first steps taken by the Bayside IIC to prepare this year's budget.

2. Analyze the "asking" budgets of each I & R Unit in terms of the budgetary criteria of clarity, equity, and utility.

3. Describe immediate and long-range steps that should be taken by the I & R Units, the IIC, and the SPC in providing adequate resources for Bayside School.

Case 8

Remodeling of Riverdale School

James M. Lipham

Riverdale Elementary School is an attractive, single-floor school of wood and stone exterior on a beautifully landscaped lot at the suburban fringe of a large metropolitan school district. The citizens have great pride in their school which they affectionately dubbed "our motel" because of its impressive entrance and neat, angular design. The more than adequate multipurpose cafetorium is often used by community groups for recreation and meetings after school. The parent-teacher organization has placed several planters at strategic locations to beautify the hallways and offices.

The school was constructed in four phases. The most recent addition comprises four spacious rooms which were added to the west wing in 1970 when kindergarten programs became state supported (See Figure 10.1 and Table 10.1). The main part of the west wing, added in 1967, contains two rows of four classrooms each.

The main part of the school, built in 1960, contains 12 classrooms, the multipurpose room, offices, nurse's room, faculty lounge, kitchen, and several storage areas. Under a portion of the east wing there is an excavated basement, approximately one-half of which is used for the heating plant. The furnace is placed adjacent to the windows which the architect changed to frosted glass. The remainder of this spacious area is used for storage of desks, maintenance equipment, risers, and other materials. Since presently there is only one entrance to this area, fire regulations preclude its use for instructional purposes. In one corner of the room is the custodian's desk and "office."

Except for the recent kindergarten rooms, the classrooms are uniform in size. The building has no instructional materials center, since it had been district policy during the 1960s to decentralize library materials to each room in the elementary schools. In 1971, a slightly larger classroom in the newest addition was converted to a library which can barely accommodate thirty students at a time.

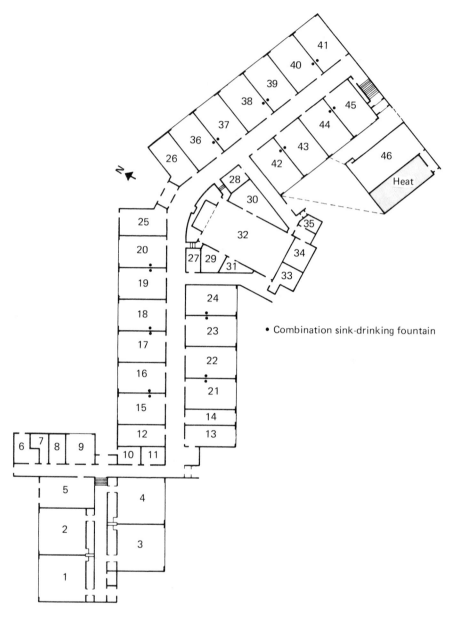

Fig. 10.1 Floor plan of Riverdale School.

In constructing the school, excellent materials were used, so maintenance costs are minimal. Corridor floors are terrazzo, classroom floors are quality tile, and offices are carpeted. Ceilings are made of acoustical tile which partially controls noise. Fluorescent lighting is used throughout the

Table 10.1 Space Configuration of Riverdale School

Number	Space	Square Feet	Number	Space	Square Feet
1	Classroom	1296	24	Classroom	890
2	Classroom	1296	25	Boys' Lavatory	648
3	Classroom	1296	26	Girls' Lavatory	648
4	Classroom	1296	27	Storage	162
5	Classroom	890	28	Nurse's Room	162
6	Equipment Storage	270	29	Kitchen	274
7	Boys' Lavatory	284	30	Storage	274
8	Girls' Lavatory	280	31	Storage	152
9	Storage	500	32	Cafetorium	2600
10	Conference Room	274	33	Faculty Lounge	324
11	Conference Room	243	34	Principal's Office	405
12	Boys' Lavatory	567	35	General Office	324
13	Girls' Lavatory	567	36	Classroom	890
14	Storage	405	37	Classroom	890
15	Classroom	890	38	Classroom	890
16	Classroom	890	39	Classroom	890
17	Classroom	890	40	Classroom	890
18	Classroom	890	41	Classroom	890
19	Classroom	890	42	Classroom	890
20	Classroom	890	43	Classroom	890
21	Classroom	890	44	Classroom	890
22	Classroom	890	45	Classroom	890
23	Classroom	890	46	Basement Storage and Furnace Room	4326

school. Walls in the west wing are made of cement block and tile and in the other parts of the building, wood stud/pressed wood. Interior classroom partitions are not bearing walls.

The current enrollment of the school is 651 students, assigned to five I & R Units, as follows:

	Unit A (K-1-2)	Unit B (1-2-3)	Unit C (3-4)	Unit D (4-5-6)	Unit E (4-5-6)
K—80 (1/2 day)	80				
1—86	43	43			
2—92	45	47			
3—97		30	67		
4—99			50	20	29
5—95				45	50
6—102				62	40
	168	120	117	127	119

After approximately a year and a half of awareness activities, extensive involvement, and intensive planning, the decision was made to adopt IGE at Riverdale School. The multiunit organizational structure was established, excellent unit leaders chosen, and an effective IIC formed. The school was divided into five I & R Units. Each unit includes the unit leader, four staff teachers, and instructional aide, and approximately 130 students.

Through efforts of the SPC, a positive decision was made by the Board of Education in July to allocate $15,000 during the changeover year for Phase I, immediate remodeling of Riverdale School, to accommodate the IGE program. Recognizing that this amount would not be adequate to cover other desirable changes, the board further indicated that a similar amount would likely be available next year for a Phase II, long-range Riverdale remodeling plan.

In their early work with the SPC, the Riverdale IIC gave considerable attention to the need for several facility changes. With approval of the allocation by the Board, the IIC held several intensive planning sessions, and drafted the following overall criteria for the remodeling plan:

1. Square footage allocation of space should be as equitable as possible among the I & R Units.

2. All remodeling must conform to existing fire and safety codes which preclude the placement of instructional equipment in corridors.

3. An instructional materials center should be provided. If possible, it should be easily accessible to the primary units.

4. A substantial share of the Phase I funds should be used to remove walls between classrooms.

5. Desirable, but not critical, items, such as carpeting, moveable dividers, and staff office spaces should be delayed until Phase II.

6. Preliminary cost estimates, subject to upward revision due to inflation, are as follows:

   a. Removing a wall with plumbing $1000.00
   b. Removing an ordinary wall   800.00
   c. Carpeting a typical classroom   700.00
   d. Building a storage wall   600.00
   e. Installing a moveable divider   600.00
   f. Building a stairwell   3000.00

7. Each unit leader, working with the I & R Unit staff, will prepare a plan to be reviewed, discussed, and approved by the IIC.

8. The approved final plans for the Phase I remodeling will be submitted by November 1 to the Superintendent and the Board of Education, so that contracts can be let for the work which hopefully will be accomplished during the winter vacation, December 15–January 5.

Now, it is October 1. As principal, you are aware that each I & R Unit has been working hard on the remodeling plans, since you have met several times with them to respond to their questions and suggestions. The IIC will be meeting soon to make and approve the final plans. You realize that you must be able to react realistically and helpfully to the many suggestions. As you examine the Riverdale floor plan again, ask yourself, "What changes *really* should be made?"

CASE ANALYSIS

1. Prepare a new floor plan for the Phase I, immediate remodeling of Riverdale School, which you will present to the IIC.
2. Defend each proposed change, taking into account the criteria of the committee, including such factors as equity, cost, proximity, utility, and flexibility.
3. Prepare a list of desirable options to be included in the Phase II Plan, long-range needs for future remodeling. On the basis of research regarding facility and equipment needs for IGE schools, assign priorities to each option.

Glossary

Accountability   A point of view that indicates that persons may be held responsible for their task performance.

Accountability, educational   The idea that teachers and school systems may be held responsible for actual improvement in student achievement and that such improvement is measurable.

Affective outcomes of education   Results which involve feelings more than understandings. Likes and dislikes, satisfactions and discontents, ideals and values are some of the affective outcomes that education may develop in the individual.

Aide, clerical   A paraprofessional whose duties are mainly secretarial.

Aide, instructional   A paraprofessional member of the I & R Unit who, working under the direct supervision of the teachers, performs various routine duties. These duties, which depend on the experiences and skills of the aide, may include working with children in a one-to-one or small group situation, administering and scoring tests, and helping students in the media center or on the playground.

Assessment   Application of a measurement procedure; obtaining data through measurement; does not include a judgment and therefore is non-evaluative measurement; assessment is also used by some writers as a synonym for either evaluation or measurement. See **Postassessment.**

Attitude   An orientation toward or away from some object, concept, or situation; a readiness to respond in a predetermined manner to the object, concept, or situation.

Basic skills   Skills such as those involved in reading, language, and arithmetic. Their development is regarded as essential to the further study of content subjects, and they tend to be emphasized during the elementary school years.

Behavior   (1) The action or activities of an individual; that is, anything that an individual does, including overt, physical action, internal physiological and emotional processes, and implicit mental activity; (2) those activities of an organism that can be observed by another organism or by an experimenter's instruments. Included within behavior are verbal reports made about subjective, conscious experiences.

Behavior, exploratory   Behavior characterized by activities designed to find out more about something. In classroom groups these exploratory behaviors may be indicated as expressions of thought processes or as overt physical activities.

Center, instructional materials (IMC)   (1) An area set up by a school system consisting of at least a library and an audiovisual center which contain a variety of instruction material and equipment; *syn:* **educational materials center; multimedia center; learning resource center;** (2) an area set aside within a single school in which the multimedia approach is utilized for individual and group teaching-learning activities.

Center, learning   An area in the classroom or some designated area in the school where there is a wide assortment of resources for learning.

Cognitive outcomes of education   Results from education in the intellectual domain including factual knowledge, comprehension, and various intellectual skills; not to be confused with an *objective* of education, which is a desired result of education.

Comprehension   The process of acquiring or developing the meaning of various types of material, including words, sentences, paragraphs, and longer material.

Concepts   Abstractions based on the properties or relationships common to a class of objects or ideas. Concepts may be of concrete things, e.g., the term "poodle dog" referring to a given variety of dog, or of abstractions, e.g., equality, justice, number, implying relationships common to many different kinds of objects or ideas.

Control group   A group not subject to the experimental treatment but is otherwise as nearly as possible like the experimental group or groups.

Criterion   A standard or norm established as a basis for making qualitative or quantitative comparison.

Criterion, mastery   A standard that explicitly indicates full or complete attainment of an objective or objectives, usually in the cognitive or psychomotor domain: e.g., 90 percent correct on a 30-item test that measures attainment of three objectives in science; walking a mile in 15 minutes without stopping to rest or running. Mastery criteria are usually set when it is known or presumed that one objective, or set of objectives, must be attained fully before the next one can be undertaken successfully.

Criterion-referenced test   See **Test, criterion.**

Criterion, variable   A standard that implies that either (a) not all students must attain the same level of knowledge, skill, or affective outcome, or (b) that a particular lesson or unit contains several objectives, not all of which are to be attained to the same specified level. Variable criteria are generally set in connection with expressive objectives, objectives in the affective domain, and objectives in the psychomotor domain. In general only a limited number of objectives in the skill subjects are to be attained to mastery by all students at one time during their elementary school years, and even here exceptions are made for exceptional students; e.g., blind, deaf, emotionally disturbed, mentally retarded.

Decision making   The act of making a choice among defined alternatives concerning a defined issue or problem.

Decision making, involvement in   The extent to which one engages in defining a problem, suggesting alternatives, making decisions, and evaluating decision outcomes.

Definitions, operational   Operations, actual or mental, which give meaning to concepts.

Developing Mathematical Processes **(DMP)**   A comprehensive instructional and management program in elementary mathematics that integrates arithmetic, geometry, and probability and statistics.

Differentiated staffing   Dividing the roles of school personnel into different professional and paraprofessional subroles according to specific functions and duties to be performed in the school and according to particular talents and strengths evident within the human resources of any given school community.

Evaluation   The science of providing information for decision making; the process of delineating, obtaining, and providing useful information for judging decision alternatives.

Evaluation criteria   The standards against which a person, a group, a procedure, or an instrument may be checked.

Evaluation cycle   The cycle which begins with an initial determination of educational objectives for a particular course or program and ends with a final evaluation of its effectiveness.

Evaluation, formative   Evaluation of a student's learning during an instructional sequence; evaluation of an instructional product—textbook, film —while it is being developed; evaluation of a process while it is being carried out.

Evaluation, informal   Appraisal of an individual's status or growth by means other than standardized instruments.

Evaluation, initial   Evaluation of a student's characteristics and level of achievement before determining appropriate instructional objectives for the student; evaluation of an instructional product, e.g., a textbook, a film, before using it; evaluation of a process, e.g., planning an instructional program for a student, planning for the use of materials by the IIC, before beginning the actual process.

Evaluation instrument   Any of the means for obtaining information on the progress of a learner and the effectiveness of instruction; quantitative and qualitative data, objective measures, subjective impressions, tests, observations, anecdotal records, case studies, and sociometric methods may all serve as instruments for deciding whether instructional objectives have been obtained.

Evaluation, of a curriculum   The assessment of learning activities within a specific instructional area for the purpose of determining the validity of objectives, relevancy and sequence of content, and achievement of specified goals; leads to decisions associated with planning, programming, implementing, and recycling program activities.

Evaluation, of staff   An estimate of the quality of a person's performance based on one or more criteria such as achievement, adjustment, behavior, and the judgment of school officials, parents, students, and the role incumbent.

Evaluation, of an instructional program of a student   An estimate of the quality of the instructional program arranged for a particular student that uses as the criterion the student's attainment of the stated objective(s) of that program.

Evaluation, of a student   A process in which information derived from many sources is used to arrive at a value judgment; includes not only identifying the degree to which a student possesses a trait or to which the student's behavior has been modified but also evaluating the desirability and adequacy of these findings.

Evaluation, summative   Evaluation of a student's learning at the end of an instructional sequence (this would also be considered part of the formative evaluation of an instructional program comprising more than one sequence); evaluation of an instructional product—textbook, film, total instructional program of a student—after it is completed or finished; evaluation of a completed process.

Facilitative environments   The intra- and extraorganizational agencies, groups, and individuals who contribute to installation, refinement, and renewal of innovative educational programs.

Goal   An end state or condition toward which the motivated behavior sequence is directed and by which the sequence is completed.

Group, instructional   A social system exhibiting the general characteristics of groups with the particular quality of the group being shaped by the fact that it is essentially a formal work group functioning within the institutional setting of the school.

Group morale   A sense of satisfaction and motivation which results from personal identification with rationally determined organizational goals. Morale is relative. It may be described as high or low relative to another point in time or another situation.

Individually Guided Education (IGE)   A comprehensive form of schooling that is an alternative to the age-graded, self-contained form of schooling; it is designed to produce higher education achievements and to attain other educational objectives through providing well for differences among students in rate of learning, learning style, and other characteristics.

Individually Guided Motivation (IGM)   A program for focusing a school's efforts on motivation in accordance with instructional programming for the individual student; four motivational-instructional procedures are designed to increase children's interest in learning related to any curricular area and also to promote their self-direction.

Individualization   See **Instruction, individualized.**

Inservice teacher education   A school, system, or area teacher training plan that may include such activities as workshops and seminars for individuals who are already teaching; it is designed to increase staff competency or to inform them of recent developments.

Instruction, individualized   As commonly used, any type of teaching-learning situation in which consideration is given to planning and arranging instruction for the individual student; more strictly, the kind of teaching-learning situation in which each student receives instruction of a different kind or at a different rate from other students, for example, in guided independent study and in proceeding through a sequence of instruction at the individual's own rate; this is in contrast to instructional programming for the individual student in which children who have similar needs and readiness to attain the same objectives are grouped for instruction.

Instruction and Research (I & R) Unit   An element of the multiunit school organization typically consisting of a unit leader, three to five staff teachers, an instructional secretary, a teacher aide, and 100–150 students; the I & R Unit replaces the age-graded, self-contained classroom organization for instruction. The staff of the unit is a hierarchically organized team with clearly defined job descriptions.

Instructional Improvement Committee (IIC)   The organizational element of the multiunit school organization structure at the school level. It is composed of the principal, the unit leaders, and a parent representative. The IIC carries out many planning and evaluating functions regarding instruction previously performed by the principal or teachers independently.

Instructional program   (1) A statement or description of instructional activities over a given period of time designed to enable the students to attain specified instructional objectives; (2) that which is being taught or has been taught by the school or teacher in question and the manner of instruction.

Instructional program, for an individual student   (1) The teaching-learning activities by which the student attains one or more instructional objectives over a short period of time (students with the same needs and readiness may have the same instructional program in a given curriculum area); (2) the combination of all the student's teaching-learning activities in the various curriculum areas for any given period of time.

Instructional Programming, for the individual student   The process of identifying objectives, planning and carrying out a series of related activities and use of materials (learning experiences) by which a student is to attain the objectives to a stated criterion; the amount of time may or may not be specified.

Instructional Programming Model (IPM)   A seven-step model for planning, carrying out, and evaluating instructional programs for the individual students of a school (see **Instructional program, for an individual student**). The model takes into account these conditions: that some but not all instructional objectives should be attained by all students during the elementary school; that some, but not all, objectives should be attained by students to a criterion of mastery, and that some, but not most, objectives are attained in a fixed and invariant sequence.

Intelligence   (1) That which a properly standardized intelligence test measures; (2) according to Binet, the characteristics of thought processes that enable persons to take and maintain a direction without becoming distracted, to adapt means to ends, and to criticize their own attempts at problem solution.

Intergroup cooperation   Relationships within a group characterized by strong motivation to complete the group task, greater division of labor, high communication, expression of friendliness.

Learning   A relatively permanent change in behavior that occurs as the result of practice. Behavior changes due to maturation or temporary conditions of the organism (e.g., fatigue, the influence of drugs, adaptation) are not included.

Learning, independent   Learning that occurs by an individual without assistance from another person.

Measurement, educational   (1) A term indicating the testing, scaling, and appraisal of aspects of the educational process for which measures are available and of the individuals undergoing the educational process; (2) the end product obtained through applying a measure to any aspect of the educational process or the individuals undergoing it.

Motivation   A general term used to indicate the activation and direction of effort, usually toward a goal.

Motive   Any condition of the organism that affects its readiness to start upon or continue in a sequence of behavior.

Multiunit school organization   A three-level instructional organizational pattern consisting of the Instruction and Research unit; the Instructional Improvement Committee within the building; and the System-wide Program Committee within the school district.

Objective, behavioral   An instructional objective that includes a description of observable or measurable behavior: the behavior may be measurable, not necessarily only overt behavior that is directly observable.

Objective, educational   An aim stated for education in general, for a school division, or for a subject in general.

Objective, expressive   An instructional objective stated in terms of the kind and/or number of activities to be engaged in.

Objective, instructional   A statement describing the desired results that may be expected from the particular unit or sequence of instruction.

Objective-based instruction   A system of instruction in which instructional activities and evaluation procedures are based on clearly stated objectives.

Outcomes, educational   The immediate, long-range, and ancillary outputs of the school or the educational process.

Outcomes, instructional   Outcomes that result from the instructional program, planned in terms of pupil growth in all areas.

Paraprofessional   Any person who works within an I & R Unit who is not being employed as a certified teacher and is not an intern or student teacher; also see **Aide, clerical** and **Aide, instructional.**

Performance   Overt or readily measured behavior as distinguished from knowledge or information not translated into action.

Personality   The individual characteristics and ways of behaving which, in their organization or patterning, account for an individual's unique adjustments to the total environment (*syn.,* individuality).

Postassessment   The process of gathering various kinds of data to understand the individual after a sequence of instruction; some of the information is used to evaluate the student's attainment of particular instructional objectives.

Preassessment   The process of gathering various kinds of information to understand the individual prior to the start of an instructional sequence; some of the information is used to evaluate the student's readiness for attaining particular instructional objectives.

Preservice teacher education   The program planned and implemented by an institution of higher learning which terminates in a degree and teacher certification.

Program, education, of a building   A short statement of the terminal objectives that all students are to attain at a specific point in time; e.g., after seven years of schooling, after one year of schooling, and the related learning experiences by which the various objectives are to be attained. Common objectives which are to be attained by all students and other objectives to be attained by some but not all students should be indicated.

Program planning   A process by which the nature and sequence of future educational programs are determined.

Psychomotor domain   The area of learning or instruction pertaining to muscular activity that follows directly from a mental process.

Rating scale   A device by which raters can record a judgment of other persons or of themselves on the traits defined by the scale.

Reference group   The group with which individuals compare themselves when making self-estimates of status. Most people have several reference groups. A reference group may or may not be a membership group.

Regional IGE Coordinating Council (RICC)   The intermediate group in a three-level organizational arrangement; the group is composed of representatives of the Systemwide Program Committees of the school districts of the region, a representative of the intermediate agency of the region, a representative of at least one teacher education institution of the region, and a representative of the state education agency.

Role   The dynamic aspect of a status or position which is defined by the expectations held for one's behavior.

Role playing   A method for teaching principles affecting interpersonal relations by having the subject assume a part in a spontaneous play, whether in psychotherapy or in leadership training.

Socialization   The shaping of individual characteristics and behavior to conform to expectations that the social environment provides.

Staff development   Continuous improvement of teacher knowledge, skills, and attitudes as planned for and with the I & R Unit, the school, and the school district.

State IGE Coordinating Council (SICC)   The state group in a three-level organizational arrangement; it is chaired by the chief state school officer or a designee, and composed of at least one state IGE coordinator, other key personnel of the state agency, and representatives of each RICC including a teacher educator, a representative of an intermediate agency, and a representative of an SPC.

Subpublic   A group holding similar positions, membership, and value orientations.

Systemwide Program Committee (SPC)   The element of the multiunit school organization at the school district level; it is chaired by the superintendent of schools or a designee and consists of representative central office consultants, principals, unit leaders, teachers, and community representatives.

Team teaching   A type of instructional organization involving teaching personnel and the students assigned to them in which two or more teachers are given joint responsibility for all or a significant part of the instruction of the same group of students; the team may include paraprofessionals and student teachers; the I & R Unit is a hierarchical team with clearly defined roles for all members, and it has functions in addition to instruction.

Test, achievement   An instrument designed to measure a student's accomplishment or proficiency related to some body of knowledge or skill; often used to measure achievement in arithmetic, chemistry, English, typing, and other subjects of study; most tests made by teachers for classroom use are achievement tests.

Test, aptitude   An instrument designed to determine the potential of an individual for development along a special line or the extent to which the person is likely to profit from instruction along that line. Tests of academic aptitude, scientific aptitude, music aptitude, clerical aptitude, and other special aptitudes are available.

Test, criterion   The instrument used to measure the end result of an instructional sequence or an experimental treatment.

Test, diagnostic   An instrument designed to reveal specific weaknesses or failures to learn in some subject of study such as reading or arithmetic. In a diagnostic test the main interest is in scores on individual items or on small groups of highly similar items.

Test, mastery   An instrument not intended to indicate how much a student has achieved relative to other students, but only whether or not the student has achieved enough to satisfy the minimum requirements of the teacher or the examining agency.

Test, nonverbal   Usually an intelligence test, a test which aims to minimize the importance of language skills as a factor determining the test score. In the purest form of nonverbal test there is no use of words, written or spoken, either by the examiner giving the test or by the subjects responding to it. More commonly, a nonverbal test is one in which no written directions are employed and to which the subject responds without using language. Such tests are commonly used in testing small children, illiterates, and others with language deficiencies.

Test, objective   A test that can be provided with a simple predetermined list of correct answers, so that subjective opinion or judgment in the scoring procedure is eliminated. The scoring of true-false, multiple-choice, or matching exercises is completely objective. The scoring of short-answer or completion items is partly objective.

Test, performance   A test to which students ordinarily respond by overt action, that is by motor or manual behavior. More broadly, any test intended to measure actual accomplishment rather than potential ability.

Test, work-sample   A nontest product of student learning, such as a handwriting sample, a science project, or a written report.

Theory   A set of assumptions (axioms) advanced to explain existing data and predict new events; usually applicable to a wide array of phenomena and experimental situations.

Understanding   The process of acquiring or developing the meaning of various types of material.

Unit Leader   A certified teacher who in addition to teaching children from 51 to 80 percent of the time, is responsible for serving as the instructional leader of an I & R Unit, chairing meetings of the unit, and serving on the IIC of the school building; a main instructional responsibility is to lead the unit staff in planning, carrying out, and evaluating instructional programs for individual students.

Wisconsin Design for Reading Skill Development **(WDRSD)**   A reading program which describes six areas of reading skills and related behavioral and expressive objectives; it provides machine-scorable, criterion-referenced tests for assessing student attainment of behavioral and expressive objectives; it also provides the means for managing objective-based instruction in reading.

Indexes

Author Index

Subject Index

q·8·766

372.1394
L764   98766

Lipham, J. M.
The PRINCIPAL + INDIVIDUALLY GUIDED
EDUCATION